AF560235

AUTHORITY AND KINGSHIP UNDER THE SULTANS OF DELHI

Authority and Kingship under the Sultans of Delhi (thirteenth–fourteenth centuries)

IQTIDAR HUSAIN SIDDIQUI

MANOHAR
2006

First published 2006

ISBN 81-7304-688-3

Published by

Ajay Kumar Jain for
Manohar Publishers & Distributors
4753/23 Ansari Road, Daryaganj
New Delhi 110 002

Typeset at

Digigrafics
New Delhi 110 049

Printed at

Lordson Publishers Pvt. Ltd.
Delhi 110 007

Distributed in South Asia by

FOUNDATION BOOKS

4381/4, Ansari Road
Daryaganj, New Delhi 110 002
and its branches at Mumbai, Hyderabad,
Bangalore, Chennai, Kolkata

Contents

Preface

The Ghurian conquest of north India towards the close of the twelfth century AD, led to the introduction of Sultanate polity which had evolved in Central Asia. It was a complex system of governance in which rights, functions and duties of different components of state and society were specified. The concept of absolute monarchy was repugnant to this system. In the Indian environment changes were introduced whenever it was thought necessary. As the land chiefs constituted an important element in the polity, they were befriended and given a share in power, if they acquiesced to the Centre's authority. The close relationship between the royal court and the landed aristocracy led to the development of the culture of shared values which came to be known as India's composite culture.

The discovery of fresh evidence in non-conventional contemporary literature, hitherto unknown, calls for a reappraisal of the system of governance during the Sultanate period. It really enables us to make a departure from the conventional approach. Amongst the non-conventional sources, the anthologies and *diwans* of poets, *tazkiras*, both of the sufis and poets, religious literature, and *malfuzat* (collection of utterances) of the sufi saints who belonged to different fraternities illumine the atmosphere of culture around the royal court on the one hand and the life of people on the other. In studying the complex socio-political phenomena during the Sultanate period, all the conventional and non-conventional sources have been used carefully. I have avoided entering into controversy whether the Sultanate was more important historically than the Mughal period. The institutions were built on a sophisticated political system and they survived the Sultanate with necessary modification. The bureaucratization of the ruling elite and military professionalism that had become the distinct features of the Sultanate polity have been discussed in some detail. Likewise the significance of traditions and rituals connected with it were important as their performance enhanced the *dabdaba-i-shahi* (pomp and splendour of the royal court) on the one hand and which also led to social development on the other, has been analysed for the first time. The nature of *iqta* system has been reappraised because it could not receive adequate attention from the modern scholars.

As for the modern works on the history and culture of Delhi Sultanate, I have sparingly referred to them, in order not to increase the volume of the work. I hope this study will open new visitas for further investigation in the history and culture of Delhi Sultanate.

Aligarh IQTIDAR HUSAIN SIDDIQUI

Introduction

Implicit in the title of this monograph is the study of the political structure of the Sultanate founded in the wake of the Ghurian conquest of north India towards the close of the twelfth century AD. The introduction of the new politico-social institutions led to important changes in the country's traditional system. A uniform administrative system was established under a bureaucracy, the members of which were transferred from one territory to the other. The job cpportunities created by the Sultanate attracted people of talent and learning from the neighbouring countries who settled in different towns and cities. It is worth recalling that nowhere were the old residents evacuated to make room for the new settlers, but their settlements added a new element to the demography of the caste towns and cities. Included among the immigrants were scholars, poets, scientists, artists, and traders engaged in international over-land and over-seas trade. Thus, the mingling of people belonging to different countries and cultural traditions let loose the process of cultural synthesis that provided variety and richness to life. Since the land chiefs were accommodated as an important element in the Sultanate polity, the new cultural influence spread through them far and wide. Moreover, with their accommodation, political pluralism seems to have become the characteristic feature of the Sultanate polity.

No doubt modern scholars have paid attention to the study of political institutions, important events such as decisive battles and efforts made by individual Sultans to centralize power through the control of the nobility, but these aspects have been studied in separate compartments. The institutions, rituals, and practices associated with the Sultanate polity have not been studied properly, with serious attention not paid even to conventional historical sources. An attempt has been made here to have an argument on the nature of Sultanate polity and its impact on medieval Indian society. Attention has particularly been focused on the causes that led to the modification of the Central Asian polity in the Indian environment.

In studying the various strands of the Sultanate polity, we have to take notice of the different models evolved in Central Asia and Khurasan. The Ghaznavid and Saljuq dynasties are important in this context because two different models of polity developed under their hegemony. These models influenced and inspired the rulers of the succeeding dynasties, known as the Khwarazm Shahi and the Ghurid dynasties respectively.

The rise of Sultan Mahmud to power in Ghazna (reigned: AD 997–1030), marks the beginning of a new phase in the development of the Sultanate polity in the Persian-speaking lands of the Muslim world. Sultan Mahmud appears to have been the first ruler to assume the title of the Sultan. He made a compromise with the religious leadership over the division of power. The *ulama* (religious leaders) were conceded the right to perform legislative as well as interpretive functions with regard to the enforcement of the *Sharia* (Islamic canon law). The administration of justice and the interpretation of law became the exclusive province of the *ulama*, who were appointed by the state as *qazis* (judicial officers) and *muftis* (expounders of the law). The Sultan was not expected to interfere with them in this regard. However, the Sultan was allowed to wield discretionary power only in dealing with the offenders against him or the state. Such cases were generally not referred to the *qazi's* court.[1] As regards the Sultan's claim to authority, he had become the fountainhead of political power. His claim to authority rested on his ability to provide his followers with military leadership and his ability to maintain peace and order in the realm.[2] Now the political theory crystallized the concept that it was the duty of the Sultan to provide relief to people in times of calamity such as famine, control prices of essential commodities, and suppress anti-social elements.[3] Similarly, the patronage extended by the Sultan to the men of learning and talent turned the Ghaznavid court into a centre of intellectual and cultural activities. The association of scholars, poets, scientists, and artists with the court became an attribute of sovereignty, and it inspired succeeding generations of Sultans in Iran, Central Asia, and India.

The centralization by Sultan Mahmud of political power and

authority, and the bureaucratization of the army, are also noteworthy features of the Sultanate polity under the Ghaznavid Sultans. All officers and soldiers were paid in cash; revenue assignment in lieu of cash salary to army personnel or any other employee does not seem to have been a practice. In fact, the process of military professionalization began with the concentration of the war-making function in the monarchy. The crack troops of the centre, who belonged to different ethnic groups and followed different religions, including Hinduism,[4] were highly bureaucratized, with rules and regulations governing the recruitment of officers and soldiers, their promotion schedules, as well as their rates of pay.[5] Barthold rightly observes: 'The concept of the state was brought to its extreme expression under the Ghaznavids, and especially under Mahmud. The population was divided into the army (mainly multinational), which received a salary from the monarch, who in return demanded its faithfulness.'[6]

As regards the provincial government, the administrative-cum-military charge of the *vilayet* (extensive territorial unit) was assigned to a military general, designated as *sipahsalar*, while the responsibility of revenue collection and the administration of justice were made the concerns of the provincial *diwan* (finance officer) and the *qazi* respectively. The *sipahsalar* was accountable to the Sultan, the diwan to the wazir at the centre, and the *qazi* to the *qazi-al-quzat* in Ghazna.[7] It is noteworthy that the army was deputed from the centre to serve in the province and every one of its soldiers was expected to be loyal only to the Sultan as his servant. The *sipahsalar*, as the representative of the Sultan, could command respect and obedience on the battlefield, but not loyalty to him against the Sultan. Baihaqi's account of the appointment of Ahmad-i-Yenaltagin as *sipahsalar* by Sultan Masud in AD 1031, and his rebellion afterwards, may be quoted at some length because it casts an interesting light on the conduct of different provincial officers and the provincial army. Baihaqi tells us that after his selection, Ahmad-i-Yenaltagin

> took the oath of allegiance and signed the articles of agreement which were entrusted to the record keeper. Thereafter, the Khwaja (i.e. Khwaja Ahmad-i-Hasan Maimandi, the Wazir) said to him: 'You are a general and must act according to the articles of your agreement. You must not

say anything to any person respecting political or revenue matters. But you must perform all the duties of the commander so that the Qazi, may not be able to drag you down. His Majesty deems it advisable to send with you some of the Dailami Chiefs and some others of whom apprehensions are entertained. . . . You must take them all and treat them very kindly but they need not be allowed to go beyond the river Chenab without the King's order or without your permission. You must be careful not to let them mingle with the garrison of Lahore and not allow them to drink or play at Chaugan.[8]

Later on, when Yenaltagin revolted against the Sultan in AD 1033, he was not supported by the army of the province. The Sultan deputed the Hindu general, Tilak, at the head of a strong force, against him. Unable to face Tilak, the rebel took to flight but was pursued and killed.[9] Having destroyed the rebel, Tilak returned to Ghazna in accordance with the royal *farman*. On his return in 1035, he was honoured with an expensive robe of honour. A grand feast was also arranged in his honour.[10] Relevant evidence contained in contemporary sources, although brief, further shows that the activities of the provincial and central officers were watched by spies, who kept the Sultan well informed about all important developments in the empire. There was a well-organized department of secret intelligence that functioned under a minister, called the *sahib-i-barid*.[11] To conclude, it may be stated that in the Sultanate polity under the Ghaznavid Sultans, military success and the establishment of law and order justified the Sultan's claim to authority and provided legitimacy to it as well.

The other ruling dynasty that left behind a tradition of its own with regard to the polity was that of the Saljuq Turks. Originally nomads, the Saljuq Turks took a long time to throw off their uncivilized ways even after they had entered the fold of Islam.[12] They appear to have become acquainted with the political system of the Ghaznavid Empire, and inspired by the captivating power of civilization by the time they defeated Sultan Masud in the battle of Dandaniqan in 1041. Yet Tughril, the founder of the Saljuq dynasty (reigned: AD 1039–63) had to show regard to the concept of equality among his tribesmen and he was cautious in continuing with the Ghaznavid institutions. For example, he found the *diwan-i-barid* (the bureau of the intelligence service) repugnant to the psychology of the tribesmen because they did not like to be watched by spies. Moreover, brothers, cousins, and other relations were to share power with him; they were given territorial appanages with full autonomy.[13] Tughril's brother, Daud, could not be prevented from having the *khutba* read in his own name in his territory. Thus, in the Saljuq polity introduced by Tughril, the transmission of sovereignty to the princes and the tribal chiefs was a common feature. The princes nominally acknowledged the suzerainty of the Sultan.[14] Later, under the great Saljuq Sultans, Alp Arslan (reigned: 1063–72) and Malik Shah (reigned: 1072–92), the Saljuq Empire reached the zenith of its glory, owing to the overhauling of the administrative system by the celebrated wazir, Nizam-ul-Mulk Tusi, the polity remained basically unchanged. A learned man, adept in the political culture of his time, Nizam-ul-Mulk founded institutions of higher learning and public welfare, yet the hold of the centre could not be tightened over the provinces during his *wizarat*. He distributed *iqtas* (land assignments) among the soldiers in lieu of cash allowances. The *iqtas* seem to have been given on a permanent basis.[15] A.K.S. Lambton observes that Nizam-ul-Mulk introduced the practice of assigning the *iqtas* to the army men and regularizing them in order to unify the army and the administrative unit (*iqta*). The *iqta* system became the dominant feature of the Saljuq Empire.[16] It is, however, to Nizam-ul-Mulk's credit that he prevented the army men from oppressing the peasants and artisans in their *iqtas*. He kept himself and the Sultan well informed about the conditions in the provinces through the intelligence officers whom he was able to appoint during the reign of Malik Shah. He writes in the *Siyasatnama*: 'It is the King's duty to inquire into the condition of his peasantry and army, both far and near, and to know more or less how things are.'[17] He also writes about the need for the King to have an elaborate system of espionage:

> In the past it has often happened that governors, assignees, officers and army commanders planned rebellion and resistance, and plotted mischief against the King; but spies forestalled them and informed the King, who in turn was able to immediately act with all speed and, coming upon them unawares, to strike them down and frustrate their plans; and if any foreign King or army was preparing to attack the country, the spies informed the King and he took action and repelled them.[18]

As regards the organization of the army, the Saljuq Sultans could not establish their effective control over it, like the Ghaznavids. Consequently, the Sultanate polity under them was always one of collective sovereignty.

The defeat and capture by the Ghuzz Turks of the last Saljuq Sultan, Sanjar, in 1153 cleared the way for the rise of two different ruling houses in Central Asia and Khurasan. The ruling dynasties of these houses are known in history as Khwarazm Shahi and Ghurid respectively. The former was founded by Atsiz, whose ancestor was a Turk slave, entrusted with the government of Khwarazm and Qipchaq provinces. Unlike him, the founder of the latter dynasty was the descendant of the Chieftain of Ghur (in present-day Afghanistan), a vassal of the Ghaznavid Sultan since the time of Sultan Mahmud. Their association with the courts of their paramount lords had a civilizing influence on them. They learnt political wisdom and adopted the prevailing aristocratic culture. Let us briefly examine the nature of the polity of the Khwarazm Shahi Empire.

The region of Khwarazm was peninsular in shape and had enjoyed a higher culture, at least since the tenth century AD. It shared borders with the Turkish steppes, inhabited by the Turkish tribes of the Qipchaqs, the Qanqlis, the Yimeks and others associated with them. The Turkish steppes were called Turkestan and its inhabitants generally followed either Shamanism or were still pagans.[19] Though Atsiz, the real founder of the dynasty, remained a nominal vassal of Sultan Sanjar till his death in 1156, he laid down the foundations of the Khwarazm Shahi Empire, which became a great military power under his successors. A man of many talents, he not only increased his military strength but also evinced a keen interest in the economic development of the territory under his rule. He was also a man of refined literary taste, composing verses in Persian and extending patronage to men of learning.[20] The benevolent rule of Atsiz and his immediate successors brought prosperity to Khwarazm. Foreign travellers were amazed to discover general prosperity, progress, and culture there. The Arab geographer Yaqut found Khwarazm ahead of other Muslim lands in urban and agricultural progress and prosperity. 'The walled cities and fortified villages, canals, and irrigation works discovered by Soviet archaeologists confirm the view that the area of cultivated land had expanded in the course of the 12th century.'[21]

It is, however, noteworthy that neither Atsiz nor his son and successor Sultan Tekish, doubtless a mighty and capable ruler, made any change in the political structure of the Saljuq Empire. If the Saljuq Sultans depended on the military contingents supplied by their vassals in war, the Khwarazm Shahi rulers looked towards the Turkish tribes of the Qipchaq, Qanqli, Yimek, and other associated tribes for support during times of conflict with any neighbour. Atsiz and Tekish also continued to acknowledge the non-Muslim Gur Khan, the king of the Qara Khitai Turks, as their suzerain and paid him nominal tribute. The annexation by Tekish Khwarazm Shah of territories along the border of Iraq as well as his relations with Gur Khan caused conflict between him and the Caliph of Baghdad. Though the Caliph was not powerful enough to take military action against the Khwarazm Shah, his opposition seems to have made him unpopular among the Muslim elite outside Khwarazm. According to Juzjani, the strained relations between them caused harm to the Khwarazm Shahi dynasty during the reign of his successor.[22]

Notwithstanding his military might, Tekish and his successor appear never to have tightened their control over the governors and vassals in the provinces outside the region of Khwarazm. They relied heavily upon the Turkish chiefs of Qipchaq, Qanqli and other Turks for military support. Indeed, they shared power with them. Also, the relatives of the Sultan such as his cousins were given territories to rule over, with full autonomy. In fact, this segmentary polity became the cause of the weakness of the empire on the eve of the Mongol invasion in 1219–20. Many non-Turk nobles who had been constrained to submit to Khwarazm Shah after the assassination of Sultan Muizuddin Muhammad bin Sam showed reluctance in supporting the Khwarazm Shah against Chinggis Khan. For example, Muhammad bin Ali Khar Pust, a Ghurid noble, is reported to have conveyed to Yamin Malik, a cousin of Sultan Muhammad Khwarazm Shah, then seeking shelter in the territory of Ghazna: 'We are Ghurids and you are Turks. We cannot live together.' This led to a conflict.[23] In such conflicts Muslim warriors fought against one another and thousands of them were slain. The Turkish allies from the steppes were unpopular among the Muslims for their ruthlessness. Juvaini writes about the Qanqli Turks: 'Wherever they passed, that country was laid in ruin. . . . Indeed, it was their cruelty, violence and wickedness that brought about the downfall of the dynasty.'[24] The Sultan did not take any action against them even when it had become necessary because he was not confident that the Qanqlis would submit to punishment.[25] It may also be added that the assignment of land revenue as maintenance *iqtas* to a military general or the favourite of the Sultan weakened the centre's hold over the province. The *muqta* (the assignee) maintained his army contingent and enjoyed autonomy within his charge. He was charged only with the responsibility of maintaining an army contingent for the service of the centre at call, besides the maintenance of law and order in the territory assigned to him in *iqta*. We find no shred of evidence in our sources to suggest that the *muqta* was required to pay the *fawazil* (surplus revenue) collected in the *iqta* to the state exchequer or that his account papers were checked by the audit officers. To conclude, it may be said that like the Saljuq Empire, the Empire of the Khwarazm Shahs began as well as ended as a loose confederation of semi-independent kingdoms over which the Sultan exercised nominal authority.

It follows from the above discussion that the two models of Sultanate polity were evolved in Central Asia under the hegemony of the Ghaznavid and the Saljuq Sultans. After them, these models served as examples for the Sultans of the dynasties that followed. Since the Ghurid Princes had acquired a higher level of urban culture of the Islamic elite on account of their association with the Ghaznavid court, they were inspired by the Ghaznavid tradition outside Ghur. Sultan Muizuddin Muhammad bin Sam, the conqueror of India, followed the Ghaznavid tradition both in Ghazna and in his Indian dominions. No doubt the Sultan trusted his Turkish slave generals for their loyalty, yet they do not appear to have outnumbered the Tajiks. Moreover, they were Persianized generals, having nothing in common with the freeborn Saljuq or Ghuzz Turks of Central Asia. They were bought in Muslim lands in their childhood. They were brought up as Muslims and trained in Muslim culture and manners; the education of a slave was a good investment because an educated and cultured slave fetched a higher price. This is why in India the Turkish slave generals became great patrons of Persian culture and poetry. As the Sultanate founded by his lieutenant, Malik Qutbuddin Aibek (reigned: 1206–10), in India was Sultan Muizuddin Muhammad bin Sam's legacy, a separate chapter is devoted to the history of the ruling house of Ghur.

As for the following chapters, Chapter 1 deals with the nature of kingship and authority, highlighting the different models that the Ghurid rulers followed in their ancestral principality of Ghur and in the conquered territories after they had built an empire. Chapters 2 to 4 offer an analysis of the Sultanate polity and its cultural orientation in India. The question about how the political institutions of foreign origin at the centre and in the provinces underwent change and were modified has been addressed in terms of the need of the times. Due emphasis has been laid on the historical significance of public welfare that inspired the Sultans of strong personality to take an interest in promoting material culture and win the loyalty of their subjects and the grateful remembrance of posterity. Some of the Sultans were certainly ahead of their counterparts in other parts of the civilized world as regards the concept of public welfare. Chapter 5 examines the Delhi Sultanate's relations with foreign countries and is based on a critical study of the relevant evidence contained in sources hitherto unknown as well as known chronicles. Chapter 6 describes the network of spies and the intelligence apparatus organized under a minister designated the *sahib-i-barid*. Chapters 7 and 8 deal with the organization of provincial units; each one of them was composed of a number of fiscal-cum-administrative units such as the *pargana* and the village with fixed boundaries, and the construction of canals and water works respectively. If the provincial organization helped the establishment of a sound and uniform administrative system, the construction of a network of canals and water reservoirs turned certain regions of arid climate into granaries.

It is hoped that this volume will arouse scholars' interest in undertaking further investigation and research into this field.

NOTES

1. Cf. Muhammad Nazim, *The Life and Times of Sultan Mahmud of Ghazna*, rpt., New Delhi, 1971, pp. 147–9 for details.
2. The Sultan should enjoy the confidence of the army by virtue of his competence as a military general. His failure on the battlefield could be disastrous for him, as the defeat inflicted by the Saljuq Turks on Sultan Masud in 1040 shows. The Sultan was killed by army men on his way to India (1041). *Tabaqat-i-Nasiri*, vol. I, p. 234.
3. Fakhr-i-Mudabbir, *Adab ul-Harb wal-Shuja'a*, ed. Ahmad Suhail Khwansari, Iran, 1346 Shamshi, pp. 103–10.
4. The Hindùs served in large numbers in the Sultan's army and were granted religious freedom. Al-Ma'arri describes the scene of a Hindu woman's *sati* (immolation on the pyre of her dead husband) in Ghazna. *Risalat-ul-Ghufran*, p. 153, as cited by Nazim, *The Life and Times of Sultan Mahmud of Ghazna*, op. cit., p. 140, fn. 7.
5. Ibid., pp. 141–2.
6. V.V. Barthold, *Four Studies in the History of Central Asia*, Eng. tr. V. and T. Minorsky, Leiden: E.J. Brill, 1956, vol. 1, p. 70.
7. *The Life and Times of Sultan Mahmud of Ghazna*, op. cit., pp. 147–9.
8. Abul Fazl Muhammad al-Baihaqi, *Tarikh-i-Masudi*, Tehran, 1324 Shamsi, pp. 266–7.
9. Ibid., p. 433.
10. Ibid., p. 434; Gaadezi, *Zainal-Akhbar*, p. 497.
11. The spies are said to have kept watch even on the private affairs of the nobles. Nizam-ul-Mulk Tusi was impressed by the honesty and integrity of the *barids*. Cf. Nizam-ul-Mulk Tusi, *Siyasatnama*, ed. Jaffar Shiar, Tehran, 1348, pp. 93–4.
12. Minhaj-i-Siraj Juzjani, *Tabaqat-i-Nasiri*, 2 vols., ed. Abdul Hai Habibi (Kabul, 1963, 1964), vol. I, pp. 245–7; Muhammad bin Ali bin Sulaiman al-Ravandi, *Khulasa i-Rahat ul-Sudur-o-Ayat-ul-Surur*, ed. Nazir Ahmad, in Qand-i-Parsi, no. 9 (Iran House, New Delhi, 1374 Bahar), pp. 24–5.
13. *Tabaqat-i-Nasiri*, vol. I, op. cit., p. 248.
14. Cf. A.K.S. Lambton, 'The Internal Structure of the Saljuq Empire', *The Cambridge History of Iran*, ed. J.A. Boyle, Cambridge, vol. 5, 1968, pp. 217–18.
15. Nizam-ul-Mulk Tusi, *Siyasatnama*, ed. Jaffar Shiar, Tehran, 1348, pp. 93–4. Also W.W. Barthold, *Turkestan down to the Mongol Invasion*, Eng. tr. T. Minorsky and ed. C.E. Bosworth, London, 1968, p. 307.
16. Cf. A.K.S. Lambton, 'The Internal Structure of the Saljuq Empire', in *The Cambridge History of Iran*, ed. J.A. Boyle, Cambridge, 1968, vol. 5, p. 231.
17. *Siyasatnama*, Eng. tr. H. Darke, London, 1960, pp. 66–7.
18. Ibid., p. 78.

19. In his *Muqadimah* to the *Shajra-i-Ansab*, Muhammad bin Mansur, known as *Fakhr-i-Mudabbir*, describes the length and breadth of Turkestan as well as the life of Turkish tribes. Interesting information is furnished about their trade relations with the Muslim countries, their Turkish language, the scripts prevalent among the sedentary Turks, along with descriptions about the life and conditions of those who lived in the remote areas and remained pagans till the close of the twelfth century. It may also be pointed out that in view of its historical importance, E. Denison Ross critically edited this *Muqadimah* and published it with an introduction and notes in English but incorrectly identified its author, Muhammad bin Mansur bin Sa'id, with his contemporary poet and scholar, Fakhruddin Mubarak Shah Marvarrudi, the author of *Bahr-ul-Ansab* and, therefore, called it *Tarikh-i-Fakhr al-Din Mubarak Shah*. I have used the Persian text edited by E. Denison Ross (London, 1927) but called it *Tarikh-i-Fakhr-i-Mudabbir. Cf.* text, London, 1927, pp. 37–8, hereafter cited as *Tarikh-i-Fakhr-i-Mudabbir.*
20. Cf. *Tabaqat-i-Nasiri*, vol. I, pp. 299–300.
21. Cf. C.E. Bosworth, *The Cambridge History of Iran*, vol. 5, op. cit., ed. J.A. Boyle, Cambridge, 1968, p. 142, for Khwarazm.
22. Minhaj-i-Siraj quotes the following satirized verses composed by Zahiruddin Faryabi, a contemporary Persian poet:

    O Lord, after you have captured Ajam (Iran), you depute your army towards the burial place of the Prophet. You should desecrate the holy Kaba (grand mosque at Mecca) and destroy the sacred spout. Reduce the edifice of the holy Kaba to dust and throw it to the wind. Bring the tattered sheet cover of the Kaba to your treasure house and then send a few yard-long mats (made of split reeds) for the shrine of the Prophet. You attack the abode of the Caliph, cut-off his head and send it to the Khita (i.e. Gur Khan) and then become a confirmed infidel.

    Tabaqat-i-Nasiri, vol. I, p. 301.
23. Ata Malik Juvaini, *Tarikh-i-Jahan Qusha*, Eng. tr. John Andrew Boyle, vol. II (Manchester University Press, 1958), pp. 460–1.
24. Ibid., vol. II, p. 465.
25. Ibid.

CHAPTER 1

The Ruling House of Ghur and its Legacy in India

The mountainous region in central Afghanistan, situated to the east and south-east of Herat, south of Gharjistan and Juzjan, and about the headwaters of the Farah Rud, and Marghab, was known as Ghur. It was the homeland of the Sultans of Shansabani dynasty. The members of this dynasty started as petty chiefs during the period of Ghaznavid hegemony but gradually rose to prominence. They acquired a place for themselves in history by establishing their political domination first over the entire region of Ghur and then conquered the lands of higher culture around their principality. In the twelfth century AD, Sultan Ghiyasuddin Muhammad bin Sam and Sultan Muizuddin Muhammad bin Sam raised their kingdoms of Ghur and Ghazna to the ranks of world powers. This chapter seeks to reconstruct the history of the rise of the royal house of Ghur and its impact on the life and culture of India.

The ethnic origin of the Ghurid Sultans and the history of the Islamization of the region of Ghur is a controversial subject. Modern scholars have generally taken the evidence, furnished by medieval writers, at its face value and have therefore failed to escape pitfalls in interpretation. The problem calls for a closer probing of the sources of information. In fact, important factors that helped the process of acculturation have been ignored by modern scholars.

In 1930, Professor Mohammad Habib published his pioneering article on the royal house of Ghur, in which he pointed to the legendary nature of Minhaj Juzjani's account of the ethnic origin of the Shansabani dynasty and its conversion to Islam during the Caliphate of Ali, the fourth Caliph of Islam. He states:

The traditions assume that the Ghurians were converted to the faith in the first or second generation of Islam and that the Shansabani dynasty was prominent from the very first. Both claims can be definitely disproved. The extant volume of Imam Abul Fazl Baihaqi's *Tarikh-i-al-i Subuktigin,* written some two hundred years before the *Tabaqat-i-Nasiri,* gives us a very different picture of the heroic and disunited hill tribes. . . . The chiefs, moreover, instead of being pious Muslim devotees of the house of the Prophet, were staunch infidels imbued with the strength of their native hills and inspired by the love of their gods.[1]

Three decades later, K.A. Nizami followed Mohammad Habib on the subject of the infidelity of the Shansabanis during the early Ghaznavid period, but differed from him on the point of the ethnic origin of the Ghurid Sultans. He accepted uncritically Minhaj Juzjani's statement that Zahak (the legendary figure of Firdusi Tusi's *Shahnama*) was the ancestor of the Shansabani dynasty. Though Zahak in the *Tabaqat-i-Nasiri* is said to have lived during prehistoric times, Nizami would have us believe that he was admitted into the fold of Islam by Ali.[2] In an interesting article, C.E. Bosworth, rejecting the stories about the descent and the time of the conversion of the Shansabanis to Islam as 'myths of a type familiar within the Islamic World', describes the Ghurids of eastern Iran as being of Tajik stock. 'It seems that the language of these Tajiks had considerable dialectical divergences from the Persian spoken in Khurasan and because of that familiar to the Ghaznavid Sultans; for his campaigns of 1020 into Ghur Prince Masud had to employ local interpreters.'[3] However, Bosworth is more or less in agreement with Mohammad Habib about the beginning of the process of Islamization in Ghur since the time of Sultan Mahmud of Ghazna (AD 999–1030). He says, 'Until the 11th century it was a pagan land.' Islamization of the region began with Mahmud of Ghazna.[4] It may be pointed out that Bosworth has not consulted the early Arab geographical works that tell us about the presence of Muslims in Ghur since the tenth century.

A careful examination of the relevant evidence tends to suggest that Islam had begun to spread in the border areas of Ghur since the beginning of the ninth century AD, though the hill areas inside the mountain chains (the mountains rising to 10,000 feet and even higher eastwards to the Hindu Kush) remained inaccessible until the beginning of the eleventh century. The hill chiefs who entered the fold of Islam in the border areas do not seem to have been deeply influenced by the Islamic culture of the neighbouring countries; old local customs and practices must have continued there for quite long. The predatory activities of the chiefs of Ghur provoked Sultan Mahmud of Ghazna to retaliate. For their refractory nature against the Ghaznavid Sultan, the historians of Ghazna describe the people of Ghur as bad-tempered, uncivilized, and heathenish. But the Arab names of the Ghurid chiefs, mentioned by Ghaznavid historians, leave no doubt about their being Muslims, even though superficially. For instance, Al-Utbi mentions Ibn Suri, the Shansabani chief of Ahangaran (principality) and his followers as being inclined towards infidelity on account of his rebellion against Sultan Mahmud in AD 1010.[5] It may be pointed out that Ibn Suri's eldest son, Abu Ali, to whom the Sultan assigned the charge of Mandish territory after the defeat and death of his father, is portrayed as a good Muslim and as being submissive to his paramount lord.[6] Similarly, Baihaqi condemns outright the Ghurids as infidels for their persistent recalcitrance, yet the details furnished by him of the campaign by Prince Masud in AD 1020, against the rebel Shishani chief of Warmesh-pat of Jurwas (also in Ghur) contain the names of Muslim chieftains of the same region who were loyal to the Sultan and who joined the Prince against their own fellow chiefs. The loyal chieftains were Abul Hasan Khalaf and Sherwan. The former is reported to have brought with him a gift consisting of choice shields and cuirasses made in his principality. Both of them joined Prince Masud at Ribat-i-Razi near the border of Gharjistan and Ribat-i-Karvan on the border of Guzgan respectively.[7] It is a pity that Minhaj Juzjani's overemphasis on the pre-eminence of the Shansabani dynasty led him to omit any mention of the other powerful chieftains of Ghur who were eventually forced to submit to the overlordship of the Shansabani ruler of the valley of Mandish. His incidental reference to the bad temper and unruly nature of the different clans of Ghur in the account of Qutbuddin Hasan (bin) Abbas shows that the confederacy of the chiefs had been established under the leadership of the Shansabani Prince sometime in the latter half of the eleventh century.[8] As far as the process of urbanization accompanied by acculturation in Mandish is concerned, it seems to have started earlier under the patronage of Abu Ali, the son and successor of Ibn Suri.

Minhaj Juzjani gives Abu Ali credit for having initiated the process of urbanization in his principality. He had a *Jama* mosque (congregational mosque) and *madrasas* (colleges), important agents, no doubt, in the process of urbanization and acculturation, constructed in the region. Furthermore, he extended patronage to the men of learning (the *ulama*) and venerated dervishes. Many endowments (*auqaf*) were established by him for the upkeep of religious and educational institutions. But he was ousted by his nephew, Abbas, who ruled over Ghur for more than seven years.[9] No contemporary or later writer mentions the date of the capture of power by Abbas in Ghur. As he was destroyed by Sultan Ibrahim of Ghazna (d. AD 1099), the date of Abbas's rise to power may be set approximately in the middle of the eleventh century AD. The scanty relevant information furnished by Minhaj Juzjani tends to suggest that by this time the Shansabani chief had established his political domination over the entire region of Ghur and that the local chiefs acknowledged his overlordship. Further, they acquired the aristocratic culture and began to evince an interest in learning the popular sciences in the tradition of their overlords, the sultans of Ghazna and the Saljuq dynasty. Amir Abbas, though harsh and cruel by temperament, was a patron of the sciences, as will be discussed subsequently.

Since Abbas antagonized the nobles and chiefs of Ghur by his oppressive rule, they invited Sultan Ibrahim of Ghazna to undermine him. The latter was waiting for an opportunity to re-assert his overlordship because Abbas had withheld the dispatch of annual tribute to Ghazna. Sultan Ibrahim entered Ghur and the chiefs and nobles betrayed Abbas to the Sultan. Later they requested the Sultan to entrust the government of Ghur to Muhammad, the son of Abbas, who possessed noble qualities that contrasted with his father's vices. Thus, Muhammad was made by Sultan Ibrahim the Amir of Ghur in place of his father. The elevation of Muhammad to the emirate of Ghur ushered in a period of prosperity. He ensured justice to his people and created conditions conducive to cultural and economic development.[10]

On the death of Amir Muhammad, Qutbuddin Hasan succeeded

to the chieftainship of Ghur with the title of Malik.[11] The adoption by him of the title of Malik suggests that being a cultured and ambitious man he wanted to tighten his grip over the other chiefs. The chiefs, who had little regard for the paramount lord, rose in rebellion against him. Therefore, the new Malik fought against them and suppressed their recalcitrance with military force. However, in one of the battles, fought between his army and the rebels of Takab (situated in the north-east of Kabul) in the territory of Wajiristan (present-day Ajaristan in the west of Ghazna), he was wounded and killed. But the army of the Malik defeated the rebels and destroyed them completely. Their village was also razed to the ground along with its castle and never permitted that it be rebuilt.

It may be recalled that, in spite of the establishment of the political supremacy of the Shansabani house, the local chiefs in the region do not seem to have reconciled themselves to the loss of their freedom. Every year, according to Minhaj Juzjani, the chief stopped the payment of annual dues and military force was then used for their collection. Their refractory nature did not change till the fall of the dynasty.[12] Moreover, the Shansabani rulers also never seemed to have been serious about their total destruction. Perhaps they regarded the chiefs as pillars of their dynastic rule even after they had extended it up to the lands of higher culture. The local chiefs held complete hold over their tribal following in their respective areas. They lived together and could be destroyed together. Their destruction in any area could deprive the paramount ruler of tribute. As Ghur was sparsely populated, and the difficult conditions of life in this mountainous region could not attract new settlers from the neighbouring countries, the Shansabani rulers tried to keep themselves contented with them. The most powerful of them were allowed to hold important positions in the army and administration on a hereditary basis. For instance, the head of the Shishani family continued to hold the post of *sipahsalar* in Ghur till the fall of the dynasty.[13] In short, the polity in Ghur always remained fragmented. Even Sultan Ghiyasuddin Muhammad bin Sam and his brother, Sultan Muizuddin Muhammad bin Sam, who behaved as absolute monarchs outside Ghur did not change the traditional political pattern *vis-à-vis* the chiefs of Ghur.[14]

The successor of Malik Qutbuddin Hasan was his son, Malik Izzuddin Husain, who is reported to have been a great patron of learning. He also had his seven sons instructed in the popular sciences and trained both in warfare and statecraft. Being a peace-loving man, he avoided the conflict of arms with his powerful neighbours, the Saljuq Sultan and Sultan Bahram Shah of Ghazna. He regularly sent annual tribute and gifts, comprising choice weapons, coats of mail, armours, helmets, and the famed dogs of Ghur that resembled lions in bodily strength.[15]

Malik Izzuddin Husain was survived by his seven sons, born of different mothers. His eldest son, Fakhruddin Masud, was born of a Turkish slave girl, while the mother of the second son, Qutbuddin Muhammad, originally happened to be the maid-servant of the chief wife of the Malik. The latter was a Shansabani princess and the mother of the remaining five sons. The sons born of her were named Saifuddin Suri, Bahauddin Sam, Ala-uddin Husain (later Jahansuz), Shihabuddin Muhammad, and Shujauddin. The claim to chieftainship of Ghur of the two senior sons was passed over in favour of Saifuddin Suri on account of the princely status of the latter's mother. However, Saifuddin Suri equitably divided his ancestral territory among his brothers. Being civilized and cultured men, everyone of them took an interest in the social and cultural development in his territory. Qutbuddin Muhammad, who had got the territory of Warshad, selected the village of Firuz Kuh on the right bank of the Heri Rud for his headquarters.[16] He laid down the foundations of a fort and a new city there. He also adopted the title of Malik-ul Jabal. The fort and city were still under construction when Malik-ul Jabal became infuriated with Saifuddin Suri; in disgust he handed over his territory to his stepbrother, Bahauddin Sam, the governor of Sangah, in the valley of Mandish, and left to join the court of Sultan Bahram Shah of Ghazna.[17]

Bahauddin Sam was an equally ambitious man. He not only brought to completion the fort of Firuz Kuh, along with other buildings, but also had four other forts constructed at different sites of strategic importance. They were Qasr-i Kajuran on the border of Girmsir, the Qila-i Bindar on the hills of Ghajistan, and the Qila-i Firuz between Ghajistan and Paris (i.e. between Madin and Nadin).[18] The famous fort of Saifrud (in Ghur), which had the distinction of having withstood the siege by the Mongols of Chinggis Khan for quite long in the thirteenth century, was also built by him after the departure of Saifuddin Suri for Ghazna.[19]

Prince Qutbuddin Muhammad joined the court of Sultan Bahram Shah. Being a sophisticated man of refined manners, he endeared himself to the notables of Ghazna. His popularity increased among both the nobles and commoners in the city on account of his magnanimity and munificence. Some of the courtiers of the Sultan, who grew jealous of him, poisoned the Sultan's ears, alleging that he had cast evil eyes on his harem and distributed money among people in order to win their support. Bahram Shah had him poisoned to death. His death was the cause of war between the two ruling houses.[20] This war is important inasmuch as it paved the way for the rise of the royal house of Ghur to prominence. The facts as described by the contemporary or near contemporary writers about it are:

> Being informed of the death of his brother in Ghazna, Saifuddin Suri vowed to wreak vengeance against the ruler of Ghazna. He marched towards Ghazna and defeated Bahram Shah in AD 1148. Sultan Bahram Shah escaped to the region of the Afghans in the south of Ghazna. Saifuddin Suri occupied the Ghaznavid capital and assumed the title of Sultan. Since then, the Shansabani rulers assumed the title of Sultan successively. Being a just and enlightened ruler, Saifuddin Suri treated the residents of the city kindly and made no distinction between the nobles of Ghur and those of Ghazna. In return to his kindness and generosity, the nobles of Ghazna also assured him of their loyalty but only outwardly; in their heart of hearts they were still committed to the cause of the descendant of Sultan Mahmud. Trusting them, Saifuddin Suri sent back his Ghurid nobles to Ghur. A little later, the roads became blocked by snowfall and then the nobles of Ghazna invited Bahram Shah, who had gathered a large force comprising hundreds of elephants and Hindu chiefs, his vassals, from his Indian dominions. On Bahram Shah's arrival near Ghazna, Saifuddin Suri was betrayed by the nobles of Ghazna; he was placed on a feeble cow and paraded in the streets of the city. He was killed while his wazir, Saiyid Majduddin Alevi, was hanged.[21]

It was now the turn of Bahauddin Sam, the successor of Saifuddin Suri in Ghur, to take revenge for the murder of his brothers. He collected his forces in Firuz Kuh, which had been made the new capital of Ghur in place of Ishtiyar, and left for Ghazna. But he fell ill on the way and died. Now the leadership of the Shansabani house devolved on Alauddin Husain in AD 1150. The latter decided to destroy Ghazna or die. He marched via Zamindawar. Bahram Shah also moved with a view to intercepting him. The rival armies faced each other in the vicinity of Zamindawar. Before fighting started, Bahram Shah is reported to have sent a message to Alauddin Husain that he should go back and rest contented with his ancestral territory because he would not be able to face his large army, containing war elephants. Alauddin Husain sent the following reply: 'If you have brought Pheel (elephants), I have got Kharmail (i.e. the famous warriors or champions of Ghur, named the Kharmail Sam Banji, etc.) You have done wrong by killing my brothers, though I have killed none of your men.'

The battle was fought near Takinabad in which the Ghurid soldiers fought on foot under the leadership of their celebrated champions, the two Kharmails. The Ghaznavid soldiers suffered heavy losses and then they took to flight. Bahram Shah also fled away. He stopped on the way, reorganized his army and again took a stand at a place called *Jush-i-ab-i garm* (hot water spring) some distance from Takinabad. This time, too, his army was worsted and he fled to Ghazna. In Ghazna, besides the soldiers, the residents also rallied around him to fight against the invader. As they were no match against the Ghurid soldiers, Bahram Shah was defeated for the third time. Ghazna was seized by Alauddin Husain while Bahram Shah fled to the Punjab (India). The city of Ghazna was set ablaze and it burnt for seven days. Hence, Alauddin Husain's sobriquet Jahan Suz.

Minhaj Juzjani writes about the enormity of Jahan Suz's oppression. For seven nights and days, 'On account of the deep darkness caused by smoke, the atmosphere was so black that the day seemed to be night, whereas the flames of fire (ignited in the evening) would turn the night into day. During these days there was committed rapine, pillage, killing and extreme oppression and barbarism.'[22] According to the author of *Adab-ul-Harb-wal-Shuja'a*, the residents of Ghazna were subjected to tyranny and then killed mercilessly; the number of Muslims killed rose to 60,000. Those who could escape slaughter were reduced to penury. Having punished people in this frightful way, Jahan Suz left one of his army commanders, Amir Khan, to further punish the people and he returned to Ghur. Amir Khan was ordered to destroy Ghazna completely so that its ruins could remind wayfarers of the cause of its destruction. But the commander fled away in mysterious circumstances without carrying out his master's order because the local sufi dervish, Abul Mujjid, had prayed to God for the survival of the people left there.[23] As the author of *Adab-ul-Harb wal-Shuja'a* also drew for his material on popular folk tradition, we should not give any credence to his statement. It is also not supported by the circumstantial evidence available in the *Tabaqat-i Nasiri*. Jahan Suz composed verses on his way back home, bragging about his victory over Bahram Shah and showing mercy to the citizens of Ghazna at the time of his departure to Firuz Kuh.[24] Further, it may be pointed out that the title of Khan was something foreign to the Muslim rulers in Central Asia and Iran till the end of the twelfth century. It was adopted in the Persian-speaking Muslim countries in the thirteenth century under Mongol influence.

Flushed with success, Alauddin Husain Jahan Suz assumed the title of Sultan al-Muazzam (the great king).[25] Displaying arrogance, Jahan Suz not only withheld the dispatch of the annual gift to the Saljuq Sultan, Sanjar, but also attacked the border territory of the Saljuq Empire. Provoked by his misconduct, Sultan Sanjar marched against him. Jahan Suz gave him battle. The Ghuzz, other Turks and the Khaljis, who formed the right wing of the Ghurid army and were 6,000 in number, defected to Sultan Sanjar. Jahan Suz was defeated and taken captive. He was put in a golden cage on his own request. In prison, he managed to endear himself to the Saljuq Sultan through his ready wit and verses composed by him in praise of his captor. Ultimately, the Sultan was pleased to make him his courtier. After two years, when Sultan Sanjar was to march against the rebellious Ghuzz Turks, Jahan Suz was favoured with a rich gift and allowed to return to Firuz Kuh.[26]

During Jahan Suz's absence in Ghur, the nobles selected his nephew, Malik Nasiruddin Husain, the chief of Madin, for his throne. As he was a weak man, he was used as a puppet by the nobles, who squandered the treasures collected by Jahan Suz. He was also killed before Jahan Suz returned to Firuz Kuh.[27]

On his return, Jahan Suz decided first to punish the chiefs of Ghur. As the Saljuq Sultan Sanjar was defeated and taken captive by the Ghuzz Turks, Jahan Suz embarked on a career of conquests. He conquered Bamiyan, Takharistan, Zamindawar, Bust, and the fort of Tulak in the territory of Herat. After Tulak, he captured the fort of Gharjistan and married Hur Malik, the daughter of Sher Ibrahim bin Ardshir Shapur. His nephews, Ghiyasuddin Muhammad bin Sam and Shihabuddin bin Sam, were ordered to be imprisoned at this time. Both were sent to the fort of Gharjistan with fixed maintenance allowances.[28]

Despite the tyranny to which he subjected people of Ghazna, Jahan Suz was not a monster of brutality. By this time, the Shansabani princes had adopted the best of the aristocratic culture developed in Central Asia. Jahan Suz had a ready wit and composed verses in Persian extempore at the slightest excuse. His verses are found in the *Tabaqat-i Nasiri* and the medieval *Tazkiras* and anthologies, but they do not rank highly in quality. By this time, many poets and scholars of eminence had joined the service of the Ghurid princes. Some of them produced works that are included in the classics of Persian literature such as *Chahar Maqala*.[29]

Before his death, sometime in AD 1161, Jahan Suz seems to have adopted the Ismaili faith. Minhaj Juzjani tells us that he invited the *da'is* (preachers) from the fort of al-Maut to propagate Ismailism in Firuz Kuh towards the close of his reign. On his death soon afterwards, Jahan Suz's son, Sultan Saifuddin Husain, who was a committed Sunni Muslim, had the Ismaili *da'is* executed and also suppressed the followers of the Qaramitah (Carmathian) sect.

Sultan Saifuddin Husain was a just and benevolent ruler. He befriended all those who had been oppressed by his father. His cousin, Prince Ghiyasuddin Muhammad bin Sam, and his younger brother, Shihabuddin Muhammad bin Sam, were also set free in Gharjistan.[30] Having had the Ismaili preachers in his kingdom put to death, he promoted the interests of orthodox Sunni leaders. But his was a short-lived reign. When he started on a military expedition in AD 1163. against the Ghuzz Turks who had been carrying on predatory encroachments in his territories, he was killed by Abul Abbas Shishani,[31] the younger brother of Sipahsalar Darmish Shishani. The latter had earlier been killed by Sultan Saifuddin Husain. Following the murder of the Sultan, the Ghuzz Turks defeated the Ghurid army.[32]

Having escaped from the battlefield, Sipahsalar Abul Abbas Shishani proceeded to Afshin in Gharjistan, where he placed Prince Ghiyasuddin Muhammad bin Sam (son of Sultan Baha-uddin Sam) on the throne with the title, Sultan Ghiyasuddin Muhammad bin Sam. The new Sultan was joined by his younger brother, Shihabuddin (later Sultan Muizuddin Muhammad bin Sam), who had been living with his uncle in Bamian. He was appointed *Sar-i Jandar* (commander of the royal bodyguards) by his brother, with the *vilayet* of Istiya and Kajuran as his administrative charge.[33] Abul Abbas had become overbearing and was in alliance with the rebel chiefs in Ghur, and thus the brothers became disgusted with him. They began to plan as how to get rid of him. The commander, Abul Abbas, found them too clever to be used as puppets. The local historian of Ghur, Minhaj Juzjani, would have us believe that the Sultan Ghiyasuddin Muhammad bin Sam and his brother had developed hatred towards Abul Abbas for the murder of Sultan Saifuddin Husain and directed their Turk guards to kill him at the time of his visit to the court. But Minhaj-i-Siraj Juzjani's senior contemporary, Sadiduddin Muhammad Awfi, who hailed from Bukhara and had taken shelter in India after the Mongol conquest of his home-land, supplements the information contained in the *Tabaqat-i Nasiri*. He states: The *sipahsalar* (Abul Abbas) proclaimed the two bothers, Sultan Ghiyasuddin Sam and Muizuddin Sam, as rulers after the martyrdom of Sultan Saifuddin Husain. Both the brothers owed their elevation to him. When their position became secure with power and influence, Abul Abbas grew jealous of them. In fact, he wanted to have them put on the throne as puppets. He forged an alliance with their uncle, the ruler of Bamian. He wrote letters to him and his sons and hatched a plot against the Sultan of Ghur. The royal brothers got an inkling of the plot, and having consulted the trusted nobles, decided to have the commander, Abul Abbas, eliminated without any delay. He was summoned to the court and on arrival was killed.[34]

As for their uncle, Fakhruddin Masud of Bamian, he had already started from Bamian along with his allies, Malik Alauddin Qimaj Sanjari, the Saljuq governor of Balkh, and Tajuddin Yildoz of Herat at the invitation of Abul Abbas, but could not achieve success. His young nephews were powerful enough to foil his move. As Qimaj and Yildoz moved from their sides ahead of the army of Bamian, they were intercepted and defeated by the Ghurid armies one after the other. The head of Qimaj was sent to Fakhruddin Masud, who was still on his way to Ghur. Disappointed by the turn of events, Fakhruddin Masud decided to return but was surrounded by the army of Ghur. Left with no option, he came to terms with his nephews and returned to Bamian, where he soon passed away.[35] His son, Malik Shamsuddin, was confirmed by Sultan Ghiyasuddin Muhammad bin Sam in the government of Bamian, Takharistan, Balkh, Chighariyan Khash, Jarun, and Badakhshan. As he continued to be loyal to the Sultan of Ghur, he was honoured with the title of Sultan.[36]

During the reign of Sultan Ghiyasuddin Muhammad bin Sam, the Ghurid power reached its zenith. First, the young Sultan marched towards the territories of Girmsir and Zamindawar and annexed them to his kingdom. Thereafter, he started towards Herat at the invitation of its residents, who were not pleased under the rule of Bahauddin Tughril, one of the Saljuq nobles. It was also annexed without any difficulty. After Herat, the territories of Qadas, Jalivan, Tiwar, and Saifrud were conquered. Besides, the entire region of Gharjistan, Talqan and Jarzvan also came under his occupation. The Sultan assigned the charge of the government of Jarum and Takinabad to his brother, Muizuddin Muhammad bin Sam.[37] On his return from Sijistan (or Sistan), where the local chief had acknowledged his suzerainty, he started deputing his horsemen to attack the Ghuzz Turks in the region of Ghazna and plunder it. Having harrased the Ghuzz for sometime, he summoned the armies from different parts of Ghur and Khurasan and moved with them for the conquest of Ghazna in AD 1173. Having occupied Ghazna, he entrusted its charge to his brother with the title of Sultan Muizuddin Muhammad bin Sam. The latter began his rule with benevolence; people were provided with employment in the army and administration. The maintenance of peace and order in the region attracted traders and merchants who had fled to different lands during the tyrannical Ghuzz rule.

A contemporary writer, Muhammad bin Mansur, known as Fakhr Muddabbir, states that Sultan Muizuddin Muhammad bin Sam not only cleaned Ghazna of the rapacious Ghuzz but also provided security of life and property to people against the menace of the Carmathians, who plundered travellers and villages. The roads were rendered safe for the merchant caravans. Consequently, the merchants again started moving about, loaded with merchandise through Ghazna and its territory. The revival of trade and commerce led to all-round prosperity in the region. The scarcity of essential goods that had caused much hardship to the people in Ghazna and its dependency was now over. Learning and scholarship got a fillip as the result of the Sultan's large-hearted patronage. The revival of old crafts led to improvement in general conditions, with the result that one who could not afford to own one domestic slave previously, could now have, besides camels and horses, both male and female slaves.[38] As for the conquests made by Sultan Muizuddin Muhammad bin Sam in India, the Carmathian kingdom of Multan and Uchh (Upper Sind) was the first to be conquered, in AD 1175–6. In the year 1178–9 he attacked the Hindu kingdom of Gujarat through the desert of Sind, but was defeated and driven away. This defeat led him to change his military strategy with regard to the conquest of India. As the Ghaznavid Lahore could strategically serve as a base better than any other town or city, in 1178–80, he captured Peshawar from where he could easily advance towards Lahore. The following year he attacked Lahore, which was a fortified city but he had to return from there unsuccessful in 1180–1. As the Carmathians (Qaramitah) had fled to lower Sind from Multan and Uchh, and posed a threat to the Ghurid officers in the region, the Sultan decided to destroy their power before the conquest of Lahore. In 1182, he left Ghazna and entered Sind. The entire region of lower Sind, including the seaport of Debul, was cleaned of the Carmathians. From Sind the Sultan returned to Ghazna loaded with booty.[39] Though Khusrau Malik, the last Ghaznavid ruler, was weak, yet he managed to defend Lahore against the Sultan till 1186. Unable to conquer it by the use of military power, Muizuddin Muhammad bin Sam took recourse to strategem for the seizure of Lahore. Prince Malik Shah, son of Khusrau Malik, who had been staying in Ghazna as hostage for his father, was allowed by the Sultan to return to Lahore with a message of goodwill from the latter for his father. He was still on his way when the Sultan started for Lahore by a different route. Having bypassed Malik Shah, he reached the vicinity of Lahore. Khusrau Malik, who had received the news of the release of his son, was besides himself with joy and spent the night in merrymaking. The following morning, when he got up from sleep and was informed about the situation, he lost his nerve and surrendered to his rival. He was sent to Gharjistan as a prisoner. In 1192, Khusrau Malik was killed along with his son, Malik Shah. His capture of Lahore opened the way for the expansion of his rule in north India.[40] Now the rivals who needed to be fought against were Hindu Rajput rulers.

About the year 1190, the capture of the fort of Tabarhinda (present-day Bathinda in Indian Punjab) by the Sultan provoked Prithvi Raj, the powerful ruler of Ajmer, to defend his frontiers against the foreign invader. He started with a huge army to liberate Tabarhinda from foreign rule and laid siege to its fort. Malik Ziauddin Tulaki, whom the Sultan had posted there, defended it with courage. Sultan Muizuddin, who was still on the way, got the news from Tabarhinda and turned back to fight against Prithvi Raj. In 1191, a fierce battle was fought between the rival armies in the plain of Tarain (in present-day Haryana state). The horses of the Ghazna army were frightened by the sight of elephants and could not stay on the field. As a result, the mounted soldiers and officers of the Sultan's army lost courage and began to run away. In an attempt to boost the morale of his men, the Sultan with spear in hand charged to the centre of the army and displayed undaunted courage, but he was severely wounded. One of the Khalji mounted soldiers saw him falling down from his horse, and he came to his rescue; taking him up on his horse, he galloped out of the battlefield.[41]

Possessed of a bull's tenacity, no setback or defeat could dampen Sultan Muizuddin's courage and fighting spirit. In fact, his failure made him think of changing his military strategy and tactics, and then he was able to retrieve his honour. On his return to Ghazna, he set about reorganizing his army, and having brought to completion his preparation, he again moved to fight against Prithvi Raj in 1192. Again, Prithvi Raj came to fight in the plain of Tarain. This time the Sultan adopted quite a different tactic. According to Sadiduddin Muhammad Awfi, the Sultan kept the fire burning in front of his camp throughout the night so that his rival thought that he was in the camp, and then he moved out of the camp with his horsemen and reached the rear of the enemy army when it grew quite dark. At dawn, he surrounded the enemy camp and fell on it all of a sudden. The Rajputs were caught napping. Thrown into confusion, they could not make a stand, and Prithvi Raj decided to run away. But he was captured and killed.[42] This second battle proved decisive, and in the following ten years the Sultan and his Turkish generals defeated all the powerful chiefs in north India and established their political hegemony from Sind up to the Bay of Bengal.

The booty looted in the wake of military campaigns led by the Sultan and his Turkish generals in the conquered territories was enormous; it helped the Ghurid kingdom rise to the status of a world power. Every time the larger part of the booty was sent by Muizuddin to his brother in Firuz Kuh. It comprised, among other things, the choice products of India. For instance, out of the booty acquired in Ajmer in 1192, Sultan Muizuddin sent to his brother a wheel, a chain, a huge melon with a circumference of five yards into five yards, and two large drums, all made of gold. Sultan Ghiyasuddin Muhammad bin Sam ordered the wheel, the chain, and the melon to be hung by the gate of the Jama mosque of Firuz Kuh. Later, when the mosque was damaged by flood water, the gold drums, the melon, the wheel, and the chain were sent to Herat with instructions that they should be melted and the money gained by their sale should be spent on the construction of a new Jama mosque there.[43]

Brief mention should be made of the fact that the increase in the power and glory of the Sultanate of Ghur led to the establishment of close diplomatic relations between the Abbasid Caliph of Baghdad and Sultan Ghiyasuddin Muhammad bin Sam. The Caliph still commanded immense respect among the Sunni elite the world over, and he was regarded as the lawful sovereign and the head of the entire Islamic world. The grant of a diploma of authority and its investiture by him to a Sultan in any country legitimized the latter's rule over the Muslims. It was also a source of prestige. The emissaries from Baghdad came to Firuz Kuh twice and returned with gifts from the Sultan.[44] The other rulers of Central Asia, Sultan Tekish Khwarazm Shah (d. AD 1200) and the Sultan of Samarqand who were the vassals of the non-Muslim Qarakhitai ruler, were looked down upon and considered by the Caliph as unworthy Muslims, who deserved to be destroyed.[45]

Realist by nature and pragmatic in his approach, the Ghurid Sultan Ghiyasuddin Muhammad bin Sam could not be instigated by the Abbasid Caliph to start an armed conflict against Khwarazm so long as Sultan Tekish was alive. On the latter's death in AD 1200, the Ghurid brothers decided to launch a war against Tekish's son, Sultan Alauddin Muhammad Khwarazm Shah. They advanced with their combined forces on Nishapur in Khurasan, seized it easily, and entrusted its charge to Malik Ziauddin Muhammad, a Shansabani prince and the son-in-law of Sultan Ghiyasuddin Muhammad bin Sam. The following year, they captured Marv Shah Jahan and posted Malik Nasiruddin Kharang there. Thereafter, the territory of Sarakh was occupied and the Shansabani prince, Malik Tajuddin Zangi, the grandson of Fakhruddin Masud of Bamian, was posted to hold it. Now the whole of Khurasan was brought under the control of the Ghurid Sultan. From Khurasan Sultan Muizuddin marched towards Tus and occupied it, too. The details furnished by Juvaini of the Ghurid conquest shed light on the discipline among the Ghurid army men, which contrasted with that of the Khwarazmian army. Juvaini tells us that having seized the place, the soldiers began to plunder but the *shahnas* (prefects) were sent by the Sultan to protect the houses of the holy men in the city. 'They continued to pillage till midday, when a proclamation was made that they should desist. And such was the discipline of the army that each soldier at once let go of what he was holding; and all the spoils having been gathered together, as soon as anyone recognized his goods, they were at once restored to him, for this was the policy in their plundering.'[46] As for Sultan Alauddin Muhammad Khwarazm Shah, he made overtures of peace indicating his willingness to rule over his territories as a vassal if Khurasan was left to him, but his offer was spurned.

He extended large-hearted patronage to the scholars of religious and secular sciences and collected a fairly large number of them at his court. He was fond of their company. Moreover, men of piety and learning in different cities of Khurasan, Ghazna, and India received stipends and gifts from him every year.[54]

The Shansabani rulers also seem to have emulated the sultans of the neighbouring empires in having beautiful cities and castles constructed in Ghur and in the conquered territories as well; they evinced a keen interest in popular sciences, at least since the middle of the eleventh century AD. For instance, Amir Abbas bin Shis, though known for his tyrannical rule, took pains to acquire mastery over the popular science of astronomy. He is also given credit for having invited skilled architects from different places for the reconstruction of the fort in Sanga in the Valley of Mandish.

> The walls, after the manner of a parapet, were carried from that castle, on two sides, to the strong ground on the summit of the mountain of Zar-i Margh, and, at the foot of that mountain, on a knoll, a lofty Qasr (palace) was directed to be raised, with twelve towers, and in every tower, like the zodiac circles in the firmament, there were thirty openings—there were six towers towards the east and the north, and six others towards the west and the south—marked out; and these were so arranged that, everyday, the sun would shine through one of those openings approximating to the position of its rise. By this means, he used to know in what degree of what sign of the zodiac the sun was on that particular day.[55]

Sultan Ghiyasuddin Muhammad bin Sam not only maintained this tradition in promoting the progress of art and culture, but he also tried to excel even the grand rulers of Central Asia and Iran in this regard. He had pleasure gardens laid out and beautiful palaces and pavilions erected in different parts of his empire. He is reported to have selected Zamindawar for his winter capital. Between Firuz Kuh (his summer capital) and Zamindawar he developed the entire region into a hunting ground. Near Zamindawar he had a pleasure garden laid out with beautiful pavilions and named it Bagh-i Iram. According to Minhaj Juzjani, no garden in the world could bear comparison with it in pleasantness and freshness. It was very long and its glades were beautified with pine, juniper trees, shrubs, and odoriferous herbs.

'Once every year, at the Sultan's direction, a semi-circle of about one hundred miles was drawn and more than ten thousand beasts were driven into the plain adjoining the garden. Then the Sultan came to the pavilion of the garden and held a convivial entertainment while his officers and slaves were permitted, one by one, to enter the plain and kill the game before him.'[56]

In his youth he loved to sip wine but later on he gave it up. However, the sparkling of a crystalline glass and the grace of good company always held an attraction for him. In later days, while his companions were served with wine, the juice of pomegranate was served to him with the same ostentation.[57] Charity was another substitute for wine, meant to soothe his spirit. Minhaj Juzjani tells us: 'He distributed his gifts among the pious and the needy in east and west, in Arabia, Iran, Turkestan, and India.'[58]

As for the nature of kingship under the last Ghurid Sultans, it underwent change with the accession of Sultan Ghiyasuddin Muhammad bin Sam in AD 1163. Like his uncle Jahan Suz, he entrusted the charge of the conquered territory of Ghazna to his younger brother, Shihabuddin Muhammad, as his appanage and also conferred upon him the title of Sultan Muizuddin Muhammad bin Sam in AD 1173. Later on, his cousin Malik Shamsuddin, son and successor of Fakhruddin Masud of Bamian, was also honoured with the title of Sultan.[59] In other territories, the sipahsalars were appointed from amongst the nobles in the tradition of the Ghaznavids. The latter carried on the administration on behalf of Sultan Ghiyasuddin Muhammad bin Sam in their respective provinces.[60]

On the death of Sultan Ghiyasuddin Muhammad bin Sam in AD 1202. Sultan Muizuddin Muhammad bin Sam became the head of the Shansabani dynasty of Ghur. He distributed the territories ruled over by his brother among the royal princes in accordance with his own judgement of each prince. Neither did he do away with the tradition of fragmented polity within the region of Ghur (the chiefs continued to enjoy their privileges there), nor did he abandon the doctrine of collective sovereignty by setting aside the right of the Shansabani princes to get a territory each as an appanage to rule over in his own name. Therefore, the territories conquered by Jahan Suz and Sultan conquered to the east of Lahore. For instance, Sultan Muizuddin entrusted the charge of Tabarhinda, seized from the vassal of Prithvi Raj of Ajmer in AD 1191,[64] to Malik Ziyauddin Tulaki along with other officers. After the second battle of Tarain in AD 1192, Malik Qutbuddin Aibek was posted as *sipahsalar* in Kuhram to govern it and its dependencies, including Hansi.[65] On his master's return to Ghazna, Qutbuddin Aibek pacified the region included in his charge. He defeated a powerful rebel chief in Hansi and then seized the territories of Meerut and Baran from the Dor chiefs, who were not willing to acquiesce. In the same year, Delhi was also occupied and made the headquarters of his army. In AD 1193, he conquered Kol (Aligarh) and appointed his lieutenant, Malik Hussamuddin Ughalbak, as *sipahsalar* there.[66] As Raja Jai Chand of Qanauj was defeated and killed by Qutbuddin Aibek (AD 1194), the commander of the advance guard before the main army under the command of the Sultan could reach there, the Sultan rewarded him with the charge of Jai Chand's territories.[67] However, in 1195, the fort of Thankar (later Bayana) was not made part of the *sipahsalari* of Aibek after its conquest; instead it was assigned to another slave general, Malik Bahauddin Tughril, with the instruction to seize Gwalior and include it in his *sipahsalari*.[68] Mohammad Habib rightly observes that up until now the Sultan's policy had been not to allow any of his officers to become too powerful. Hence, there were different Ghurid governors independent of each other in India.[69] It was after the death of Tughril that Aibek was made the *sipahsalar* of Hindustan,[70] i.e. the region east of the Sutlej. After the assassination of Sultan Muizuddin in AD 1206, Aibek was accepted as the Sultan by the *sipahsalars* in the Panjab because he had already gained a reputation for the invincibility of his arms and nobody had the courage to question his claim to the throne.

NOTES

1. Mohammad Habib, 'Shihab Uddin of Ghur,' originally published in *Aligarh Muslim University Journal*, No. 1, January 1930, pp. 10–15, now available in the *Collected Works of Professor Mohammad Habib*, ed. K.A. Nizami, New Delhi, 1981, vol. 2, p. 140.

2. K.A. Nizami, *Some Aspects of Religion and Politics in India during the Thirteenth Century*, New Delhi, 1961, p. 31.
3. C.E. Bosworth, 'The Early Islamic History of Ghur', *Central Asiatic Journal*, vol. VI, 1961, Wiesbaden, p. 118.
4. Ibid., pp. 118–25.
5. Al-Utbi, *Tarikh-ul Yamini* (Arabic text), Lahore, 1300 H., pp. 242–4. Also *Tarikh-ul-Yamini's* thirteenth-century Persian translation by Abu-s-Sharaf al-Jurbazqani, ed. Jaffar Shi'ar, Tehran, 1345 Shamsi, pp. 312–13.
6. Minhaj-i-Siraj Juzjani (hereafter cited Minhaj Juzjani), *Tabaqat-i Nasiri*, ed. Abdul Hai Habibi, Kabul, 1963, vol. I, p. 330.
7. Khwaja Abul Fazl Baihaqi, *Tarikh-i Baihaqi*, eds. Ghani and Fayyaz, Tehran, 1324 Shamsi, pp. 114–15; C.E. Bosworth, 'The Early Islamic History of Ghur', *Central Asiatic Journal*, 1961, op. cit., 127 (fn. 34).
8. *Tabaqat-i Nasiri*, vol. I, p. 333.
9. Ibid., p. 330.
10. *Tabaqat-i Nasiri*, vol. I, pp. 322–3.
11. Minhaj Juzjani is silent on the nature of his relationship with his immediate predecessor. Perhaps he was not his son but a nephew or a brother. *Tabaqat-i Nasiri*, vol. I, p. 333.
12. Loc. cit.
13. *Tabaqat-i Nasiri*, vol. I, pp. 351–3, 354, 355.
14. Sadiduddin Muhammad Awfi states that after the murder of Sipahsalar Abul Abbas Shishani by the order of Sultan Ghiyasuddin Muhammad bin Sam, his son was brought up and then honoured with their family position. Cf. *Jawami'ul Hikayat wa Lavami'ul-rivayat*, vol. 2, ed. Amir Bano Musaffa and Mutahir Musaffa, Tehran, pp. 467–8.
15. *Tabaqat-i Nasiri*, vol. I, pp. 332–3; before Minhaj Juzjani, Ahmad bin Umar Ibn Ali An-Nizami Al-Aruzi. As-Samarqandi also mentioned the dogs of Ghur, famous for their fighting qualities. Cf. *Chahar Maqala*, ed. Mirza Muhammad Qazvini, Tehran (rpt.), 1348 Shamsi, p. 61.
16. The fact that Firuz Kuh was founded on the northern limits of Ghur, adjoining the territory of Gharjistan, has been established by the French archaeologists, Mariaq and Wiet.
17. *Tabaqat-i Nasiri*, vol. I, pp. 335–6.
18. Ibid., vol. I, p. 337.
19. Ibid., vol. II, Kabul, 1964, p. 135.
20. *Tabaqat-i Nasiri*, vol. I, p. 336.
21. Mohammad Habib, *Collected Works*, vol. 2, op. cit., p. 106, also *Tabaqat-i Nasiri*, vol. I, pp. 394–5.
22. *Tabaqat-i Nasiri*, vol. I, pp. 343–44.
23. *Adab-ul Harb-wal-Shuja'*, ed. Ahmad Suhaili Khwansari, Tehran, 346, Shamsi, pp. 437–8.
24. *Tabaqat-i Nasiri*, vol. I, pp. 344/45, for the verses composed by Jahansuz in Persian.

25. Ibid., vol. I, pp. 344–6.
26. *Tabaqat-i Nasiri*, vol. I, p. 346. Also *Chahar Maqala*, op. cit., pp. 87–8. Aruzi Samarqandi himself was with Jahansuz's army.
27. *Tabaqat-i Nasiri*, vol. I, p. 348.
28. Ibid., vol. I, p. 346.
29. Its author was in the service of Prince Abul Hasan Ali bin Fakhruddin Masud to whom the *Chahar Maqala* was dedicated.
30. *Tabaqat-i Nasiri*, vol. I, p. 351.
31. Ibid.
32. Ibid., pp. 325, 326, 327, 350, 351–2. The brother of Abul Abbas Shishani betrayed Sultan Saifuddin Husain and paid allegiance to Malik Nasiruddin Husain after Sultan Alauddin Jahansuz had been taken away by Sultan Sanjar as prisoner.
33. Ibid., p. 354.
34. Cf. Iqtidar Husain Siddiqui, *Perso-Arabic Sources on the Life and Conditions in the Sultanate of Delhi*, Munshiram Manoharlal, New Delhi, 1992, pp. 22–3; for Awfi's *Jawami'ul Hikayat's* English translation; *Tabaqat-i Nasiri*, vol. I, pp. 355–7, 386.
35. *Tabaqat-i Nasiri*, vol. I, p. 387.
36. Ibid., vol. I, p. 357.
37. Ibid., vol. I, pp. 357–8.
38. *Tarikh-i-Fakhr-i Mudabbir*, pp. 19–20.
39. Cf. Muhammad Habib, *Collected Works*, vol. 2, op. cit., pp. 110–17.
40. *Jawami'ul Hikayat wa-Livami'il-Rivayat*, op. cit., vol. I, part II, p. 409 (hereafter cited as *Jawami'ul Hikayat*); *Tabaqat-i Nasiri*, vol. I, p. 400.
41. *Jawami'ul Hikayat*, vol. I, part II, pp. 409–10. Minhaj's account of the battle is brief. *Tabaqat-i Nasiri*, vol. I, p. 400.
42. *Tabaqat-i Nasiri*, vol. I, p. 400.
43. Ibid., p. 375.
44. Cf. Ata Malik Juvaini, *Tarikh-i Jahan Qusha*, ed. Mirza Muhammad Qazwini, part II, Leiden, 1916, p. 86.
45. *Tabaqat-i Nasiri*, vol. I, pp. 401–2.
46. John Andrew Boyle, *The History of the World Conqueror*, op. cit., vol. 2, p. 316.
47. *Tabaqat-i Nasiri*, vol. I, pp. 402–3, *Tarikh-i Jahan Qusha*, op. cit., pp. 56–7; also C.E. Bosworth, 'Qara Khitay', *Encyclopedia of Islam*, new edition, Leiden, 1978, vol. IV, pp. 581a–583b, for details about Qara Khitais.
48. *Tabaqat-i Nasiri*, vol. 1, p. 403.
49. Iqtidar Husain Siddiqui, *Islam and Muslims in South Asia: Historical Perspective*, Delhi, 1984, pp. 15–16, for the contemporary and later sources on the conversion of the Khokkar chief to Islam.
50. Hasan Nizami, *Taj ul-Maasir*, Ms., British Library, London, Add. 7623, ff. 266b–288b; *Tabaqat-i Nasiri*, vol. I, p. 403.

51. Cf. C.E. Bosworth, 'The Rise of the Karamiyyah in Khorasan', *Muslim World*, vol. I, 1 January 1960, pp. 5–14.
52. Cf. Iqtidar Husain Siddiqui, 'Abu Abdullah Muhammad bin Kiram Aur Unki Talimat' (Urdu), *Tahqiqat-i Islam*, Aligarh, Oct.–Dec. 1991, pp. 226–36.
53. *Tabaqat-i Nasiri*, vol. I, p. 362.
54. Ibid., vol. I, p. 361.
55. Ibid., vol. I, pp. 331–2; also Eng. tr., Major H.G. Raverty, vol. I, p. 331.
56. Ibid., vol. I, p. 364.
57. Ibid., vol. I, p. 365; Mohammad Habib, 'Shihabuddin of Ghur', *Collected Works of Professor Mohammad Habib: Politics and Society during the Early Medieval Period*, 1981, pp. 125–6.
58. *Tabaqat-i Nasiri*, vol. I, p. 361.
59. Loc. cit.
60. *Tabaqat-i Nasiri*, vol. I, pp. 357–8, 387.
61. Ibid., vol. I, p. 390.
62. Ibid., vol. I, p. 411.
63. The *Amir-i-dad* seems to have been posted in every territorial unit to supervise the division of booty between the state and the soldiers. Besides, he was charged with the duty of keeping a strict watch on the conduct of shopkeepers in the bazaars, public morality, and police administration in a city. Cf. Muhammad bin Mansur entitled Mubarak Shah known Fakhr-i-Mudabbir, *Adab ul-Muluk wa-kifayat-ul-Mamluk*, ed. Muhammad Sarvar Maulai and published under the new title *A'in-i-Kishvardari* (Bunyad-i-Farhang-i-Iran, no. 212), pp. 40–1; *Tabaqat-i-Nasiri*; vol. I, pp. 444, 460; vol. II, pp. 41–2; *Jawami ul-Hikayat in Perso-Arabic Sources on the Life and Conditions in the Sultanate of Delhi*, op. cit., pp. 32–3.
64. *Tabaqat-i Nasiri*, vol. I, p. 419.
65. Ibid., vol. I, p. 400.
66. *Tarikh-i-Fakhir-i-Mudabbir*, p. 22.
67. *Tabaqat-i Nasiri*, vol. I, p. 423.
68. *Tabaqat-i Nasiri*, vol. I, pp. 422–3; also Hasan Nizami, *Taj ul-Maasir*, British Library, London, no. Add. 7623, ff. 55b–56a, for the first appointment of Hussamn Uddin Ughallak as *sipahasalar* in Kol in 1193 and the *parwana* issued to him by Aibek regarding his appointment.
69. *Collected Works of Mohammad Habib*, vol. 2, pp. 116–17.
70. Minhaj Juzjani means by Hindustan the region east of the river Sutlej. He does not include in it the territorial units of Lahore, Multan, and Uchh. *Tabaqat-i Nasiri*, vol. I, p. 419.

CHAPTER 2

Evolution of the Sultanate Polity in India during the Thirteenth Century

The examination of the thirteenth-century Indo-Persian literature on statecraft suggests that the purpose of the writers was to familiarize the Turkish Sultans and their lieutenents, mostly emigrants, about the political traditions that had developed under the Ghaznavid rule in the Panjab. Doubtless, the early Indo-Persian writers were inspired by the early Arabic classics as well as the writings of Imam Ghazzali and Nizam-ul-Mulk Tusi on the system of governance, yet the transmuting of the old ideas caused by the Indian environment is implicit therein. They appear to have realized the need for cooperation between the Sultan and the hereditary land chiefs, Hindu and Muslim alike. Their works are indeed important; in them we find clues to the state policies and the important changes resulting from them. The insights provided therein take us back in time. In this regard, mention may be especially made of the works of Fakhr-i Mudabbir, the *Muqaddimah* (hereafter referred to as *Tarikh-i Fakhr-i-Mudabbir*) and the *Adab-ul-Muluk wal-kifayat-ul-Mamluk*, the *Chachnama*[1] (Persian translation by Ali Kufi of an Arabic work), and the *Jawami'ul-Hikayat wa-Lavami'ur-Rivayat,* compiled by Sadid-uddin Muhammad Awfi. Fakhr-i Mudabbir presented his first work, *Shajra-i-Ansab* with a detailed introduction (*Muqaddima*) to Sultan Qutbuddin Aibek (reigned: 1206–10) in Lahore and the *Adab-ul-Muluk wa-Kifayat-ul Mamluk* to Sultan Shamsuddin Iltutmish (reigned: 1211–36) respectively. In the *Muqaddima* (or the *Tarikh-i-Fakhr-i-Mudabbir*), the duties of the Sultan, such as the execution of justice and the maintenance of peace and order in the Sultanate, are described before the achievements of Sultan Qutbuddin Aibek in India. According to him, the foremost duty of the Sultan is to establish the rule of law and ensure impartial justice to all and sundry, suppress both the pernicious people and evils in society, construct mosques and *madrasas* (schools and colleges) in the urban centres, build bridges, ribats (later khanqahs, established by the state for the comfort of travellers), and forts for the safety of roads against robbers and highwaymen. Further, he states that the Sultan should strive to his utmost to create conditions favourable for the prosperity of the *raiyat* (peasants and commoners). As regards the *Adabul-Muluk wal-Kifayat-ul-Mamluk*, the later recension of which is well known as *Adab-ul-Harb wal Shuja*,[2] it deals with the duties of the Sultan, his ministers, state apparatus, mode of warfare, weapons, and war horses, etc.

The *Chachnama* seems to have been translated by Ali bin Hamid al-Kufi with a view to providing the new rulers of the region, Sultan Nasiruddin Qubacha and his officers of foreign birth, with information about the political traditions followed by the early Muslim rulers (the Arab conquerors) since the eighth century AD. The translator brings into greater relief the need for the Muslim rulers not to interfere with the social system of the Hindus in India. For example, Muhammad bin Qasim is said to have sanctioned the privileges of the high castes and the degradation of the low castes. The Brahmans were granted full religious freedom and also appointed to important positions in Sind and Multan regions.[3] It is also worth noting that there is a great deal of touching up of the original Arabic text in the *Chachnama* in connection with the relations between the Muslim ruler and the hereditary land chiefs, called the Rais, Thakurs, and Ranas.[4] It suggests by implication that the Sultan should foster cordial relations with the hereditary local potentates, for they constituted an important element in Indian polity. Ali bin Hamid al-Kufi seems also to imply that the victorious Muslim ruler should regard his victory over the chiefs as a prelude to a rapproachment and not to their annihilation.

Likewise, Sadiduddin Muhammad Awfi, an emigrant scholar from Central Asia who wrote a number of books, incorporates interesting details in his magnum opus, the *Jawami'ul-Hikayat wa-Lavami'ur Rivayat*, about the patterns of political behaviour, resulting from the concern of the duty-conscious Sultans in Central

Asia and India for the welfare of the people under their rule. His statement that the Sultan should fashion friendly ties with the land chiefs tends to suggest that he had also realized the fact that the consolidation of the Sultan's power in India was not easy without the cooperation of the local chiefs. He praises Sultan Nasiruddin Qubacha for forgiving the rebel Khokkar chief in the Salt Range after his victory over him.[5]

We may now turn to a discussion about how the traditions developed and the concepts evolved in Central Asia and India under the Arabs and the Ghaznavids with regard to statecraft and how these influenced the polity of the Sultanate in India. Sultan Qutbuddin Aibek, who laid down the foundation of an independent Sultanate in India after the assassination of his master, Sultan Muizuddin Muhammad bin Sam, was an heir to the political traditions of Ghazna. Possessed of excellent qualities of head and heart, he did not only provide successful military leadership to the army but also evinced a keen interest in the well-being of the people under his rule. According to Fakhr-i-Mudabbir, he always inspired enthusiasm and devotion among the army men by his own personal example. Hasan Nizami invented an ornate style, making use of the conceits of Arabic and Persian prose and poetry, for producing the history of Aibek's reign so that it could agree with the greatness of the Sultan. His style was soon considered by the literati an ideal style for writing the history of the great kings in India as well as outside India.[6] Undoubtedly, Aibek had emerged as a charismatic leader on account of his outstanding achievements in India.[7] Yet he never seems to have claimed any super human power inhering in his person. Moreover, there is no shred of evidence to show that the Sultan was ever considered by his followers as a super human being. His strong personality and good qualities made him acceptable to the nobles and armymen.

The details furnished by the contemporary writers about the rituals associated with sovereignty tend to suggest that their performance both by the Sultan and the people reminded them of their responsibility towards each other. Fakhr-i-Mudabbir, mentioning the response of the people to Aibek's claim to the throne in AD 1206, refers to a well-established ritual regarding allegiance paid by people in general to the new Sultan. He states that on his arrival from Delhi to Lahore, the notables of the city, the *qazis* (judges or judicial officers), *imams* (religious divines), saiyids, *Ahl-i-Sufa* (men of piety), officers and military men, traders and merchants, high and low, powerful and weak, rich and poor, came out to show their allegiance to him.[8] Indeed, this ritual implied operational legitimacy and suggested as well that the ceremony of *bait* (general allegiance) still had symbolic importance. The same author also indicates the importance that Lahore had acquired under the later Ghaznavids and states that the city served as the winter capital of Sultan Muizuddin Muhammad bin Sam as well and that it could better serve as the capital of the Sultanate. Minhaj Juzjani also describes Lahore as the centre of learning and culture wherein a large number of merchants had taken residence. They carried on trade as far as the Mongol lands.[9] According to Majduddin Abul Ma'ali Muaiyid bin Muhammad Jajarmi, the thirteenth-century translator of Imam Ghazzali's *Ihyaul-Ulum id-din*, besides the traders, the *ulama* belonging to different schools of religious thought, particularly Hanafi, also lived in Lahore in sizeable numbers.[10] In short, Lahore was the most prestigious city,[11] while Delhi was still a pargana headquarters of no historical significance.[12]

Equally interesting is the evidence about the policy adopted by Sultan Aibek towards the religious elite, nobility, and the hereditary landed aristocracy in the new Sultanate. After his accession to the throne, Aibek issued the *mithal* (royal mandate) regarding *imlak* (land grants) held by the *a'ima* (religious scholars), stating that they would be retained by the old grantees. Likewise, all those amongst the deserving people (of piety and religion) who received stipends and monthly allowances from the state were also not touched. Further, he made new land grants to the scholars, and ordered that fixed food grain and monthly allowances in cash be given to dervishes, widows and orphans for their maintenance.[13] Attracted by his patronage to men of learning, many scholars came from the neighbouring countries and got lucrative positions in the civil administration of the expanding Sultanate. The following incident narrated by Muhammad Awfi casts light on the Sultan's attitude towards the emigrant scholars:

> During the reign of the just and benevolent Sultan, Qutbuddin (Aibek), an émigré *danishmand* (scholar of canon law) named Sharaf was found guilty of cheating a slave merchant. The compiler had met the

danishmand. The latter got hold of a slave girl by deceiving the merchant. The *qazi* (judge) sentenced him to imprisonment. When the matter was reported to the Sultan, a *farman* (royal mandate) was issued that the price of the slave girl be paid to the merchant from the royal treasury on behalf of the offender. Thereupon, the *danishmand* was brought out from prison and ordered by the Sultan to serve in the royal kitchen as a water-carrier by way of punishment. . . . After a week, he was forgiven and employed as a judge.[14]

As regards the composition of the ruling elite under Sultan Aibek, the officers, both civil and military generals, who had been serving since long were retained. They are said to have belonged to different ethnic groups, such as the Ghurids (i.e. Taziks or modern Tajiks), Turks, Khurasanis (i.e. emigrants from the region now included in present-day Afghanistan), Khaljis,[15] and the Indian *Ratagan* (or Rawats) and *Takaran* (or Thakurs), i.e. the Hindu land chiefs.[16] It shows that the ruling elite of the Sultanate was ethnically heterogeneous in the beginning and remained so subsequently. Thus, the Tajiks from Ghazna and the area around, the Turkish slaves from Turkestan (or the steppe), the Khaljis from Garmsir and the area south of Ghazna (in present-day Afghanistan), the Ghurids from the region of Ghur, the Indian Muslims, and the Hindu chiefs constituted the sources of recruitment to the ruling elite. These different ethnic groups could be used by the strong Sultan to counterpoise the influence of any powerful group of nobles and this helped him maintain balance between them. The successful Sultan welded them into a harmonious whole and benefited from their services to him and the state. The tradition set by Sultan Aibek in this regard inspired his successors.[17]

The nobles, high as well as petty, who had been serving under Aibek since the time of Sultan Muizuddin Muhammad bin Sam were rewarded with promotions after his accession to the throne. The new Sultan is reported to have conferred upon them the rank and position of *sipahsalar* along with the privileges of possessing *sarapardah* (tent enclosure like that of the king), *kos* (kettledrum) and *alam* (banner).[18] The other nobles of lesser ranks were elevated to the posts of *kotwal* in important forts of strategic importance.[19] As the Sultan was famous for his generosity, the soldiers and the *raiyat* (or common people) also benefited from his benevolence.[20]

An important *parwana*[21] issued by Aibek to Malik Hussamuddin Ughalbak regarding his appointment as deputy *sipahsalar* of Kol after its conquest in 1193 casts light on the concern that the Sultan or his deputy in India had for the welfare of people under his rule. As this became a model for the drafting of royal *farmans* during the Sultanate period,[22] and contains interesting information concerning the conduct of *sipahsalars* (or governors), its contents may be briefly analysed:

The deputy *sipahsalar* is directed through the *parwana* to provide protection to the *raiyat* and the traders and ensure impartial justice to all and sundry under his rule. He would earmark some portion of money out of the revenue for distribution in charity to deserving persons.

> Every effort should be made to render the roads safe and protect the highways and bridges for the convenience of traders who serve as liaison between different countries and come from abroad with choice products of other countries. The worthy and virtuous people should not be neglected. The travellers and guests should be looked after, no discrimination be made between the rich and the poor in this regard. Money should be saved for charitable purposes, for benevolence serves as a provision for man in the life hereafter.[23]

In the tradition of the Ghaznavids, the *sipahsalar* could be transferred from one territorial unit to another in case the need arose. For instance, Malik Hussamuddin Ughalbak was transferred from Kol to Benaras, a more extensive unit, in reward for his services to the state.[24] Though the *sipahsalar* is not reported to have been assigned an *iqta* in lieu of cash salary, yet the circumstantial evidence available in the contemporary sources reveals that he could favour an intrepid warrior with a small *iqta* and thus raise his morale.[25] Such *iqtas* were small, each comprising one, two, or three villages. The term used for such assignees seems to have been *iqtadar*[26] and not *muqta*.

Sultan Aibek is also credited with having alleviated the burden of taxes on the peasantry and streamlined revenue administration in the light of the *Sharia* law (Muslim canon law). The extra taxes not permitted by the canon law were abolished. The new Sultan is reported to have ordered the collection of *ushr* (one-tenth of the agricultural produce) from the cultivators. It is further reported that the *nim-ushr* (one-twentieth of the produce) was collected from those who had paid *ushr* previously. It seems that *ushr* and *nim-ushr* were collected from the Muslim cultivators in the *khittas* of Multan and Lahore while the non-Muslims still paid *kharaj* (one-fifth) in accordance with *Sharia* law.[27] Likewise, the customs and practices that were prevalent and found detrimental to the interests of the peasantry were declared unlawful. For example, revenue officials were forbidden to demand chicken or lamb or even beds from the peasants.[28] In short, Sultan Aibek preferred moderation to severity in formulating the state policy. His agrarian policy seems to have been followed by his successors because the thirteenth-century writers found the revenue administration so well known to their readers that they did not think it necessary to mention it in their writings. Generally, they took notice of the reforms or regulations introduced by a Sultan if they had an impact on the life and conditions in the country. It was during the reign of Sultan Alauddin Khalji (AD 1296–1316) that the demand of the state's share in agricultural produce was raised to one half in the wake of the new land settlement taken up, and described in detail by contemporary writers.

The conclusion that we may draw from the above discussion is that the founder of the independent Sultanate in India was an enlightened and far-sighted ruler, the state policy followed by him brought the members of the foreign ruling class and the Hindu landed aristocracy close to each other, and thus paved the way for the development of harmonious relations between them, on the one hand, and the exchange of ideas and culture, on the other.

The accidental death of Sultan Aibek in AD 1210 led to the breakup of his Sultanate into parts held by different nobles. Aibek's son and successor, Aram Shah, was probably a minor and seems to have been removed by the supporters of Iltutmish in Delhi under mysterious circumstances after his accession to the throne.[29] His removal laid down a tradition that a minor was not fit for the throne. Of the contenders for power, three nobles, Nasiruddin Qubacha, the Turkish slave of Sultan Muizuddin Muhammad bin Sam and the son-in-law of Aibek, occupied the whole of the Punjab and Sind regions, while Iwaz Khalji assumed the title of Sultan Ghiyasuddin and ruled over Bihar and parts of

Bengal as an independent ruler. The third was Iltutmish whom the nobles of Delhi invited from Badaon and accepted him as their Sultan. He assumed the title of Sultan Shamsuddin Iltutmish. In an attempt to legitimize his claim to sovereignty, the latter married the daughter of Aibek[30] and then prepared to fight against his rivals.

All the three Sultans (mentioned above) retained the existing administrative system in their respective territories. They had *sipahsalars* in the provinces and paid them in cash. Like Aibek, they seem to have rewarded intrepid *sawars* and petty army officers with land in *iqtas* as a mark of honour. The relevant evidence supplied by the contemporary foreign accounts of Shihabuddin Nasawi (the compiler of *Sirat-i-Jalaluddin Mangbarni*) and Ata Malik Juvaini (the compiler of *Tarikh-i-Jahan Qusha*) reveal that Sultan Nasiruddin Qubacha favoured only individuals with small *iqtas* for their extraordinary achievements.[31]

As regards Sultan Shamsuddin Iltutmish (AD 1211–36), he was opposed by the old nobility, mentioned as the Muizi and Qutbi nobles. They held important territories around Delhi. They gathered together outside Delhi and were also joined by other Turks and Tajiks not willing to accept the usurper (i.e. Iltutmish). Sultan Shamsuddin Iltutmish just feigned an inability to face them by not coming out from Delhi and then on a certain day fell on the hostile nobles and defeated them.[32] After this victory, Sultan Iltutmish seems to have acted tactfully. He fought against his rivals one by one. Though the enemies of the Sultan have not been mentioned by name, they were certainly the nobles of Sultan Muizuddin and Sultan Aibek, such as Hussamuddin Ughalbak, the *sipahsalar* of Benaras. Minhaj-i-Siraj Juzjani's brief reference to these nobles in the eastern Doab implies that they were the old Turkish and Tajik nobles whom the Delhi army of Iltutmish destroyed one after the other.[33] On the destruction of his opponents in the vast region from Delhi up to Awadh between AD 1211 and 1220, Sultan Iltutmish became quite powerful because in every territory the old nobles were killed and their treasures were seized for the royal treasury.[34] Thereafter, Iltutmish was in a position to depute his army on military expeditions against his rivals and for plundering the alien territories. One plundering expedition was led against the Rajput ruler of Jalore in western Rajputana[35] in AD 1215. In the same year, Iltutmish defeated and captured Tajuddin Yildoz.[36]

A feature added to the evolving polity of the Sultanate in India during the reign of Iltutmish was the adoption of the Central Asian practice[37] of getting undesirable nobles eliminated in case they were considered a threat to the royal person or to peace in the country. But in fear of antagonizing public opinion, he did not have them murdered publicly without sufficient legal justification and, therefore, assassins were employed to kill them. Minhaj Juzjani incidentally intimates his readers about this fact in his biographical account of Iltutmish's slave general, Malik Saifuddin Aibek, that the latter was directed by the Sultan to seize the property of murdered nobles for the state. He also says that the noble being a God-fearing man detested the job assigned to him.[38] Awfi also refers incidentally to the assassins in the service of Iltutmish.[39] Al-Kasani, another contemporary emigrant scholar from Transoxiana, also indirectly corroborates Minhaj Juzjani's account when he states:

> During the one and a half year that I have spent in this Hazrat[40] (i.e. Delhi), several persons who rose in revolt against this just and pious monarch, all of them disappeared from the scene, with the result that the fear and grandeur of his royalty got hold of the hearts of the *raiyat* (commonality), Turks, Tajiks, noble and low-born people alike. All of them became subservient to him. Consequently, peace prevailed and people were saved from confusion and tyranny. The country prospered owing to the establishment of law and justice. Likewise, the *rais* (land chiefs) of Hindustan acquiesced and the grandeur of the realm increased through their cooperation.[41]

By the year AD 1229, Sultan Iltutmish had destroyed his powerful rivals from Bengal up to Sind and the Punjab. In AD 1226, Sultan Ghiyasuddin Iwaz Khalji and his son Ali Sher-i-Iwaz Khalji of Bengal were defeated and killed,[42] and two years later, Multan and Sind were seized from Sultan Nasiruddin Qubacha. Nasawi, the biographer of *Sirat-i-Jalaluddin Mangbarni*, informs us that Sultan Iltutmish drove away Jahan Pehlvan, the lieutenant of Khwarazm Shah, from the Salt Range (in the Punjab), while Hasan Qarllugh, also the Khwarazmian officer and the *vali* of the region to the north of the Indus, joined Iltutmish's service in

AD 1229.[43] In AD 1230, Daulat Shah (formely Balka Khalji), whom Iltutmish had allowed to assume the title of Sultan and rule over a part of Bengal (i.e. deltaic Bengal) as his vassal, was also destroyed for daring to rise in rebellion.[44] Thereafter, Sultan Iltutmish seems to have taken an interest in undertaking projects of public utility and treated people in a generous way in the territories seized from his rivals. No town or city was pillaged after its conquest, and everywhere people were granted amnesty.[45] Tanks and lakes were constructed both for domestic and irrigation purposes.[46] As a result, the extension of Delhi's control over north India and even beyond the river Indus, the maintenance of peace, and the suppression of highwaymen endeared the Sultan to the people under his rule.[47] The Sultan's hold over the entire region within the frontiers of the Sultanate had become effective.[48]

A superficial study of the contemporary literature gives the impression that the Sultanate under Iltutmish was the sum of *iqtas* (also called *khittas* and *vilayets* in the sense of extensive provinces), each held by a slave general. The latter, generally called *muqta*, was commissioned by the Sultan to take charge not of a well-controlled local territorial unit but of a local situation. That the only obligation on the assignee or *muqta* was to defend his *iqta* (or administrative charge) against internal and external exigencies, because the Ghurian conquest was still partial, the towns and strategic forts were garrisoned by the Sultan's army while Hindu chiefs reigned supreme in the countryside. However, a careful study of the information culled from different sources suggests that the terms *iqta*, *khitta*, and *vilayet* have been generally used as synonyms for extensive territorial units and not for revenue assignment made to a noble in lieu of cash salary and allowances for the maintenance of his personal army contingent. The term generally used with regard to the delegation of power or the right to govern the territory assigned to a *muqta* or *vali* is *iyalat* (administrative responsibility or governorship). The *muqta* or *vali* was a bureaucrat dismissible and transferable at the Sultan's pleasure.[49]

Following the traditions of Sultan Muizuddin Muhammad bin Sam and Sultan Aibek, Iltutmish appointed a number of officers with specified functions and decreed that they would be independent of each other. They also seem to have acted as a check on each other. For example, each *khitta* or *vilayet* was placed under the charge of a *sipahsalar* along with other officers. The contemporary sources hitherto neglected or unknown supplement the information contained in the *Tabaqat-i Nasiri*. Awfi and the contemporary poet Siraji Khurasani say that Prince Nasiruddin Mahmud, the eldest son of Sultan Iltutmish, was posted in Hindustan (i.e. the eastern territories) to control it. Both of them also mention him as holding the title of Sultan during the lifetime of his father.[50] Awfi also tells us that the Prince was still a minor and was born of the daughter of Sultan Aibek (who was married to Iltutmish). For his protection and guidance, the veteran general Bahauddin al-Jamji, an emigrant elite noble from Khurasan who had been in India since the time of Aibek's reign, was sent from Delhi as a *sipahsalar* to take up the command of the Hashm-i-Hindustan in AD 1220. He suppressed the Qutbi nobles and their supporters among the land chiefs, seized the wealth of the alien territories, and had the *khutba* read in the name of the Prince, calling him Sultan-i-Muazzam Nasir ul-Dunya wad-Din, Sultan-ush-Sharq, and the lord of the earth and the sea. In recognition for his services to the state, Sultan Iltutmish conferred upon him the rank and title of Malik and also sent royal gifts along with the robe of honour. The *khitta* of Bahraich is also said to have been conquered by al-Jamji.[51] On the conquest of Gwalior in AD 1231, Majd ul-Mulk Ziyauddin Junaidi was appointed in Gwalior as *amir-i-dad*, Sipahsalar Rashiduddin Ali as *kotwal* (superintendent of police administration), while Minhaj Juzjani was entrusted with *qaza* (the responsibility of administering justice as a judge), *ihtisab* (officer charged with the duty of maintaining public decency), and religious affairs. The function of the *amir-i-dad* was to supervise the division of booty between the state and the army as well as render possible coordination between different officers.[52] Later on (AD 1231) Malik Nusratuddin Taisi, a Turkish slave-general of the Sultan, was entrusted with the charge of the *khitta* of Bayana along with the *shahangi* (military control) of the Gwalior territory and the *sipahsalari* (command) of the armies stationed in the territorial units of Qanauj and Mahro-Mahavan (later Mathura), so that he could lead military campaigns against the hostile chiefs of Kalinjar, Chanderi, etc. Malik Taisi is also reported to have been ordered by the Sultan to take residence in the fort of Gwalior.[53] The army stationed in each province was from the centre. Its every soldier was loyal only to the Sultan.

The relevant evidence contained in the inscriptions and *qasidas* composed by the poets in praise of the Sultan, the princes, and the grandees sheds light on certain high nobles who acted as *sipahsalars* but their position in the nobility has not been mentioned by the contemporary chroniclers. One such noble who may be included among the early architects of the Sultanate was Malik Izzuddin Bakhtiyar, most probably a free-born non-Turkish emigrant. Of the thirteenth-century writers, Hasan Nizami tells us that in AD 1211, when Sultan Iltutmish was challenged and opposed by the nobles of Sultan Muizuddin Muhammad bin Sam and Sultan Aibek, Malik Izzuddin Bakhtiyar was sent along with Nasiruddin Mardan Shah, Hazbaruddin Ahmad Suri, and Ikhtiyaruddin Muhammad Umar against them.[54] As regards Minhaj Juzjani, he mentions Izzuddin Bakhtiyar in the list of the leading nobles of Iltutmish's court but omits all details about his career. The little information available in the *Fawaid ul-Fuad* is interesting in so far as the construction by this noble of the buildings of public utility and for religious purpose is concerned. He is said to have had a mosque and a hot bath constructed in Delhi.[55] The epitaph found near Mehrauli where Izzuddin Bakhtiyar seems to have been buried casts light on the high status he held, that of the rank and post of *sipahsalar*.[56] The *qasida* composed by Siraji in his praise not only corroborates the evidence available elsewhere but also supplements it. It tells us that the Sultan had raised him over and above the other nobles because he was granted the privilege of commanding the King's army on his behalf.[57]

Since the state system did not undergo any important change with regard to provincial organization until AD 1242, we may refer to the existence of different officers in a vast province having a large and important urban centre as its headquarters. For example, the *khitta* of Lahore continued to have a number of officers, independent of each other, until its sack by the Mongols in AD 1241. During the reign of Sultan Raziya, Malik Ikhtiyaruddin Qaraqash was entrusted with the *iyalat* of Lahore, while Aqsanqar, a veteran general, served there as *kotwal* and another officer, Muhammad, was *amir-i-akhur*, i.e. officer-in-charge of the royal horses maintained for the use of the Lahore army.[58] Once Shaikh Nizamuddin (Chishti) told his visitors about a leading scholar, Maulana Raziuddin Sighani, who served in the territorial unit of Kol as *naib-i-mushrif* (assistant account officer either during the reign of Aibek or early years of Iltutmish's reign) that Maulana Sighani could not get along with the *mushrif* and resigned.[59] This suggests that besides the *sipahsalar*, the *amir-i-dad*, and the *amir-i-akhur*, there was a *mushrif* also accountable to the central *wazir* or his subordinate, the central *mushrif*.[60]

It is also noteworthy that the territories in the north-west of Delhi that were peaceful and almost free from recalcitrant elements seem to have been brought under Khalsa (central administration through the *diwan-i-wizarat*, i.e. the revenue ministry). Minhaj Juzjani once uses the term *khalsat* [61] (plural of *khalsa*) and then refers to such well-controlled and peaceful units as the *khittat-i-mahrusa*.[62] The designation of the supreme officer in a *khalsa* unit was the *shahna* and not other *vali* or the *sipahsalar*. The *shahna* was certainly a second-ranked noble while the *vali* or the *sipahsalar* was a first-ranked officer, as discussed above.

As regards the assignment of an entire province in *iqta* (revenue assignment) in lieu of cash salary, only Nizam-ul-Mulk Junaidi, the distinguished *wazir* and *sadr*[63] under Sultan Iltutmish, was assigned the territorial unit of Kol. An inscription, now damaged, fixed on a building constructed in Kol during the reign of Iltutmish refers to Kol as being under the *iyalat* (governorship) of Khwaja Jahan Nizam-ul-Mulk (Junaidi).[64] The occurrence of the term *iyalat* would suggest that the *wazir* held the *iyalat* in addition to the two posts of *wazir* and *sadr* at the centre. Though Minhaj Juzjani does not state that the *iyalat* of Kol was entrusted to the *wazir*, he says that in 1236, after the death of Sultan Iltutmish, Nizam-ul-Mulk Junaidi fled from Delhi to Kol. It shows that he had his establishment in Kol and thence he proceeded to join the rebel Malik Izzuddin Salari, the *muqta* of Badaon.[65] The contemporary historian also tells us that Junaidi's successor, Muhazzabuddin (Tajik), reserved the *iqta* of Kol for him during the reign of Sultan Alauddin Masud Shah (AD 1242–6), although he had been elevated by Sultan Raziya to the *wizarat* with the title of Nizam-ul-Mulk.[66] He seems to have been given it because his predecessor had held Kol earlier, perhaps in his *iqta*. Another noble whom the Sultan is said to have assigned a small *iqta* was Malik Kabir Khan Ayaz. Minhaj Juzjani states that in 1227–8 he was entrusted with the *iyalat* of the *khitta* of Multan but that he incurred the royal displeasure and was deprived of his privileged position in consequence. As he was a slave general of the Sultan, he was assigned Palwal (a small pargana town) in *iqta*.[67]

The category of lesser assignees called *iqtadars* also deserves to be discussed. Incidentally, Barani refers to the soldiers of the *hashm-i-qalb* (central army) as *iqtidars*, to some of whom Sultan Iltutmish had assigned one or two villages in lieu of cash salary and horse allowance for their distinguished service to the state. They held their villages in the vicinity of Delhi and were a few thousands in number.[68] Apart from this reference, there is no shred of evidence to suggest that *iqtas* were assigned to the nobles in lieu of cash salary on a large scale. For example, Minhaj Juzjani informs us that when Khwaja Saifuddin Aibek was elevated to the post of *sar-i-jandar* (chief of the royal bodyguards), his salary was fixed at three lakh *jitals*.[69] In fact, Iltutmish seems to have been an advocate of the centralized polity, like his predecessors.

The exchange of emissaries between Sultan Iltutmish and foreign rulers was also a significant development in the Sultanate polity. Sultan Tajuddin Yildoz, the successor of Sultan Muizuddin Muhammad bin Sam in Ghazna, sent his emissary to Delhi with a robe for Iltutmish. The latter is said to have accepted the robe and acknowledged his suzerainty for the time being because he had to face many rivals around Delhi during his early years.[70] In AD 1221, Sultan Jalaluddin Mangbarni, the fugitive ruler of Khwarazm, arrived in India and desired to enter into alliance with the rulers of India against Chinggis Khan. His message for Iltutmish was:

> The vicissitudes of fortune have established my right to approach thy presence, and guests of my sort arrive but rarely. If, therefore, the drinking place of friendship be purified upon either side and the cups of fraternity filled to the brim, and we bind ourselves to aid and assist one another in weal and woe, then shall our aims and objects be attained; and when our opponents realize the concord that exists between us, the teeth of their resistance will be blunted.

He also requested that a place might be assigned to him in which he could remain for a few days. Iltutmish avoided being dragged into a conflict with the Mongols and forced the Khwarazm Shah to retreat towards the Panjab and Sind.[71] Minhaj Juzjani would also have us believe that Chinggis Khan also sent his envoy to Delhi but his statement is neither corroborated by the foreign accounts nor by the circumstantial evidence contained in the contemporary Indo-Persian sources.[72]

Mention should be made of the visits by the emissaries from the Caliph of Baghdad to Delhi. Minhaj Juzjani refers to their arrival with an investiture for Iltutmish and his nobles in AD 1229. Sparing any details of the important ceremony, attendant upon this conferment, the *Tabaqat-i-Nasiri* states that Delhi was lavishly decorated and that there was a banquet to feed the citizens.[73] Emphasizing the importance of this event, A.B.M. Habibullah and K.A. Nizami say that it is not known whether Iltutmish requested the Caliph to do him the honour or whether the latter had sent the gift to Delhi on his own.[74] Indeed, they do not seem to have gone through the entire *Tabaqat-i-Nasiri* carefully because Minhaj-i-Siraj Juzjani mentions in his account of the younger brother of Sultan Balban that a senior officer, Rashiduddin Abu Bakr Habshi, was sent by Iltutmish with presents and a request for investiture.[75]

Muhammad Awfi is more detailed about this event. He writes:

> One of the manifestations of the grandeur and elegance of Sultan Shamsuddin, Abul Muzaffar Iltutmish is that costly gifts were sent to the exalted court of the Caliph of Baghdad. None of the preceding kings had ever dispatched so many costly gifts to the Caliph (as he did). In return, the Caliph sent standard, ring, vest, a special turban, saddled camels, Arabian horses, and robes of honour for the Sultan, the princes, and the dignitaries of the court. All this may be considered the proud privilege of the royal dynasty. And the credit for this achievement goes to the prudent statesmanship of the *wazir* (Nizam-ul-Mulk Junaidi), for the emissaries were sent (to Baghdad) at his instance.[76]

The grant of investiture by the Abbasid Caliph to a Sultan in any country had ritualistic value. The Caliph, being the descendant of the uncle of the Prophet, commanded immense respect among the Sunni Muslims and was considered the political head of the community the world over. Therefore, his recognition of any

Sultan as the 'Right Hand of the Caliph and Helper of the Commander of the Believers' legitimized the latter's claim to authority, on the one hand, and further raised his prestige in the community, on the other. Moreover, the exchange of the choicest goods as presents between the countries led to the modification of indigenous crafts and the introduction of new ones. Trade relations improved and cultural exchange became more frequent.[77]

The treatment meted out by Iltutmish to Berke Khan's emissaries from Qipchaq was not good. Berke Khan, a grandson of Chinggis Khan, who had embraced Islam and held the government of Qipchaq on behalf of his older brother, Batu Khan, sent his Muslim emissaries to Delhi in order to establish friendly relations with Iltutmish. Since Berke Khan was not an independent ruler, and Iltutmish was fearful of Mongol designs against non-Mongol rulers, he placed the Mongol envoys under arrest in Gwalior. During Raziya's reign, they were shifted to Qanauj where they were poisoned by the order of Sultan Muizuddin Bahram Shah (AD 1240–2).[78] Again, Berke Khan sent an Arab, Imam Maghrabi, to the court of Sultan Nasiruddin Mahmud in AD 1259. As Berke Khan had become independent of the Mongol emperor and his commitment to Islam also became well known, this time his envoy seems to have been shown due consideration. He was now at war against his cousins.[79]

On the death of Iltutmish in AD 1236, the centre became weak on account of the incompetence of his immediate successors. The nobles became king-makers; in ten years, five Sultans were placed on the throne in succession. As a result, the centralized polity of the Sultanate began to undergo important changes that ultimately led to its decentralization. Sultan Raziya (1236–40) being a purdah-observing lady was not expected to command the army in person in the beginning, and therefore she appointed Malik Saifuddin Baihtu as *naib-i-lashkar* (deputy commander-in-chief). On the latter's death soon afterwards, Qutbuddin Hasan Ghuri was appointed in his place as *naib-i-lashkar*.[80] During the reign of Sultan Muizuddin Bahram Shah (1240–2), the Turk slave general, Malik Ikhtiyaruddin Aitikin, created the post of *naib-i-mumalikat* or regent for him and usurped all royal powers. The *naib-i-mumalikat* reduced the Sultan to a mere figurehead on the throne. The latter got the *naib* assassinated and took up the reins of government in his own hands.[81] This led the nobles to depose the Sultan and place Prince Alauddin on the throne with the title of Sultan Alauddin Masud Shah instead. The office of the *naib* was revived and entrusted to Qutbuddin Hasan Ghuri.[82]

It was during the reign of Sultan Alauddin Masud Shah that armed conflict between the Turkish and the Tajik nobles took place. The leader of the Tajiks was the Wazir Muhazzabuddin, entitled Nizam-ul-Mulk. The *wazir* tried to consolidate his power by appointing non-Turks, particularly Tajiks, to important posts at the centre. The Turks turned against him and killed him in the army headquarters at Hauz-i-Rani.[83] His fall cleared the way for the establishment of the Turkish ascendancy in the Sultanate of Delhi. According to Barani, forty Turk nobles, called by him the *Turkishan-i-Chahalgani* (forty Turkish families) rose to prominence and they monopolized the key positions and got extensive territorial units assigned to themselves in maintenance *iqtas*. The *muqta* (assignee) governed his large *iqta* as an uncrowned king.[84] Of the non-Turk nobles, only Qutbuddin Hasan Ghuri was able to retain his *iqta* of Meerut and the post of *naib* (regent)[85] not because of his seniority or connection with the Shansabani dynasty but due to his ability to maintain a balance between the rival groups among the Turks themselves.

It is also imperative to point out that the Turks who were brought to India by the slave merchants for sale never seem to have been in large numbers. Unlike the Central Asian lands during the period under review, India did not receive an exodus of emigrant Turkish tribes. In Central Asia, Asia Minor, and Azerbaijan, the Turks came in large numbers, generally free born. In every region they retained their language and also compelled others to adopt it (Turkish language). Fakhr-i-Mudabbir is right when he says that Muslims in the lands of higher culture learnt Turkish language in order to gain access to the Turk officers and enjoy their patronage.[86] Conversely, in India the Turks being comparatively in smaller number than the non-Turk Persian-speaking emigrants from the neighbouring countries, they could not impose Turkish language on the non-Turks. They were generally purchased in their childhood and Persianized by the slave merchants. That is why the Turkish slaves in the service of the Sultans from the beginning of the Sultanate were at home in

Persian and many could write it also.[87] Later on, in the fourteenth century, Hindvi, mixed with Persian and Arabic words, was also spoken by the ruling elite. In fact, Hindvi had become a link language in the whole of the Sultanate.[88]

A close analysis of the information about the political events that occurred during the reign of the next ruler, Sultan Nasiruddin Mahmud, available in different contemporary sources leaves no doubt about the new Sultan being an imbecile prince, incapable of providing leadership.[89] First, he was used as a puppet by his stepfather, Qutlugh Khan, his mother (remarried to Qutlugh Khan) and their colleague, Malik Bahauddin Balban (later Sultan Balban) and others in alliance with them. Bahauddin Balban also gave his daughter in marriage to the Sultan. It was because of the close cooperation between them that Prince Jalaluddin, whom they had transferred from Qanauj to Badaon, became apprehensive of their designs and fled away to Korakoram, and there joined the court of the Mongol Emperor, Monge Qaan. The latter ordered the *noyens* of Khurasan to help him. The Mongols seized Lahore and Jalandhar territories and installed him there as a Mongol vassal.[90] Soon relations between Bahauddin Balban and Qutlugh Khan became strained. Sher Khan, the cousin of Bahauddin Balban, seized Uchh from Izzuddin Balban Kishlu Khan, son-in-law of Qutlugh Khan, and thus revolted against the centre in AD 1251–2. Thereupon, Bahauddin Balban was ordered by the Sultan to leave for his *iqta* of Hansi. Soon he was replaced by Prince Ruknuddin in Hansi and transferred to Nagaur, while Sher Khan Sunqar was driven away from Uchh and Multan (1252–3). The latter went to Turkestan to join the Mongol court at Korakoram.[91] Rivalry between Qutlugh Khan and Bahauddin Balban dealt a shattering blow to the short-lived ascendancy of the Turk slave generals. Both of them won over supporters among the non-Turks nobles who had been relegated to the background. If Bahauddin Balban appealed to the non-Turks and Turks of foreign birth, Qutlugh Khan approached the land chiefs of India through Imaduddin Rayhan, an Indian by origin.[92]

Freed of his powerful rivals in Delhi, Qutlugh Khan tried to extend his power with the support of the non-Turks, including Hindu land chiefs. He had Ain-ul-Mulk Junaidi, son of the late Nizam-ul-Mulk Junaidi, entrusted with the *wizarat*, while Imaduddin Rayhan, an Indian eunuch, was elevated to the ministerial post of *vakil-i-dar*. The latter could act as a liaison between the centre and the land chiefs. Rayhan had his protégé Qazi Shamsuddin of Bahraich appointed the chief *qazi* in place of Minhaj Juzjani. As Junaidi, the *wazir* failed to retain the confidence of Qutlugh Khan, he was soon replaced by Sadr-ul-Mulk Nizamuddin Abu Bakr in the *diwan-i-wizarat*. Though Qutlugh Khan was able to create goodwill among the Hindu land chiefs for himself, and could enjoy their support against Bahauddin Balban, the latter was more than a match for him in shrewdness. Bahauddin Balban could out manoeuvre his rival.

In Nagaur, Bahauddin Balban, having strengthened his position, asserted his power against his rivals in Delhi. He established an alliance with Prince Jalaluddin, now entitled as Sultan. His cousin, Sher Khan Sunqar, had also returned from Turkestan and joined Sultan Jalaluddin in Lahore. Many nobles in Delhi were already secretly in alliance with Bahauddin Balban. Assured of support from Turkish and non-Turkish nobles of foreign origin, Bahauddin Balban moved from Nagaur towards Hansi. He was joined by Turk nobles and Sultan Jalaluddin and Sher Khan Sunqar near Hansi. Qutlugh Khan also took the Sultan with him and proceeded against his rivals. When the two armies were face to face with each other, certain nobles in the royal camp who were secretly in alliance with Bahauddin Balban frightened the Sultan with accounts of the military superiority of the rival army and also persuaded him to make a compromise. At their instance, Bahauddin Balban's condition with regard to Rayhan's transfer from Delhi to some *iqta* was accepted by the Sultan, and then Balban returned to Delhi. As for Sultan Jalaluddin, who seems to have been promised the throne of Delhi, he was deceived by Sher Khan Sunqar. The latter won over a large number of Jalaluddin's followers to his side and forced him to return to Lahore in disappointment.[93]

In Delhi, Bahauddin Balban got the upper hand against Qutlugh Khan and had Imaduddin Rayhan transferred from Badaon to Bahraich. Qutlugh Khan was also ordered through the royal *farman* to move to Awadh along with the Queen Mother.[94] On their departure in AD 1254, Bahauddin Balban got Qutbuddin Hasan Ghuri assassinated because he was thought to be a hurdle in his way to the throne.[95] His murder enabled Bahauddin Balban to get for himself the coveted post of the *naib* and the title of Ulugh Khan Azam. According to Isami, he was granted by the Sultan the privilege of using the royal umbrella as well.[96] Thereafter, the nobles who held *iqtas* and were opposed to Ulugh Khan Azam were either eliminated or forced to run away from their *iqtas*. Imaduddin Rayhan was killed in Bahraich while his supporters, Qutlugh Khan and the Queen Mother, were chased out of Awadh. Ultimately, they fled to Central Asia. Their ally, Izzuddin Balban Kishlu Khan, transferred his allegiance to the Mongol Emperor through Hulegu, the Il-Khan of Iran, in order to save himself from the Delhi army.[97] Besides him and Sultan Jalaluddin Masud Shah, Hasan Qarlugh and his son and successor, Sultan Muhammad, had been the loyal vassals of the Mongols since AD 1236. The latter ruled over Kuh-i-Jud (the Salt Range).

Ulugh Khan Azam seems to have waited for an opportunity to destroy the Mongol protectorates in north-western India and re-annex them to the Sultanate. Informed of the dissolution of the Mongol empire, caused by the conflict of arms between the descendants of Chinggis Khan, particularly between Hulegu and Berke Khan, he established friendly relations with Hulegu and also received his envoys.[99] A no-war pact was also concluded between Hulegu and Delhi with the help of Sultan Muhammad Qarlugh.[100] This no-war pact created a false sense of security in the minds of the Mongol vassals in India. Then Ulugh Khan Azam invaded Multan and easily occupied it. Sultan Jalaluddin was also destroyed. As Sultan Muhammad Qarlugh was suspected by the Mongols of treachery towards their vassals in India, he was killed and Kuh-i-Jud was occupied by the Mongols.[101]

The elimination of the rivals cleared the way for Ulugh Khan to remove the puppet Sultan from the scene. The latter died in mysterious circumstances,[102] leaving the throne vacant for the *naib-i-mumalikat*. The latter ascended the throne of Delhi with the title of Sultan Ghiyasuddin Balban in AD 1266. His reign was marked by political stability, peace, and order. Apparently, it appears that under the new Sultan, the polity of the Sultanate was once again centralized and the *valis* or *muqtas* in the provinces were denied discretionary powers. However, a careful analysis of contemporary sources in conjunction with circumstantial evidence tends to reveal that Sultan Ghiyasuddin Balban had to make compromises with the changes that the Sultanate polity had already undergone during the preceding period.

Ziauddin Barani, who is the only near-contemporary to intimate us about Sultan Balban's theory of kingship, is fulsome in his praise of the steps that the Sultan took to raise the prestige of the crown. According to him, the new Sultan organized his court on a grandiose scale, and introduced customs of ancient Sassanid origin, such as *paibos* (kissing of the king's feet) and *sajda* (prostration) before the Sultan. The choicest carpets, curtains of exported silk fabric, and other costly trappings added to the grandeur of the royal court. It is said that he was fond of holding convivial gatherings before his accession to the throne, but that he now gave up this practice because he wanted to maintain a distance between himself and the nobles. All the nobles had to observe the etiquette laid down by the Sultan whenever they came to pay obeisance. The Sultan is also reported to have employed the sturdy and awe-inspiring Siestani Pehlvans (warriors) as his bodyguards. They stood in the royal *darbar* with drawn swords, and also moved in the royal procession in the capital city in the same manner. The Sultan did not allow anybody to make jokes in his presence nor did he himself act in this way; he would not even smile while holding the court or conducting the business of the state. Unlike Sultan Aibek and Sultan Iltutmish, he avoided having any association with the leading merchants, both Indian and foreign, because they dealt with people in the *bazaar*, and hence in his eyes they were no better than those of base stock. Likewise, he was against the employment of low-born people in the royal service; noble birth was the essential qualification in this regard.[103] Ziauddin Barani says that in consequence of the measures adopted by the Sultan, he inspired fear, and both the nobles as well as the people became law-abiding.[104] The grandeur of the court and the performance of state rituals, such as hosting of mangificent banquets captured the imagination of the nobles and the people alike. Further, the Sultan concocted his genealogy, claiming descent from the legendary Turkish ruler, Afraisiyab. Emphasizing the dignity of the Sultan, he declared that the heart of the Sultan was the repository of divine manifestation.[105] In making displays of royal grandeur, Sultan Balban is said to have surpassed even Sultan Iltutmish.[106] It may, however, be stated that the details furnished by Barani about the state system under him suggest that Sultan Balban was serious only about demanding complete obedience from and submission by his nobles. He neither abolished the *iqta* system nor curtailed the powers of the *muqtas*; the latter enjoyed autonomy in their *iqtas* so long as they followed the general norms and did not incur the royal displeasure.

The reforms introduced by the Sultan in the central departments and institutions substantiate the above analysis. The first important institution that attracted the Sultan's attention was the *qalb-i-ala* or the *hashm-i-qalb* (central army). Its efficiency as a fighting machine was badly affected on account of slackness that had crept into every department at the centre during the preceding period. The Sultan reorganized the central army. Every effort was made to raise its morale. A few thousand of the distinguished soldiers were chosen by the Sultan to be honoured with the assignment of *iqtas,* each consisting of a few populated villages in the vicinity of Delhi in lieu of *mavajib* (allowances in cash).[107] Barani also refers to the assignment of lands to the Afghan soldiers posted in the new *tahanas* (later *thanas*) in lieu of cash payment, as will be discussed subsequently. The assignment of land to the soldiers carried with it a great deal of prestige; it was a symbol of authority wielded by the assignee. As regards the payment of allowances to other soldiers, those serving in the central army might have been paid in cash, though there is no direct evidence about it. While discussing Balban's order with regard to the resumption of *iqtas* held by the old army men or their descendants, called *iqtadars*, A.B.M. Habib Ullah says: 'The chronicler leaves us only to infer that cash payment henceforth became the rule for Balban's military personnel.'[108] This is not supported by the circumstantial evidence contained in Barani's *Tarikh*. The veteran soldiers in the *qalb-i-ala* or those posted in the *thanas* were assigned land instead of cash payment, as already referred to.

The relevant evidence concerning the assignment of large *iqtas*, each comprising the entire extensive territorial unit, to high-ranking nobles in lieu of cash salary and allowances[109] tends to indicate that Sultan Balban was not able to centralize the polity to the extent that it had been during the reigns of Aibek and Iltutmish. In fact, he had to adjust to the changed reality since the death of Iltutmish. The *khittas* or *vilayets* (provinces) had been assigned by him to his Turkish partisans among the old nobles during Nasiruddin Mahmud's reign, and they were continued to be held by them after his accession to the throne in AD 1266. Any change effected by him in the state policy might have antagonized the nobility. The only modification or re-enforcement of an old regulation under him seems to have been the payment of *fawazil* (surplus revenue) by the *muqta* to the state exchequer. The latter having deducted his own share had to transmit the *fawazil* to the centre.[110] Further, Barani's statement that the whole empire during Balban's reign was divided into *iqtas* and land grants, assigned to the nobles, armymen, and other persons depending on state patronage (such as religious divines, poets, etc.), suggests that Balban retained the *iqta* system that obtained prior to his accession.[111] The only territories that seem to have been brought under *khalsa* were the newly carved-out *iqta* of Amroha in the Katehar region and the *vilayet* of Sunam and Samana. Barani says about the latter unit that when Bughra Khan was taken by the Sultan with him on his expedition to Bengal against the rebel *muqta*, Tughril, the *vilayet* of Sunam and Samana, was first divided into *shiqqs* and then each *shiqq* was further parcelled out into *iqtas* and assigned to the armymen stationed there. Malik Sonj, the *sar-i-jandar*, was appointed over the armymen as the *sar-i-lashkar* (or commander). As the armymen, both the soldiers and their officers, were the employees of the centre, the second-ranked Malik, the *sar-i-jandar* (chief of the royal bodyguards), was selected as their commander.[112] The land left out after it had been parcelled into *iqtas* must have been managed by the *diwan-i-wizarat* through its revenue officials.[113] Thus the provinces (or *khittas*) entrusted to the nobles as *iqtas* under Balban prevented the Sultan from centralizing the polity. As a matter of fact, no *muqta* is reported to have been interfered with in conducting the affairs of his province so long as he followed the established norms. He governed his administrative charge through his own servants. A.B.M. Habibullah is not correct in his observation that 'Balban's despotism was of an extreme kind in which the right of the military aristocracy even to a share, not to speak of domination in the government, could find no place.'[114] The relevant evidence found in Barani's *Tarikh* clearly reveals that royal pomp and grandeur (*kokaba* and *dabdaba*, the terms used by Barani) exercised the imagination of the people in Delhi while the *muqta*'s court mattered in the province.[115]

The difference between the position of the *muqtas* of large *iqtas* and the lesser assignees, called by Barani *iqtadars*, may be discussed here. The *muqtas* being senior and higher-ranking trusted nobles of the Sultan were allowed autonomy within their administrative charges with certain obligations to fulfil. They were charged with the duty of maintaining peace and order in the *iqta* and also of defending it against external invaders. They were also expected to be loyal to the Sultan; no one howsoever great could be tolerated in case he was found assuming an air of independence. To keep himself well posted of the internal conditions in a large province held by a noble as his *iqta*, Sultan Balban reorganized the intelligence service (espionage system). He employed efficient *munhiyan* (spies) and *barids* (intelligence officers) and posted them everywhere to keep a strict watch on the behaviour of the state officers at the centre and in the provinces alike. Even his own sons, posted in Multan and Samana, were not spared in this regard. Barani states: 'Everywhere in the territories, the *muqtas, valis*, officials (*kardaran*), *amils* (revenue collectors), or their sons, relatives or slaves, did not have the courage to hurt anyone without reason.'[116] Apart from the *barid* or a *qazi* (judicial officer), no other officer seems to have been posted in a large *iqta* to serve as a check on the *muqta*.

The Sultan is reported to have held that the foremost duty of the king was to ensure impartial justice to all and sundry under his rule. He saw to it that people were safe from tyranny. In an attempt to impress upon the people that everyone was equal in the eyes of the law and that no discrimination would be allowed between man and man on the basis of birth or status. The high-ranking nobles found guilty of crimes were punished by the Sultan in an exemplary manner. For instance, Malik Baqbaq, the trusted slave general and the *muqta* of Badaon, was put to death because he had killed his own *farash* (in-charge of floor coverings) under the influence of alcohol. The *barid* posted in Badaon was punished for he had failed in informing the Sultan about the crime committed by the *muqta*. Another slave general, Haibat Khan, the *muqta* of Awadh was flogged five hundred times and then handed over to the widow and children of the man killed by him. Haibat Khan was saved after the widow accepted money (one thousand *tankas*) as the price of her husband's blood. Haibat Khan died in frustration because he was not able to regain the confidence of the Sultan.[117] Barani says that the sense of justice demonstrated by the Sultan as well as his concern for public welfare had made him popular among the people.[118] However, the murder by the order of the Sultan of Amin Khan for his failure in defeating Tughril, the rebel *muqta* of Lakhnauti, caused indignation among the people for the latter was innocent and helpless. He had been unsuccessful because many of his followers had defected to the rebel out of greed for money.[119]

It is also worth recalling that the Sultan had eliminated every one of the powerful nobles whom he considered a threat to him or to his dynastic interests afterwards. For example, his own cousin, Sher Khan Sunqar, a veteran general who had defeated the Mongol invaders several times, was poisoned by his own cup-bearer at the instigation of the Sultan.[120] Many other senior nobles who survived the reign of Nasiruddin Mahmud on account of their alliance with him were also eliminated because they were not trusted. As the public killings of the nobles could tarnish the Sultan's image in the eyes of the people, the assassin's dagger was resorted to.[121]

In the tradition of his predecessors, both in Central Asia and India, Sultan Balban appears to have established friendly relations with the *ulama* (religious divines). Not only did the *ulama* enjoy the privilege of occupying the *quzat* (judiciary), the *sadarat* (ministry of *auqaf* or endowments, etc.) and manning educational institutions, but they could also sway public opinion in the Sultanate. The Sultan is said to have paid a visit to the leading *ulama* and joined the funeral procession whenever any one of them died. Their sons or dependants were not deprived of the land grants or state patronage after their death.[122] Some distinguished scholars were associated with his court, and he took his dinner in their company and listened to their discussion of issues related to religious philosophy and the law.[123] Every Friday he went to pay a visit to Maulana Burhanuddin Balkhi at his residence. Like Maulana Balkhi, Maulana Sharafuddin Valvalji, Maulana Sirajuddin Sijzi, and Maulana Najmuddin Damashqi were held in high esteem by the Sultan. Another distinguished scholar of Delhi, Maulana Kamaluddin Zahid, is said to have spurned the royal invitation to join the court as *imam*, remarking that the only asset he possessed was his prayer to God but that the Sultan wanted to deprive him of it.[124] The following anecdote described in the *Malfuzat* of a contemporary Chishti saint, Shaikh Hamiduddin Nagauri, indicates that the Sultan had to tolerate even those *ulama* whom he disliked in case they commanded respect among the people. Once Shaikh Hamiduddin Nagauri told his disciples that Sultan Balban used to say about the three *qazis* associated with the state in Delhi that 'One of them fears neither God nor me (i.e. the Sultan). Of the remaining two one fears me (the Sultan) and not God, while the third one fears only God.' According to him, Minhaj Juzjani, the chief *qazi*, feared neither God nor the Sultan, while the *qazi-i-lashkar* (*qazi* in the army) feared only God.[125] As Qazi Minhaj Juzjani was held in high esteem both by the *ulama* and the *mashaikh*, Sultan Balban had cultivated friendly relations with him even prior to his accession to the throne. Indeed, he was his ally during his conflict with Qutlugh Khan, and therefore lost his position as *qazi* during Qutlugh Khan's short-lived regency.[126]

Another important development of social and economic importance that resulted from the political behaviour of Sultan Balban was the establishment of colonies of Afghan soldiers in the new *thanas* or military posts at strategic points in the Sultanate for rendering the highways safe against dacoits and other anti-social elements. The operations of dacoits and rebel villagers created a problem of great magnitude for the early Sultans. It was imperative that a solution to this problem should be found.

Isami informs us about the construction of military posts and the placing of garrisons there in these words: 'The successful Sultan had many fortresses constructed. The fortifications of Jarati and Zarki were raised anew, besides the construction of Gopalgir fort. As a result, innumerable recalcitrant people were captured.'[127] Barani adds: 'The fortification was raised in Gopalgir. A number of *thanas* were established around Delhi and the jungles cleared so that the dacoits or highwaymen could not get shelter there. The road to east India was opened, with the result that the *karvanians* (grain dealers, moving in caravans) and merchants could move freely.' This was possible owing to the establishment of *thanas* in the densely forested areas. Ibn Battuta's reference to Afghanpur, a *thana* established on the bank of the river Ram Ganga in the *iqta* of Amroha, tends to suggest that every territory affected by the activities of the anti-social elements had *thanas*.[128] *Thanas* are also reported to have been built at Jalali (in Aligarh district), Shamsabad, Kampil, Patiali, Bhogaon, and Bhojpur. These military posts were also colonized by the Afghans. *Madrasas* and mosques were also constructed for the diffusion of culture and education among the Afghans.[129] The *madrasa* was a catalyst of social change. In fact, the *thana* played an important role in the process of urbanization. The relevant evidence about *thanas* available in our medieval sources suggests that they were established in forested areas abounding in anti-social elements or on the borders of the Sultanate near a village. After the establishment of a *thana* and its staffing with a strong military force, it rapidly developed into an important township. The safety ensured by the presence of a garrison against dacoits or highwaymen encouraged merchant caravans, loaded with their merchandise, to move around. It also provided market and credit facilities to peasants, and therefore new villages sprang up around the new town and prospered. The rise of the rustic Afghans as an important component of the ruling elite in the Sultanate of Delhi may be traced to Balban's reign.[130]

In fact, the strong sense of duty and justice possessed by the Sultan led him to take effective steps to provide security of life and property to travellers. The dacoits and highwaymen—whose operations hampered the progress of trade and commerce and in fear of whom the merchant caravans could not move from one *khitta* to the other without sufficient military force—were suppressed.

The composition of the ruling elite also underwent important changes during the period under review. The employment of the Afghans as the *shahnas* of the *thanas* paved the way for their rise in the nobility of the Sultanate. Not only did the Afghans begin to rise socially and politically under the patronage of Sultan

Balban, but so did the Khaljis and the Tajiks, who were once again favoured with high posts in the administration and at the royal court. It may be pointed out that the Khaljis seem to have been evacuated from Bengal after the suppression by Sultan Iltutmish of the revolt of Daulat Shah (Balka Khalji) in 1230 and scattered in other parts of the Sultanate.[131] The civil administration continued to be manned by the non-Turks, the Tajiks, and others even during his ascendancy at the court of Sultan Nasiruddin Mahmud.[132] The Sultan's own contingent before his rise to sovereign status in AD 1266 seems to have comprised his own slaves and the Afghans and the Khaljis.[133] Later on, important individuals among his old servants were elevated to high positions in the Sultanate along with the old nobles whose loyalty to him was above doubt.[134] It was during the early years of his reign that the dependents of Sultan Muhammad Qurlugh of Kuh-i-Jud (the Salt Range in the Panjab) joined his service as nobles after they had been driven away by the Mongols. Malik Hizbaruddin, the grandson of Hasan Qarlugh, Malik Ali Shah Kuh-i-Judi, and Malik Jalaluddin Firuz Khalji[135] are mentioned among his nobles. Like these officers of the Qarlugh ruler of Kuh-i-Jud, the Mongol followers of Berke Khan (the ruler of the Golden Horde, mentioned in the sources as *nau-Mussalmanan* (Mongol converts to Islam),[136] also sought refuge after their resistance had been overcome in the region south of Ghazna, although their leader, Negudar, had joined the Chaghataids of Transoxiana.[137] Berke Khan had had friendly relations with the Sultan of Delhi since 1259, when Ulugh Khan Azam (Balban) was the regent in Delhi, as already referred to.[138]

With the entry of the non-Turks into the nobility under Balban, the position of the Turk slave generals or their descendants was considerably weakened. The nobility was, however, made quite broad based. A.B.M. Habib Ullah's observation that the Delhi Sultanate under Sultan Balban 'was extremely a Turkish concern' and that the Sultan 'considered himself more the custodian of Turkish sovereignty than a king of the Mussalmans',[139] is nothing short of historical oversimplification. In fact, it was the result of Balban's policy towards the nobility of aristocratic birth that the non-Turks like Malik-ul-Umara Fakhruddin Kotwal became so powerful that they could place Kaiqabad, their choice, on the throne against the will bequeathed by Sultan Balban. Besides the members of the family of Malik-ul-Umara Fakhruddin Kotwal and the Wazir Khwaja Khatir, other non-Turks also seem to have become so powerful that the Turk slave generals of Balban could not view their future without apprehension. In dismay, they conspired to eliminate the leaders of the non-Turks through treachery and safeguard their own interests. It was, however, too late. Their conspiracy was revealed and then Shaista Khan, the *amir-i-ariz* (former Malik Jalaluddin Khalji), seized the throne.[140] His accession to the throne in AD 1290 marked the beginning of a new phase in the development of the polity of the Delhi Sultanate.

Another aspect of the Sultanate polity that calls for an explanation is the position of the Hindu landed aristocracy in the state system, and the Sultan's policy towards Hindus in general and Hinduism in particular. It is here worth recalling that the ruling elite of the Sultanate differentiated the *raiyat* (or Hindu masses) from the high-caste Hindus, the Brahmans and the land chiefs. W.H. Moreland rightly points out that Barani uses 'this word (Hindu) in a narrow sense, to denote the classes above the ordinary peasants, so that in fact it is almost a synonym for chiefs and headmen in this context'.[141] Long before Barani, Minhaj Juzjani's reference to the Hindus also implies hereditary land chiefs.[142] Besides the land chiefs, Barani's Hindus included the Brahmans as the religious leaders of the Hindus.[143] Barani's junior contemporary, Shaikh Muzaffar Balkhi (the spiritual successor of Shaikh Sharafuddin Yahya Maneri), also uses the term Hindu for the non-Muslim land chiefs.[144] As regards the general Hindu masses, comprising the peasantry and the artisans, etc., they are mentioned as the *raiyat*, deserving the sympathy and consideration of the ruling elite. Both Minhaj-i-Siraj Juzjani and Barani shower praises on those Sultans and officers who took a keen interest in the well-being of the *raiyat* and encouraged them to extend cultivation.[145] Most probably, the low-caste or non-caste Indians were not recognized as Hindus by the high-caste Hindus. The testimony of the thirteenth-century Tibetan pilgrim, Dharma Svamin, is of significance in this regard. Once the pilgrim from Tibet, while fording a river in Bihar, was carried away by the current towards the opposite bank. He shouted to a man standing on the bank, 'Save me from the river.' The man shouted back, 'I am of low caste', and did not help him. It is also reported that it was improper for a man of low caste to 'touch' with his hands a person of high caste. If a person of low caste were to look at a person of high caste eating, then the food had to be thrown away. A sign of low caste was the absence of perforations (holes) in the ears.[146] Low-caste Indians and high-caste Hindus lived in two different social worlds.

As regards the Sultan's policy towards the hereditary Hindu land chiefs, it was influenced by the traditions set by the early Muslim rulers of the Sind and the Punjab regions.

The relevant evidence found in the contemporary work *Lubab-ul-Albab* shows that Sultan Qutbuddin Aibek, the founder of the independent Sultanate in India, appointed a Rana from the Benaras territory as the *sahib-i-barid* (the head of the intelligence department), although his Muslim associates were opposed to an Indian's appointment to such an important post.[147] The Sultan certainly wanted to win over the confidence of the influential Hindus in the conquered territories. Fakhr-i-Mudabbir praises Sultan Aibek for befriending those Hindu chiefs who agreed to submit to his authority.[148] Hasan Nizami's reference to the presence of the Hindu *rais* at Aibek's court is of corroborative significance. He states in his rhetorical style: 'The carpet of the auspicious court became the kissing place of the *rais* of Hindustan.'[149]

Sultan Aibek's immediate successors in different parts of north India appear to have seriously followed his policy in this regard. Describing the conflict between Sultan Nasiruddin Qubacha and the Khokkar chief in the Panjab, Muhammad Awfi says that the Sultan turned his powerful enemy, who commanded 50,000 warriors, into his friend by pardoning him after his defeat.[150]

The evidence yielded by the contemporary sources about friendly relations between Sultan Shamsuddin Iltutmish and the Hindu land chiefs is a bit more detailed. The details furnished by Minhaj Juzjani about the revolt by Rana Jahir, the powerful chief of Kalinjar during the early years of Sultan Nasiruddin Mahmud's reign (AD 1246–65), show that the Rana was allowed by Iltutmish to retain the territory on *ijara* (farming). Malik Bahauddin Balban (later Ulugh Khan Azam) led a military expedition against him, defeated him, and forced him into submission to the centre.[151]

Dharma Svamin also bears testimony to the existence of cordial relations between the Sultan and the land chiefs in Bihar. According to him, the Turk soldiers posted in Bihar at strategic places were small in number and did not interfere with the local Hindus. They also showed regard to the chiefs in the area nearby; the Hindu and Buddhist land chiefs had acquiesced to the authority of the Sultan.[152] The relevant evidence contained in the *farman* issued by Sultan Firuz Shah (AD 1351–88) shows that Iltutmish was content with the nominal acknowledgement of his suzerainty by the chiefs. In an attempt to reconcile the land chiefs to the centre, Firuz Shah announced through a *farman* that he would have the tribute and taxes collected from 'the class of zamindars, comprising *muqaddams*, *mafruzian*, *malikan* and their like' in accordance with the state demand fixed by Sultan Shamsuddin Iltutmish.[153] Thus, only powerful land chiefs who refused to come to terms with Iltutmish were destroyed. As the powerful land chief Birtu of Awadh sided with the Muslim nobles posted in the eastern region and opposed Iltutmish, he was destroyed after the suppression of the Muslim rebels.[154]

Sultan Ghiyasuddin Balban (AD 1266–87) also seems to have followed his predecesors' policy towards the landed aristocracy. Amir Khusrau tells us about his maternal grandfather, Imad-ul-Mulk, Sultan Balban's Rawat-i-Arz (i.e. *amir-i-ariz*), that he was able to keep the *rais* attached to the centre through his friendly behaviour.[155] The details available in the *Futuh-us Salatin* reveal that the establishment of friendly relations and cooperation between the state and the landed aristocracy gave rise to the concept of shared values, which went a long way towards the fusion of two aristocratic cultural traditions, the Hindu and the Central Asian Muslim traditions. These details also reveal that the matrimonial relations between the two further cemented the friendly ties. For example, Rai Kaloo, the father-in-law of Prince Muhammad Khan (known as Khan-i-Shahid) in the Punjab, recovered the dead body of his son-in-law from the Mongols after his death on the battlefield by paying a huge amount of money from his own treasury.[156] It is also worth mentioning that Sultan Balban was greatly concerned about the protection of people in the north-western frontier territories against the Mongol invaders from across the border. As the nobles failed to defend the territories against the Mongols after the death of Sher Khan, he posted his own sons there in order to raise the morale of the army and the people. Thus, he exposed his own sons to risk.[157]

A word may be added here about the origin of the term zamindar for the class of hereditary land chiefs and its historical significance. The term zamindar occurs for the first time in a document drafted by Amir Khusrau entitled *Fathnama-i-Lakhnauti* during the reign of Sultan Balban; Khusrau refers in this document to the powerful land chiefs of Orissa as zamindars.[158] Its occurrence in the fourteenth-century writings shows that the term was coined to indicate the importance of the hereditary ruling princes considered by the Sultan as an important element in the Indian polity. For instance, the description by Khusrau of the visit of Rai Ramchandra of Deogiri to the court of Sultan Alauddin Khalji after his defeat by the Delhi army in AD 1307 shows that his territory was restored to him in the form of zamindari.[159] Barani also refers to the land chiefs as zamindars in his account of Sultan Firuz Shah's reign, implying that they enjoyed complete autonomy in their feudal territories.[160] Ain-ul-Mulk Mahru states in one of the official documents of the reign of Firuz Shah that the class of chiefs included the *muqaddams, mafruzian*, *chaudhriyan*, and *ranagan*, and that all of them were collectively called zamindars.[161] The early fourteenth-century Persian lexicon *Farhang-i-Qawwas*, explains that the term zamindar was adopted for a big land chief as a substitute for *kirang*, who enjoyed a privileged position and commanded prestige in Iran and Central Asia.[162]

In short, the feudal system that existed in India before the foundation of the Sultanate continued with little modification. The obligations and duties of the land chiefs towards the centre seem to have increased with the passage of time. Similarly, we are informed by the same source that the *khut* in the village was not a chief but a village headman, the equivalent of which in Iran or Khurasan was called *dehqan*.[163] He was selected by the Sultan and paid a commission for collecting land revenue from the peasants for the state at the time of harvest. This term seems to have found its way into India with the invaders from Ghazna, as the *khut* existed there in the village as an intermediary between the peasants of a village and the Sultan.[164]

With Sultan Balban on the throne, the Hindus of talent and good families also seem to have been employed and taken into confidence by the Sultan. Barani mentions, incidentally, Kotwal Birinjtan and Hatya Paik, the two leading warriors (*pehlwans*) of Sultan Balban among the details of the conspiracy hatched in the *khanqah* of Sidi Maula against the person of Sultan Jalaluddin Khalji (AD 1290–6). He tells us that each one received one lakh *jitals* (perhaps annually) as his salary, and that they were dismissed by the Khalji Sultan along with other nobles for their opposition to the new regime. They were arrested along with the Muslim nobles for their involvement in the plot.[165] Many other Hindus seem to have received such favours from the Sultan. At another place, when describing the jubilation in Delhi caused by Sultan Balban's triumphant return from Bengal after the destruction of the rebel Governor Tughril, Barani says that all those of the Muslims, Hindus, Turks, and Tajiks who commanded respect, enjoyed fame, held land grants, and received rewards from the state came out to felicitate the Sultan with offerings of horses, camels, and other costly gifts and cash.[166]

Efforts made by Sultan Balban for the establishment of peace and conditions favourable for prosperity seem to have created goodwill among the people towards the Sultan and his dynasty. This is explicitly expressed in a Sanskrit inscription found at Palam. This inscription, dated 1337 Vikram Era (AD 1280–1), states that in his Sultanate 'everywhere the earth bears the bounty of sylvan spring'. And that 'Vishnu himself has retired from the care of the world and gone to sleep on the ocean of milk.'[167] If the Hindu land chiefs were befriended, the Hindu moneylenders, bankers, and traders flourished due to the policy of non-interference followed by the Sultan. The burden of tax levied on the merchants was also alleviated; it was collected from the merchants at the time of their entry or departure from the borders of the Sultanate.[168] Barani's allusion to the Multani merchants tends to suggest that the Hindus were in a majority among them. He says that the Multanis and the Shahs (moneylenders) became rich on account of the extravagant tastes and habits of the nobles; the latter borrowed money from them and paid exorbitant rates of interest.[169] Barani's senior contemporary, Amid Lowiki Sunami, tells us that the moneylenders charged 24 per cent interest per month during his time (thirteenth century).[170]

Similarly, the relevant evidence about the Sultan's non-interference in the religion of the Hindus, clearly shows that the Hindus enjoyed full religious freedom. Even the custom of *sati* (burning of the widow with the bier of her dead husband) prevalent among the caste Hindus was not interfered with even by Sultan Mahmud of Ghazna, who had a Hindu army in Ghazna. He allowed the Hindus to continue this practice in his capital.[171] Ibn Battuta was surprised to see the prevalence of *sati* in the Sultanate, although it was obnoxious to the Islamic system of law. He writes: 'In the Sultan's dominion they (Hindus) ask his permission to burn her (the widow), which he accords them and then they burn her.'[172]

As regards the spread of Islam through proselytizing amongst Hindus belonging to the lower strata, the overall impression created by our sources is that neither the Sultan nor his nobles ever acted as preachers of their religion. If the *ulama*, in an attempt to impress the rulers by their feigned love or concern for the progress of Islam, suggested that they should champion the cause of their religion by converting non-Muslims to it, the rulers evidently sidetracked the issue in some subtle way. For example, Barani writes, either on the basis of a popular oral tradition or some written source not extant now, that a group of emigrant *ulama* paid a visit to Sultan Iltutmish, and in the course of their conversation they suggested that the non-Muslims be offered the choice either accept Islam or accept death. Thereupon the Sultan asked his *wazir*, Nizam-ul-Mulk Junaidi, to discuss the matter with them. Shrewd and practical as the *wazir* was, he satisfied the *ulama* by saying: 'The Muslims are so few that they are like salt in a dish. If the Hindus would combine together, in case they are confronted with the alternative of Islam or death, the Muslims would not be able to suppress them.' Thus the *ulama* were silenced.[173]

Further, freshly available contemporary evidence found in Dharma Swamin's work helps us correct the historiographical error according to which it was believed that the Muslim invaders destroyed religious and educational institutions such as Nalanda.

Dharma Swamin found Nalanda intact, and studied Buddhist literature there under the guidance of eminent scholars during the reign of Iltutmish.[174] A later Tibetan pilgrim Taranath states that 'years after the establishment of Turkish rule in Bihar, the Tirthankars who had a quarrel with the Buddhists during a religious sermon burnt Buddhist temples, religious places and Ratanodadhi, one of the three buildings of the Nalanda University library.'[175] As a matter of fact, the destruction of Hindu religious or quasi-religious places does not seem to have been a state policy during the entire Sultanate period. The tolerant religious policy followed by the Sultan of Delhi resulted in the establishment of communal harmony and cultural integration.

Lastly, we may discuss the political dimension of the capital city during the period under consideration. Delhi emerged as the centre of culture and trade after it was chosen the capital of the Sultanate by Sultan Iltutmish in AD 1211. The exodus of the elite from Central Asia and Khurasan to India, caused by the Mongol irruption there, helped Delhi rise to the status of a metropolis, with citizens representing different cultural traditions. The progress of education and the diffusion of learning seems to have created political awareness among the citizens of Delhi, which ultimately led to the development of a political community, namely, the urban political community. The display of political awareness among Delhi's citizens took place for the first time during the short-lived reign of Iltutmish's immediate successor, Sultan Ruknuddin Firuz Shah. The citizens rose against him, threw him into prison, and placed his stepsister Raziya on the throne in AD 1236.[176] The second time, the citizens of Delhi turned against the political ascendancy gained by the Khaljis under the leadership of Jalaluddin Khalji in 1290, for they had developed an attachment to the dynasty of Sultan Balban. In fear of the Delhites' opposition to his rule, Sultan Jalaluddin Firuz Shah Khalji did not enter the old capital until after he had pacified the people through his acts of benevolence and feigned simplicity.[177]

The details furnished by Isami and Barani about the conspiracy hatched by the notable citizens against Sultan Jalaluddin Firuz Shah Khalji (AD 1290–6) in the *khanqah* (mansion) of Sidi Maula, an emigrant dervish, also cast light on the existence of the political community in Delhi. According to Barani, the sons of the slave generals of Sultan Balban, Qazi Jalaluddin Kashani who commanded immense respect among the people, and Kotwal Brinjtan and Hatya Paik, conspired to change the political system by killing the Sultan, Jalaluddin Firuz Shah Khalji, and making Sidi Maula the Caliph of the Sultanate instead. Their conspiracy was revealed to the Sultan, the conspirators were arrested, and Sidi Maula killed.[178] The political awareness of the citizens of Delhi increased, and the urban political community grew stronger during the fourteenth century.[179]

To conclude, it may be stressed that political pluralism in the Sultanate polity promoted the concept of partnership in political power, on the one hand, and helped the growth of a composite culture, on the other. In fact, it brought the Hindu and the Muslim socio-political elites closer together. Further, the Sultan was never able under this polity to emerge as an absolute monarch. He had to make compromises with the *ashraf*, the cultural and religious elite in urban centres. Political power could only be centralized through the imposition of checks on the bureaucracy. Also, it needs to be emphasized that the typologies applied by the new orientalists in the West to their studies of the state and society in South Asia, such as the patrimonial and bureaucratic empire or the decentralized feudal polity, are not applicable to the state system under the Muslim rulers. In fact, the orientalists have failed to take note of the political and cultural dimensions of the capital city in general and the role performed by the *ashraf* as well as the conventions and practices developed with regard to the relationship between powerful sections of the society and the crown. Royal authority always remained bound up with the rule of law, defence of conventional moral values, and the safeguarding of material prosperity, resulting from the proper fulfilment of his duties by the Sultan and his officers. An incompetent or a minor Sultan was never acceptable during the period of the Delhi Sultanate.

NOTES

1. Ali bin Hamid al-Kufi, *Fathnama-i-Sind* (popularly known as *Chachnama*), ed. Nabi Bakhsh Baloch, Islamabad, 1983. Hereafter cited as *Chachnama*.

2. It may be pointed out that the comparison of *Adab-ul-Muluk wal-Kifayat-ul-Mamluk* with *Adab-ul-Harb wal-Shuja* suggests that the scribe, probably at the instance of some bookseller, separated the first six chapters from the former, copied the remaining ones dealing with diplomacy and the art of warfare, and then introduced these as *Adab-ul-Harb wal-Shuja*. This recension has attracted adequate attention as an important source of information on the mode of warfare. In the year 1346, Shamsi, Ahmad Suhaili Khwansari published its critically edited text from Iran. In 1354 Shamsi, Muhammad Sarvar Maulai published the six and three other chapters of the *Adab-ul-Muluk wal-Kifayat-ul-Mamluk* with notes under the new title '*Ain-i-Kishvardari:* Cf. *Ain-i-Kishvardari* (*Shash bab bazyafta*), Buniyad-i-Farhang-i-Iran, Publication no. 212.
3. Yohanan Friedmann is the first scholar to point out that the *Chachnama* presents a clear-cut picture of the establishment of friendly relations between the Arab ruler and the Hindus of Sind and Multan. He says that Muhammad bin Qasim gave his unqualified blessing to the characteristic features of the Hindu society that he encountered, and sanctioned both the privileges of the high castes and the degradation of the low castes.

   Cf. *The Origin and the Significance of the Chachnama, Islam in Asia*, ed. Yohanan Friedmann, Jerusalem, 1984, vol. I, p. 31.
4. *Chachnama*, text, op. cit., pp. 159, 160, 161, 162, etc.
5. Cf. *Perso-Arabic Sources of Information on the Life and Conditions in the Sultanate of Delhi*, pp. 27–8; hereafter cited as *Perso-Arabic Sources of Information.*
6. Cf. Iqtidar H. Siddiqui, 'The Origin and Growth of Islamicate Historiography in India: Analysis of the Thirteenth-Century Indo-Persian Historians' Approach to the History of the Foundation of Muslim Rule in the South Asian Subcontinent', *Journal of Objective Studies*, New Delhi, vol. 1, nos. 1–2, July–October 1989, pp. 71–5.
7. *Tarikh-i-Fakhr-i-Mudabbir*, p. 26.
8. Ibid., pp. 35–6.
9. *Tabaqat-i-Nasiri*, vol. II, pp. 163–4.
10. *Perso-Arabic Sources of Information*, op. cit., p. 48.
11. Minhaj Juzjani mentions Lahore as the winter capital of Sultan Muizuddin Muhammad bin Sam. That is why Aibek also made it his capital. It was a prestigious city. *Tabaqat-i-Nasiri*, vol. I, p. 405.
12. Isami says that before Iltutmish, Delhi was one of the parganas in the region. It emerged as a magnificent metropolis during Iltutmish's reign. *Futuh-us-Salatin*, ed. A.S. Usha, Madras, 1948, p. 108 (lines 6 and 7).
13. *Tarikh-i-Fakhr-i-Mudabbir*, pp. 33–4, 35, 73.
14. Cf. *Perso-Arabic Sources of Information*, p. 27.
15. *Fakhr-i-Mudabbir* and the early Arab and Persian writers mention the Khaljis as being of Turkish origin. However, Ziauddin Barani's statement

that the Turks in Delhi did not regard the Khaljis as being of Turkish race nor the latter's claim to be one with them has led modern scholars to regard them as being of non-Turkish stock. K.A. Nizami would have us believe that the Khaljis entered the fold of Islam when they arrived in India, although they are reported to have served as Muslim warriors in the Ghaznavid, the Saljuq, and the Ghurid armies since earlier times. As a matter of fact, the long stay of these Turkish people in the region now included in Afghanistan cut them off from their homeland, and they seem to have changed their lifestyle and adopted the local Persian dialect spoken in the region around Ghazna. *Tarikh-i-Fakhr-i-Mudabbir,* p. 48; Iqtidar Husain Siddiqui, *Nobility Under the Khalji Sultans, Islamic Culture*, Hyderabad, January 1963, pp. 52–5; idem, 'The Turks and their Migration to Central Asia and India: Analysis of the Historical Information on the Turks and Turkistan in Early Medieval Indo-Persian Sources', *Proceedings of the Indian History Congress*, 55th Session, Aligarh, 1994, Delhi, 1995, pp. 178–83; K.A. Nizami, *Royalty in Medieval India*, Munshiram Manoharlal, New Delhi, 1997, p. 5.

16. *Tarikh-i-Fakhr-i-Mudabbir*, p. 33.
17. Irfan Habib, 'Formation of the Sultanate Ruling Class of the Thirteenth Century', *Medieval India* 1: Researches in the History of India, New Delhi, 1992, pp. 1–21, 8–13 for details.
18. *Tarikh-i-Fakhr-i-Mudabbir*, p. 26.
19. Ibid., p. 51.
20. Ibid., p. 52.
21. Generally, the terms used for the official documents issued by the Sultan were *farman* and *mithal*, while *nishan* and *parwana* signified the orders in writing issued by the princes and nobles posted in the provinces as governors respectively.
22. A comparative study of the available documents from the Sultanate period shows that Aibek's *parwana* continued to serve as a model. *Perso-Arabic Sources of Information*, pp. 167–89, for details.
23. *Perso-Arabic Sources of Information*, op. cit., pp. 168–9.
24. *Tabaqat-i-Nasiri*, vol. I, pp. 422–3.
25. In his account of the conquest of Bihar and Bengal by Muhammad (bin) Bakhtiyar Khalji in the beginning of the thirteenth century, Minhaj Juzjani says that he joined Malik Hussamuddin Ughalbak's service in Benaras and got two villages in *iqta* for his maintenance on the border of Bihar. *Tabaqat-i-Nasiri*, vol. I, p. 423.
26. Barani refers to the warrior sawars of the *hashm-i-qalb* whom Sultan Iltutmish assigned villages in *iqtas* in lieu of cash salary and allowances and stated that they were called *iqtadars*. Ziauddin Barani, *Tarikh-i-Firuzshahi*, Calcutta, 1862, p. 62. Hereafter cited as Barani.
27. *Tarikh-i-Fakhr-i-Mudabbir*, p. 33.
28. Loc. cit.
29. The contemporary historians Hasan Nizami and Muhammad Awfi,

who brought to completion their respective works *Taj-ul-Mathir* and *Jawami-al-Hikayat wa-Lavami-al Rivayat* respectively during the reign of Iltutmish, omit any mention of Aram Shah's accession to the throne because a reference to it was thought disparaging to the reigning Sultan. Minhaj Juzjani mentions him as the son and immediate successor of Aibek but omits the details of his disappearance because he also presented his book to the son of Iltutmish, Sultan Nasiruddin Mahmud in AD 1259. If read between the lines, Minhaj Juzjani's brief account suggests that Aram Shah was killed after Iltutmish had come to Delhi at the invitation of Amir-i-Dad Ismail. *Tabaqat-i-Nasiri,* vol. I, p. 144.

30. Minhaj Juzjani states that the youngest daughter of Aibek was married by Iltutmish after he had occupied Delhi and Aram Shah was no more. *Tabaqat-i-Nasiri,* vol. I, p. 418.
31. Cf. Iqtidar H. Siddiqui, 'Relations Between Sultan Jalaluddin Khwarazm Shah and the Turkish Rulers of North India', *Aligarh Journal of Oriental Studies*, Aligarh, vol. III, Spring 1986, pp. 55–66, 60–1, for details.
32. *Tabaqat-i-Nasiri*, vol. I, p. 444. Also *Perso-Arabic Sources of Information*, pp. 60–1, for other sources of information.
33. *Tabaqat-i-Nasiri*, vol. I, pp. 444–5.
34. According to Sadiduddin Muhammad Awfi, Malik Bahauddin al-Jamji, a distinguished warrior, was deprived of his huge treasure and thrown into prison. Cf. *Lubab al-Albab*, ed. E.G. Browne and Muhammad Qazwini (London, 1906), part 1, pp. 113–15, for details about his career.
35. *Perso-Arabic Sources of Information*, p. 61.
36. *Tabaqat-i-Nasiri*, vol. I, p. 445.
37. *Jawami-al-Hikayat wa-Lavami-al Rivayat* contain interesting information about the elimination by the Sultan of the nobles and his rivals through treacherous means in case their existence should pose a threat to the person of the king or peace in the Sultanate. Cf. *Perso-Arabic Sources of Information*, pp. 22–3.
38. *Tabaqat-i-Nasiri*, vol. II, p. 8.
39. *Lubab-al-Albab*, part 2, pp. 114–15.
40. During the early medieval period, every city chosen by a Sultan for his capital in Central Asia was called *Hazrat* out of respect. In the Central Asian tradition, Delhi is mentioned by the early writers as *Hazrat* after Sultan Iltutmish had made it his capital. In fact, Delhi began to be called Hazrat-i-Delhi before any saint came to be buried there.
41. Abu Bakr bin Ali Usman al-Kasani, *Farsi Tarjuma-i-Kitab ul-Saidna of Al-Biruni,* ed. M. Sotudeh and Iraj Afshar, Iran, 1352 Shamsi, pp. 11–13.
42. Neither Minhaj-i-Siraj Juzjani nor any later writer mentions Ali Sher 'Iwaz Khalji as the ruler of Bengal. A recently discovered inscription in Bengal mentions Ghiyasuddin 'Iwaz's son Ali Sher. Z.U.A. Desai observes that the rare coin of Bengal carrying the name of the reigning Sultan is

Ali Sher-i-Iwaz Khalji and not Ghiyasuddin; this suggests that the father was dead and that his son Ali Sher had succeeded to the throne sometime in 1221. He also refers to a coin issued by Ali Sher, pointing out that the date AH 621, had not been correctly deciphered by Hoernele. The date AH 621 corresponds to AD 1224. Disagreeing with Desai, Abdul Karim establishes the fact that Ali Sher was the governor of the territory and that his father Sultan Ghiyasuddin was reigning when Iltutmish invaded Bihar and Bengal. It is to be pointed out that the Crown Prince could be granted by his father the title of Sultan during this period. Sahiduddin Mohammad Awfi mentions the eldest son of Iltutmish as Sultan.

Cf. *Epigraphia Indica: Arabic and Persian Supplement*, 1975, ed. Z.U.A. Desai, New Delhi, 1983, pp. 7–11; Abdul Karim, *Corpus of the Arabic and Persian Inscriptions of Bengal*, Asiatic Society of Bangladesh, 1992, pp. 21–5.

43. *Sirat-i-Jalaluddin Mangbarni*, fourteenth-century Persian translation from the Arabic text, ed. Minovi, Tehran, 1956, p. 121.
44. *Perso-Arabic Sources of Information*, p. 33.
45. Ibid., pp. 29–30.
46. Iqtidar Husain Siddiqui, 'Water Works and the Irrigation System in Pre-Mughal India', *Journal of the Economic and Social History of the Orient,* Leiden, vol. XXIX, pp. 53–5.
47. Awfi tells us that India abounded in dacoits and highwaymen whose operations not only hampered the progress of trade but also made difficult the transmission of information between the centre and the provinces. He praises Iltutmish for taking effective measures against them. The roads were rendered safe and the robbers suppressed, cf. *Perso-Arabic Sources of Information*, p. 31.
48. A.B.M. Habib Ullah, who could not explore the evidence in Nasawi's work, says that Iltutmish's hold over the Panjab was not effective. Cf. *Foundation of Muslim Rule in India*, p. 97.
49. *Tabaqat-i-Nasiri*, vol. II, pp. 5-6, where Minhaj Juzjani states that in 1228 Sultan Iltutmish assigned the *iyalat* of the *khitta* of Multan to Malik Izzuddin Kabir Khan Ayaz but that later he was demoted and then assigned the charge of Palwal, a small pargana town near Delhi (now in present-day Haryana).
50. In his *qasidas* (panegyrics), Siraji, Khurasani mentions Prince Nasiruddin Mahmud with the royal titles of Sultan and Shah. For instance, mentioning the defeat of the chief of Awadh by his army, the poet says: O King! A single Turk (of the army) dispersed the army of Hardu Dal. Thy sword made the sighs of Hardu Dal reach the heavens. *Cf. Perso-Arabic Sources of Information*, pp. 59–60.
51. Ibid., pp. 6–9, for details about Malik Bahauddin al-Jamji.
52. *Tabaqat-i-Nasiri*, vol. I, pp. 448–9, vol. II, pp. 40–1.
53. Ibid., vol. II, pp. 10–11.

54. Cf. *Perso-Arabic Sources of Information*, pp. 60–1.
55. Hasan Sijzi, *Fawaid ul-Fuad*, Lucknow, AH 1302, pp. 50–1.
56. *Epigraphia Indica: Arabic and Persian Supplement*, op. cit., pp. 2–4.
57. *Diwan-i Siraji Khurasani*, ed. Nazir Ahmad, Aligarh, 1972, *qasida* no. 130, pp. 37–8.
58. *Tabaqat-i-Nasiri*, vol. II, pp. 23–4.
59. *Fawaid ul-Fuad*, pp. 103–4.
60. *Foundation of Muslim Rule in India*, p. 237.
61. *Tabaqat-i-Nasiri*, vol. II, p. 20.
62. Ibid., vol. II, pp. 3, 25, etc.
63. Cf. *Perso-Arabic Sources of Information*, pp. 28–33, for the position of Nizam-ul-Mulk Junaidi at Iltutmish's court.
64. *Epigraphia Indica: Arabic and Persian Supplement*, 1966, p. 9.
65. *Tabaqat-i-Nasiri*, vol. I, p. 456.
66. Ibid., vol. I, p. 469.
67. Ibid., vol. I, p. 456.
68. Ziauddin Barani, *Tarikh-i-Firuzshahi*, Calcutta, 1862, pp. 61–2, hereafter cited as Barani.
69. *Tabaqat-i-Nasiri*, vol. II, p. 8.
70. Minhaj-i-Siraj Juzjani states that after Iltutmish had established himself in Delhi in AD 1211, Tajuddin Yildoz sent an umbrella and *durbish* (royal staff) for him. The acceptance by Iltutmish of Yildoz's gift led to the establishment of peace between them. Again he states that in AD 1215, Tajuddin Yildoz marched from Lahore towards Delhi, but Iltutmish gave him battle in the plain of Tarain, and defeated and captured him. Cf. *Tabaqat-i-Nasiri*, vol. I, pp. 444, 445.
71. Cf. Iqtidar H. Siddiqui, 'Relations between Sultan Jalaluddin Khwarazm Shah and the Turkish Sultans of North India', *Aligarh Journal of Oriental Studies*, vol. III, no. 1, Spring 1986, pp. 55–66, 58.
72. Ibid., p. 64.
73. *Tabaqat-i-Nasiri*, vol. I, p. 447.
74. K.A. Nizami, *Some Aspects of Religion and Politics in India during the 13th Century*, New Delhi, 1961, pp. 122–3.
75. *Tabaqat-i-Nasiri*, vol. II, pp. 45, 48.
76. *Perso-Arabic Sources of Information*, p. 31.
77. *Tabaqat-i-Nasiri*, vol. II, p. 45.
78. Ibid., vol. II, p. 214.
79. Ibid., vol. II, p. 218.
80. Ibid., vol. I, p. 459.
81. Ibid., vol. I, p. 463.
82. Ibid., vol. I, p. 468.
83. Ibid., vol. I, p. 469.
84. Barani, pp. 27–8.

85. *Tabaqat-i-Nasiri*, vol. I, p. 468; vol. II, p. 46, for the *vilayet* of Meerut held by him.
86. *Tarikh-i-Fakhr-i-Mudabbir*, p. 44.
87. *Tabaqat-i-Nasiri*, vol. II, pp. 3-88, the section related to the nobles.
88. The Hindvi dialect had begun to develop as a link language in the Sultanate in the thirteenth century. With the establishment of Muslim colonies by the Sultans of Delhi in the conquered territories, from Malwa and Gujarat up to the Deccan, it gained currency everywhere through the old residents of the north settled there to stabilize the Sultan's power. Cf. Iqtidar H. Siddiqui, '*Urdu Zaban ka Irtiqa Tarikhi Haqaiq ki roshni mein Fikro Nazar*', Urdu Quarterly, vol. 27, no. 2, Aligarh, 1990, pp. 33–48.
89. Sultan Nasiruddin Mahmud was born after the death of Nasiruddin Mahmud, the oldest son of Iltutmish. The latter gave the name of his deceased son in order to perpetuate his memory. *Tabaqat-i-Nasiri*, vol. I, p. 472.
90. Cf. Iqtidar H. Siddiqui, 'Politics and conditions in the territories under the occupation of Central Asian rulers', *Central Asiatic Journal*, vol. 27, nos. 3–4, Wiesbaden, 1983, p. 290.
91. *Tabaqat-i-Nasiri*, vol. I, p. 487, vol. II, p. 44.
92. Malik Tajuddin Sanjar Sewistani, a veteran general from Sind, was an ally of Bahauddin Balban. He was a non-Turk from an old family of Sind and was trusted by Balban. In 1254, he attacked Imaduddin Rayhan in Bahraich and destroyed him. *Tabaqat-i-Nasiri*, i/49.
93. Both Minhaj Juzjani and Amid Loeki Sunami (the contemporary poet) mention Jalaluddin as Sultan Masud Shah. *Tabaqat-i-Nasiri*, vol. I, p. 489; vol. II, pp. 68–9; *Perso-Arabic Sources of Information*, pp. 69–70, for Amid Loeki.
94. *Tabaqat-i-Nasiri*, vol. I, p. 489.
95. Loc. cit.
96. *Futuh-us-Salatin*, pp. 160–4.
97. *Tabaqat-i-Nasiri*, vol. I, pp. 490, 494.
98. Cf. Iqtidar H. Siddiqui, 'The Qarlugh Kingdom in North-Western India', *Islamic Culture Quarterly*, Hyderabad, vol. LIV, no. 2, April 1980, pp. 75–90, for details.
99. *Tabaqat-i-Nasiri*, vol. II, pp. 213–14, 218.
100. Ibid., vol. II, pp. 83–4.
101. *Islamic Culture Quarterly*, vol. LIV, no. 2, April 1980, op. cit., p. 86.
102. Isami reports that Balban occupied the throne after having killed the Sultan. Ibn Battuta, who arrived in India in AD 1333, was told by the responsible people in Delhi that Balban had killed his master. Cf. *Travels of Ibn Battuta*, tr. Sir Hamilton Gibb, Cambridge, 1971, vol. III, pp. 632–3; *Futuh-us-Salatin*, p. 163.
103. Ziauddin Barani, *Tarikh-i-Firuzshahi*, Calcutta, 1862, pp. 29–34, hereafter cited as Barani.

104. Barani, pp. 28–9.
105. Ibid., p. 73.
106. Ibid., p. 31.
107. Ibid., p. 29.
108. *Foundation of Muslim Rule in India*, op. cit., p. 166.
109. Barani, pp. 80, 81, 119.
110. Barani incidentally refers to the term *fawazil* in his account of Sultan Kaiqubad and Sultan Jalaluddin Khalji's reign (1290–6), suggesting that by their time it had become a well-established practice in the Sultanate. Sultan Jalaluddin did not make any change in the state system during his reign. Barani, pp. 164, 220–1.
111. Barani, p. 50.
112. Barani's reference to Kamal Mahiyar's rejection by the Sultan for the post of accountant in the *iqta* of Amroha indicates that Amroha was made a *khalsa* unit because in the khalsa unit officials were appointed by the centre and not by the *muqta*. It may also be added that on his promotion to the post of *sarjandar*, Jalaluddin Khalji was assigned Kaithal as *iqta* in lieu of cash salary and the charge of Samana *shiqq* in addition. Barani, pp. 36, 195.
113. Ibid., p. 37.
114. *The Foundation of Muslim Rule in India*, p. 164.
115. Barani, p. 29.
116. Ibid., p. 45.
117. Ibid., pp. 40–1.
118. Ibid., p. 29.
119. Ibid., pp. 83–4.
120. Ibid., p. 65.
121. Ibid., pp. 47–8.
122. Ibid., p. 47.
123. Ibid., p. 46.
124. Saiyid Muhammad Mubarak Kirmani, known as Mir Khurd, *Siyarul-Auliya*, Delhi, AH 1302, p. 106.
125. Anonymous, *Surur-us-Sudur*, MS Habib Ganj Collection, Maulana Azad Library, Aligarh, p. 24. Folios have not been marked. It may be stated that the internal evidence contained in the *Tabaqat-i-Nasiri* shows that its compiler, Minhaj Juzjani, was not devoid of concern for Islam. Shaikh Nizamuddin Auliya is also reported to have praised him for delivering religious sermons, which had an impact on the Shaikh himself. *Fawaid-ul-Fuad*, pp. 191–2, 233, 253.
126. *Tabaqat-i-Nasiri*, vol. I, pp. 470–1, vol. II, pp. 2–3.
127. *Futuh-us-Salatin*, p. 164; Barani, pp. 57–8.
128. *Travels of Ibn Battuta*, Eng. tr. H. Gibb, Cambridge, 1971, vol. 3, p. 762.
129. Barani, pp. 57, 58–9.

130. Cf. Iqtidar H. Siddiqui, 'The Afghans and their Emergence in India as a Ruling Elite during the Delhi Sultanate Period', *Central Asiatic Journal*, vol. 26, nos. 3–4, Wiesbaden, 1982, pp. 241–61 and 251–2.
131. Minhaj Juzjani mentions only two Khalji nobles, Malik Nasruddin, son of Malik Chaush Khalji, and Malik Daulat Shah (i.e. Balka Khalji), in the list of the leading nobles of Sultan Iltutmish. Both of them seem to have submitted to the authority of the Delhi Sultan in AD 1226, when Bihar and Bengal were conquered and annexed to the Delhi Sultanate. In 1230, Daulat Shah revolted and was killed by Iltutmish. Thereafter no Khalji is mentioned by the medieval sources to have survived as an important man in Bihar or Bengal. Dharma Swamin's account suggests that the military operations against the rebels in Bihar and Bengal continued till 1234. Most probably, the Khaljis were evacuated and scattered in other territories under the control of the Sultan. *Tabaqat-i-Nasiri*, vol. I, pp. 450, 451; *Biography of Dharmasvamin (Chaglo-tsa-ba chos-rje-dpal): A Tibetan Monk's Pilgrimage*, Eng. tr. G. Roerich K.P. Jayaswal Research Institute, Patna, 1959, pp. 62, 65.
132. It is worth mentioning that the Tajiks and others, who themselves or whose fathers had come from abroad, were against the rise of the converts to Islam in the state service. During the short-lived conflict between Qutlugh Khan and Bahauddin Balban, the Tajiks lent their support to the latter because they could not tolerate Imaduddin Rayhan (an Indian convert to Islam), the protégé of Qutlugh Khan, holding the ministerial post at the centre. On his restoration as regent in Delhi in AD 1254, Balban had the non-Turkish supporters favoured with important positions. In this regard, mention should be made of Tajuddin Sanjar Sewistani, Alauddin Ayaz Zinjani, and Jamaluddin Nishapuri, the *amir-i-ariz*. The former was promoted from the post of deputy *hajib* to that of *vakil-i-dar*. *Tabaqat-i-Nasiri*, vol. I, p. 493; vol. II, p. 60.
133. *Tabaqat-i-Nasiri*, vol. II, pp. 83, 86.
134. Barani, pp. 115–16.
135. Barani, p. 126; Iqtidar H. Siddiqui, 'Politics and Conditions in the Territories under the Occupation of Central Asian Rulers in North-Western India', *Central Asiatic Journal*, Wiesbaden, 1983, vol. 27, nos. 3–4, p. 292, for Jalaluddin Khalji.
136. Barani, p. 133; Isami, *Futuh-us-Salatin*, ed. Usha, Madras, 1949, pp. 186, 187–8.
137. Cf. Peter Jackson, 'The Dissolution of the Mongol Empire', *Central Asiatic Journal*, Wiesbaden, 1978, vol. XXII, nos. 3–4, pp. 223–43.
138. *Tabaqat-i-Nasiri*, vol. II, p. 218.
139. *The Foundation of Muslim Rule in India*, p. 179.
140. Barani, pp. 172–3.

141. W.H. Moreland, *The Agrarian System of Muslim India* (rpt.), Delhi, 1968, p. 225.
142. *Tabaqat-i-Nasiri*, vol. II, p. 70.
143. Ziauddin Barani, *Fatwa-i-Jahandari,* ed. A.S. Khan, Lahore, 1972, p. 18.
144. Shaikh Muzaffar Balkhi, *Muktubat-i-Shaikh Muzaffar Balkhi*, MS. Khuda Bakhsh Oriental Library, Patna, letter no. 151; also Syed Hasan Askari, 'Maktub and Malfuz Literature', Khuda Bakhsh Annual Lecture Series 6, Khuda Bakhsh Oriental Public Library, Patna, 1976, pp. 18–21. Saiyid Hasan Askari leaves out the sentences to the effect that Hindu landlords possess estates and in case they are given high positions in the government, the Muslims will be deprived of their source of livelihood.
145. *Tabaqat-i-Nasiri*, vol. II, pp. 41, 52; Barani, p. 45.
146. *Biography of Dharma Svamin*, tr. George Roerich, K.P. Jayaswal Research Institute, Patna, 1959, p. 85.
147. Sadiduddin Muhammad Awfi, *Lubab ul-Albab*, eds. E.C. Browne and Mirza Muhammad Qazvini, London, 1960, vol. I, pp. 113–14.
148. *Tarikh-i-Fakhr-i-Mudabbir*, p. 26.
149. *Taj-ul-Masir*, MS. F.133b.
150. *Cf. Perso-Arabic Sources of Information*, p. 28.
151. *Tabaqat-i-Nasiri,* vol. I, pp. 485–86, vol. II, p. 61–2.
152. Cf. *Biography of Dharma Svamin*, op. cit., pp. 65, 98.
153. Ain-ul-Mulk Mahru, *Insha-i-Mahru*, ed. Shaikh Abdur Rashid, Lahore, 1965, document no. 6, p. 17.
154. *Cf. Perso-Arabic Sources of Information,* pp. 59–60.
155. *Muqaddimah-i-Ghurat al-Kamal*, MS., British Library, London, Add. 21, 104, f. 176b.
156. *Futuh-us-Salatin*, pp. 180–1.
157. Barani, p. 108.
158. *Ijaz-i-Khusravi*, Lucknow, 1876, vol. 5, pp. 5–13.
159. *Dewal Rani wa-Khizr Khan*, p. 70.
160. Barani, p. 539.
161. *Insha-i-Mahru*, op. cit., pp. 16–17.
162. Cf. *Perso-Arabic Sources of Information*, pp. 81--2.
163. Loc. cit.
164. Muhammad bin Mansur, known as Fakhr-i-Mudabbir, *Adab-ul-Harb wa Shuja,* ed. Ahmad Suhaili Khawansari, Iran, 1346 Shamsi, p. 481.
165. Barani, p. 210.
166. Ibid., p. 108.
167. Cf. *Epigraphia Indo-Moslemica*, 1913–14, pp. 35–45.
168. Ibn Battuta, vol. 3, Eng. tr., op. cit., pp. 602, 605.
169. Barani, p. 120.
170. Cf. *Perso-Arabic Sources of Information*, p. 69.

171. The Hindu army men lived in a separate quarter of Ghazna. 'Al-Ma'arri describes the scene of a Hindu woman's sati in Ghazna. *Risalatu'l Ghufran*, p. 153, as cited by Muhammad Nazim, *The Life and Times of Sultan Mahmud of Ghazna*, op. cit., p. 140, f.n. 7.
172. *The Travels of Ibn Battuta*, vol. 3, Eng. tr. Sir Hamilton Gibb, Cambridge, 1971, p. 614.
173. Ziauddin Barani, *Sahifa-i-Na'at-i-Muhammadi* MS., Raza Library, Rampur, ff. 390a; also Nurul Hasan, 'A note on Sahifa Na'at-i-Muhammadi', *Medieval India Quarterly*, nos. 3–4, Aligarh, 1950, pp. 102–3.
174. *Biography of Dharmasvamin*, op. cit., pp. 73, 90–1.
175. Cf. Taranath, as cited by Hasan Nishat, *The Comprehensive History of Bihar*, vol. 1, Patna, 1983, p. 40.
176. *Tabaqat-i-Nasiri*, vol. I, p. 456.
177. Barani, pp. 172, 175–6.
178. Isami says that the dervishes of Delhi became jealous of the popularity of Sidi Maula and spread the calumny that people wanted to make him the Shah-i-Hindustan in place of Sultan Jalaluddin Khalji, *Futuh-us-Salatin*, p. 216; Barani, pp. 208–11.
179. Cf. Iqtidar H. Siddiqui, 'Social Mobility in the Sultanate of Delhi', *Medieval India*, vol. 1, ed. Irfan Habib, New Delhi, 1993, pp. 35–6.

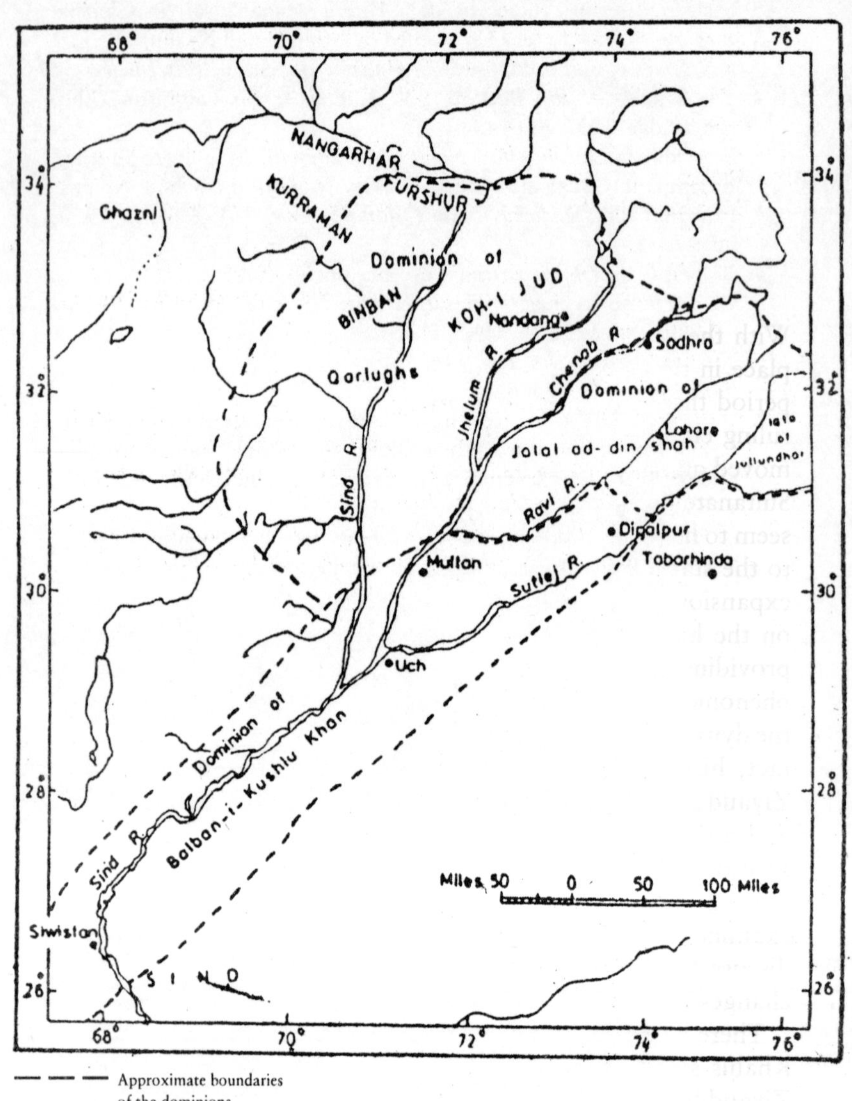

THE DOMINIONS OF THE QARLUGHS AND OTHER MONGOL ALLIES

CHAPTER 3

Kingship and Authority under the Khalji Sultans

With the rise of the Khaljis to power, important changes took place in the Sultanate polity. The dynastic change ushered in a period that had not only an impact on the composition of the ruling elite but also on their thought process. The new leaders moved quickly and turned the Sultanate around. Once again the Sultanate became a tightly centralized entity; the political ideals seem to have been harnessed with a view to imparting dynamism to the state apparatus through the process of development and expansion of the empire. The changed atmosphere had an impact on the historiography of the period, which widened in scope, providing its reader with insights into the complex socio-political phenomena. The reader comes away with a fresh perspective on the dynamics of a new age in the history of the Delhi Sultanate, in fact, history seized in all its dynamism. Amir Khusrau and Ziyauddin Barani successfully depict the transformation of ideas and attitudes adopted by the rulers towards the polity, social relationships, productivity, and distribution, and their policies towards war, faith, the social and political order. Before we examine the nature of kingship and authority, we should briefly discuss the ethnic origin of the Khaljis because it also led to changes in the system of governance.

There has been a controversy about the Turkish origin of the Khaljis since medieval times. The fourteenth-century historian Ziyauddin Barani would have us believe that the Khaljis were immigrant Muslims of non-descript origin,[1] while the modern Afghan scholar Abdul Ha'i Habibi insists on their being of Afghan stock.[2] It is now necessary to offer some explanation about the problem in the light of evidence contained in the miscellaneous sources.

The early Chinese and Arabic sources tell us that the Khaljis were Turk by origin but were driven from their ancestral homeland, called Turkestan. They entered and settled down with their livestock in the region around Ghazna (now included in present-day Afghanistan). Besides the Chinese sources, Minorsky also refers to al-Masudi and Kashghari; according to the former, the Khalji Turks lived in the region adjoining Siestan and stretching towards Garch and Bust. Kashghari says: 'The Oghuz (Turks) consisted of 24 clans but the two Khalaj clans separated from the federation, and therefore these two are not (evidently now) counted as of the Oghuz.' Further, the passage quoted by Minorsky from the rare manuscript copy of the early thirteenth-century work, *Jahan nama*, by Muhammad bin Najib Barkan is conclusive. 'The Khaljis (Kh.L.J.) are a tribe of Turks who from the Khalukh limits emigrated to Zabulistan (present-day Afghanistan). Among the districts of Ghaznin, there is a steppe where they reside. Then on account of the heat of the air their complexion has changed and tended towards blackness; the language, too, has undergone alterations and become a different dialect. A tribe of this group went to the limits of Bavard and founded some settlements. By mistake (in writing) people call them the Khallukh Khalaj.'[3]

It is also worth mentioning that Fakhr-i-Mudabbir, who wrote more than a century before Barani, includes the Khaljis in his list of the sixty-four Turkish tribes.[4] Likewise, the fourteenth- and fifteenth-century Indo-Persian lexicons also mention them as being of Turkish origin. For instance, the *Dastur-ul-Afazil*, explaining the meanings of Khalaj, says that it is the name of the *vilayet* of Turks (in present-day Afghanistan).[5] The fifteenth-century compiler of *Zafan-i-Goya* mentions Khalaj as a territory of Turks, known for the beauty of its inhabitants and musk.[6] As regards the fifteenth-century historian, Shihab Hakim, he calls Sultan Alauddin Mahmud Khalji of Malwa (reigned: 1436–69), the descendant of the Turkish general, Qulij Khan, the so-called general of Chinggis Khan:

> His Majesty is the descendant of Khalaj Turks who happened to be the chiefs in Turkestan. His ancestor belonged to the clan of Qulij Khan; through corruption became Khalaj. He was a leading noble and son-in-law of Chinggis Khan. He had descended from Afrasiyab (the legendary king of the Turks). Having quarrelled with his wife, the daughter of

Chinggis Khan, he left with 30,000 *sawars* (horsemen) and took up abode in Kabul. After the death of Chinggis Khan, he proceeded to Samarqand.[7]

Excepting the part relating to the Turkish origin of his sovereign patron, the other details may be rejected as a concoction.

Influenced by Shihab Hakim, the sixteenth-century historian Nizamuddin Ahmad also describes the Sultan of Malwa as a descendant of Qulij Khan. However, he adds that the Khan settled in the hilly country of Ghur and Ghurjistan after the defeat of Khwarazm Shah by Chinggis Khan, his father-in-law. And that by a change of letters and frequency of use Qulij became Khalaj.[8] Writing early in the seventeenth century, Firishta, who was quite meticulous in sifting and verifying historical evidence from the earlier sources, does not accept the version given by Shihab Hakim and Nizamuddin Ahmad. He states on the authority of *Saljuq nama* (no longer extant) that the Khaljis were Turks. Further, he states that the Khaljis have often been mentioned in the histories of the Sultans of Ghazna and Ghur.[9] It may now be concluded that the Khaljis were of Turkish origin, yet they were considered by the Turkish nobles as their rivals and thus a threat to their monopoly of power in the Sultanate.

A word may be added here about the Islamization of the Khaljis. Mentioning their marauding activities during the reign of Amir Subaktigin, al-Utbi calls them *sahranashin* (nomads) and infidels. Sultan Mahmud of Ghazna had to lead military expeditions against them and then they entered the fold of Islam. They seem to have been enlisted in the army and exposed to the higher culture of Ghazna.[10] The Khalji horsemen, serving in the armies of the Ghurid and Khwarazmian Sultans, were highly disciplined and urbanized officers.[11]

Minhaj Juzjani's account of the Khalji conquerors, who carved out an independent Sultanate in Bengal and Bihar after the death of Sultan Qutbuddin Aibek in AD 1210, tends to show that they were not willing to acknowledge the suzerainty of Sultan Shamsuddin Iltutmish of Delhi (1211–36) because the latter was originally a slave and a mere upstart in their eyes. Freeborn Muslims and the followers of Sultan Muizuddin Muhammad bin Sam, as the Khaljis were, they must have thought highly of themselves. They had not only conquered eastern India but had also consolidated their rule there. Within a short period, *madrasas*, mosques, *khanqahs* (hostels for the comfort of travellers), roads, and bridges were built in Bihar and Bengal.[12] In fact, they were the first dividers of water from the lands in this region of overwhelming rivers and boundless swamps. They are reported to have built dykes, which made possible the reclamation of tracts of land in Bengal. The dykes made the movement of people and cattle possible during the rainy season. Moreover, the large-hearted patronage extended by the Khalji rulers of Bihar and Bengal to scholars and men of talent was proof of their being men of culture. The interest evinced by the Khalji rulers in the economic and cultural development of the region seems to have made their rule acceptable to the local people. That is why Khalji power could not be destroyed completely after the annexation of Bihar and Bengal by Sultan Iltutmish to his Sultanate in 1226. Sultan Iltutmish of Delhi assigned the vast territory of Bengal to a Khalji noble named Balka Khalji, granting him permission to assume the royal title of Daulat Shah and rule as his vassal in order to reconcile the Khaljis to him, but in vain. Daulat Shah waited for an opportunity. In 1230, on the death of Prince Nasir-uddin Mahmud, the son of Iltutmish and the supreme governor of the eastern territorial units, he revolted and drove away the Delhi army. Sadiduddin Muhammad Awfi states:

During this reign (of Sultan Iltutmish), may it last until the day of judgement, the rebellion by Daulat Shah against his benefactor, the Sultan of the World, heir to Solomon, Shams al-Dunya wad-Din, the Shadow of God, is a case in point. The mean-minded wretch turned ungrateful, in spite of the fact that he was elevated through royal benevolence to the highest position; his short-lived power and prosperity had filled him with arrogance. Previously, he could not afford to possess even one horse but now he looked a Champion and ruled as a Prince on account of the favour done to him by the Sultan [Iltutmish]. He was allowed to enjoy power and exercise authority. The devil, however, led him astray. He seized the entire *vilayet* of Lakhnauti and Gaur, considering it an easy choice. Informed, the successful sovereign (i.e. Iltutmish), who is the shadow of the mercy of the creator, decided to march against him. He ordered the victorious army to proceed both by the land and the river (Ganges). He himself marched under the shade of his auspicious umbrella. Success accompanied the Sultan. As the royal standard reached the region (Bengal), people were seized with panic.

The unfortunate and accursed fellow (the rebel), who lacked discretion, got ready to fight because the power that he had acquired through oppression and tyranny had turned him arrogant. He was killed by the soldiers before the sun of kingship, the shadow of God, had come out to fight.[13]

After this event, the Khaljis seem to have been expelled from the region. They were probably scattered and forced to seek employment for their survival under nobles or served in petty positions.[14]

We may now discuss the significance of Barani's statement about the aversion of residents of Delhi to submit to the authority of Sultan Jalaluddin Khalji in 1290. He writes: 'Since he belonged to a different race, he had no confidence in the Turks, nor did the Turks acknowledged him as belonging to their tribe.' He also tells us that the people could not imagine that the throne of Delhi could ever be seized by a non-Turk.[15] Apart from the fact that the Khaljis looked unlike the Turks on account of their long stay in Afghanistan and were completely Persianized, Jalaluddin himself was an immigrant in Delhi and had begun his career at a lower position during the reign of Balban. The Ilkhanid historian, Rashiduddin Fazlullah, mentions him as one of the officers in the service of the Qarlugh ruler of Kuh-i-Jud and Binban.[16] According to Rashiduddin Fazlullah and Amir Khusrau, his name was Firuz.[17] On the destruction of the Qarlugh ruler by the Mongols, he resisted the Mongols for some time and then left to enter the service of the Sultan of Delhi. As he was a veteran soldier, Balban appointed him *sar-i-jandar* (commander of the royal bodyguards) and assigned to him the *iqta* of Kaithal.[18] It may also be added that there seem to have been more than one *sar-i-jandars* in the service of the Sultan. They performed their duty turn by turn.[19] Balban's successor conferred upon Malik Firuz Khalji the title of Shaista Khan and also elevated him to the ministerial post of *amir-i-ariz* (paymaster general of the army). Thus, the forces that paved the way for the rise of the Khaljis to supreme power in the sultanate of Delhi were set in motion.

As far as the Turk nobles of the reigns of Balban and Kaiqubad are concerned, none of them was competent enough to save the throne from slipping into the hands of the Khaljis in AD 1290. Though Aitmar Surkha and Aitmar Kachhan rose to cope with the situation, they failed. They were neither successful military generals nor shrewd statesmen. They conspired to do away with the non-Turk nobles who had gained the upper hand over the Turks during Kaiqubad's reign. But their conspiracy was divulged to the non-Turks, who united themselves under the leadership of Malik Jalaluddin Khalji. They killed both the Turkish leaders. Thereupon, the other Turkish nobles also decided to join the Khaljis. Barani says:[20] 'Many of the Maliks and Amirs, who were of Turkish origin, joined Malik Firuz Khalji whose title was Shaista Khan, and the Khalji force considerably increased.' Thereupon, the Khaljis got themselves recognized and succeeded in tiding over all difficulties. They established themselves firmly in the place of the Ilbarite Turks. Shaista Khan assumed the royal title of Sultan Jalaluddin.

The Significance of the Khalji Revolution

The Khaljis were realists and they seized the throne with the support of the Indians as well as the other non-Turks against the Turk nobles. Moreover, the Khaljis did not have any pretensions as to their aristocratic lineage. None of their ancestors had ever risen to a position of sovereign authority, as Jalaluddin Khalji himself realized.[21] They seized the royal sceptre because they had the power to do so. This revolution threw open the door of higher government posts to all, irrespective of race, birth, and also creed to some extent. Now the recruitment of the official class was not based on the principle of noble birth but on the survival of the fittest. The regard for noble birth disappeared entirely. Every person could now potentially rise in status and position according to his abilities.

The composition of the nobility changed drastically. The Turkish slave nobles and their sons and grandsons who held key positions at court were replaced with the relatives of the Sultan and other persons belonging to different non-Turk families. The myth that only the Turks were worthy of sovereignty was exploded. The highest title of Khan was awarded to the sons and the brother of the Sultan. The eldest son was given the title of Khan-i-Khanan, the second that of Arkali Khan, and the third that of Qadr Khan. The brother of the Sultan got the ministry (*diwan-i-ariz*) with the title of Yaghrash Khan.[22] Khwaja Khatir, the old *wazir* of Sultan

Balban whom Malik Nizamuddin, the *amir-i-dad*, had disgraced and dismissed during the reign of Kaiqubad, was now restored to the Wizarat.[23] Malik Qutbuddin Alavi was honoured with the highest position of *naib-i-mumlikat* at the court. The nephews of the Sultan, Alauddin, Almas Beg, and Ahmad Chap, were also appointed in charge of important departments. In addition, other Tajiks and non-Tajiks got important ranks and *iqtas* in the Sultanate.[24] Of the old nobles, some such as Malik ul-Umara Fakhruddin, the *kotwal* of Delhi, were retained in their posts.[25] Thus, the new Sultan was able to consolidate his power with their support.

Since public opinion mattered greatly in the capital in so far as local support or opposition to the authority of the Sultan was concerned, the Sultan had to take this factor into consideration. The residents of Delhi were quite assertive in this regard, as their support to Raziya in 1236 and their opposition to Sultan Muizuddin Bahram Shah in 1244 had shown. Again, they showed their reluctance in being forced to reconcile themselves to the dynastic change. Ram Prasad Tripathi is right in his observation: 'The Khalji Revolution brought to light for the first time that there was among the Muslims of Delhi something like a public opinion that had been unconsciously growing up.'[26] It was the fear of this hostile public opinion that seems to have led Sultan Jalaluddin Khalji to choose Kilokheri as his capital instead of Delhi. By his order the palace of Kaiqubad was brought to completion and the new city was planned.[27] Barani writes that the palace complex was beautified and the nobles and courtiers were also ordered to have their mansions built and take up residence there. Shopkeepers were brought and settled in the *bazaars* of the new city. Fortification walls were erected with towers that were garrisoned, and the nobles were assigned duties to look after them turn by turn. The fortifications were built with stone. Soon Kilokheri was transformed into a beautiful city and given the name of Shahr-i-nau.[28]

Similarly, the little relevant evidence contained in the details furnished by different medieval historians of the conspiracy[29] hatched in the *khanqah* of Sidi Maula casts light on the Sultan's views about the Sultanate polity. It reveals that many officers of the preceding regime were thrown out of their jobs because of doubts about their loyalty and also that people of certain persuasions and categories were expected to maintain their traditions. Further, it suggests that the *diwan-i-Sahib-i-barid* (the bureau of secret intelligence service) was reorganized and its charge was entrusted to Alghu, the Mongol convert to Islam and the son-in-law of the Sultan, because he happened to be a newcomer having no affinity with any group of nobles in the capital. Such a man could act in an impartial manner. When Alghu passed on the information to the Sultan, the conspirators were arrested and put in jail. A few days later, the *mahzar* (royal tribunal) was organized. The culprits, including Sidi Maula, were brought and presented. The Sultan turned to Sidi Maula and said: 'Why should a dervish make himself busy with the affairs of the empire and the business of the Sultanate?' Sidi Maula denied the charge and pleaded not guilty. Qazi Jalaluddin Kashani, who was a leading *qazi* and held in high esteem for his erudition, happened to be an over-ambitious man and given to making mischief. He was promised by the conspirators the *iqta* of Multan with the title of Qazi Khan in reward. The Sultan accused him thus: 'One who is intelligent and a man of eminence is raised to the rank of a Qazi. How could you think of rising to a greater dignity than this?' He also pleaded not guilty. The other accomplices were the sons of the Khans and the Maliks of Sultan Balban, who were dismissed from the state service and deprived of their *iqtas* and ranks. Among them were two famous Hindu warriors for whom Sultan Balban is reported to have fixed one lakh *jitals* each in reward. They were severely punished. Sidi Maula was trampled to death by elephant.[30]

However, the entry of the new element into the nobility changed its composition. It is noteworthy that the office of the *naib-i-mumlikat* was conferred on Malik Qutbuddin Alavi, who did not belong to the tribe of the reigning dynasty.[31] Likewise, Maulana Sirajuddin Savi, the poet of Samana, was appointed the *nadim-i-khas* (associate).[32] A person of the Mandahar tribe (Hindu) was appointed the *wakil-i-dar* on a handsome salary of one lakh *jitals* in recognition for the bravery that he had shown on the battlefield against the Sultan while the latter was the *muqta* of Samana.[33] Malik Saduddin Mantaqi was made a high-ranking noble, though he was only a Qalandar. The hated Mongols, who were regarded not only as thoroughly unrefined but also as the great enemies of Islam, were induced after their defeat to accept Islam and enter the royal service. Barani writes:[34] 'The advance guard of the Sultan emerged successful and many of the Mongols were put to the sword. One or two Amir-i-Hazara and a few Amir-i-Sadah were made prisoners and brought before the throne.'

After that the Sultan called Abdullah, the grandson of Hulegu, his son, and the latter called the Sultan his father and thus peace was established. Though Abdullah returned, Alghu, the grandson of Chinggis Khan, stayed in the Sultan's service with his followers. The Sultan gave him his daughter in marriage and also honoured the other Mongols with *iqtas* and ranks. They were called 'neo-Muslims' and their settlements near Kailughari and Ghiyaspur were named Mughalpur.[35]

We can now reconstruct an account from circumstantial evidence and the available information from literary sources that Sultan Jalaluddin Khalji succeeded in winning over the confidence of the old nobility and the residents of Delhi. He acted as a friend to and well-wisher of all people under his rule. Barani writes: 'Neither during the tenure of his malikship nor under his kingship did he punish (people), take away *iqta* (from a noble), or dismiss anyone of those whom he had patronized and exalted.'[36] No doubt, his mildness always governed his anger. It is also noteworthy that he was an old man of seventy years at the time of his accession to the throne and had developed an aversion to bloodshed, war, and cruelty. He liked to rule in peace. He used to hold convivial gatherings to which all the leading nobles, such as—Malik Tajuddin Kuchi, Malik Izzuddin Ghuri, Malik Firuz, Malik Nusrat Sabah, Malik Ahmad Chap, Malik Kamaluddin Abul Maali, Malik Nasiruddin Kuhrami, Malik Saduddin Mantaqi, Tajuddin Iraqi, Amir Khusrau, Muid Jarjami and Hamid Raja were invited. They were known for their sophistication and good manners.[37] His behaviour made a good impression on the senior old nobles who seem to have become enamoured of him. But the young warriors in general and the Khalji youth in particular were disappointed. They regarded him as incapable of leadership. Some of them even went to the extent of making remarks against him in private gatherings. Informed of their remarks, he would say to them: 'You do not fear me and go on talking nonsense. Why do you not fear Arkali Khan, my son, who is hot-tempered? I do not know what he will do to you.'[38] In short, the Sultan never seems to have lost his temper or shed human blood for petty reasons. If he was asked by someone from among his relations to be strict in handling the affairs of the state, he would say: 'If kingship means killing, suppression and destruction, I am not capable of this and I do not like it.'[39]

Besides his old age, Sultan Jalaluddin Khalji was faced with a financial crisis also. He found the treasury of the Sultanate almost empty because Sultan Kaiqubad had squandered all the riches left by his grandfather.[40] The organization of military expeditions for the conquest of alien territories involved huge expenditure. Certainly, the lack of treasure was also a handicap for the old Sultan. Conscious of the aspirations of his young followers, he led military expeditions to meet the expectations of the adventurous warriors. He led military expeditions against the forts of Mandore and Jhain. Both the forts were captured easily and a huge booty acquired.[41] From Jhain the Sultan proceeded against the fort of Ranthambhor. The army laid siege to it. Soon it was found that its conquest was not easy and that it also involved the considerable loss of men and material. Thereupon, he ordered the army to raise the siege and retreat to the capital.[42] His retreat disappointed the young warriors and they formed an adverse opinion about him. Barani would have us believe that the authority of Sultan Alauddin was in a way forced on the people because they did not consider the good-natured and peace-loving old Sultan worthy of exercising sovereignty.[43]

The ambitious young warriors who were eager to shine in the glory of their military exploits found their hero in Alauddin, the *muqta* (governor) of the territorial unit of Kara and Manikpur and the nephew and son-in-law of the Sultan. They succeeded in instigating Alauddin to make a bid for the throne of Delhi.[44] Therefore, after the capture of the booty, comprising a huge treasure and war elephants in Deogiri (Maharashtra), the first thing that Alauddin Khalji did was to murder Sultan Jalaluddin treacherously.[45]

The Reign of Sultan Alauddin Khalji

With the accession of Sultan Alauddin Khalji to the throne revolutionary changes took place in the Sultanate polity. In the beginning, Sultan Alauddin took care not to fling a challenge to the nobles. He decided to seek an apparent reconciliation with them and thereby dispelled any fear of revenge entertained by them regarding their dismissal. He offered generous terms to the nobles of his uncle. He possessed the treasures brought from Deogiri (in the Deccan) and distributed them among the people. He made it clear that all those nobles who would join him would be amply rewarded in gold and silver. These terms were most welcome to the majority of the old guard, and we see that Malik Tajuddin Kuchi, Malik Abaji, the Akhurbeg, Malik Amir Ali Diwana, Malik Usman, Malik Haranmar, Amir-i-Kalan, and Malik Umar Surkha, who were deputed by Sultan Ruknuddin Ibrahim Shah (the youngest son and successor to Sultan Jalal-uddin) to oppose the advancing army of Alauddin, joined him at Baran.[46] Their desertion caused dismay among the nobles in Delhi and they also began to desert.[47] In such circumstances, Sultan Ruknuddin Ibrahim Shah, Malik Ahmad Chap, and Alghu had to flee to Arkali Khan in Multan.[48]

In Delhi, Alauddin's coronation was celebrated for the second time in an extraordinary way; the festivities associated with the occasion went on with the scattering of gold and silver in the *bazaars* and streets. He assumed the title of Sultan Alauddin Muhammad Shah. Everyone in the city enjoyed the scene. People were highly impressed by the splendour of the occasion. The faithful supporters were honoured with the titles of Khan and high positions.[49] The old nobles of the preceding regime were also rewarded with gold and allowed to retain their *iqtas*. Khwaja Khatir was reconfirmed as *wazir*, Qazi Sadruddin, the Sadr-i-Jahan (the father of Davar Malik who was a prominent noble during the reign of Muhammad bin Tughluq Shah) remained the chief justice of the Sultanate. Similarly, other nobles and officers of the preceding regimes were honoured with royal favours. The old *auqaf* (charitable endowments) and land grantees and stipend holders were not touched and were issued fresh certificates. The armymen were rewarded with cash payments equivalent to six months' or one year's allowances.[50]

The old nobles who had betrayed the son and successor of Sultan Jalaluddin must have been under the impression that Sultan Alauddin would let them enjoy their position and the wealth that they had obtained as the price of their desertion. They were tolerated until his rule was consolidated. The new Sultan was a man of a different calibre. He refused to accept any noble of doubtful loyalty. He wanted complete obedience, fidelity, and subservience to the master. It was his desire to create a new nobility that would be loyal to him and his throne. He believed in absolute despotism so far as the exercise of executive, military, and financial powers was concerned. He wanted the centralization of these powers in his own hands. All the powers were to be in the hands of the iron-willed Sultan, and the state officers and military generals were to act according to the orders that they got from the throne. Therefore, in the second year of his reign, when he found his throne safe after the imprisonment of the sons of Sultan Jalaluddin and the capture of Multan, he had the old nobility destroyed root and branch with the exception of three nobles. Their property and effects were declared forfeited to the state exchequer and their sons were left without anything. Their army contingents were placed under the command of the new nobles. Khwaja Khatir was replaced by Nusrat Khan in the *wizarat*. The new *wazir*, Nusrat Khan, treated the old nobles of dubious character with high-handedness. They were arrested and forced to surrender their wealth. Even the orchards, villages, and houses owned by them were taken away and brought under *khalsa*. They were blinded, killed, or thrown into prison.[51] The three fortunate nobles who were spared were Malik Qutbuddin Alavi, Nasiruddin Rana, the *shahna-i-peel* (in-charge of the royal elephants), and Amir Jamal Khalji. They were left unharmed because they had shown full loyalty to the son of Sultan Jalaluddin and had never accepted Alauddin's gold. They enjoyed security of life throughout the Sultan's reign.[52]

Barani's statement below about the Sultan's state policy is revealing:

(The Sultan) held firm to the viewpoint that kingship is separate from Sharia and religious tradition (canon law). The affairs of the state concern the King while the enforcement of Sharia comes within the jurisdiction of the Qazis and the Muftis (the expounders of the law). Accordingly, he did whatever he thought proper and in the interest of the Sultanate. It did not matter whether it was in conformity with the Sharia.[53]

This statement may lead the reader to think that even the nominal regard for the *sharia* was cast aside.[54] But this is not corroborated by a careful study of the sources.

As a matter of fact, the Sultan never appears to have interfered with the court of the *qazis*. The judicial and legislative powers continued to be exercised by the *qazis* and the *muftis*. Four of the leading *ulama*--Qazi Ziauddin of Bayana, Maulana Zahir Lung, Maulana Mashayed Kuhrami, and Qazi Mughis of Bayana—were included among his associates and they were consulted. They enjoyed great respect and shared meals with the Sultan.[55] Barani seems to imply that he exercised his discretionary powers regardless of the *sharia* in meting out punishment to the offenders such as the rebels.[56] His discussion with Qazi Mughis of Bayana regarding the severe punishment inflicted on the innocent children and wives of the rebels and other culprits in violation of the *sharia* tends to suggest that the *ulama* were critical of the Sultan. Qazi Mughis had the courage to tell the Sultan that sons and wives could not be punished for the crimes committed by husbands and fathers. The Sultan being annoyed said: 'Oh Mullah Mughis, you are a wise and learned man but not an experienced one. I am not a learned man but I have gained much experience.' He justified his action on the ground that rebellion disturbs peace and leads to the killing of a larger number of people. As regards the corrupt *amils* (revenue collectors) and the *mutasarifs* (finance officers), the Sultan saw that they were paid handsome allowances and wages that allowed them to live comfortably, yet they indulged in corruption. They embezzled state money. Therefore, he did what he thought proper in the interests of the Sultanate.[57]

It is also wrong to assume on the basis of Barani's statement that after the resumption of land grants made to the *ulama* (religious divines, called *aima*) and the abolition of *auqaf* (charitable endowments) established by the preceding Sultans the practice was given up. This is a half truth. No doubt, the land grants held by the *ulama* and those belonging to the *auqaf* were resumed and brought under the *khalsa* (i.e. under the control of the revenue ministry) in the beginning of the reign.[58] But this is contradicted by the evidence contained in the *Ijaz-i-Khusravi* of Amir Khusrau and the *Futuh us-Salatin* of Isami. As the land grants were made on the recommendation of the chief *sadr* of the Sultanate, Amir Khusrau refers to these grants along with the name of the minister for theological affairs as *Sadr-i-Sadur-i-Jahan Ziya ul-Haque* (*wad-Din*) within whose purview they fell.[59] Isami's grandfather enjoyed the grant of two villages until it was resumed by Sultan Ghiyasuddin Tughluq Shah (reigned: 1320–4).[60] Barani also completes his statement with regard to the land grants made by Sultan Alauddin in his account of the reign of Sultan Ghiyasuddin Tughluq Shah. He says that whatever people got as rewards—stipends, grants in cash, lands, or villages—during the reign of Sultan Alauddin, they were allowed to enjoy them. But the grants made during the reigns of Sultan Qutbuddin and Khusrau Khan were resumed by Sultan Ghiyasuddin Tughluq Shah. Even their claims were looked into and the deserving persons were not deprived of their land grants.[61] It was also during Sultan Alauddin's reign that the rationalist sciences gained popularity in Delhi. The Sultan and his nobles came under the influence of rationalist thinkers.[62]

The Composition of the Nobility

Sultan Alauddin's nobility was a broad-based nobility. It included common people as well as men of old aristocratic families. It is, however, worth mentioning that the fathers and grandfathers of many high-ranking nobles of the Sultan had not held high offices during the preceding period, although they might have worked in the lower government posts, which were meant for petty officials in the civil administration and the army. The new Khalji Sultan seems to have realized the fact that the services of competent persons, whether of aristocratic families or not and irrespective of creed, would be required for the administration of the expanding empire. He had already benefited from his composite contingents in his campaigns against the Rajas of Bhilsa and Deogiri during the reign of Sultan Jalaluddin. Mahmud Salim, a 'low-born wicked person of Samana', and Ikhtyaruddin Hud, the murderers of Sultan Jalaluddin, had been Alauddin's trusted men during his governorship of Kara and Awadh.[63] His four leading nobles,

Almas Beg, entitled Ulugh Khan, Hizbaruddin Khalji, entitled Zafar Khan, Nusrat of Jalesar, entitled Nusrat Khan, and Sanjar entitled Alap Khan, were self-made men, known for their loyalty to Alauddin.[64] They carried out his orders faithfully. They rose in social status on the basis of merit. Their rise to positions of high dignity and importance may be attributed to the Khalji revolution.

During Alauddin's reign, the experiment of raising low-born persons to important posts proved successful. Believing that they owed their advancement to the liberal policy of the Sultan, they gave him their unwavering loyalty.[65] It was due to their efforts that Malik Naik, a Hindu general and the governor of the territorial unit of Samana and Sunam,[66] won a victory over the large army of the Mongols led by Ali Beg and Tartaq. Malik Ghazi, the famous warrior (later Sultan Ghiyasuddin Tughluq Shah), also fought under the command of Malik Naik.[67] Moreover, this well-disciplined and strong army not only guaranteed security against the Mongol invasions and held the refractory land chiefs in check but also proved superior to the Mongols in military tactics and arms. The Mongols were known for their rapid mobility, superior organization, and physical strength. In many countries, the rulers and their armies were not able to resist their onslaught. But it was only the Indian soldiers under the tried and skilled Indian generals who could stop the Mongols from crossing their borders. By now the Indians had also become adept in their tactics, such as the use of scorched-earth tactics against foreign invaders.[68] This was not all; the Indians also began to commit aggression in the land under the rule of the Mongols and became a terror for them, with the result that the Mongols were so harassed that they gave up dreaming of the conquest of India.[69] The Khalji officers also displayed remarkable administrative talent in dealing with the complex and exacting problems of the empire. They established a uniform and sound bureaucratic administrative system in the whole empire. All the nobles, military generals, and civil officers were paid their salaries and allowances in cash from the state exchequer.[70] The system of land assignment in lieu of cash salary or allowances was abolished. The only exception was Malik Kafur whom the Sultan had elevated to the position of *naib* (regent). He was assigned the *iqta* of Rapri as a special mark of honour and distinction.[71] It is also noteworthy that the Sultan consulted his courtiers, and took a rationalist approach to tackling all problems faced by him. He accepted their advice after careful deliberation. The fixation of the soldiers' allowances and price controls were enforced according to their suggestions.[72]

The evidence furnished by Isami and Barani about Haji Maula's rebellion in 1301 provides us with an insight into the change that had taken place in the socio-political outlook of the Delhi residents towards the state and society. The flow of wealth resulting from the progress of trade and commerce, and the huge treasures obtained in south India as a result of conquests, seem to have created resentment among those who served in low posts in and around Delhi and who were denied the chance to climb the social ladder quickly. Haji Maula, originally a slave, served as *shahna* (officer-in-charge of a *thana* or police post) at Ritaul (district Meerut). He decided to take advantage of the discontent among the people at the lower rungs of the social ladder. Though Barani puts the blame on the oppressive *kotwal* of old Delhi for alienating the people from the Sultan, the spread of discontent among the low-paid employees of the *kotwali* and other departments is also implicit in his narrative. According to him, Haji Maula came from Ritaul, won over the *kotwaliyan* (policemen attached to the *kotwali*) to his side, and raised a tumult. He proceeded with a few foot soldiers with drawn swords to the residence of the *kotwal* in the afternoon and called him, saying that he had come with a royal *farman* from the Sultan for him. When Tirmizi, the *kotwal* (of Delhi) came out, the soldiers fell on him and killed him. The commoners also turned out to support him. They opened the gate of the central jail and then the prisoners also joined him. However, Haji Maula's supporters were no match for the Sultan's disciplined army. Though he was killed by Malik Hamiduddin and the Sultan's authority was restored, his rebellion appears to have led the Sultan to become pragmatic in his approach to the solution of the problems, that he faced and he adopted a progressive policy towards the recruitment of officers and their promotion to higher positions irrespective of birth and class background. His new policy seems to have increased social mobility in the Sultanate.[73]

But it is also wrong to assume that only the Indians or the

common people were taken into the state service. Foreigners and the descendants of the old aristocracy were also given high posts. The flow of Muslim immigrants from the neighbouring countries still continued.[74] Even the Mongol converts to Islam came in search of fame and fortune and entered the Sultan's service as soldiers.[75] The fact that should be highlighted here is the adoption by the Khalji Sultan of a policy that was different from that of the early Turkish Sultans with regard to the recruitment of officers. Therefore, the nobility under the Khalji Sultan was not a charmed circle into which the entry of meritorious people rising from below could be denied. Thus, with the dynastic change, the political system also underwent a change. Now the people of so-called base stock could aspire to the highest positions in the official hierarchy on account of their competence. Dividing Alauddin's reign into three phases, Barani says that the last phase was dominated by low-born officers. 'The last part of Alauddin's reign', says he, 'lasted for four or five years. In these years the Sultan remained unwell, and the whole administration was conducted by Malik Naib (Kafur). All the important posts were held by indecent and low-born persons. With the ascendancy of low-born *shiqqdars* and officers, the whole administration was disturbed and the people suffered.'[76]

Even ministerial posts of a religious and quasi-religious nature, such as those of the chief *qazi* (chief justice), called *quzzat-i-mamalik*, and the *sadr-us-sudur* (minister for theological affairs), called *sadr-i-jahan*, could be entrusted to the charge of those educated people who had no claim to noble descent, although these posts had been the exclusive privilege of the members of certain old respectable families of Shaikhs and Saiyids. Criticizing Sultan Alauddin Khalji's policy with regard to the appointment of officers, Barani suggests that the offices of the *quzzat* and the *sadr-i-jahan* could only be held by learned men belonging to certain noble families who commanded respect in the country for their piety and learning. Sultan Alauddin followed this tradition in the beginning of his reign; Qazi Sadruddin Arif, the father of Daud Malik and a grandson of the daughter of Sadr-i-Jahan Minhaj Juzjani (author of *Tabaqat-i-Nasiri*), was given joint charge of both offices. The offices of the *quzzat* and the *sadr-i-jahan* acquired lustre and prestige thereby. Even if the incumbent was not considered a distinguished scholar, yet, being a capable man of a noble family, he commanded respect and discharged his duties properly. He was succeeded by Qazi Jalaluddin Livalji in the office of chief *qazi* and Maulana Ziauddin of Bayana as *sadr-i-jahan*. The latter had served as *qazi-i-lashkar* (*qazi* in the army). Since both of them lacked high family status, the departments lost much of their influence and prestige. Then Barani would have us believe that, during the last phase of the reign, the *quzzat* of the empire, which was in every way an important and lofty position and for which no one but a member of a well-established family of noble descent, traditionally known for its learning and religiosity, could be considered fit, was entrusted to Malik ut-Tujjar (chief of the merchants), Hamiduddin Multani. The latter had served in the royal household as *pardadar* (in-charge of curtains) and *kaliddar* (keeper of the keys). Any mention of this Malik-ut-Tujjar (Hamiduddin Multani) is not worthy of a place in history. Nobody had the courage to point out (to the Sultan) that only education and knowledge were not sufficient grounds for appointment to this position.[77] It is interesting to note that Shaikh Nasiruddin Chiragh-i-Dilli, the contemporary Chishti Sufi, had a different and better opinion of the same minister's good qualities. Hamiduddin Multani is said to have been helpful to scholars and other deserving persons as *sadr*, and to have performed the functions of chief justice with honesty and integrity.[78] It is worth recalling that Barani was a conservative man who thought only noble families had been chosen by God to rule the rest of mankind. He considered low-born persons unworthy of holding government posts and saw them as destined to do menial services.[79] Barani contradicts himself in his account of Sultan Qutbuddin Mubarak Shah's reign where he says: 'Rebellions could not break out in the Sultanate because the old nobles known for their experience and competence held the provinces.'[80] In short, the spread of education helped to undermine the social barriers created by Muslim immigrant families in the early days of the Sultanate.

It may also be mentioned here that the elevation of members of unprivileged families and slaves to high positions in the army and the administration created conditions favourable for the entry of others of the same class. For example, the appointment of Khusrau

Khan Parwari as the *naib-i-sultanate* (regent) under Sultan Qutbuddin Mubarak Shah Khalji (reigned: 1317–20) paved the way for the short-lived ascendancy of the Hindu Parwaris of Gujarat at the imperial court.[81] Though the murder of Sultan Qutbuddin Mubarak Shah by the Parwaris brought about their downfall, no reaction seems to have occurred against the appointment of Hindus to government posts. Ghazi Malik came to power with the slogan of punishing the Parwaris, and made use of the obvious advantage in condemning the religious affiliations of the Parwaris. Yet Ghazi Malik himself had Hindu Khokkars as officers and *sawars* in his provincial army in Depalpur. They supported him in his struggle for the throne against the Parwaris.[82]

Crime and Punishment

As discussed earlier, Sultan Alauddin never interfered with the *qazis* and *muftis* in the administration of justice, which was left as solely their concern. He also did not seek guidance from them in deciding how the rebels and others charged with committing crimes against the state were to be punished. He exercised his discretionary power in dealing with them. The rebels deserved no mercy; even their children and wives were to suffer, in spite of their innocence. Children were slaughtered alongwith their mothers.[83] The disregard shown by the Sultan towards the *sharia* law in punishing the children and the women of the rebels led Barani to portray the Sultan as a tyrant, having no fear of God, and not to give him credit for the general prosperity and affluence that resulted from his policies. But the Sultan won through his good deeds the loyalty of the common people. He was gratefully remembered by people after his death, as will be discussed later. We may, however, express our gratitude to Barani for the details that he furnishes. Among the courtiers that he mentions were Malik Hamiduddin and Malik Izzuddin, the sons of the chief *dabir* (in-charge of the royal chancery) and Ain-ul-Mulk Multani, men of ideas who had far-reaching insights into the way that the system of government worked. The polity was centralized, particularly the military, executive and financial powers were the concern of the Sultan alone. The secret intelligence service received special attention; spies were posted everywhere to keep watch on the nobles and other people who counted in the affairs of the state.[84] The Sultan was informed about the conduct of the nobles in the whole of the empire through the spies; nothing, not even the goings-on inside their houses, could remain concealed from him.[85] Since modern scholars have paid adequate attention to the market control system, the new land settlement system, the restrictions imposed on social gatherings in the houses of the nobles, the ban on the sale and purchase of liquor and other alcoholic drinks in Delhi,[86] we may confine our discussion to the new policy adopted towards the *khuts* and *muqaddams* in the countryside. The Sultan had a grievance against the *khuts* and the *muqaddams*—that they defied his authority and did not pay revenue to the state unless threatened by force.[87] He took strict measures to force them into submission, as will be discussed later.

In short, Sultan Alauddin Khalji exerted himself to the utmost in creating conditions favourable for progress and prosperity in the Sultanate. The contemporary writers glow with pride in describing his achievements resulting from his concern for the welfare of the people. Mentioning the reforms introduced by the Sultan to enable poor people to meet their daily requirements easily, they also inform us about the Sultan's interest in the conservation of old monuments for posterity. The corbelled domes of the tombs and mosques that had collapsed were reconstructed on the basis of the arcuate system of architecture. 'All mosques that lay in ruins—the vaults of some had fallen to the ground, the walls of others had crumbled down after having been repeatedly patched up and repaired, the [interior of] some was compelled by the winds to perform an ablution with dust every day, . . . were built anew.'[88] Isami also informs us that the peace and prosperity in the Sultanate during his reign attracted people from foreign countries to migrate to India. 'Anyone who arrived from two Iraqs (i.e. southern Iran and Iraq proper), Sind and Arabia to this "garden of happiness", developed so much attachment to it (the Sultanate) that he hardly even remembered his native land. World travellers, who did not stay at any place even for a month, settled down in India after they had been overcome by its charm.'[89]

Likewise, we find interesting information contained in the

Futuh-us-Salatin about the increase in Delhi's population, the progress of crafts, indigenous as well as new, and the supply of essential and luxury goods in the *bazaars*.[90] As regards the expansion of the metropolis, Isami says that it had become the largest city of the country, that none of its quarters would look empty even if a hundred divisions were raised there and sent out.[91] Many of its scientists and men of arts and learning had acquired fame in foreign countries.[92]

Even Barani, who was angry with and disliked the Sultan for his indifference to the *sharia* in meting out punishment to the children and women of the rebels, could not avoid describing the blessings of his reign. Although Barani believed that in history only the achievements of the noble born or men of aristocratic families were to be recorded, that history means the study of the *ashraf* (elite), yet he was constrained to praise the artisans of Delhi for their skills. Indeed, he glows with pride while claiming that Delhi's artisans had excelled the master craftsmen of foreign countries in manufacturing weapons, garments, rosaries, caps, etc.[93] All this led the residents of Delhi to love and respect the Sultan. They regarded him as being endowed with spiritual power. After his death, they paid visits to his grave, made wishes, and tied threads.[94]

The Sultan's Policy towards the *Khuts*, *Muqaddams*, and *Rais*

Barani brackets the *muqaddams* with the *khuts* and creates an impression that both of them belonged to the same class of landlords (*zamindars*), that the *khuts* and *muqaddams* were reduced to insignificance, and that there was left no difference between an ordinary peasant and them. But a careful study of the contemporary Indo-Persian literature reveals that the *khut* belonged to a different class and that his post was of foreign origin, introduced by the Muslim rulers after the foundation of their rule. Fakhr-i-Mudabbir mentions the *khut* in a village near Tiginabad as being the head of the villagers during the later Ghaznavid period.[95] The contemporary scholar of Sultan Alauddin's reign, Fakhruddin Mubarak Shah, known as Qawwas Ghaznavi, helps us understand the difference between the *khut* and the *muqaddam* (landlord). In his lexicon, *Farhang-i-Qawwas*, he provides us with a clue that the *muqaddam* was the equivalent of the newly created term *zamindar* (a hereditary land chief). The term *zamindar* was adopted to distinguish a powerful chief. Explaining the meaning of *kinarang*, he says that it meant *marzban*, i.e. *shahna-i-vilayet-o-zamindar* (either it means the *shahna* of the *vilayet* or the *zamindar*).[96] The *shahnas* or the *kinarang* used to be powerful hereditary chiefs in Iran and Khurasan. Further, he says in regard to the difference between a *khut* and a *muqaddam* or *zamindar* that the *khut* was a village headman whose counterpart in Khurasan was called *dehqan*.[97] In the Sultanate of Delhi, the *khut* was given certain privileges because he helped the *amils* (revenue collectors) in collecting taxes in the countryside. His was not a hereditary post, and he acted as an intermediary between the state and the peasantry.

Qawwas Ghaznavi's contemporary Amir Khusrau also mentions the *zamindar* in the sense of a powerful chief. In his *masnavi*, *Daval Rani wa Khizr Khan*, while describing the royal favours showered by Sultan Alauddin Khalji on Rai Ram Chandra of Deogiri in Delhi in 1307, Amir Khusrau says that the territory of Deogiri was restored to the Rai in *zamindari*.[98] According to Ain-ul-Mulk Mahru, the class of land chiefs in India included the *muqaddams*, *mafruzian*, *chaudhriyan*, and *rangas*, and all of them were collectively called *zamindars*.[99] Sultan Alauddin seems to have abolished the office of *khut* by depriving them of their perquisites. Thus, the *khut* and the Chaudhri (also a commission agent having the charge of a number of villages) were reduced to poverty. They were treated like other peasants and had to pay *charai* (pasture tax) and *ghari* (house tax) in addition to the state's share in agricultural produce.[100]

As for the *muqaddam*, he does not seem to have been deprived of his hereditary rights as in the case of the *zamindar* because Sultan Alauddin is reported by Amir Khusrau to have been very generous towards the *zamindars* who voluntarily acquiesced to his authority in the conquered territories. He writes about the land chiefs of Malwa: 'Many powerful *zamindars*, fitted with gifted keenness of vision, threw aside their boldness and impudence, came to the imperial court with open eyes and turned its threshold into antimony by rubbing their black pupils upon it;

at the same time they saved their bones from becoming boxes for the dust. The emperor regarded every one of them with an affectionate glance, and threw on them a ray of his favour, which their eyes had never expected to behold.'[101] In the Deccan also, the Sultan allowed the powerful chiefs to retain their territories if they acknowledged his suzerainty and surrendered elephants and treasures. His advice to Malik Naib (Kafur) on the Telangana expedition (1309) sheds light on his policy. 'Be quick and do not persist in exacting too much. Do not insist on Lader Deo's presenting himself in person or on bringing him to Delhi for the sake of your fame and honour.'[102] The *rai* was the title held by a big chief holding sway over a large territory. Sultan Alauddin's son and successor, Sultan Qutbuddin Mubarak Shah, was more favourably inclined towards them; in order to cement his ties with them, he married their daughters.[103]

The Reign of Sultan Qutbuddin Mubarak Shah

Upon the death of Sultan Alauddin in 1316, Malik Naib (Kafur) placed a five- or six-year-old child, Prince Shihabuddin, on the throne and took up the reins of government in his hands as the regent. The grown-up princes were either blinded or put in prison,[104] but he retained the old system of governance without any change. The ministers in-charge of the *diwans* of *risalat, wizarat, diwan-i-arz*, and *diwan-i-insha* were ordered to function in accordance with the rules and regulations of the preceding reign.[105] But Malik Naib's rule did not last for more than thirty-five days. He was killed by the palace guards, and Prince Mubarak Khan, aged seventeen or eighteen years, was brought out from prison and made the regent. After a few months, Shihabuddin was blinded and sent to Gwalior prison, and then Mubarak Khan ascended the throne with the title of Sultan Qutbuddin Mubarak Shah (1317–20).

In an attempt to gain popularity, the young Sultan abolished price controls and repressive legislation. Thousands of prisoners who had been languishing in the dungeons in the capital and other towns and cities were set free. The burden of heavy taxes on the peasantry and others was alleviated considerably, and the *diwan-i-wizarat* was forbidden to mulet officials and others to collect state dues.[106] The shopkeepers, merchants, and brokers became free to conduct their business. People were happy, but the administrative machinery became slack, at least in the capital. The officers became corrupt; the revenue collectors and the *mutassarifs* (finance officers) began to indulge in bribery. The secret intelligence agents had no work to do, and the *diwan-i-risalat* gave up functioning. Barani writes:

'People were no longer in fear of receiving orders such as:
'Do this but don't do that; say this but don't say that; put on this dress but don't put on that dress; eat that but don't eat this; sell this way but don't sell that way. Behave this way but don't behave that way.'[107]

The restrictions imposed on the nobles were lifted; they could invite their friends and entertain them. They drank wine publicly and indulged in pleasure. But Sultan Qutbuddin Mubarak Shah Khalji did not change his father's policy with regard to the recruitment of government servants and their promotion to higher positions. He also tried to balance the old nobility by creating a counter-nobility. In this connection, he seems to have preferred competent persons belonging to non-privileged families over the descendants of the old nobility. For example, he elevated his father's slave Shahin with the title of Wafa Malik and appointed him his regent to safeguard the capital when he left for Deogiri to quell the rebellion of Harpal Deo.[108] Likewise, Khusrau Khan, a Parwari slave, was so greatly favoured that he was made the leading noble of the Sultanate. He was distinguished from the other nobles when he was conferred all the privileges that Malik Kafur, the favourite of Sultan Alauddin, had enjoyed. Khusrau Khan was also assigned Malik Kafur's *iqta* of Rapri, a mark of special favour because other nobles were paid their allowances in cash even in the provinces where they served as governors.[109] In this reign, the low-born nobles also increased in large numbers. According to Barani, 'they got ascendancy over the members of the old aristocratic families'.[110] Barani seems to be right in so far as their ascendancy at court is concerned, because they did overshadow the old nobles of Alauddin's reign there. The Parwaris who belonged to the caste of Khusrau Khan were invited from Gujarat and Malwa to join the state service. Khusrau Khan had them placed in important posts, and they came to acquire the position of a pressure group within a short time. It was their strength that encouraged Khusrau Khan to get rid of the Sultan and capture the throne. Upon the murder of the Sultan by the Parwaris, Khusrau Khan killed all the surviving princes and occupied the throne. The nobles present in Delhi, Muslims and Hindus both, paid allegiance to him.[111]

Lastly, in conclusion it may be said that the polity remained tightly centralized even after the death of Sultan Alauddin. Neither Sultan Qutbuddin Mubarak Shah nor Khusrau Khan, the regicide, assigned *iqtas* to the nobles in lieu of cash salary. Similarly, the provincial armies obeyed the command of the military governor so long as he enjoyed the confidence of the Sultan. The little relevant evidence available tends to show that Sultan Qutbuddin Mubarak Shah followed his father in appointing different but trusted officers to govern an extensive territorial unit. For example, Malik Yaklakhi was entrusted with the governorship of the territorial unit of Deogiri but its subdivisions were placed under the charge of different executive officers, *mutassarifs* (officers) and *amils*.[112] Later on, the *wizarat* of Deogiri was entrusted to Malik-Ainul-Mulk Multani, and Malik Tajul-Mulk was appointed in-charge of the *ishraf* (account office). Malik Mujiruddin Aburija was appointed the *naib wazir* of Deogiri.[113] Similarly, the army stationed in a province was sent from the centre to work under the governor. The soldiers obeyed the governor as long as he was loyal to the Sultan; in rebellion he was seldom supported. In fact, the reign of Sultan Alauddin presents a classic example of a centralized polity that went a long way to inspire great rulers throughout the medieval period.

NOTES

1. Ziyauddin Barani says that since he (Jalaluddin Khalji) belonged to a different race, he had no confidence in the Turks, nor did the Turks recognize him as belonging to their tribe, cf. Ziauddin Barani, *Tarikh-i-Firuz Shahi*, Calcutta, 1862, p. 171 (hereafter cited as Barani).
2. Abdul Hai Habibi, 'Khaljis are Afghans', in Z. Ansari, ed., *Life, Times and Works of Amir Khusrau-i-Dehlavi*, Seventh Centenary National Amir Khusrau Society, New Delhi, 1976, pp. 67–9.

3. Cf. V. Minorsky, *Hudud al-Alam*, Eng. tr., p. 348 (commentary and notes).
4. *Tarikh-i-Fakhr-i-Mudabbir*, p. 47.
5. Hajib Khairat Dehlavi, *Dastur ul-Afazil*, ed. Nazir Ahmad, Farhang-i-Bunyad, Iran, no. 168, Tehran, 1352, p. 119.
6. *Badr Ibrahim, Farhang-i-Zafan-i-Goya*, ed. Nazir Ahmad, Patna, 1989, p. 142.
7. Ali bin Mahmud al-Kirmani, known as Shihab Hakim, *Maasir-i-Mahmud Shahi*, ed. Nurul Hasan Ansari, Delhi, 1968, pp. 8–9.
8. Nizamuddin Ahmad Bakhshi, *Tabaqat-i-Akbari*, Calcutta, 1911, vol. III, p. 116.
9. Qasim Hindu Shah Firishta, *Gulshan-i-Ibrahimi,* known as *Tarikh-i-Firishta*, Lucknow, n.d., pp. 88–9.
10. Cf. *Tarikh-i-Yamini*, early thirteenth-century Persian translation by Abush Sharaf al-Jarbaz Khani, ed. Jaffar Shiar, Tehran, 1345 Shamsi, pp. 33, 282, 285.
11. Cf. *Tabaqat-i-Nasiri*, vol. I, pp. 399, 420.
12. *Tabaqat-i-Nasiri*, vol. I, pp. 436–7; also Iqtidar Husain Siddiqui, 'The Process of Urbanization and Social Change in Pre-Mughal India', *Islamic Culture,* Hyderabad, vol. LXXVII, no. 2, April 2003, pp. 37–9, for details about the nature and function of the *khanqah.*
13. Cf. *Perso-Arabic Sources of Information on the Life and Conditions in the Sultanate of Delhi*, pp. 33–4, for Awfi's *Jawami'ul-Hikayat wa-Lavami-ul Rivayat*, pp. 33–4; also *Tabaqat-i-Nasiri*, vol. II, p. 86.
14. *Tabaqat-i-Nasiri*, vol. II, p. 86.
15. Barani, pp. 172–6.
16. Cf. Iqtidar Husain Siddiqui, 'The Qarlugh Kingdom in North-Western India During the Thirteenth Century', *Islamic Culture,* Hyderabad, vol. LIV, no. 2, April 1980, pp. 83–8.
17. Rashiduddin Fazlullah, *Jamiul-Tawarikh,* MS. British Library, London, Add. 7628, f. 385b; Amir Khusrau, *Miftah-ul-Futuh*, ed. Shaikh Abdur Rashid, Aligarh, 1954.
18. Barani, p. 194.
19. Barani mentions another *sarjandar*, Malik Sonj, under Sultan Balban. Barani, p. 85.
20. Barani, p. 172.
21. Ibid., p. 178.
22. Cf. Barani, pp. 176–7.
23. Barani, p. 133.
24. Ibid., p. 177.
25. Ibid.
26. Cf. R.P. Tripathi, *Some Aspects of Muslim Administration*, 1st edn., 1936, p. 44.
27. Barani, p. 176.

28. Earlier in his account of Sultan Kaiqubad's reign, Barani writes: 'Sultan Muizuddin (Kaiqubad) vacated the Kushak-i-lal (red palace) in the Dar ul-Sultanate (Delhi) and moved to Kailokhari. He had there a beautiful palace constructed and a garden laid out on the bank of the Jamuna. He took abode there along with his servants, courtiers, and nobles. As the nobles found the Sultan inclined to reside there permanently, they also had their mansions and palaces built in Kailokhari. After them came the heads and different craftsmen (guilds) and settled down there, with the result that within a short time Kailokhari turned into a fully developed place, thronging with people.' Cf. Barani, p. 130. It may also be pointed out that Minhaj Juzjani's reference to Shahr-i-nau, near the village of Kailokhari, suggests that the nobles and other rich people had started having houses built near the bank of the river Jamuna since the time of Iltutmish. Cf. *Tabaqat-i-Nasiri*, vol. II, p. 83. To conclude, it may be said that Shahr-i-nau could not take the shape of Barani's *Misr-i-Jami* (perfect city) during the short-lived reign of Kaiqubad. It was certainly under Jalaluddin Khalji that it became a perfect city with strong fortifications.
29. Cf. K.S. Lal, *History of the Khaljis*, Munshiram Manoharlal, rpt., New Delhi, 1980, pp. 23–6 for details.
30. Isami briefly describes the execution of Sidi Maula and does not mention the others involved in the conspiracy. Barani's account contains references to a number of conspirators. Yahya Sirhindi adds to Barani's account, certainly on the basis of some sources available to him but not extant today. For example, Barani states that one from amongst the dismissed dignitaries divulged the conspiracy to the Sultan. But Yahya Sirhindi says that the report of the plot was submitted by Alghu to the Sultan. In fact, it was the chief of the intelligence bureau through whom all the secret information was transmitted to the Sultan, as has been discussed in one of the following chapters. Isami, *Futuh-us-Salatin,* pp. 215–17; Barani, pp. 210–11; Yahya Sirhindi, *Tarikh-i-Mubarak Shahi*, Calcutta, 1931, pp. 65–6.
31. Barani, p. 195.
32. Ibid., p. 196.
33. Ibid., p. 198. Sad Mantaqi continued to be a high-ranking noble until the reign of Sultan Muhammad bin Tughluq.
34. Barani, p. 219.
35. Ibid., pp. 219–20.
36. Ibid., p. 194.
37. Ibid., p. 199.
38. Ibid., pp. 189–92.
39. Ibid., p. 193.
40. Ibid., p. 146.
41. *Futuh-us-Salatin*, pp. 215, 223–4; Barani, p. 213.

42. Barani, pp. 213–14.
43. Ibid., pp. 207–8.
44. Ibid., p. 224.
45. Alauddin was the son of Malik Shihabuddin Khalji, the elder brother of Sultan Jalaluddin. Barani, pp. 186, 234; *Tarikh-i-Mubarak Shahi*, p. 171.
46. Barani, pp. 240–4.
47. Ibid., p. 245.
48. *Futuh-us-Salatin*, pp. 247–8; Barani, p. 246.
49. Barani, p. 247, *Futuh-us-Salatin*, pp. 245, 249–50.
50. Barani, pp. 247–8.
51 Ibid., pp. 250–1.
52. Ibid., p. 251.
53. Ibid., p. 289.
54. Mohammad Habib states: 'He knew nothing about *Shariat,* and did not care to go to it for guidance.' Cf. *Politics and Society during the Early Medieval Period: Collected Works of Professor Mohammad Habib*, ed. K.A. Nizami, New Delhi, 1974, vol. I, p. 91.
55. Barani, pp. 289–90.
56. Ibid., p. 292.
57. Ibid.
58. Ibid., p. 283.
59. Cf. Syed Hasan Askari, 'Material of Historical Interest', in Ijaz-i-Khusravi, *Medieval India: a Miscellany*, Aligarh, 1969, vol. 1, pp. 12–13.
60. Isami says about his grandfather that he had held the grant of two villages since the time of the early Sultans. Each village was developed and looked into, and fresh *sanads* (documents) were issued, renewing the grant of the villages. When Tughluq Shah came to the throne, both the villages were taken back by the state. Cf. *Futuh-us-Salatin*, p. 391.
61. Barani, pp. 438–9.
62. Ibid., pp. 298, 352–3.
63. Ibid., pp. 234–5.
64. Ibid., p. 242.
65. Ibid., p. 244.
66. Amir Khusrau calls Malik Naik a Hindu and writes about his bravery: 'As he (the Mongol general) wished to injure the faith through his infields (i.e. the non-Muslim Mangol followers) fate decreed that he should meet his death at the hands of an infidel (Hindu). The soil of the wilderness drank the blood of the armies of Ali Beg and Tartaq when the two Turkish (Mongol) Khans were suddenly captured by a Hindu slave (i.e. the servant of the Sultan) and the conflagration was quelled by the sharpness of the imperial sword.' Cf. *Dawal Rani-o-Khizr Khan*, translated and quoted by Mohammad Habib in his translation of *Khazain-ul Futuh* of Amir Khusrau, Madras, 1931, pp. 27–8.

67. Barani says that the governorship of the unit of Samana and Sunam was entrusted to Malik Akhur Beg Nayak. Barani, pp. 320, 322–3.
68. Once Shaikh Nasiruddin Chiragh-i-Dilli came from Awadh to pay a visit to Shaikh Nizamuddin Auliya in 1303 before the Mongol General Targhi reached the vicinity of Delhi. On his approach, the Sultan ordered the residents of the villages nearby to be brought to Delhi. 'The soldiers were detailed to bring people from the surrounding countryside and to destroy all the villages and burn the standing crops'. Cf. Hamid Qalandar, *Khair-ul-Majalis*, ed. K.A. Nizami, Aligarh, 1959, pp. 259–60.
69. Barani, p. 323.
70. Ibid., p. 324.
71. Ibid., p. 328.
72. Ibid., pp. 303–4.
73. Ibid., pp. 367–8.
74. The ancestor of Shaikh Rizq Ullah Mushtaqi and Shaikh Abdul Haque Muhadis of Delhi, Agha Muhammad Turk, came to India with his followers in the beginning of Alauddin's reign. He was employed by the Sultan and sent to Gujarat. Cf., Shaikh Abdul Haque Muhadith, *Akhbar-ul-Akhiyar*, Delhi, AH 1283, p. 284.
75. Barani, pp. 336–7.
76. Ibid., pp. 351–2.
77. Ibid., pp. 350-51.
78. Cf. *Khair ul-Majalis*, op. cit., pp. 88, 241.
79. Barani, *Fatawai-i-Jahandari*, Eng. tr. Afsar Begum and Mohammad Habib, *Medieval India Quarterly*, Aligarh, 1958, nos. 3–4, p. 172.
80. Barani, pp. 397–8.
81. Ibid., pp. 379, 380, 402.
82. Cf. Amir Khusrau, *Tughluqnama*, Aurangabad, 1938, p. 131.
83. Barani, p. 253.
84. Cf. Chapter 6, 'Intelligence Apparatus', for more details.
85. Cf. K.S. Lal, *History of the Khaljis*, New Delhi, 1980, p. 175.
86. Barani, pp. 284–6.
87. Ibid., p. 291.
88. *Khazin-ul-Futuh*, Eng. tr., pp. 19–20.
89. *Futuh-us-Salatin*, pp. 301, 352.
90. Ibid., pp. 445–6, 452.
91. Ibid., p. 445.
92. Barani, p. 365.
93. Ibid., pp. 324–5.
94. Ibid., p. 324.
95. Cf. *Adab-ul-Harb wal-shiuja*, p. 481.
96. *Fakhr Uddin Mubarak Shah* known as *Qawwas Ghaznavi*; *Farhang-i-Qawwas*, ed. Nazir Ahmad, Raza Library, Rampur, 1999, p. 128.
97. Ibid., p. 142.

98. *Diwal Rani-o-Khizr Khan*, Aligarh, 1917, p. 70.
99. *Insha-i-Mahru*, ed. Shaikh Abdur Rashid, Lahore, 1965, pp. 16–17.
100. Barani, pp. 287, 288.
101. *Khazain-ul-Futuh*, Eng. tr. Mohammad Habib, Bombay, 1931, pp. 42–3.
102. Barani, pp. 327–8.
103. *Futuh-us-Salatin*, p. 365.
104. Barani, pp. 372–3.
105. Ibid., p. 374.
106. Isami's statement that the *dehqanian* (cultivators) were exempted from paying revenue is not correct. Barani is right when he says that the reduction in the demand of its share of the agricultural produce by the state enabled the cultivators to put on fine clothes and ride horses. *Futuh-us-Salatin*, p. 355; Barani, pp. 383, 385.
107. Barani, pp. 384–5.
108. Ibid., p. 289.
109. Ibid., pp. 390–1.
110. Ibid., pp. 402–10.
111. Ibid., p. 390.
112. Ibid., pp. 397–8.
113. The rebel Governors, Hassamuddin in Gujarat and Yaklakhi in Deogiri, were not supported by the provincial armies against the centre. They were easily destroyed.

CHAPTER 4

Sultanate Polity under the Tughluq Sultans

With the dynastic change under Ghiyasuddin Tughluq Shah (reigned 1320–4), the administrative machinery was undoubtedly reorganized on the pattern of Sultan Alauddin Khalji's model, yet changes were also introduced into it if necessary. The interest of the peasant (*the khut*), the *zamindar* (land chief), as well as that of government employees, revenue collectors, and nobles, was taken into consideration while framing the development-oriented policies. The grand success achieved by the Sultan in promoting peace and prosperity in the Sultanate during his short-lived reign of four years led Ziauddin Barani to judge him the best and ideal Sultan in the history of the Sultanate. The achievements of the Sultan both before and after his accession to the throne make it necessary to briefly describe his rise to military prominence as a general and administrator (under the Khalji Sultans).[1]

No contemporary Indo-Persian writer provides us with information about the family background of Ghazi Malik, later Sultan Ghiyasuddin Tughluq Shah. In the speech that Ghazi Malik delivered to the audience in the *hazar satun* (thousand-pillared) palace before his accession, as quoted by Amir Khusrau, he told people that in India he had begun as a *mard-i-awara* (wanderer) in search of fortune. This tends to suggest that he was an immigrant like other adventurers from the neighbouring countries. He further stated that Sultan Jalaluddin Khalji was his first employer and that by his favour he became his *muqarrab* (trusted man). Upon the Sultan's murder, he was taken by Ulugh Khan (Sultan Alauddin Khalji's brother) into his service on account of his fame as a warrior. He became a favourite of his new master as well. The role performed by him in the siege operation at

Ranthambore had raised him in the estimation of the Sultan. This is the reason why Sultan Alauddin Khalji took him into his own service after the death of Ulugh Khan in AD 1301, he was then able to rise to important positions in the official hierarchy. As regards his ethnic origin, Ibn Battuta was told by people in Multan in AD 1333 that Ghazi Malik was a Qaruna Turk.[2]

Before his posting in the newly carved-out territorial unit of Depalpur in 1306, Ghazi Malik seems to have served in different territories where he made his mark as a military general and an administrator of distinction. In the extensive territorial units of Multan and Uchh, he is said to have a large canal dug[3] and the town of Ghazipur in upper Sind founded.[4] In 1305, he was deputed to fight under the command of the Hindu general, Malik Naik against the Mongol invaders Ali Beg and Tartaq in the territorial unit of Samana.[5] After the grand victory achieved by his generals over the Mongol invaders, Sultan Alauddin is said to have entrusted the charge of each north-western provincial units to a veteran general for the defence of the frontier against the Mongols. In 1306, Malik Naik was posted as governor in the extensive unit of Samana and Sunam (extending over present-day Haryana and eastern Punjab), Ghazi Malik in the newly created extensive unit of Depalpur, while the charge of the combined extensive territorial units of Multan and Sewistan (Sind province) was assigned to Tajul-Mulk Kafuri.[6]

Ghazi Malik is praised for organizing the provincial army into an effective fighting force against the Mongol invaders. He appears to have employed on behalf of the Sultan experienced and intrepid soldiers, Indians as well as foreigners. Amir Khusrau states that the crack troops were from Mulk-i-bala (Central Asian lands, including the eastern part of Russia), including Turks, Ghuzz, Mongols (converts to Islam), Rumis (immigrants from Anatolia), Russians, Tajiks, and the Hindus of the Panjab.[7] Mention is made particularly of the Hindu Khokkars, who were the trusted and brave fighters in the army of Depalpur.[8] According to Isami, Gulchand and Sahaj Rai were men of high rank among the Khokkars.[9] With the support of this multiracial army contingent, Ghazi Malik is credited with having cleared the Kuh-i-Jud region (i.e. the Salt Range) of the Mongols and established his control thereon. The river Indus appears to have then become the dividing line between the Chaghataid Mongol empire of Central Asia and the Delhi Sultanate. Amir Khusrau states that Ghazi Malik massacred the Mongols along the Indus and, in consequence, the Hindu chiefs of the region transferred their allegiance to him and paid the tribute.[10]

By the time Sultan Alauddin died in 1316, Ghazi Malik had begun to command respect in the army in general and the capital in particular for his victories achieved in the war against the Mongols. He acted as the bulwark along the north-western frontier and, in order to do him favour, Sultan Qutbuddin Mubarak Shah conferred on his son, Juna, the rank of Malik with the post of *amir-i-akhur* in the capital. Juna resided in Delhi as the representative of and as surety for his father, according to the custom.[11] It was really Ghazi Malik's fame for the invincibility of his arms that Khusrau Khan, the regicide, feared him and wanted to get him eliminated through treacherous means. Ghazi Malik, too, could not view his future without apprehension because of his close association with the Khalji Sultans. The allusion made by Barani in the first unrevised version of his *Tarikh* to Khusrau Khan's plot against certain leading nobles reveals that, like Ghazi Malik, some other powerful governors did not come to the capital to pay obeisance to the regicide. Barani writes:

> The plot and stratagem were worked out to the effect that somehow or the other Ghazi Malik, Malik Bahram Aiba, Malik Tajuddin Hoshang (the *muqta* of Jalore), Malik Tagin (the *muqta* of Awadh), and Malik Yal Afghan should come to Delhi and fall into the trap, that they be lured with favour and money and then put under arrest all of a sudden, simultaneously. After them there would be left none of the nobles of Sultan Alauddin and Sultan Qutbuddin (Mubarak Shah) to be feared.[12]

In Delhi, Ghazi Malik's son, Malik Fakhruddin Juna, and Malik Aiba's son[13] were clever enough to perceive danger to their fathers. Malik Fakhruddin Juna is said to have sent his trusted man, Ali Yaghdi, to inform his father in Depalpur about the situation in Delhi. Directed by his father, Malik Juna took with him Malik Aiba's son and some of his own servants and fled to Depalpur. On his arrival, Ghazi Malik began preparations to fight.[14] The governors in the neighbouring provinces were invited to join the struggle, but none except Malik Aiba of Uchh province responded to the call to join Ghazi Malik. Malik Mughalati, the governor of Multan, and Malik Yaklakhi, the governor of Samana and Sunam, turned hostile towards Ghazi Malik, but in both the provinces the soldiers broke out in mutiny, killed the governors, and joined Ghazi Malik.[15]

Of the two battles fought by Ghazi Malik on his way to Delhi, the second one outside Delhi was decisive. On his return to his camp in triumph at Inderpat, Ahmad, son of Malik Ayaz, the *kotwal* of the metropolis, brought the keys of the fort of Siri and also conveyed his father's greetings to the victor. The following day, the latter arrived in the *hazarsatun* (thousand-pillared) palace where he was received by the officers and prominent citizens of the metropolis. He addressed the people and told them that the motive behind the struggle was to avenge the murder of the sons and the humiliation of the wives and ladies of Sultan Alauddin Khalji, his benefactor, and that this goal had been achieved. Then he asked them to find any surviving prince or elect one noble from amongst themselves in case none of the sons or grandsons of Sultan Alauddin still were left. As no legal heir to the throne was left, the nobles insisted that either he or his eldest son should occupy the throne. Ultimately, he agreed to wear the elective crown. He assumed the title of Sultan Ghiyasuddin Tughluq Shah, Tughluq being his surname.[16]

Although Sultan Ghiyasuddin Tughluq Shah was an Indian by adoption, he had become fully conversant with the system of governance in the Delhi Sultanate. Having passed the period of apprenticeship in the army and the administration since the reign of Sultan Jalaluddin Khalji, he could understand well the working of the political structure of the Sultanate and also the importance of the changes effected by Sultan Alauddin in the system. Possessed of intelligence and ability, he could understand the bright as well as the dark sides of the system of governance that obtained under Sultan Alauddin.[17] Therefore, after his accession to the throne, he removed its harsh features, but preserved all that he thought was necessary for the centralized polity that he had inherited. Noble and upright in his personal life, he evinced interest in the welfare of the people placed under his charge even before his rise to sovereign status. According to the contemporary sources, he had canals and water tanks dug and towns founded in different territorial units assigned to his charge under the Khalji Sultans.[18] In fact, his rise to supreme power held out hope of a prosperous future. He was different from Sultan Alauddin in his attitude towards the *zamindars*, who were treated by the Sultan on a par with the nobles. As for the *khut*, his perquisites were restored, with his function as an intermediary between the state and the peasantry. The Sultan is reported to have remarked that the *khuts* had heavy obligations laid upon their necks, and that if they were not allowed their perquisites, then no benefit for undertaking the responsibility of the office would be left.[19]

As for Sultan Tughluq Shah's attitude towards the nobility,[20] he seems to have followed the footprints of Sultan Alauddin Khalji with regard to its composition. After his accession to the throne, he bestowed royal favours upon his old followers and allies, in addition to his sons and relatives. Malik Aiba, who had joined him in the war against Khusrau Khan, was honoured with the title of Kishlu Khan and the governorship of the combined provinces of Multan, Uchh, and Sind, the latter being called Sewistan.[21] The eldest son, Malik Fakhruddin Juna, was declared heir apparent and the high-sounding title of Ulugh Khan was conferred upon him. The other sons were honoured with the titles of Bahram Khan, Zafar Khan, Nusrat Khan, and Mahmud Khan respectively. As regards the close relatives and old followers, though none of them was honoured with the rank and title of Khan, yet each one was entrusted with the charge of a ministerial post at the centre or the government of a province. The Sultan's nephew, Asad Khan, was raised to the rank of Malik and appointed *barbak* (officer-in-charge of ceremonies and conducting people in the royal presence) at the court. Bahauddin, the son of the Sultan's sister, also got the rank of Malik, the title of Gurshasp, the governorship of the province of Sunam and Samana, and the charge of the *diwan-i-ariz-i-mumalik*.[22] Shadi, the son-in-law of the Sultan, was granted the rank of Malik and assigned the charge of the *diwan-i-wizarat*. The Mongol whom the Sultan had found as an infant lying on the battlefield after his victory over the Mongol invaders was adopted and brought up as his son; he was favoured with the title of Tatar Malik and the governorship of the territorial unit of Zafarabad.[23] Burhanuddin, a scholar from Hansi who seems to have served in Depalpur under him as a civil officer, was rewarded with the title of Alim Malik and appointed the *kotwal* of the capital (*hazrat-i-Delhi*). Likewise, another old companion, Malik Haidar, got the post of *wakil-i-dar*.[24] Qazi Kamaluddin was appointed *sadr-i-jahan*,[25] while the office of the chief *qazi* (chief justice) went to Qazi Samauddin. Qivamuddin (later Qutlugh Khan), the son of Alim Malik, who had instructed the heir apparent in calligraphy, was made the *wazir*[26] of the territory of Deogiri. The experienced officers were selected from amongst the trusted nobles for important posts in other important extensive territorial units as well. For instance, Malik Tajuddin Jaffar was sent to Gujarat to act as *amir-i-ariz* of the army stationed in Arsa-i-Gujarat. As all the aforesaid nobles won the people's confidence with their competence and excellent conduct, nobody felt revulsion against their authority, according to Barani.[27]

The army being the pillar of strength received special attention. Its administration again became highly bureaucratized, with precise rules and regulations concerning the recruitment of troops and officers, their promotion, and their pay and allowances. Since the role model for the new Sultan was Sultan Alauddin, the latter's *amir-i-arz*, Siraj-ul-Mulk Khwaja Haji, became the head of the *diwan-i-arz-i-mumalik*, perhaps in place of Malik Gurshasp.[28] He was delegated full powers regarding the management of the army's affairs, periodical muster, the branding of horses, fixation of the prices of war horses, and the payment of pay and allowances in accordance with the practice of Sultan Alauddin's reign.[29]

It is also worth mentioning that Barani's somewhat cryptic statement regarding the royal order that forbade the audit staff to summon the grandees like the revenue officials to the *diwan-i-wizarat* has led some modern scholars to assume that the *iqta* system was revived, at least in favour of the governors.[30] No doubt, Barani is the only authority to furnish information about the reforms introduced and changes made by the Sultan in the system of administration, yet his statements should be examined critically in the light of the circumstantial evidence that is also contained in his work. In the first unrevised version of his *Tarikh*, he briefly refers to the Sultan's order with regard to the levy of agricultural taxes and the salaries and allowances of the bureaucracy. He writes: 'The Sultan forbade the levy of heavy taxation on the peasants and ordered the soldiers to be paid their salaries in cash from the treasury. The grandees and officers (*amirs*) also benefited from the handsome salaries, rewards, and favours that they received.'[31] The second revised version contains a detailed but a somewhat ambiguous statement. Therein we are informed that, in order to save the high grandees from humiliation, the Sultan ordered the audit staff not to summon the grandees to the *diwan-i-wizarat* as though they were revenue officials. Those whom the Sultan raised to highly dignified positions were not to be dealt with sternly in the manner in which petty officials were treated. The grandees were also advised to maintain their dignity by their honest conduct. They were allowed to take a half tenth or half eleventh, and one-tenth or one-fifteenth, of the *kharaj* in excess of their salaries in the *vilayets* or *iqtas* entrusted to their charge. Likewise, their subordinates were allowed to keep with them a half or 1 per cent in addition to their salaries. Those who were found guilty of larger misappropriation were sternly punished.[32] As a matter of fact, the references in this passage to the *valis* and *muqtas* along with the *mutassarifs* posted in the *vilayets* and *shiqqs* tend to reveal that the centralized polity revived by Sultan Alauddin did not undergo any change. The *vali* and *muqta* have been used as synonyms, meaning military governor, and the *mutassarif* who acted as finance officer independent of the *vali*, at least since the reign of Sultan Alauddin.[33] The *vali* and the *muqta* commanded the provincial army, which remained loyal to the Sultan and could mutiny against the former in case he revolted against the centre, as discussed above. It is also worth pointing out that the term *iqta* has been used by Barani in his history of the Khaljis and the first two Tughluq Sultans for a territorial unit like the *shiqq*, as will be discussed in the chapter on provincial organization.

The Sultan is also reported to have been considerate towards the old members of the ruling elite who had served the Sultanate during the pre-Khalji period but now lived in retirement with no association with the royal palace. Mention is made of Khwaja Khatir, *wazir ul-mumalik*, Junaidi[34] and Khwaja Muhazzab, who had served as *wazirs* previously. They were invited to the court and honoured with robes and costly gifts, given fixed pensions, and also provided with seats in front of the throne. The Sultan is also reported to have consulted them about state affairs from time to time.[35] It is also noteworthy that the position of Ainul-Mulk Multani whom Barani includes in the list of the leading nobles of the reign is not supported by the circumstantial evidence in the historical record. Perhaps he was not taken into royal confidence because of his dubious role in the war against Khusrau Khan. Neither Amir Khusrau nor Isami, nor any other contemporary or near-contemporary writer, refers to him as holding any position in the new dispensation.[36]

After the distribution of ranks, titles, and offices at the centre and in the provinces as well as the reorganization of the ruling elite, the Sultan looked into financial matters and the functioning of different ministerial departments. He demanded from the ministers concerned an account of actual income and expenditure. The officers from each ministry came with the relevant records and read them to the Sultan. When the report of the state exchequer was submitted, it was found that the treasury contained no money because it had been emptied by Khusrau Khan. All the treasures had been distributed to the army men and the citizens of Delhi. Barani states that severe methods were adopted to recover money from the people. These people were divided into three groups; to the first group belonged honest people, though few in number; they kept the money safe and returned it to the state exchequer on demand. Those who belonged to the second group tried to bribe the officers in order to keep the money with themselves, but in vain. They were treated with severity and forced to return all the ill-gotten money. The third group consisted of criminals who were thrown into prison and subjected to torture until they paid back what they had taken.[37] The only exception were the troops and soldiers from whom no recovery was made. But the Sultan is said to have ordered the *amir-i-ariz* to deduct in instalments the amount of money equal to one year of their allowances and to write off the remaining amount that they had been paid by Khusrau Khan. The pay and allowances of the armymen were fixed, and the increase made by Khusrau Khan was cut down.[38] Every soldier and *amir* was given a fixed allowance according to his merit.[39]

A similar policy was adopted towards the land grant holders. According to the established practice, a new Sultan could cancel the land grants held by the people and renew them in case the grantee was found deserving of the favour. Sultan Ghiyasuddin Tughluq Shah followed this practice. Isami tells us that all the land grants given to people by the preceding rulers were declared forfeited to the *diwan-i-wizarat* and thus brought under *khalsa*, and that the two villages that his ancestors had continued to hold in *inam* (reward) from an earlier time, and the grant of which was renewed by every new Sultan through a new *farman*, were also taken back. Even the *aima* (religious divines) were not spared.[40] Obviously, Isami is critical of the Sultan for personal reasons. But Barani's statement is quite different. According to him, the Sultan was always moderate in formulating the state policy but was opposed to parasitism. Barani states that the Sultan looked into the claims of all the grantees and considered each case on the basis of individual merit. All those who rendered services to the state or society in some way or the other and were found deserving got the land grants renewed. Those who got land grants during the reigns of Sultan Qutbuddin Mubarak and Khusrau Khan were found undeserving and deprived of them. Unlike them, others who could justify their claims were spared. As a matter of fact, the Sultan made land grants to and fixed financial assistance for deserving persons according to their needs. Barani says that the people who had got villages, stipends, or land in *inam* during the reign of Sultan Alauddin were not touched; their grants were forthwith renewed.[41] It may be pointed out that the recovery of money from the citizens of Delhi and the taking back of the land grants from the grantees made the Sultan unpopular in Delhi. In defending the Sultan's action and policy, Barani says that neither did the Sultan give so much that it would encourage extravagance nor too little that would not suffice. In every season, or at the time when the news of the conquest of an alien territory was received, or the birth of a prince took place, the *ulama*, jurists, men of piety, and teachers were given money as gifts. The Sultan also sent money to the hospices of the Sufi saints as *futuh* (gift) and thus the ruler shared his joy with the people. Overemphasizing the Sultan's liberality, Barani says that in comparison to his predecessors' largesse, the amount given to an individual was less but the number of people who received the gifts was much larger. Similarly, if the occasions on which money was distributed each year of the reign are counted, the amount distributed would amount to far more. The Sultan also desired that Hindus and Muslims should follow their trades peacefully, extend cultivation, and take an interest in the promotion of handicrafts. Opposed to the practice of begging, he wanted beggars to take to some proper means of livelihood.[42]

Mention should also be made here of the imperialist policy of the Sultan with regard to the expansion of the Sultanate, for it casts light on his concept of authority and the nature of kingship under him. He differed from Sultan Alauddin in this respect to some extent. It is noteworthy that the political thinkers associated with the court like Amir Khusrau propagated the idea that the annexation of far-off territories in south India was possible after the consolidation of the Sultan's power in the Maratha territory (Deogiri).[43] Tughluq Sultan was also of the same opinion. As soon as he was free from the work of the reorganization of the central structure, he dispatched a military expedition under the command of the heir apparent, Ulugh Khan, for the conquest of Telangana. The Prince moved with royal *dabdabe-o-Kokaba* (majesty and splendour), accompanied by the veteran generals of Sultan Alauddin's time under the umbrella, and *saraparda* (royal tent enclosure). In the details furnished by the contemporary writers of the events that took place in the course of the expedition, we find interesting information about Tughluq Shah's state policy *vis-à-vis* the nobility. Though Barani portrays the Sultan as a religious-minded person who followed the *sharia* law, he contradicts himself at least when he refers to the punishment inflicted on the generals who had rebelled in Telangana. Though the veteran general, Malik Timer, the *muqta* of Chanderi, and Malik Tagin, the *muqta* of Awadh, were killed by the Hindu land chiefs loyal to Delhi, other important persons were arrested and brought to Ulugh Khan in Deogiri. The latter sent them to Delhi. Before their arrival, the Sultan had their ladies and children thrown into prison. When they were brought to the capital, the Sultan held the *darbar* in the plain outside the palace of Siri, ordered Ubaid Shair and Malik Kafur Muhardar to be hanged while the others were trampled to death under the feet of elephants. This served as a warning to the people.[44] Only a few persons seem to have been forgiven; Makh Afghan was spared out of consideration for his elder brother, Malik Ikhtiyaruddin Yal Afghan, a loyal general of Alauddin's time.[45]

Upon the annexation of Telangana, the *fathnama* was received in Delhi, and then the victory was celebrated with traditional gaiety and fanfare. Ulugh Khan is reported to have stayed in Warangal for sometime, rechristened the town (Warangal) as Sultanpur, divided the entire conquered region into *shiqqs* (extensive territorial units) on the pattern of north India, and appointed one military and one financial officer with specific functions. Barani refers to these officers as *vali* and *mutassarif* respectively.[46] Thus, the centralized polity of north India was introduced into south India also. An inscription found fixed on the wall of a mosque constructed in 1322–3 at Atigi (in district Sangli in present-day Maharashtra state) tends to suggest that military posts were established at strategic places for the consolidation of the Sultan's authority.[47] Likewise, the details of the expeditions led by the Sultan in person to establish his direct control over the far-off territories through the appointment of governors (*walis* and *wazirs*) are interesting. The Sultan marched against Bengal in 1323. His adopted son, Tatar Malik, the *vali* of Zafarabad, joined him on the way and was appointed the commander of the advance guard. The latter defeated Bahadur Shah, the unpopular Sultan of Bengal, and also captured him. Thereupon, Prince Nasiruddin, the brother of Bahadur Shah, was installed in Lakhnauti as the vassal, while the territorial units of Sonargaon and Satgaon were separated and brought under the control of the centre.[48] The other contemporary writers Ikhtisan and Isami supplement the information contained in Barani's *Tarikh*. They furnish information about the conquest of Tirhut by the Sultan on the way back from Bengal. Ikhtisan accompanied the Sultan as his *dabir-i-khas* (minister-in-charge of the chancellery) and describes all the events that took place during the course of this expedition. According to him, the land chiefs of Tirhut were befriended after they had submitted to the Sultan. As regards the *rai* (ruler) of Tirhut, he writes:

> The Rai of Tirhut was arrogant on account of his resources in man and material and also strong fortification. He did not acknowledge the

overlordship of the Sultan of Delhi, let alone the payment of tribute. Informed of the march of the Delhi army under the command of the Sultan into his territory, he lost courage and sought safety in flight. He considered the forest and hills safer than his fort. A few days later, the Sultan entered the large city (*shahr-i-Muazam*) of Tirhut. He stayed there for quite some time to organize the administration of the region. The officers were posted in the newly carved-out territorial units (called *iqtas*) and the land chiefs who resisted, depending on the dense forests around their strongholds, were attacked and eliminated. But those chiefs (*muqaddams*) who acquiesced were spared and rewarded with additional land for maintaining an increased number of soldiers for the service of the centre.[49]

This tends to suggest that the *zamindars* were placed under an obligation to serve the Sultan like his nobles, with the difference that their estates were not transferable. The *zamindars* enjoyed hereditary rights.

As for Isami's account of the conquest of Tirhut, it is corroborative as well as supplementary; herein also reference is made to the *rai's* unwillingness to acknowledge the suzerainty of the Sultan on account of the thick jungle that made it difficult for the invader to penetrate into his territory. Isami says that the Sultan dismounted from his horse, and in order to inspire his soldiers took up an axe in his own hand and started cutting down a tree. Thereupon, the soldiers and officers became busy felling trees; soon a road was created for the movement of the army. In two or three days, the army appeared before the gate of the city and occupied it. The Sultan stayed there for a few weeks, and deputed the army generals to subdue the hostile *zamindars*. Thereafter, he entrusted the charge of the government to Malik Ahmad bin Talbagha, and then started on his return journey to Delhi.[50] (The Sultan met his accidental death near Delhi towards the close of 1324.)

Lastly, mention should be made of the foundation of Tughluqabad, the new capital, because by this time the construction of a new capital had become an established practice. There was a two-fold motive behind the foundation of a new capital, at least since the time of Sultan Jalaluddin Khalji.[51] The new metropolis symbolized the splendour and grandeur of the ruler, on the one hand, and provided the Sultan with protection from the loyalists of the preceding regime, on the other. This new capital called Tughluqabad seems to have been designed by the architect Ahmad bin Ayaz with the aim of surpassing the other surviving capitals of the preceding Sultans. Isami praises Tughluqabad in these words:

I am told that in years of the reign that passed with all success, the fortress was built at a distance of one *farsang* [about three miles] from the old capital [Siri]. This was built of hard stone and its foundation was laid in large rough stones. A reservoir of water was constructed beneath the fortress, its clean water gushes always in sparkling waves like the river flowing down the Caucasus mountains. The fortification was called Tughluqabad after the name of the fortunate Sultan.[52]

Barani says about its importance that the city would serve as a memorial for its beauty and strength until the day of resurrection.[53] Further, the reference made by Barani to Tughluqabad in the account of the conquest of Telangana suggests that it was completed by the end of 1322. He says that the conquest was celebrated, and the cities of Tughluqabad, Delhi, and Siri were decorated with curtain, musical instruments were played, and the people rejoiced.[54] Ibn Battuta's description is also worth quoting: 'In it (Tughluqabad) was the great palace whose tiles he had gilded, so that when the sun rose they shone with a brilliant light and a blinding glow that made it impossible to keep one's eyes fixed on it.'[55]

A survey of the remains of the buildings today reveals evidence of Indo-Muslim urban planning and its architectural elements. The town was built over a hill surrounded by a basin, the southern part of which was dammed and made into a lake. The well-preserved tomb of the Sultan was constructed within a small fortified castle over a man-made island in the middle of this lake, and was linked to the fort by a causeway about 300 metres long. The town itself had a Perso-Islamic plan with three fortified areas: the citadel (*arg*), situated to the south; the fort (*qila*) about six times the size of the citadel, and situated to the west; and the town itself (*shahristan*), spread towards the north and the east of the fort and the citadel.[56]

Earlier, the same surveyors had excavated the site of the residential and public buildings in the town. Besides the remains of the residential buildings, the Jama mosque and some other structures were outlined in the town plan. The remains of the *khaas bazaar* (main shopping street), which runs at the western side of the town from the North Gate of the fort and ends in a triangular square area in front of the Dobhani Gate, sheds light on an important change introduced in town planning. The remains 'provide the earliest examples of their kind in India. It seems that, together with the other architectural and urban design features, the form of the shops set on platforms was imported by the Sultan from the region of Khurasan.'[57]

II

With the accidental death of Sultan Tughluq Shah at Afghanpur near Delhi towards the end of the year AD 1324, a period of radical changes began under his son and successor in AD 1325.[58] The crown prince, Ulugh Khan, who ascended the throne under the title Abul Mujahid Muhammad bin Tughluq Shah was a remarkable man on several counts, a far-sighted statesman who established diplomatic and trade relations with foreign countries as far away as Egypt in the west and China in the east, and, above all, a philosopher king with a vision. In military generalship, he was a leader *par excellence*; he was a combination of military tactician and strategist. By both education and inclination he was attracted to logic and the rationalist sciences. He regarded inherited religion as a feeble thing, sapping one's manhood; instead, he took the rationalist approach to it and believed in an intuitive perception of religion. He tried to draw his co-religionists away from centuries-old stagnation and also showed regard to other people's religion. With his advent to the throne, not only did *dabdaba-i-badshahi* (splendour and royal grandeur) reach its high watermark, but the people were also assured of a bright future. Never before had a coronation ceremony been performed with such gaiety. Barani states that before the Sultan moved from Tughluqabad to old Delhi for his coronation, the *bazaars* and streets were decorated with embroidered and colourful curtains of silk and artificial trees with flowers.

> The *farman* was issued that as soon as the royal umbrella would enter the (old) city, money be showered in the streets of its quarters. Gold and silver coins were thrown on the ground as well as the roofs of the houses and also dropped in the skirts of the spectators. On the entry of

the large-hearted Sultan through the Badaon Gate with unprecedented splendour and glory, the grandees rode the elephants with dishes full of gold and silver *tankas*, placed in front of them. They moved, raining the coins in the *bazaars* and lanes of the city.[59]

Though Isami was hostile to the Sultan, he corroborates Barani's account in these words: 'In the beginning, he made a full display of his spirited munificence by having gold scattered everywhere.'[60] On his arrival in 1333, Ibn Battuta also heard about this grand celebration. In describing the noble qualities possessed by the mother of the Sultan, he says that there was such illumination in the evening on that occasion that the flashing light blinded the mother of the Sultan.[61] The illumination of the city was followed by the oath-taking ceremony in which the nobles and the people swore their allegiance to the new Sultan. This ritual provided the operational legitimacy for the new ruler. Moreover, the charm of the Sultan's personality and his fame as a successful army general must have had an effect in attaching him to the minds of the people.[62] Barani says about the personality of the Sultan: 'It seemed that the robe of sovereignty and the dress of royalty was made to his measure, and that the throne of the Sultanate formed a part of (divine) creation on account of his accession (to the throne).'[63]

The reorganization of the nobility was taken up by the Sultan on a priority basis after his accession to the throne because the nobility was an institution next to kingship in importance. The Sultan being a ruler with good knowledge and experience of the system of governance wanted to be instrumental in bringing about positive changes through the introduction of development-oriented reforms rather than continuing with the system that he had inherited. For this purpose, he selected for ministerial posts at the centre and for governorships in the provinces trustworthy men who could implement the royal policy in all seriousness. Although he does not appear to have deprived any senior noble of his rank and position, he replaced his father's ministers by men who enjoyed his own confidence. He had his own servants, slaves, and friends since he had served first as his father's representative at court and then as *amir-i-akhur* under Sultan Qutbuddin Mubarak Shah.[64] Further, on his nomination by his father as heir apparent, many *malikzadas*, members of the aristocratic families, might have been induced to rally around him in the hope of gaining his favour in the time to come. The term *malikzada* connotes a connection with the Sultanate extending over generations.[65] Of the favoured *malikzadas*, Ahmad bin Ayaz was selected to be the *wazir* of the Sultanate in place of Malik Shadi, the brother-in-law of the Sultan. Ahmad Ayaz had not only won his confidence but had also identified himself with the Sultan's political ideals and his religious philosophy. The title of Khwaja Jahan was conferred upon him.[66] In addition to the *wizarat* (revenue ministry), he was also entrusted with the governorship of the province of Gujarat (arsa-i-Gujarat), where he posted his slave Maqbal to govern it on his behalf.[67] It is noteworthy that no other *Malikzada* appears to have been favoured with a high position at court in the beginning of the reign. Promotion was earned by merit. Malik Maqbul Telangani, a convert to Islam, was entitled Qivam ul-Mulk and appointed *naib-i-wazir* (deputy *wazir*) under Khwaja Jahan. He was also attached to the Sultan since he had embraced Islam after the conquest of Telangana (1322–3).[68] After the *wizarat*, the next important ministry was the *diwan-i-arz* (department of the paymaster general); this was entrusted to a trusted slave entitled Imad-ul-Mulk Sultani.[69] The other persons who were given favours in the beginning of the reign were the sons of Malik Burhanuddin. They were Qivamuddin and his brothers. Qivamuddin, who had instructed the Sultan in calligraphy, was granted the title of Qutlugh Khan and sent to Deogiri as the *khadev* (governor-general) of all the territorial units in south India annexed to the Sultanate.[70] Qutlugh Khan's brothers, Qazi Kamaluddin and Shamsuddin and Nizamuddin, were also favoured. Since they were scholarly men and known for their righteousness, Qazi Kamaluddin was appointed as *sadr-i-jahan* and the chief *qazi* (chief justice) of the Sultanate. According to Ibn Battuta, Maulana Shamsuddin 'renounced the world for the service of God and sojourned at Mecca to the time of his death'.[71] The fourth brother Nizamuddin was also taken into the official hierarchy and granted the title of Alim Malik. He served in different territorial units. In 1344, he served as the executive officer of the seaport of Bharoach (Gujarat) and its dependencies, from where he was sent to Daulatabad with the order to conduct the government of the south Indian provinces until the arrival of new officers appointed after the recall of Qutlugh Khan. Barani calls him a simple and inexperienced man in warfare. He proceeded from Bhroach to Deogiri in accordance with the royal *farman* and took over the command of the army.[72] In this statement we find a clue to the fact that until this time non-military men like Qutlugh Khan, his brother, and Aziz Khumar could hold the charge of important provinces and conduct the government successfully with the help of the provincial army, which was loyal to the Sultan, and his loyal officers.

It is important to note that, in order to meet the needs of an expanding Sultanate, the Sultan recruited officers on the basis of merit, regardless of birth or creed. Consequently, the nobility became broad based. His enlightened policy attracted foreigners to India in search of fortune. Moreover, the Sultan encouraged educated persons who belonged to ordinary families to compete with those of aristocratic background in the state service. The favouritism shown by the Sultan to foreigners caused resentment among the Indians, yet the Sultan continued to patronize them until the end.[73] In addition to their appointment to important positions, he had some of the foreigners married to his own relations or to the daughters of his ministers. For example, Saifuddin, an Arab from Syria, was married to the Sultan's sister.[74] Azam Malik Bayazidi Bistami, who was married to the daughter of the Sultan's sister, was entrusted with the governorship of the iqta-i-Kara.[75] The two sons of Qivamuddin from Tirmiz whom the Sultan had honoured with the title of Khudawandzada were married to the daughters of the *wazir*, Khwaja Jahan.[76] Many foreign merchants who carried on overseas and overland trade between India and other countries and also had their establishments in the seaports of the Sultanate were also favoured. Mention made by Ibn Battuta of Malik ut-Tujjar (chief of the merchants), Pirwiz of Gazarun (Iran), reveals that he was appointed the governor of the port city of Cambay, with permission to carry on his private trade with foreign countries.[77] After his murder in 1334, his son and widow stayed in Cambay until their end.[78] Thus, the Sultan was able to meet the needs of an expanding empire.

Like Cambay, the other seaport of international importance was that of Lahribandar on the coast of Sind, constructed after the old seaport of Daibul had been abandoned on account of silting. Its management was entrusted to Ala-ul-Mulk, an immigrant scholar from Herat. Ibn Battuta calls Lahribandar a port of call with a large harbour.

It was visited by ships from al-Yaman, Fars (Iran), and other Middle Eastern countries. For this reason, its contribution to the treasury and its revenue are considerable; the governor Ala-ul-Mulk told me that the tax yield from this town amounted to sixty lakhs per annum. The governor receives *nimdeh-yak*, meaning the half of the tenth of this, that being the footing on which the Sultan hands over the provinces to his governors, that they take for themselves one-twentieth of the yield.[79]

Among the foreigners from Arab countries, Iran, Khurasan (present-day Afghanistan) and Central Asia were included the Kurds of Iran, the people of Iraq and Turkey, the Maldives and Spain.[80]

As regards the Kurds from the neighbouring countries, they also appear to have held important positions in the Sultanate. Some of them were men of culture and could serve as emissaries in the Arab countries on account of their proficiency in the Arabic language. Mahmud Shams Kurd and his father are reported to have visited the Abbasid Caliph in Egypt as envoys from India.[81]

Equally important is to discuss the rise of the people belonging to the lower strata of society in the bureaucracy. There was a social upsurge resulting from the liberal state policy followed by the Sultans since the advent of the Khaljis to power. In fact, the reign of Sultan Muhammad bin Tughluq is the most important period in this regard. Both Ibn Battuta and Barani mention a number of low-born persons whom the Sultan elevated to important positions in the official hierarchy. The nature of the offices assigned to them indicates that they were educated people and could perform their duties efficiently. Ibn Battuta and Barani both mention Ratan, a Hindu barber by caste; this reference is of historical significance. Despite his low origin, Ratan had distinguished himself as a mathematician and expert calligrapher. Impressed by his knowledge and competence in calligraphy, the Sultan took him into his service and ultimately elevated him to the status of a high-ranking noble. He got the governorship of Sind province with the grant of drums and flags, a privilege enjoyed by the very important nobles.[82] The following passage from the *Tarikh-i-Firuz Shahi* shows how social mobility resulted from the Sultan's attitude:

Najib, the musician of obscure origin, was so much honoured that he superseded in position and status many of the senior grandees. He was assigned the charge of Gujarat, Multan, and Badaon (territorial units, perhaps held in succession).[83] Like him, Aziz Khumar and his brother were honoured. Firuz the barber, Manka the cook, Masud Khumar the liquor brewer, Ladha the *baghban* (gardener), and many other base and mean people were elevated to important posts and assigned (the charge of) *iqtas*. Shaikh Babu, son of Nanak the weaver, was made a royal associate and thus the scoundrel became an influential man in society. Pira *Mali* (gardener), who was the meanest and most ignoble person in India, was honoured with the charge of the *diwan-i-wizarat* and raised in this way over and above the *maliks*, *valis*, *muqtas* and senior grandees.[84] Kishan Bazran of Indri who was the meanest of the meanest got the governorship of Awadh (province). Maqbal, the slave of Ahmad Ayaz, was entrusted with the governorship of Gujarat (on behalf of his master, as mentioned above), an office meant for prominent nobles and ministers, although he possessed no qualities outwardly or inwardly.[85]

Isami would have us believe that the Sultan favoured Hindus with important positions owing to his hostility towards Islam, and that therefore he subjected its followers to their tyranny.[86]

It needs to be pointed out that the nobles, described by Barani as being of base stock, were valued by the Sultan for their faithfulness in implementing his policies and carrying out his orders with greater competence and sincerity than men of aristocratic background. The rebels against the Sultan generally belonged to the old Indian aristocratic families. Ibn Battuta's account of some of the nobles who belonged to ordinary families casts light on their loyalty to the Sultan and their sincerity in performing their duties. Aziz Khumar successfully held the post of finance officer in Amroha and that of the governor of Malwa, while Maqbal managed the affairs of arsa-i-Gujarat as the *naib* (deputy) of the *wazir*, Khwaja Jahan. Aziz Khumar is described by Ibn Battuta as a man of violent temper, but Maqbal had no such shortcoming. Ibn Battuta found him a cultured and hospitable man.[87]

It is also during this reign that we come across the names of a number of Afghan nobles. The Afghans, who belonged to the second and third generations of the early immigrants from beyond the north-western frontier of the Panjab, emerged as a new element in the social formation in Indo-Muslim society at this time. By now they seemed to have become familiar with Indo-Muslim aristocratic culture.[88] They were given high posts in the state service. Many of them acquired political influence in certain regions. Malik Shahu Lodi even went to the extent of killing Malik Bihzad, the governor of Multan, and assuming the royal title in 1334. His rebellion was of such seriousness that the Sultan himself had to march against him. Thereupon, Shahu Lodi lost his courage, appealed for pardon, and sought shelter in 'Afghanistan'.[89] The other important Afghan nobles who rose to prominence were Malik Khattab, Qazi Jalal Afghan, Jhiloo Afghan, and Makh Afghan, the latter being the younger brother of Malik Ikhtyar Uddin Yal Afghan. Ibn Battuta is full of praise for Malik Khattab, the governor of Rapri, for his undaunted courage and military talent.[90] The Afghans were in such large numbers in Gujarat and the Deccan that their rebellion in 1345 led to the dismemberment of the Sultanate.[91]

Some black African slaves from Ethiopia and other countries of Africa who started out as the slaves of the Sultan could attain to the ranks of nobles, and were posted in territorial units in reward for their services. One of them served as *shahna* (commander) of the *thana* (military post) at Alapur (in Gwalior district). Being a warrior of talent, he controlled the area and guarded the highway connecting Delhi with the Deccan through Malwa. His followers were also his fellow African slaves.[92] Also, in the account of the outbreak of plague in the Sultan's camp on the way to Telangana, Ibn Battuta refers incidentally to the presence of black African slave soldiers who died in large numbers.[93]

As regards the inclusion of Hindus in the nobility in a sizeable number, it may be stressed again that, besides the members of Hindu *zamindar* families like Malik Gulchand of the Panjab,[94] low-born Hindus could also aspire to important ranks and positions, as already discussed. In fact, like the bureaucratization of the civil service, army organization was one of the important factors responsible for the increase in social mobility; brave and talented soldiers and efficient civil servants were rewarded with promotion and ultimately could rise to high positions. In the Deccan, many Hindus served the Sultan as *mutassarifs* and generals in the extensive territorial units. Barani and Isami mention a few such men incidentally in their accounts of various rebellions. Barani describes the Hindu noble Bhairon as the *mutassarif* of Gulbarga, whom Ali Shah Khalji the rebel killed treacherously. Isami adds that Bhairon also held the charge of the fort of Gulbarga.[95] The references contained in the *Futuh us-Salatin* to the *muqtas* posted in different administrative units of the Deccan tend to suggest that they were from north India as their names Seo Rai, Pithora, and Gandhar Khatri show. They remained loyal to the Sultan and fought against the rebels until the end.[96] It may be pointed out that the Khatris were from the area around Delhi, Haryana, and the Punjab. They rose to prominence during this period. They served in different regions.

Besides the maintenance of a powerful army and an efficient bureaucracy, the foundation of new urban centres, grand metropolitan cities, and the laying out of beautiful gardens had become a well-established tradition, symbolic of *dabdabashahi* (royal splendour). Sultan Muhammad bin Tughluq tried to surpass his predecessors in this respect also. He had beautiful buildings constructed under the supervision of his *wazir*, Khwaja Jahan, a renowned architect as well.[97] The first metropolitan city planned by Khwaja Jahan in order to materialize his Sultan's dream was Jahanpanah (asylum of the world), also called Adilabad. The fort of Jahanpanah was constructed on the south-east corner of Tughluqabad, on the eastern side of the lake in which the first fortress tomb of Sultan Ghiyasuddin Tughluq Shah stands. The fort of Jahanpanah is rectangular in shape, built on the rocks, commanding a lovely view of the lake. It was built in the style of Tughluqabad architecture: 'The massive walls and heavy bastions have a bolster plinth which gives an impression of a sloping wall.'[98] The graphic description given by Ibn Battuta casts light on the originality of its planning. He states that the royal palace in it was called *darsare* (auspicious palace). It contained many gates.

> At the first gate there are posted a number of men in charge of it, and beside it sit the buglers, trumpeters, and pipe-players. When an Amir or person of note arrives, they sound their instruments and so during this fanfare announce 'so and so has come'. The same takes place at the second and the third gates. Outside the first gate are platforms on

which sit the jalladun (floggers). Between the first and the second gates there is a large vestibule with platforms built along both sides, on which sit those troops whose turn of duty it is to guard the gates. Between the second and the third gates there is a large platform on which the principal *naqib* (one who conducts a visitor into the royal presence) with a gold mace in his hand. . . . The other *naqibs* stand before him, each wearing a low gilded cap on his head and a girdle around his waist and holding in his hand a whip with a gold or silver handle. The second gate leads to a large and commodious audience hall in which the people sit.

There were found record keepers at the third gate. They put down the name of every visitor. This third gate opened 'into the immense and vast hall called *hazar satun*, which means 'a thousand pillars'. The pillars are of painted wood and support a wooden roof most exquisitely carved. The people sit under this, and it is in this hall that the Sultan sits for public audience.[99] The court poet Badr Chach, praises the Sultan for his munificence, which flows from its threshold:[100]

Agar na Khuld-i-barin (a) ste in Hazar satun,
Chara Faza-i-darash Arzgah-Roz-i-Jaza (a)st.

The *hazar satun* (palace) is paradise. Had it not been so,
How could munificence flow in the plain around its gate?

Equally interesting is the evidence available in a contemporary Arabic source, *Masalik-al-Absar*, regarding city planning during Muhammad bin Tughluq's reign. Shihabuddin al-Umari was told by a traveller from India about the foundation of Daulatabad (near old Deogiri in Maharashtra):

The Sultan chalked out the plan of the city in such a wise way that sectors were to be built for different sections of people; one sector for the residence of the army, the second for the *wazirs* and secretaries, the third for the *qazis* and *ulama* (religious scholars), the fourth for the Sufis and mendicants, and the fifth for the merchants and craftsmen. There were made separate arrangements according to the needs of each sector, such as a mosque, minaret for *azan* (call for prayer), *bazaars*, public baths (*hamam*), flour mills, ovens, and various types of craftsmen's shops such as goldsmiths, dyers, and leather tanners, so that the people of one sector might not depend on those of the other in meeting their needs. Every sector was thus self-contained.[101]

The foundation of these metropolitan cities of Jahanpanah and Daulatabad were, doubtless, symbolic of the new order. In addition, the little relevant evidence contained in our sources tends to suggest that the south Indian region was divided into a number of provinces called *shiqqs*. In some *shiqqs*, new forts were constructed to serve as headquarters. In one of the *shiqqs* in present-day Karnataka was founded a town with a fort and named Ustadabad after the name of Qutlugh Khan, the *ustad* (preceptor) of the reigning Sultan.[102] These headquarters developed into important urban centres and acted as integrative nuclei in spreading Delhi's culture and creating local support for the Sultan's authority.

Some words are in order here about the construction of highways connecting the far-off provinces with Delhi. The highways were constructed along with police posts, royal villas, *dak chaukis* (postal posts), and *khanqahs* for providing comfort and security to travellers. Ibn Battuta was amazed by the beauty of the road as well as the availability of necessary things, food, fodder, etc., all along the road that connected south India with Delhi. He states:

> The road between these two cities (Delhi and Daulatabad) is bordered by willows and other trees, so that the traveller on it might imagine himself to be in a garden. For every mile of this road there are three *dawas* (Hindi *dhawa*) i.e. post stations . . . and at each *dawa* there is everything that the traveller requires, so that he seems to be making his way through one continuous bazaar forty days' journey in length. The road continues in the same manner all the way to the land of Tilang and al-Maabar (Karnataka), a six-months' journey. At each halting place there is a palace for the Sultan and a hospice (*khanqah*) for travellers, so that the poor man has no need to carry provisions with him on the road.[103]

The eyewitness account left by Yahya Sirhindi corroborates Ibn Battuta:

> From Delhi to Deogiri (Daulatabad) there was constructed a *dhawa* after every *kroh* (three miles' distance) with a settlement of people who were paid maintenance allowance out of the revenue from the area. Every official courier who came, sat on the cot, and was carried from one to the other *dhawa*. There was constructed a palace and a *khanqah* at each stage. The Shaikh (al-Islam) was posted at each stage to look after travellers; food, drinks, and betel leaves were kept ready; the traveller was served whenever he came there. On each side of the road trees were planted; the remnants can still be seen.[104]

Doubtless, in the Sultanate polity kingship was considered the agency of prosperity and public well-being. The Sultan was expected to have mosques, *madrasas*, *khanqahs* (rest-cum-charity houses), *darul shifa* (hospitals), etc., constructed for the benefit of all. Sultan Muhammad bin Tughluq surpassed his predecessors in this regard also. His generosity knew no bounds. Barani is a bit critical of the Sultan's open-handedness because it caused a heavy burden on the state exchequer, particularly on account of the money and costly gifts given to foreigners.[105] Ibn Battuta corroborates Barani in these words: '[The Sultan] is of all men the most humble and the readiest to show equity and to acknowledge the right. . . . He is one of those kings whose felicity is unimpaired and whose success in his affairs surpasses all ordinary experience, but his dominant quality is generosity.'[106] Shihabuddin al-Umari was informed by Sharif Husain al-Samarqandi, who had served Sultan Muhammad bin Tughluq: 'The acts of favour, generosity, charity, and other virtues of the Sultan are such that the world would record them on the pages of history and time would inscribe them on its dazzling forehead.' An Indian traveller also told al-Umari that the Sultan distributed two lakh *tankas* in alms at the sight of the new moon among people. In addition, 40,000 poor people got a daily allowance; every person was given one *dirham* and five *ritls* (one and a half *seer*) of wheat bread or rice, that 1,000 teachers were employed by the Sultan to teach orphans and the children of poor families, that begging was discouraged, and in case someone handicapped was found begging, he was checked and a daily allowance was fixed for him.[107] As regards the Sultan's generous patronage extended to foreigners, it has been described in detail in Chapter 6.

Also, the relevant evidence found in the sources about the function of the royal *khanqahs* sheds light on the Sultan's philanthropy. The *khanqahs* (also called *ribat*) were built by the Sultan, governors, and other philanthropists to help travellers. Sultan Muhammad bin Tughluq had spacious *khanqahs* built in the provinces and along the highways that served as an institution of public utility. The charge of the *khanqah* was assigned to a righteous man, who distributed money and provided food to the needy people on behalf of the Sultan. For the maintenance of the *khanqah*, the income from a number of villages was endowed.

The manager of the *khanqah* was designated as Shaikh ul-Islam. On his visit to Amroha, Ibn Battuta was received by the Shaikh ul-Islam, who hosted a banquet to entertain him in the *khanqah*.[108] A spacious *khanqah* was built on a hillock outside the city of Dhar (Malwa) by the order of the Sultan, and the entire revenue accruing from the city and the area around was endowed for its maintenance. Its charge was entrusted to Shaikh Ibrahim Maldibi, a saintly immigrant from Maldib (or Maldive Islands). Once the Shaikh visited the Sultan on his way to the Deccan and presented an amount of thirteen lakh *tankas*, saying that it belonged to the *bait ul-mal* (public treasury) as it had been saved out of the amount meant for feeding the people. The Sultan was not pleased because it should have been spent and not saved.[109] In Bihar, a spacious *khanqah* was also built and Majd ul-Mulk, the governor, was ordered to hand over its charge to Shaikh Sharafuddin Yahya Maneri, the famous Firdausi Sufi saint. The revenue of Rajgir was endowed for its upkeep. The great Shaikh agreed reluctantly to accept the assignment for the sake of Majd ul-Mulk, his disciple.[110] In the provinces of Sind and Uchh, Shaikh Jalaluddin Bukhari, the Suhrawardi saint (popularly known as Makhdum-i-Jahanian-i-Jahangasht), was appointed the Shaikh ul-Islam, with the charge of forty *khanqahs* scattered in different parts.[111] Mention may also be made of the state-aided hospitals (*darul-shifa* in India and *bimaristans* in the Middle Eastern countries). Al-Umari tells us that 'there were seventy *bimaristans*, called *darul-shifa* in Delhi, that 12,000 *tabibs* (physicians) got maintenance allowances in the Sultanate for rendering service to the people.[112] Ikhtisan, the *dabir-i-khas* of the Sultan, corroborates the Arab writer while mentioning his own ailment.[113] The maintenance of these institutions did enhance the prestige of the Sultan in and outside the country.

Similarly, the performance of certain court rituals are worth mentioning because certain customs and ceremonies were derived from them, and they served as metaphors for royal *dabdaba*. For example, on his return in triumph from a conquered territory or after gaining victory over a rebel, the Sultan entered the capital in procession with great fanfare. Triumphal arches were erected, wooden pavilions several stories high were installed, the streets and lanes were decorated with trappings of silk, and in each storey of the pavilions singers and nautch girls decked with ornaments sang and danced. The royal procession was led by war elephants, adorned with silk fabric, woven with gold thread and studded with precious stones. The nobles also followed with their personal servants, bands of drum beaters, and players of musical instruments. Ibn Battuta was amazed to see the procession. He says:

The space between the pavilions is carpeted with silk clothes on which the Sultan's horse treads. The walls of the streets along which he passes from the gate of the city to the gate of the palace are hung with silk cloths. In front of him (the Sultan) march footmen from among his own slaves, several thousand in number, and behind come the squadrons and mounted troops. On one of his entries into the capital I saw three or four small catapults set upon elephants throwing *dinars* and *dirhams* amongst the people.[114]

Al-Umari was told by Shaikh Muhammad al-Khujandi, who had served the Sultan:

When the Sultan moves from one place to the other, he rides the horse with an umbrella over his head. The *silahdars* (royal bodyguards) move behind him with weapons in their hands. There are twelve thousand slaves around the Sultan and they move on foot. Only the *chitrbardars* (the bearers of the royal umbrella), the *silahdars* (bearers of weapons), and the *jamadars* (bearers of garments) ride the horses.[115]

Badr Chach describes the scene in his verse, wherein we are provided with details of the decoration of the lanes, *bazaars*, and streets of the city with nautch girls performing their art for the entertainment of the public. They appeared in beautiful clothes, embroidered with gold, flashing a warm smile, dancing and singing melodious songs.[116]

The absence of any reference to the hunting expeditions led by the Sultan in the works of Isami and Barani creates the impression that perhaps the Sultan did not maintain this tradition, although it had become almost an attribute of kingship. The information furnished by foreign writers shows that the Sultan went for the hunt whenever he was free. Al-Umari writes that on hunting expeditions the Sultan took a small contingent with him, i.e. only one lakh *sawars* and 200 elephants. In addition, parts of four pavilions of wood were taken on 800 camels; 200 camels were loaded with those of each one. Every pavilion was covered with silken curtains of black colour and embroidered with gold thread. Each one consisted of two storeys and was surrounded by tents and camps.[117] Ibn Battuta's eyewitness account suggests that the Sultan regarded it as a ritual and that its performance was symbolic of royal splendour. Further, it provided jobs to many people for months. Ibn Battuta also joined the Sultan once. He says:

In accordance with the practice of the people of India, I had brought a *saracha* (enclosure of curtains). Anyone there is at liberty to pitch a *saracha*, and it is indispensable for all men of high rank. The Sultan's *saracha* is distinguished by its red colour, while the others are white, embroidered with blue. I brought also the *siwan*, which is the tent under which one shelters inside the *saracha*; it is supported upon two stout poles, and the whole thing is carried on their shoulders by men called *kaiwaniya*, everyman has to hire men who furnish him with green fodder for the animals. He hires also *kahars*, that is, those men who carry cooking utensils, as well as men to carry him in a *dula* . . . and *farashes*, whose business it is to erect the *saracha* and to furnish it with carpets and to load up the camels, and also the *dawadawiya*, whose business it is to walk ahead of him carrying torches at night.

Since Ibn Battuta did not have permanent servants, he had to hire all of them.[118]

Similarly, the arrangement of royal feasts in connection with the celebration of the Id festival, the Nauroz festival, and the marriages of the princes and princesses provided occasions for the display of royal munificence and splendour. The palace was decorated in the most sumptuous manner. Ibn Battuta describes the decoration:

Artificial trees are made of silk of different colours with artificial flowers on them; three rows of them are placed in the hall, and between each pair of trees there is placed a golden chair with a covered cushion upon it. The great throne is set up at the upper end of the hall; it is of pure gold throughout, and its legs are encrusted with jewels . . . there is placed the cushioned seat, and the parasol encrusted with jewels is hoisted over the Sultan's head. Targhi, the *shahnah-i-bargah* (superintendent of the audience hall), made seat arrangements, having a gold baton in his hand.[119]

Al-Umari adds that poets attended the function on the occasion of festivals, and to celebrate royal victories, they recited their verses composed to commemorate the event.[120]

Funerary rituals also deserve to be mentioned. The mausoleums of the great Sultans were generally built during their lifetime. The surviving mausoleums or their remnants tend to suggest that they were planned in such a way as to reflect the personality and lofty ideals of the individual ruler who were buried inside. Every effort was made to ensure that the structure would surpass those of the earlier Sultans in beauty and grandeur. The novel architectural features added to each one testify to this fact. Endowments were made for their maintenance as well as for feeding poor people and distributing money in charity after the passing away of the Sultan. The members of the ruling elite appear to have adopted some funeral rites, the performance of which was calculated to enhance the popularity of the departed soul as well as the reigning Sultan. For instance, the rite of *teja* was performed three days after the death of a person. People gathered at the grave, covered the ground around it with fine flooring, and had a canopy installed over it. People sat under it and recited Koranic verses. After the Koran had been recited, the *qazi* first prayed for the departed soul and then delivered the sermon, highlighting the noble qualities of the deceased. He closed his sermon, with a prayer for the success and long life of the reigning Sultan. People stood respectfully in case the Sultan was present there.[121] Sultan Muhammad bin Tughluq used to join the funeral processions of leading citizens and nobles. Al-Umari was told by Abu Safa Omar bin al-Shaikh that he saw once the Sultan dismounting from his horse to join the funeral procession of a pious saint.[122] He carried his bier on his shoulders.[123]

The promotion of intellectual culture and the progress of arts and crafts was also regarded one of the functions of the State. Every great Sultan evinced an interest in patronizing scholars and poets and associating them with his court. Attracted by the reputation of Sultan Muhammad bin Tughluq's love for the company of the learned, scholars came from different foreign lands to join his service. He discussed literary and philosophical problems with them. He was equally interested in the study of the rationalist sciences and obtained from different sources the classics on philosophy and medicine. Once a foreign scholar came to him with books, including Ibn Sina's celebrated work *al-shifa*. The Sultan was pleased. By chance, at that time a bag full of precious gems was presented to the Sultan. He took a handful of gems to give the foreign scholar in reward, in addition to money.[124] The Sultan was also fond of the company of poets and *tabibs* (physicians) whom he employed in his service. Interested in medical science, he studied Ibn Sina's works, discussed with leading physicians different ailments and their treatment, and also prescribed medicines to patients.[125] The poets associated with his court composed verses in Arabic, Persian, and Hindi. All were rewarded generously for reciting their poems.[126] Ikhtisan corroborates Al-Umari and also mentions the reward given to him for reciting a *qasida-i-Bahariya* on the occasion of the celebration of the spring festival. He was rewarded with sixty thousand gold coins, introduced by the Sultan at the time of his ascent to the throne and named dinar-i-Muhammadi; in addition to this amount of money, the poet also received imported Arab and Tatar horses. This *qasida* is quoted by Ikhtisan in his *Basatin ul-Urs* and by Muhammad Bihamad Khani in his *Tarikh-i-Muhammadi*, and cannot be considered as possessing outstanding merit, yet the fabulous reward was given on account of the Sultan's open-handedness.[127] Ibn Battuta also mentions the reward given to the philosopher-poet Shamsuddin al-Andukani: 'The doctor Shamsuddin al-Andukani, who was a philosopher and a gifted poet, wrote a laudatory ode and the Sultan gave him a thousand silver dinars for each verse. This is a greater reward than those related of former kings, who used to give a thousand dirhams for each verse, which is only a tenth of the Sultan's gift.'[128] The court poet, Badar Chach, does not exaggerate when he praises the Sultan in the following couplet for his efforts to attract men of learning, which made Delhi the centre of learning:

Shah-i-Muhammad an vali ahad-i-Khalifa-i-Zaman,
Ku Chu Imam-i-charmain Shahr Ulum ra durust.[129]

It may also be recalled that the Sultan was undoubtedly great patron of learning, and the scholars of the rational sciences were given preferential treatment at his court. He discussed with the rationalist thinkers matters of philosophy and questioned even the accepted truth. He appears to have held to the concept of linear time and was opposed to the view of cyclical time. He argued with the scholars at court that the past did not always have superiority over the present in terms of piety, religious morality, or progress. He was critical of the popular view generally held by the traditionalist *ulama* that superiority is either in point of time, or in matter of position, or in degree of essence, and that therefore it is not right to say that superiority consists of any one of them. The Sultan did not accept this argument and said it was contrary to that of the rationalist thinkers because, according to him, the past never had superiority over the present for any of these reasons.[130] Ibn Battuta corroborates his contemporaries in this regard. In his account of the King of Morocco, he says that he was also the patron of the learned like the Sultan of India, yet the difference between them was that the latter was fond of the company of the scholars of *ilm ul-maqul* (rationalist sciences) and held discussions with them in the morning. Unlike him, the King of Morocco was inclined to befriend the orthodox *ulama*, especially those of *fiqh* (Islamic jurisprudence).[131] In short, the Sultan was a supporter of reason. But his effort to break the cultural stagnation to which Islamic orthodoxy had fallen victim created misunderstanding about the Sultan's faith in Islam. For a proper understanding of the Sultan's religion and his religious policy, which had an impact on the life and conditions of people in the Sultanate, it is desirable to discuss briefly the Sultan's education and personality.

Let us begin with Barani's statement regarding the religious philosophy of the Sultan in the first version of his *Tarikh*. Herein, Barani portrays the Sultan as a man of transcendent genius whom no one among his contemporaries could equal in military generalship, learning, penmanship, oratory, horse riding, and large-hearted generosity.[132] In addition, he had a very good understanding of the history of the past Sultans because he had studied historical literature, including the works *Tarikh-i-Nasiri* and *Tarikh-i-Mahmudi*. He discussed philosophical problems and made critical comments on the views and theories of philosophers. He had authoritative knowledge of *ilm-i-tibb* (medical science) and prescribed medicines for patients; innumerable patients were cured by him of their ailments. As a general, he was known for the invincibility of his arms; he led the army, charged the rival army in person, and could smash it.[133] As regards Sultan Muhammad bin Tughluq's advocacy of rationalism, he tells us in both the versions that under the influence of the rationalist thinkers, the Sultan had lost faith in the recorded traditions and was guided by his personal judgement. The first version is free from harsh condemnation of the rationalist thinkers; in the second revised version they are blamed by Barani for misleading the righteous and enlightened Sultan from the traditional religious path. He states in the second version that Sad Mantaqi (the logician) who was a misguided person, Ubaid Shair (the poet) who was an atheist, and the thinker poet had become his associates long before his accession to the throne. Another scholar, Maulana Alimuddin, the most learned of the philosophers, spent much of his time discussing philosophy with him. These scholars believed in rationalism, and under their influence the Sultan discarded the traditional sciences (*ilm-i-manqul*) and became a great supporter of reason. To him religious scripture and the Prophetic traditions that infuse in man the spirit of compassion and make him moderate in life had no meaning.[134] Contrary to this assessment, Barani is full of praise for these men in the first version. He writes:

> He (Sultan Muhammad bin Tughluq) came from Depalpur (to Delhi) during the reign of Sultan Alauddin (Khalji) when he was still a youth. Sultan Qutbuddin Mubarak Shah, son and successor of Sultan Alauddin made him courtier and also appointed him the *amir-i-akhur* (officer in charge of the royal stable). He was thus able to join the circle of the scholars associated with the court. By temperament he was inclined towards the acquisition of learning. He joined the circle of scholars associated with the court. He joined the circle of Malik Saduddin (*Mantaqi*), Maulana Najmuddin Intishar (also a poet), Maulana Alimuddin, and Ubaid the poet. These four scholars belonged to the rationalist school of thought (*ilm-i-maqul*). Each one had mastery over the rationalist sciences. Maulana Alimuddin, Sad Mantaqi, and Najm Intishar the poet had been the distinguished scholars of *ilm-i-kalam* (scholastic theology) and logic. No one could rival them in mastery over these sciences. They were found most of the time preoccupied with the study of philosophical literature. As for 'Ubaid' the poet, he was without any faith in religion. It was under his influence that the Sultan was attracted towards the study of the rationalist sciences.[135]

It is also noteworthy that Barani does not cast any doubt on the

Sultan's faith in Islam. In both the versions he emphatically states that the Sultan was a devout Muslim and performed the obligatory rituals punctually, that he stood respectfully when he heard the call for prayers and did not move until it was over. Thereafter, he offered prayers and then sat to recite *aurad* (continual praises of God).[136] The compiler of the *Masalikal-Absar* was also informed by a traveller that the Sultan had committed the Koran to memory, was punctual in offering prayers five times a day, and observed fasts during the month of fasting.[137] The Sultan considered the *hadith* (the Prophetic tradition) as the source of law. Ibn Battuta refers to the visit by Maulana Abdul Aziz Aradwili, the disciple of Imam Ibn Taimiya, to his court. The Maulana was a scholar of the *hadith*. Once the Sultan referred to him a certain *hadith* for comment. He reeled off so many on that subject that the Sultan was highly impressed and rewarded him with a large sum of money.[138] The Sultan had a very good understanding of Islamic jurisprudence in general and Hanafi law in particular. He could quote the rulings from the *Hidaya* off-hand.[139] It was the Sultan's interest in Islamic jurisprudence that led Sultan's *dabir-i-khas*, Ikhtisan, to call his royal patron *Nauman-i-Sani* (the title of Imam Abu Hanifa, the founder of the Hanafi school of law).[140] The little relevant evidence available also suggests that in his personal life the Sultan was almost a puritan, free from all vices; he neither drank nor maintained a large *haram*. He does not seem to have married more than once. Equally interesting are the allusions, direct and indirect, made by the great contemporary Sufi saint Shaikh Sharafuddin Maneri about the Sultan in that we find the latter a thinker in quest of religious truth. The Shaikh writes in one of his epistles addressed to his *murid*, Qazi Shamsuddin: '[Sultan] Muhammad Shah can say whatever he likes to Khwaja Jahan (the *wazir*), but if you or I were to say what he says, our heads would not remain attached to our bodies.'[141] In another epistle, he remarks, 'Every day you walk pompously out of some school and enter a cloister in order that your cap of lordship, as well as the beginnings of piety, knowledge, and rank (state of spiritual excellence) might become higher and more exalted.'[142]

Unlike the aforesaid writers, Indian as well as foreign, the upholders of Islamic orthodoxy in general seem to have been hostile to the Sultan in regard to his religious policy. They publicly denigrated him as the enemy of Islam and were charged with having incited rebellions. Amongst them were included the *fuqha* (scholars of canon law), Saiyids, and Sufi saints; the Sultan had them executed, showing no regard for their birth or social status.[143] But Isami and the Sufi Shaikh, Gesudaraz would have us believe that those whom the Sultan had murdered were innocent people and that the Sultan was fond of shedding Muslim blood. Isami contemptuously calls the Sultan a philosopher who had lost faith in Islam and turned hostile against its followers.[144] Saiyid Muhammad Gesudaraz is reported to have said after the death of the Sultan that he wanted to claim Prophethood for himself. The following statement is found contained in his *Malfuzat* (collection of utterances):

Maulana Kamaluddin, the sister's son of my preceptor (Shaikh Nasiruddin Chiragh-i-Dilli), told: Once late in the evening, we were studying *Bazdawi* under the guidance of Qazi Shamsuddin, the brother of Qutlugh Khan. In the meantime, Qutlugh Khan sent for him (the Qazi). He (i.e. the Qazi) asked us to stay and wait. On his return, the Maulana said: 'Listen to what the great Khan (Qutlugh Khan) told me: He was summoned by the Sultan to the palace. As he entered the royal chamber, he found the Sultan seated in the dark at a distance from the torch and lost in thought. He made the customary obeisance and sat down. (Then the Maulana said), 'I was worried, thinking that he wants either my brother or someone of my dependants to be killed but hesitates to tell me out of respect'. All of a sudden, the Sultan raised a query: 'If a man comes up and declares that Muhammad was not the Prophet but I am, how would you argue to prove his claim false?' I thought if I argue, he would also argue and the discussion would be prolonged, so I should rather say something that would make him realize the impossibility of him attaining to that status (Prophethood). Therefore, I said: 'There would be no need to have any argument with such a mad and stupid fellow because the power and authority of the Sultan is so well established that in the city even the slaves of the caterers and cooks would kill him with their breeches. Thereupon, the Sultan bowed his head and kept quiet.' Maulana Shamsuddin said: 'I asked (the Khan) if the ill-fated Sultan makes such a claim, how would you respond?' He said in reply that he would be the first to revolt against him. The Sultan held him (the Khan) in high esteem. Malik Mansur, the father of Malik Sad Mansur, was also shown great respect. Once the Sultan said to him: 'What did Abu Bakr and Osman do that he could not do?' Malik Mansur retorted that they were pious people, implying that the Sultan was impure. The Sultan got infuriated and used vituperative language. The Malik kept quiet.

Moreover, the Sultan had the *Mashaikh* (Sufi saints), *ulama*, Saiyids, and men of religion murdered, owing to his heretical views. His aim was to get all those eliminated who held religion dear to their heart. Instead, the Sultan gathered around him the Hindus and slaves who were not different from Hindus, so that they might obey and carry out whatever he ordered them. But he met his death before he could fulfil his desire. As his end arrived, the angel of death was ordered to take away his soul. (Soon after) the angel submitted: O my Lord! I have taken away the souls of notorious infidels, adulterers, and great sinners, but the stench from the mouth of this ill-fated man prevents me from reaching him.' Thereupon, God asked him to get it done by one of his assistants. Again, the angel told God that none of his assistants had the courage to reach him. At last, the Devil was sent to take away his soul.[145]

Either all this is a figment of the Shaikh's imagination or else it is based on propaganda started by the late Sultan's opponents to tarnish his image and bolster the position of his successor. We know that the intelligence service was so elaborate and effective that the remarks made by nobles and others even in the privacy of their homes were reported to the Sultan, as will be discussed later. Qutlugh Khan's brothers occupied important positions in the bureaucracy; none of them would cause the ruin of his family by telling his students about such delicate matters. It is to be recalled that the Sultan could tolerate criticism and every variety of opinion. In such a case, criticism or adverse opinion expressed by someone did not mean defiance of his administrative orders. He read the comments made by Shaikh Sharafuddin Maneri on his pursuit of philosophy and having been impressed by his epistles, he requested him to write something on spirituality for him. In reply, the Shaikh addressed the Sultan as 'my brother' and politely expressed his inability to write more than what had already been put down in the *Maktubat-i-Sadi*: 'Realize, my brother, that the knowledge of this group (i.e. the Sufis) is extremely precious and exalted, and cannot be contained in letters and words.'[146] Sultan Muhammad bin Tughluq was bold enough to confess that at an early stage he had passed through a state of scepticism. He wrote in a letter: 'Doubts cropped up about the existence even of the Creator. They agitated the mind, causing grief. Ultimately, the truth dawned, the attributes of God became perceptible, and the mind was convinced of the existence of Almighty God. The faith in the Prophethood which leads man to God was revived.'[147] As a matter of fact, the Sultan was ahead of his time and the *ulama* were unable to comprehend the significance of the progressive ideas and conceptions emerging during the reign of the enlightened Sultan.

Also important for discussion is the impact of the religious policy of the Sultan on the Sultanate's polity. The treatises produced in India and other Muslim countries on statecraft suggest that the close interrelationship between religion and politics, and between the order of law and the order of belief, had created deeply complex religio-political controversies among the Muslim elite. The *ulama* desired to have a system patterned on the model of the Prophet and his immediate successors, the pious caliphs. But those who gave serious thought to the problem, especially the political thinkers, thought differently. Ibn Sina (d. AD 1037), whose works inspired the Sultan,[148] considered a philosopher-king with a strong personality an ideal king, because from his political behaviour results in peace, stability, and prosperity for the country. Like his Muslim predecessors Ibn Sina regarded the *sharia* as the form of instruction to be taken by the ruler as the consummation of perfection partially attainable by the exercise of human reason or as a rule to fall back upon when man's sense of natural fellowship fails him. Strangely enough, Imam Ibn Taimiya (1226–1327), who was a protagonist of the strictest orthodox view, had of necessity to reconcile himself to the need and advise his co-religionists to cooperate with the Sultan, whose existence was thought necessary for the maintenance of law and order. He writes in his treatise *Al-Hisba fil-Islam*:

None of mankind can attain to complete welfare, either in this world or in the next, except by association (*ijma*), cooperation, and mutual aid. Their cooperation and mutual aid is for the purpose of acquiring things of benefit to them, and their mutual aid is also for the purpose of warding off things injurious to them. For this reason, it is said that 'Man is a political being by nature'. But when they unite together there must of necessity be certain things which they do to secure their welfare and certain other things which they avoid because of the mischief which lies in them, and they will render obedience to the one who commands them to the attainment of those objects and restrains them from those actions of evil consequence. Moreover, all mankind must of necessity render obedience to a commander and restrainer. Those who are not possessed of divine books or who are not followers of any religion yet obey their kings in regard to those matters wherein they believe that their worldly interests lie, sometimes rightly, sometimes wrongly.[149]

He also suggested that for a sound system of governance, the *sharia* should be made the basis for the framing of rules and regulations.

Ibn Taimiya's contemporary in India, Barani, also a political thinker who was associated with Sultan Muhammad bin Tughluq as his *nadim* (councellor and courtier), places due emphasis on the need for the Sultan to formulate rules and regulations regardless of the *sharia* but in accordance with the requirements of changed time. Barani's treatise *Fatwa-i-Jahandari* is free from didactic elements, and his approach to the problem herein is that of a rationalist thinker.[150] Much concerned with the needs of his own world of the Delhi Sultanate, he appears to have held views in blunt opposition to the Muslim theological view regarding the doctrine of causality in history. Having mentioned the patterns of political behaviour displayed by the preceding Muslim rulers of Iran and Central Asia, he emphatically states that the Prophetic tradition can no longer be followed in managing the affairs of state. According to him, the first four pious caliphs belonged to the age of the Prophet and they followed him faithfully, but the change of time in his own days had made it necessary for the Sultan to formulate new rules and regulations in the interests of the state and the people.[151] Barani's advocacy of framing new rules and regulations in view of the changed time seems to have appealed to Sultan Muhammad bin Tughluq, who rewarded him with the post of his *nadim*.

As regards Sultan Muhammad bin Tughluq, he wanted to act as the exponent of the essence of the Prophetic tradition in formulating rules and regulations. But he was against taking the tradition literally under the changed conditions. Barani tells us in the first version of the *Tarikh* that he wanted to combine in himself the functions of the Caliph of the Prophet (*Khilafat-i-*

Nubuwat) and the office of the Sultan. Barani also tells us that the Sultan wanted the diffusion of the essence of the Prophetic tradition (*sunna*) from his capital in other Islamic countries.[152] It is worth mentioning that the Sultan calls himself on his coins *Muhy-i-Sunan Khatim al-Nabiyin* (Reviver of the Traditions of the Prophet). If this claim made by the Sultan on the coins is read in conjunction with Barani's first version where the Sultan's desire to link khilafat with kingship is mentioned, it would imply that he wanted to assume for himself the role of a *mujtahid* (interpreter of law) in accordance with the needs of the time. But the orthodoxy came in his way; for its members any deviation from the established tradition was a revolt against religion. The *ulama* believed in a strict adherence to the Hanafi law, interpreted by their predecessors in foreign lands long before them. The Hanafi law was the state law. They opposed the Sultan and issued *fatwas* (religious decrees) justifying rebellion against him.[153] The *ulama* and the Sufis who opposed the Sultan were charged with treason and punished like other offenders. Ibn Battuta mentions them in detail and says that they were executed after they had confessed their crime in the court of the *qazi*.[154] Ibn Battuta also bears testimony to the fact that the Sultan went out of his way to establish the rule of law. He writes about his sense of justice:

> One of the Hindu chiefs brought a claim against him (the Sultan) that he had killed the chief's brother without just cause, and cited him to appear before the *qazi*. Whereupon he went on foot and unarmed to the *qazi's* tribunal, saluted, and made the sign of homage. The Sultan kept standing and the *qazi* gave judgement against him. The chief got the price of his brother's blood and then forgave the Sultan.[155]

This is an interesting piece of information showing that all were equal in the eyes of *sharia* law. Ibn Battuta mentions the cases of a number of *ulama*, Saiyids, and Sufis who were found guilty of siding with the rebels. They were arrested and executed by the order of the *qazis* after they had confessed their crimes.[156]

A word may be added here about the Sultan's policy towards non-Muslims in general and Hindus in particular. The Sultan not only followed his predecessors in fashioning friendly relations with Hindu chiefs but also appears to have been the first Muslim ruler to participate in Hindu festivals in order to bridge the gap between the royal court and the Hindus. Though disdainful in his references to the Sultan's interaction with Hindus, Isami states: 'He (the Sultan) celebrates with Hindus the festival of Holi, is fond of the company of the Hindu jogis (*yogis*), and shows regard for their religion.'[157] Moreover, the Hindus were financially helped in maintaining their places of worship. An invaluable Sanskrit inscription sheds light on this matter. It belongs to the period when Malik Gurshasp, the cousin of the Sultan, revolted in Sagar.[158] Some of the followers of Gurshasp did damage to the temple of Madhukesvara. After the suppression of the rebellion, the *wazir*, Khwaja Jahan, whom the Sultan had deputed to restore order, helped the custodians of the temple to reinstall the deity (Shivlinga). He also made a proclamation on behalf of the Sultan that as worship in the temple was the religious duty of the people, it would be allowed without any hindrance.[159]

Equally important is the inscription dated1385 VS (corresponding AD 1328) from Batihagarh (district Muh in Madhya Pradesh). It informs us about the construction of a cow temple (*gau math*) along with a step-well, surrounded by a garden, by the order of Sultan Muhammad bin Tughluq. The officer under whose charge the place fell is mentioned as Hussamuddin, son of Malik Zulchi.[160] It tends to show that the Sultan made no distinction between Hindu and Muslim places of worship in regard to land grant or financial aid for their maintenance. Likewise, the inscription in Persian and Sanskrit from Karakhdi (in Padra taluka in Baroda district) dated AH 740 (1339) is worth quoting in that we find information about the permeation of the culture of shared values in Gujarat also. The Sultan is mentioned in the inscription as the Khalifa of the world along with Malik Muzaffar, the governor of the territorial unit of Baroda. The latter was ordered by the Sultan to have a mosque and well constructed and to endow a part of revenue for their upkeep. It is noteworthy that the village official, Moka Mehta (a Hindu), son of Kita Mehta, was appointed the trustee of the endowment.[161]

Like the Hindus, the Jains and the Shi'i Muslims also received friendly treatment from the Sultan. Since Agha Mehdi Hasan has discussed the patronage extended by the Sultan to Jains in detail, I need not repeat it here.[162] As regards the Shi'is, they seem to have remained underground since the assassination by the Ismaili

Shia agents of Sultan Miuzuddin Muhammad bin Sam, as already discussed. Sultan Muhammad bin Tughluq lifted the ban on Shi'ism and encouraged its followers to migrate to India. They were appointed to important posts in the Sultanate. Ikhtisan states that the Jafari faith (i.e. the Shi'i creed) began to bloom as a result of his ascent to power.[163] Ibn Battuta's testimony is of importance; according to him many Shi'is came from Iraq and Hejaz and were rewarded with money. Most of them served in the Deccan. Many of them took up residence in Delhi as well.[164]

Also worth reconsidering is the problem related to the revolt of *amiran-i-sada*. Their revolt resulted in a serious conflict within the nobility and shook the foundation of the Sultanate during the last years of the reign. Our sources of information do not specify the position and function of the *amir-i-sada* in the administrative set-up. Mention made by Ibn Battuta of *sadi* in place of *pargana*,[165] an administrative-cum-fiscal unit, composed of a number of villages, gives the impression that each *sadi* had a military commandant called *amir-i-sada*. But Ibn Battuta does not mention him in the *sadi* of Hindpat where he was assigned the revenue of its two and a half villages. He says that the *sadi* is managed by a chaudhri, a Hindu, and a *mutassarif* who is a Musalman.[166] Neither Ibn Battuta nor any Indo-Persian writer ever mentions any *amir-i-sada* as having operated in any northern territorial unit. The circumstantial evidence and the general impression suggest that this post was created in the provinces of Malwa, Gujarat, and south India, which were not stabilized provinces like those in the north. The *amiran-i-sada* were required to help the revenue officers because of the presence of powerful land chiefs there. The provinces in north India could be managed by civil officers like Ratan Barber, Aziz Khumar, and Ain-ul-Mulk Mahru. Ain-ul-Mulk Mahru is mentioned by Barani as an honest and competent non-military officer who had endeared himself both to the Sultan and the people. He held the governorship of the combined provinces of Awadh and Zafarabad.[167] It was after the consolidation of his rule in the southern provinces[168] that the Sultan decided to deny the *amiran-i-sada* participation in revenue collection because they were reported to have started indulging in corruption and defying royal authority.[169] In 1345, the Sultan reorganized the administrative units into four *shiqqs* (extensive territorial units) and appointed a governor in each with orders to implement the new rules and regulations and collect revenue on the enhanced rate. The governors were Malik Mukhlis ul-Mulk, Malik Yusuf Bughra, Malik Sar Dawatdar, and Aziz Khumar. The latter was transferred from the territorial unit of Amroha. Besides, Imad ul-Mulk Sartez was transferred from Multan to Daulatabad as the *wazir* (or viceroy) in place of Qutlugh Khan.[170] Apart from Yusuf Bughra and Imad ul-Mulk, none of them seems to have had fighting experience or proper military training. Another bureaucrat without any military training, Maulana Nizamuddin entitled Alim Malik, the brother of Qutlugh Khan, was ordered to proceed from Bharoach (Broach) to Daulatabad and look after the affairs of the Deccan until the arrival of Imad ul-Mulk Sartez there.[171]

Aziz Khumar was assigned the combined charge of the province (*arsa*) of Malwa and the newly created *shiqq* of Deogiri region, adjoining Malwa. At the time of his departure from the capital, the Sultan addressed him: 'Aziz, do you see that there is an outbreak of disturbance and trouble? I know that the rebel counts upon the support of the *sada amirs*. They join him out of greed for loot and plunder. You would keep a watch upon them.' Aziz Khumar, having reached Dhar (the capital of Malwa), summoned the *amiran-i-sada*, blamed them for sedition, and killed eighty-nine of them. Some of them were renowned warriors and belonged to the *Hashm-i-Dhar*. Aziz Khumar could not understand, says Barani, that his action taken in haste would make the *amiran-i-sada* of the neighbouring provinces apprehensive, and that they would join hands and rise in revolt. Consequently, the Sada Amirs of Gujarat and Deogiri rose in rebellion. In Gujarat, they killed the officers and seized the treasure and horses being carried to Delhi.[172] It may be pointed out that so far the rebels who had arisen in different provinces from time to time were individuals and none of them appears to have received military support from his fellow nobles. The case of the *sada amirs* was quite different; their rebellion forced the Sultan to command the army against them in person.

Having realized the gravity of the situation, the Sultan decided to lead the expedition against the rebels in person. Barani says that Qutlugh Khan, the preceptor of the Sultan, sent a message to the Sultan through him stating that the Sultan should not march against the *amiran-i-sada* (of Gujarat) because they were small fry; they would be frightened by the Sultan's arrival and run away to the neighbouring provinces and instigate the *sada amirs* to join them in rebellion, and that if he was ordered to deal with them, he would persuade them to submit. He would bring them to the capital like the rebels Shihab Sultani and Ali Shah (Khalji). The Sultan did not agree to this suggestion. But it was not that easy. The rebels had committed grave crimes. They were guilty of killing officers and plundering important places, including Cambay, the principal seaport of the Sultanate. The Sultan knew that none of his nobles was fit to fight against the rebels. Only he could provide leadership to the army against the rebels, among whom were included veteran warriors. He ordered the army to march.[173]

At the halt in Sultanpur, about 30 miles from Delhi, the Sultan received the petition of Aziz Khumar to the effect: 'The *sada amirs* of Dahboi and Baroda have raised a tumult and are in revolt, and as I am present in the nearby region, I shall organize the army of Dhar and march for their suppression.' This upset the Sultan. He realized that Aziz did not know how to conduct the battle and could be killed. In the meantime, the news was received of his defeat and murder.[174] The details furnished by Isami show that the Sultan's apprehension proved to be correct. According to Isami, neither Maqbal, the deputy governor of Gujarat, nor Aziz Khumar could face the rebels successfully. Aziz Khumar commanded 6,000 sawars while the rebels were only 700 in number. The rebels were defeated. When they took to flight, Jalal Afghan, one of their leaders, hid himself in a cotton field with fourteen companions. As the troops of the royal army busied themselves in pursuit, Jalal Afghan found Aziz Khumar with a few followers; he sallied out from the field and fell on him. In the meantime, Jalal's companions, Jhalhu Afghan and some others, also turned back, arrested Aziz Khumar, killed him, and plundered his camp.[175]

As expected, the Sultan's arrival demoralized the rebels. The loyal nobles who had shut themselves up in the fortresses were encouraged. The rebels were defeated and killed in large numbers. Some of them were killed by the Hindu land chiefs; only a few escaped and joined the rebels in the Deccan.[176] After the defeat of the rebels, their well-wishers and moral supporters were ordered to be found out and punished. Honest judges and jurists were appointed to enquire into the allegations and when the guilt of a person was proved, he was dealt out punishment. Even the popular Sufi saints like Shaikh Ali Haidari (a qalandar Sufi) were killed in accordance with the judgement delivered by the judges.[177] Those of the *ulama* who sought shelter in the Deccan seem to have incited the people to oppose the Sultan with a vengeance. Isami, who writes as the spokesman of the opposition, states: 'The Emperor, being the friend of the mean and hostile to the faith, has gone astray from the path of religion. Annoyed with him, the people are in revolt and the doctors of law have declared his destruction lawful.'[178]

In the Deccan, the rebels elected Makh Afghan, a man of culture and experience, as their Sultan; the latter assumed the title of Sultan Nasiruddin.[179] The rebels defeated the officers posted in Daulatabad, and seized the treasure and the city. Informed about the situation, the Sultan marched from Gujarat against the rebels. The supporters of Makh Afghan were defeated and he took shelter in the inner fortress of Daulatabad, called Dharagir, and erected on top of a hillock. He was left with a few hundred *sawars*. The Sultan was determined to destroy the rebels in the entire region of the Deccan. But the rebellion of Targhi (a Turk slave) in Gujarat diverted the Sultan's attention to Gujarat.[180] On his departure from Daulatabad, the rebels rallied round Hasan Gango and succeeded in destroying the nobles left by the Sultan in Daulatabad and in other territories. As regards the Sultan, he chased Targhi from Gujarat to Sind. In Sind, the Samma chief, Jam Unar I, was also in revolt. Targhi joined him in Thatta. The Sultan started operations in Sind but fell ill and died in 1351. Before he died, he said to Barani: 'People are hostile to me, although I have given them so much. No one considers me his well-wisher. I know it for certain that they have become my enemies.'[181]

In conclusion, it may be said that the history of the reign is marked by political crises caused by the Sultan's religious and state policies. The religious elite followed tradition blindly and opposed the Sultan vehemently when he acted as the interpreter of the canon law in order to update it. The development-oriented schemes framed by the Sultan looked fantastic, and even the officers defied the royal orders with regard to their implementation. This led to their punishment.[182] Barani rightly observes that if the progressive ideas conceived and the schemes framed had been implemented, the results would have been good and economic growth would have been possible.[183] Doubtless, the period of his reign was marked by rebellions and the failure of his projects.[184] The Sultan was at least successful in his foreign policy; diplomatic and trade relations were established with different countries, and the frontiers of the Sultanate became secure with the acknowledgement of his suzeranity by the rulers of Herat and Ghazna.[185] It is also noteworthy that with the Sultan's death, the Sultanate polity underwent change; it was decentralized both in the Bahmani kingdom and the Sultanate of Delhi.[186]

III

It is well known that the succession of Firuz Shahi to the throne took place in an abnormal situation in Sind. Yet the question to be addressed is whether he was ever declared by Sultan Muhammad bin Tughluq his heir apparent, as Barani would have us believe. The relevant evidence contained in the sources, though brief and laconic, about the reaction against Muhammad bin Tughluq's political behaviour and the response of the ruling elite to his successor needs to be analysed more closely than has been done before. Barani seems to have been with the Sultan in Sind. But his account of the last days of his royal patron's life, particularly with regard to the succession issue, is marred by inconsistency. In the details of the military campaigns led by the Sultan in person against the rebels of Gujarat and the Deccan, he says that Malik Kabir and Khwaja Jahan acted as regents in Delhi during the Sultan's absence. Upon the victory achieved by the Sultan against the rebels in Daulatabad, the regents sent Barani to convey their greetings, petitions, and *khidmati* (offering) on their behalf to the Sultan. The Sultan was pleased and showered his favours upon him.[187] He further informs us that he accompanied the Sultan from place to place and the latter would discuss the state problems with him even in the course of the journey. Once the Sultan told him that his country had fallen ill and that it was difficult to find a cure for its illness; if it was treated for a particular disease, it would soon catch some other disease. He is also supposed to have told Barani that he would divide sovereignty between Malik Kabir, Khwaja Jahan, and Firuz Shah and leave on pilgrimage for Arabia after the disturbances had been pacified.[188] Again, he states in the account of Firuz Shah's reign that the Sultan selected three persons to rule over the Sultanate after him. They were Malik Kabir, Khwaja Jahan, and Firoz Shah. Of them Malik Kabir died in the lifetime of the Sultan, while the second nominee, Khwaja Jahan, was disqualified on account of his old age; he was more than eighty years old. Firuz Shah was, therefore, declared by the Sultan his successor.[189] Barani seems to have invented this story after his release from prison because he wanted to flatter Firuz Shah and save himself from the ostracism that he had to face.[190]

As a matter of fact, the events that look place after Malik Kabir's death and Khwaja Jahan's return from the royal camp to Delhi as regent have been described by Barani halfway. Barani states that in 1349, Firuz Shah was summoned to the camp in Sind along with certain dignitaries, including the *ulama*, the *mashaikh*, and the families of the nobles, but he is silent about the reason behind the episode. However, if the hints and allusions made by him regarding the issue of succession before the death of Muhammad bin Tughluq are pieced together and examined, it becomes clear that the Sultan wanted to nominate as his successor someone from amongst his nobles, emulating the tradition set by the first two caliphs of Islam.

Ibn Battuta directly and Barani indirectly provide us with hints about the preferential treatment given by Sultan Muhammad bin Tughluq to Malik Kabir and Khwaja Jahan. Being the premier noble, Malik Kabir was granted the privilege of standing behind the throne of the Sultan with a fly-whisk in his hand to drive off the flies.[191] Ibn Battuta further says that he stood high in the Sultan's esteem and enjoyed immense prestige and vast wealth.[192] Barani writes that none of the Sultan's nobles equaled Malik Kabir in status at court. The Sultan raised him over and above the others, made him the representative of the caliph, and addressed him as Qabul-i-Khalifati (i.e. the favourite of the caliph). He was originally a slave but became an exemplar in righteousness, magnanimity, piety, humanism, large-hearted generosity, wisdom, knowledge of state affairs and experience in conducting the government, and possessed an angelic nature. He acted as *naib* in the absence of the Sultan because of the ruler's confidence in him.[193]

The evidence found in the contemporary Sufi literature also needs to be examined as it tends to reveal that the Sultan was hostile to all of them, including Shaikh Nasiruddin, the spiritual successor of Shaikh Nizamuddin Auliya. Besides Firuz Shah, the *ulama*, etc., Shaikh Nasiruddin (Chiragh-i-Dilli) was also summoned to Thatta; his followers were worried and prayed for his survival. Shaikh Muhammad Gesudaraz says that his preceptor, Shaikh Nasiruddin, asked him at the time of his departure for Thatta to pay a visit to the shrine of Shaikh Qutbuddin Bakhtiyar (Kaki) and pray there daily.[194]

Of the later historians, Abdul Qadir Badaoni writes, obviously on the basis of some early source, that Firuz Shah was declared the Sultan in place of Sultan Muhammad by Shaikh Nasiruddin and others. When the Sultan received news about it in Gondal on his way to Sind, he ordered Firuz and his supporters to be arrested and brought to the camp. In Sind, they were sentenced to death but survived because the Sultan himself passed away before their execution.[195] Though Shaikh Nasiruddin's inclusion amongst the supporters of Firuz Shah is not acceptable because the Shaikh avoided taking an interest in such matters, spirituality always remained a serious concern to him. It is, however, possible that some visitors to his *khanqah* or his murids were involved in a conspiracy, hatched when Delhi was left without a ruler after the death of Malik Kabir and before the arrival of Khwaja Jahan. Ibn Battuta's testimony in this regard is significant. In his account of the execution of Shaikh Shihabuddin al-Jam, Ibn Battuta tells us that even the visitors to the Shaikh Jam's *khanqah* were suspected, put under arrest, and then an enquiry was instituted into whether they harboured enmity towards the Sultan. Ibn Battuta himself was put under house arrest because he also had once visited Shaikh Jam's *khanqah*. He survived, for nothing was found against him.[196] It may also be added that as the journey was arduous and the Shaikh was quite aged by this time, his friends are reported to have asked him to seek divine help against the Sultan. The Shaikh said in reply: 'It is meritorious religiously to bear hardship rather than enjoy the comforts of life.' He further said: 'Sultan Muhammad Tughluq is the sapling nurtured by my *pir*. It is not good for me to wish him disaster. It is not good and would be a cause of harm (to me).'[197]

It is also noteworthy that of the historians contemporary with Sultan Firuz Shah whose works are extant, neither Barani nor the anonymous compiler of the *Sirat-i-Firuz Shahi*, mentions any surviving son or grandson of Sultan Ghiyasuddin Tughluq Shah. Because Barani wanted to please the reigning Sultan at any cost, while the other appears to have been an official historian expected only to highlight the good works of Firuz Shah. Only Shams Siraj Afif, who wrote after the dissolution of the Sultanate and was nostalgic, mentions Dawar Malik, the son of Sultan Ghiyasuddin Tughluq's daughter. He and his mother were in the royal camp in Sind, and she is reported to have claimed the throne for her son but she was silenced by the hostile nobles.[198] Afif was born sometime in the reign of Firuz Shah and does not appear to have been interested in mentioning those princes who did not question Firuz Shah's succession and disappeared from the scene unmourned and unsung. Mention made by Ibn Battuta of the Sultan's brother, Mubarak Khan, and one nephew leaves no doubt about the concealment of the fact concerning the succession crisis. According to Ibn Battuta, Mubarak Khan and his nephew moved in the royal procession ahead of Firuz Shah in order of precedence.[199] In fact, mention made by a contemporary writer of any direct descendant would have incurred the displeasure of the reigning Sultan and his supporters.

As regards Khwaja Jahan's (Ahmad bin Ayaz's) opposition to Firuz Shah, the main cause was his faithfulness to his master's political philosophy and memory. Firuz Shah seems not to have been acceptable to him and a few other nobles present in Delhi for his lack of ability to rule as a Sultan. There is no shred of evidence to show that he ever received military training or was assigned the command of any military campaign, or even participated in any battle before his ascent to power. Nor does he seem to have acquired administrative experience because he is never reported to have been assigned the charge of any province. Afif's statement about his relation with Khwaja Jahan shows that he flattered him and that Khwaja Jahan was considerate to him, so much so that he treated him in a fatherly manner. In short, Firuz Shah seems to have behaved like an unambitious man. Sultan Muhammad bin Tughluq was kind to him and appointed him simply the *naib hajib* at court. His duty was to supervise the arrangement of royal feasts.[200] In short, a general impression formed on the basis of circumstantial evidence is that certain senior nobles who were seriously concerned about the fate of the Sultanate, which by this time looked a world of weal and woe on account of rebellions, could not accept a weakling and a non-entity to head the complex centralized polity. Their apprehension came true when the old *iqta* system was revived, old privileges were conceded to, the assignees and the assignments became hereditary in practice, if not in theory, with the result that the Sultanate polity was completely decentralized.

As long as the nobles present in the capital remained attached to Khwaja Jahan, he did not lose courage. He made preparations for an armed struggle with whatever was left in the royal treasury. As regent, he summoned the governors with the provincial armies but only a few, like Malik Khattab Afghan,[201] appear to have obeyed him. Malik Mahmud Bak, the governor of the province of Sunam and Samana, delayed the compliance on some excuse. But as soon as Firuz Shah entered the territory of Sirsuti (present-day Sirsa), he left his headquarters with the provincial army and rushed to join him. In the capital of Delhi itself, Malik Maqbul, the *naib wazir* and one of the most trusted men of Khwaja Jahan, turned treacherous; he fled along with his sons and sons-in-law, the important nobles, Malik Katbagha, Amir Muhan, and others, and joined Firuz Shah's camp. Their treacherous role dampened the courage of Khwaja Jahan.[202]

It may be pointed out that even before the fall of the opposition in Delhi, some of the most trusted associates of Sultan Muhammad bin Tughluq were placed under arrest just after the accession of Firuz Shah in Sind. Ikhtisan, the *dabir-i-khaṣ* whom Mir Khurd calls a man without faith in Islam, was eliminated and buried in Sind,[203] while Barani was placed under arrest and sent as a prisoner to the fort of Bhatner. He describes his plight in prison:

'I was confined inside the fort of Bhatner where I spent five months in traumatic conditions. When I got up at dawn I worried whether I would survive till the sunset; as it grew dark I had no hope of seeing the dawn the following day.'[204] The other nobles who were killed or put in prison after surrendering by Khwaja Jahan have been mentioned by Barani and other writers. Barani writes, briefly in the first version, obviously to flatter the reigning Sultan in the hope of retrieving his lost position, that Firuz Shah was kind to all. He compares Firuz Shah with his predecessors:

> Although the martyred Sultan (*Shahid Sultan*) Muhammad bin Tughluq Shah was the most remarkable of the Sultans of the past, yet during his reign people were ruined and eliminated or got into prominence and got wealth owing to his paradoxical qualities; all this has not happened since the beginning of the present regime. None has been murdered or harmed, except five or six persons who had allied themselves with Ahmad bin Ayaz in fomenting trouble. They were either eliminated or banished.

In the second revised version, he adds that the great Sultans, like Sultan Iltutmish and Sultan Balban, got their nobles of doubtful loyalty assassinated and their assets declared forfeited to the state exchequer, but that no such incident had happened since the advent of Firuz Shah to power. Only Ahmad (bin) Ayaz, (Malik) Nathu Sondhal, Hussain Adhrang, and two slaves of Ahmad (bin) Ayaz had been killed. Their sons and family members were spared.[205] Yahya Sirhindi adds that Ahmad bin Ayaz was handed over as prisoner to the custody of the *kotwal* of Hansi, while Malik Khattab Afghan and (Malik) Nathu Sondhal were separated from each other and sent as prisoners to Tabarhinda and Sunam respectively. Shaikh Zada Bistami was sent into exile. Hussam Adhrang and Masan were also thrown into prison.[206] Afif tells us on the basis of what he heard from his senior family members that Firuz Shah wanted to forgive Khwaja Jahan but the nobles pressed him to order his execution.[207] Afif also informs us that Sultan Muhammad bin Tughluq's sister who was in the camp claimed the throne for her son on the basis of the law of inheritance, but that she was snubbed and silenced.[208]

With the murder of Khwaja Jahan and the imprisonment of the ardent and faithful followers of Sultan Muhammad bin Tughluq, the era of centralized polity ended and the ruling elite could look forward for that of happier days and its own power.

Let us discuss briefly the changes in the state policy followed by Firuz Shah with a view to impressing upon the people his dislike of and opposition to the system of governance during the preceding regime. Both the *ulama*, their descendants, the sons and grandsons of the thirteenth-century Suhrawardi and Chishti Sufi saints, and the servivors of the Sufi *dargahs* (shrines) were the first recipients of the favour of the new regime.

In the course of his return journey, in every town and city from Sewistan to Delhi, Sultan Firuz Shah only ordered the restoration of land grants, gardens, and villages to the descendants of the *ulama* and Sufi saints because they had long ago been brought under *khalsa*, and the claimants were not considered deserving. In Sewistan (Sehwan), Bhakkar, Uchh, Multan, Depalpur, Ajodhan, and Hansi, the descendants were done a great favour; they not only had their family grants restored to them but were also shown respect. The new claimants were also given land grants and stipends.[209] In an attempt to assure the members of the ruling elite about his dislike for the policy of his immediate predecessor, the foreigners who came from the neighbouring countries, such as Sistan, Khurasan, Aden, and other lands to seek their fortunes in India, were turned back from the frontier.[210]

Since Afif's father and uncle were the foster brothers of Sultan Firuz Shah and he himself enjoyed the royal favour, he writes as a panegyrist. His history of the reign reads like the biography of a Sufi saint, composed by the saint's *murid*.[211] In fact, the socio-economic growth that resulted from the peaceful conditions and the process of urbanization started by Sultan Firuz Shah and his *wazir*, Khan-i-Jahan Maqbool, made him paint him as a blessed ruler. It was, however, the dissolution of the great Sultanate that turned him not only nostalgic but also forced him to build mild criticism of Firuz Shah's policy towards army organization and the nobility. For example, he says, while referring to the revival of the old *iqta* system during Firuz Shah's reign that previously no one was given a village or land in lieu of cash salary. According to reliable sources, Sultan Alauddin (Khalji) was of the view that a village should not be given in lieu of cash salary because in each village two or three hundred men resided and they became attached to the *wajahdar* (the state employee entitled to salary) and that, in case some *wajahdars* united to rise in revolt, they would create a disturbance. For this reason, no one was assigned a village; all the armymen received their pay and allowances in cash from the royal treasury every year. But the doors of benevolence were thrown wide open for the armymen during the reign of Firuz Shah. All the villages, towns, and the extensive territorial units were divided among them. Moreover, if an armyman died, his post and land went to his son; in case there was no son, then any close relation, or even his slave, succeeded.[212] The *iqta* system and the state service became hereditary. On the death of a noble, his son succeeded him in his office and *iqta*. In 1368–9, on Khan Jahan's death, his eldest son, Juna, was granted his title of Khan Jahan (hereafter mentioned as Khan Jahan the younger) and also appointed the *wazir*. He was allowed to inherit his father's large maintenances *iqta* comprising villages, towns (*parganas*), gardens, canals, *bazaars*, and mansions, built at different places. In addition, he was conferred upon, like his father, the privilege of having an umbrella and elephants, previously a royal prerogative. The only condition mentioned in the *farman* concerning his appointment was that he would retain in service the old servants of his father.[213] Likewise, Malik Hussamuddin succeeded his father as the *kotwal* of Delhi.[214] On the death of Zafar Khan, the governor of Gujarat, his son Darya Khan got his father's post with his title of Zafar Khan.[215]

Besides the grant of *iqta* and privileges to the nobles on a hereditary basis, the age-old practice of appointing spies to watch their activities was given up. The intelligence bureau, the functioning of which was so necessary in a centralized polity, became ineffective; indeed if may have been abolished. Barani states that nowhere was any spy seen and that the people have been relieved of their threat.[216] Thus, the freedom from the surveillance of the intelligence officers and spies encouraged the officers to act in an arbitrary manner, and they began to amass wealth by indulging in corruption. It may, however, be conceded that the grant of *iqtas* to the nobles on a permanent basis led to economic progress. The assignees took an interest in the development of their *iqtas* because there was no fear of the transfer of the *iqta* from one individual to another. They became self-contented. The revenue of the *parganas* increased many times the actual yield, assessed at the time of their assignment in *iqta*. For example, describing the misconduct and corruption of Zia ul-Mulk Abu Rija, the auditor general of the Sultanate, Afif says that he took bribes from the assignees and that even the agents of the leading nobles were not spared. They were put in prison on the charges of misappropriation of the surplus that was rightfully supposed to be deposited with the state exchequer. They were not set free unless bribes were paid to him since he was the favourite of the Sultan. The *wazir*, Khan Jahan, the younger did not have the courage to check him. At last, Malik Abdullah, whose servants were also subjected to torture, brought the matter to the notice of the Sultan. When asked to defend himself, Zia ul-Mulk Abu Rija told the Sultan that the revenue accruing from the two *parganas* of Malik Abdullah was much more than he was entitled to, but that no amount had been paid to the state exchequer out of the *fawazil* (surplus). Thereupon, Malik Abdullah said in his defence that owing to the blessing of God in the auspicious reign prosperity had increased so much that the revenue increased ten times everywhere, but that the auditor general was oppressive to all those who did not pay him bribes. The *wazir* and other nobles came to the support of Abdullah. Pressed by the high-ranking nobles, the Sultan dismissed Zia ul-Mulk Abu Rija and handed him over to the custody of the *wazir*.[217]

Also worth mentioning is the writing off the *sondhar* (loan) advanced by Sultan Muhammad bin Tughluq for carrying on cultivation on the wasteland around Delhi. The money given in *sondhar* amounted to seventy lakh *tankas*. Afif adds that after the situation had been brought under control, the chief *yandar* (inspector general) in the *diwan-i-wizarat* brought to the notice of the Sultan that the *sondhar* and the money and valuables distributed by Khwaja Jahan among the citizens of Delhi amounted to two crore *tankas* according to the figures mentioned in the account registers. The Sultan consulted Khan Jahan and sought his advice. The latter said that every new Sultan declared amnesty to all those who had been guilty of default or any such crime. On his advice the *sondhar* and the money distributed by Khwaja Jahan was written off, and the state papers were washed clean under the public gaze. The most abominable act done by Firuz

Shah on the advice of his counsellors was to further tarnish the image of the late Sultan. All the persons and the descendants of those who had been executed or whose body parts had been severed off for various crimes during the preceding regime were approached. They were given money, land, etc., and asked to forgive the late Sultan and sign the letters of forgiveness. These letters were put in a box and placed beside the head of the grave.[218] All this was done to impress upon the people the reaction against the preceding regime and to reassure them that the new regime was the dawn of the era of benevolence.

As regards the composition of the nobility, it does not seem to have undergone any drastic change. Only the induction of foreigners in the nobility was abandoned for the appeasement of the local element. Barani's statement that Firuz Shah employed nobles of noble birth, and that Hindus and Muslims were thus saved from the tyranny of the officers of base stock, is not substantiated by the evidence available in the sources.[219] Barani is inconsistent, particularly in his account of Firuz Shah's reign. Writing in 1357, he laments that by that time the *ajlaf* and *lutran* (people of low origin and base stock) dominated the world.[220] Barani also contradicts himself when he mentions Ikhtiyaruddin Madhu, a barber whom he had met during his imprisonment in Bhatner. Madhu was in-charge of the fort and Barani was amazed to see in his stable thirty horses of good breed, each worth one thousand to two thousand *tankas*.[221] In fact, the nobility became self-perpetuating, with the posts and *iqtas* becoming hereditary in practice. It was towards the close of the reign that Khan Jahan the younger became all powerful and the old Sultan was reduced to a mere figurehead on the throne. The *wazir*, Khan Jahan, began to get his opponents eliminated; this caused discontent among the nobles and the royal slaves, who numbered about one lakh in the capital itself. All of them rallied around Prince Muhammad (son of Firuz Shah), and thus the war of succession began. Khan Jahan who was defeated ran away. He was killed, and Prince Muhammad assumed the title of Sultan Nasiruddin Muhammad Shah even during the lifetime of Firuz Shah. Since by this time the slaves had organized themselves into a pressure group, they turned against the new ruler and also forced him to run away to the hills of Sirmur. After him, the son of Prince Fath Khan was installed in his place. This succession crisis encouraged the governors of the outlying provinces to become independent for all practical purposes. The case of Malik Mufarrah Sultani of Gujarat is a case in point. He was replaced by Sikandar Khan, the favouite of Prince Muhammad. When Sikandar Khan reached Gujarat, he was killed by the followers of Malik Mufarrah Sultani. Soon after, Malik Mufarrah was reconfirmed by Tughluq Shah II as the governor of Gujarat.[222]

Like the nobles, the Hindu land chiefs were also reconciled; they were in revolt, created disturbances, and plundered people along the highways. Barani writes in the first version of the *tarikh* that the class of *rais* (powerful chiefs), *muqaddams*, chaudhries, and *zamindars* was reconciled. They came to pay obeisance and 'used the dust of the royal court as collyrium for their eyes. They presented Tatari horses and other precious gifts, and were rewarded in return with embroidered robes (*zarbaft*), horses of fine breed, and ranks in the nobility. They signed the bonds regarding the payment of half of the revenue of their territories to the centre. The bonds were deposited with the *diwan-i-wizarat*; peace was established.'[223] Barani further informs us in the details of the first Bengal expedition (AD 1353) that on the Sultan's arrival in Awadh, all the *rais*, *rangan*, and *muqaddams* of Hindustan (eastern region) who were in revolt and who did not pay tribute turned up with *sawars* and footmen and joined the expedition against Bengal. Of them, the *rai* of Gorakhpur, a leading and powerful chief, came and paid also obeisance. The *rai* of Kharosa whose *zamindar* area formed a part of the *shiqq* of Awadh also joined the expedition. They were in revolt and did not pay tribute. Now they came with *khidmati* (offerings or presents). The *khidmati*, presented by the *rai* of Gorakhpur included an elephant also. In return, he was showered with royal favours such as the grant of umbrella, crown, a robe made of brocade, and horses of fine breed. The *ranas* among his followers were also dressed with robes of honour. Likewise, the *rai* of Kharosa (now a village in Gonda district in present-day Uttar Pradesh) and his lieutenants, the *muqaddams*, got robes to wear. All of them paid arrears amounting to several lakh *tankas* and signed the documents for the payment of tribute in future. The tribute was fixed and revenue collectors were appointed for their respective territories. Soon after, the *rai* of Tirhut also followed their example.[224]

Also interesting is the documentary evidence about the new policy towards the class of *zamindars*, big as well as small. The *farman* issued in 1353 in the course of the first Bengal expedition contains the proclamation: 'The *zamindars,* amongst whom are included *muqaddams*, *mafruzian*, *malikan*, etc., from the bank of the river Kosi up to the boundary of Lakhnauti (Bengal), who come and join us would be exempted from the payment of revenue (tribute) for the current year. Moreover, the privileges enjoyed by their ancestors during the reign of Sultan Shamsuddin Iltutmish would be restored and the tribute refixed accordingly.' As regards the taxes that were collected in addition to the tribute and which considered harmful were promised to be abolished. It was also proclaimed that anyone amongst the leading men of the area who would join the Sultan would have his estate doubled in reward.[225] This *farman* seems to have evoked a positive response, as discussed earlier. Besides, in the regions of present-day Haryana and Punjab, where irrigation facilities were provided through the construction of canals, the sons of *zamindars* were employed to collect the irrigation tax from the cultivators.[226]

The odd bits of information pieced together dispel the generally held view that Firuz Shah was biased against the Hindus. The *jizya* levied by him on the Brahmans in Delhi city is cited as proof of his hostility towards them. The fact that the Brahmans acted not only as priests but were also the servitors of temples and belonged to different professions should not be lost sight of. It is noteworthy that Isami and Barani use the term *jizya* in the sense of cultivation tax as well.[227] Peter Jackson is right to say that *jizya* was compounded with land tax and, as regards the urban centres, its levy was confined to the city of Delhi alone.[228]

Doubtless, the state policy conceived of by Khan Jahan Maqbool and implemented in the name of Firuz Shah yielded positive results. The expansionist policy was abandoned; only the stabilized provinces of Malwa and Gujarat in the south of Delhi, the *shiqqs* of Sewistan (upper Sind), Multan, Depalpar, and Lahore in the west and the north-west, south Bihar in the east, and the *shiqqs* of Sambhal and Saharanpur in the north were retained within the frontiers of the Sultanate. All efforts were made for the conservation of resources, with the result that socio-economic growth became possible. The burden of taxes was alleviated and irrigation facilities augmented; agriculture and horticulture made great progress.[229] It was certainly the outcome of the ferment of thought and possibility created by Sultan Muhammad bin Tughluq. A favourite noble of Sultan Muhammad bin Tughluq, Khan Jahan Maqbool appears to have been influenced by the Sultan's development-oriented policies. He implemented them with modification during Firuz Shah's reign. However, in the long run, the decentralized polity weakened the foundations of the Sultanate of Delhi. The tendency among the land chiefs to stop the payment of tribute to the centre and defy the central power revived during the last years of the reign. Even the land chiefs of the Doab, which formed the hinterland of the capital itself, began to defy the centre. After Firuz Shah's death in 1388, the Sultanate polity fractured into regional sultanates and principalities. The governors declared their independence and founded new ruling dynasties in the provinces. This was the result of Firuz Shah's policy, which led the contemporary Firdausi Sufi Shaikh Muzaffar Balkhi (d. 400) to warn Sultan Ghiyasuddin Azam Shah of Bengal, who emulated Firuz Shah in befriending the land chiefs and elevating them to ministerial positions in the Sultanate. The land chiefs were assigned important posts and assigned *iqtas* in lieu of cash salary. Referring to the dissolution of the Sultanate of Delhi, the Shaikh wrote to the Sultan of Bengal: In spite of its vast length and breadth, peace and resources (the Delhi Sultanate) has disappeared. Thereafter, he also wrote to the Sultan that the interest of the Muslim nobles who were a source of strength for him should not be sacrificed for the sake of the land chiefs because the latter possessed their own territories where their writ ran large.[230]

Lastly, it may be noted that the Sultan who occupied the throne with the support of powerful nobles had to share with them his power in order to keep them satisfied. The land assignment in *iqtas* carried with it the right of the assignee to rule over its inhabitants; this was a source of prestige, and he was able to live in a kingly style.

It was really the charm of the *iqta* system that led the founder of the Bahmani Sultanate to assign territorial units in *iqtas* to the nobles in the Deccan in lieu of cash salary because he wanted to alienate them from the Sultan of Delhi. He organized his court on the pattern of the Delhi Sultan; the title of Khwaja Jahan was conferred upon his *wazir* while the *amir-i-ariz* got the title of Imad ul-Mulk. In emulating their Sultan, the nobles also distributed villages and land among their lieutenants and *sawars* as *iqtas* in lieu of cash payment of their pay and allowances.[231] The models of centralized and decentralized polity developed in the Sultanate of Delhi during the thirteenth and fourteenth centuries retained their appeal. They provided a cultural reference point to the rulers of the regional Sultanates that arose after the disintegration of the Delhi Sultanate. It was during the sixteenth century that again efforts were made by Sultan Ibrahim Lodi and Sher Shah Sur to revive the centralized polity.[232]

NOTES

1. Amir Khusrau, *Tughluqnama*, ed. Saiyid Hashmi Faridabadi, Aurangabad, 1933, pp. 137–8.
2. Ibn Battuta, *The Travels of Ibn Batuta*, Eng. tr. Sir Hamilton Gibb, Cambridge, 1971, vol. III, p. 605.
3. Cf. Chapter 9, 'Waterworks and Irrigation System', in this volume.
4. Mention made by the anonymous compiler of the *Sirat-i-Firuz Shahi* of the fortified town of Ghazipur in upper Sind tends to suggest that it was founded by Ghazi Malik before AD 1306. Cf. Anonymous, *Sirat-i-Firuz Shahi*, Facsimile of the rare MS., Khuda Bakhsh Oriental Public Library, Patna, 1999, p. 84.
5. Isami mentions Ghazi Malik as one of the companions of Malik Naik in the battle. Khusrau and Barani describe the battle fought under the command of Malik Naik, but do not refer to the other Indian participants. *Futuh-us-Salatin*, pp. 302–4; Amir Khusrau, *Khazain-ul-Futuh*, Eng. tr., pp 26–8; Barani, p. 320.
6. Barani, p. 323.
7. *Tughlaqnama*, p. 84.
8. Ibid., p. 128.
9. *Futuh-us-Salatin*, p. 378.
10. *Tughluqnama*, p. 138.
11. Amir Khusrau mentions him as Malik Fakhruddaula, while Barani writes that he was known as Malik Fakhruddin Juna. *Tughluqnama*, p. 38, Barani, p. 411.
12. Rampur MS., p. 260; in the second revised edition only the name of Ghazi Malik occurs. Cf. Barani, p. 411.
13. His name has not been mentioned by any contemporary writer. He

resided in Delhi as his father's representative at court in accordance with the custom.

14. *Tughluqnama*, pp. 38, 41, 43; *Futuh-us-Salatin*, pp. 376–8; Barani, pp. 314–16.
15. Cf. *Tughluqnama*, pp. 62, 63, 64, 68–72.
16. *Tughluqnama*, pp. 143–4; Barani, p. 423, *Futuh-us-Salatin*, p. 388; also Agha Mahdi Husain, *Tughluq Dynasty*, Calcutta, 1963, pp. 48–9.
17. Even before his appointment as Governor of Depalpur and Lahore province he had governed the provinces of Sind and Multan. After its sack by Mongols in 1241, Lahore ceased to be an important place. Sultan Balban rebuilt its fort and included it in the territorial unit of Multan. Sultan Alauddin Khalji created a new unit of Depalpur out of the *vilayet* of Multan that included the former unit of Lahore also.
18. Highlighting his sense of duty and love for justice, Barani states that during his career as a noble he served in different provinces and that in each one he exerted to his utmost for the prosperity of people. The canals were dug, gardens laid out, towns founded and buildings of public utility constructed, the desolate villages were rehabilitated and dead land was again bought under plough. Barani, pp. 441–2.
19. Ibid., pp. 430–1.
20. It is painful for me to point out that my friend, late S.B.P. Nigam's work on the nobility of the Sultanate suffers from confusion and misleading interpretation of the source material. The changes that took place in the Sultanate polity from time to time did not receive adequate attention, moreover, ambiguity is marked in his observations at different places. For example, it is not clear what he wants to make out when he observers [*sic*] 'The dearth of the hereditary nobles which during the reign of the Ilbaris had forced the Sultans to choose influential members of the bureaucracy out of a band of trusted slaves and domestic servants had long withered away and a hereditary class had gradually stepped into the arena of politics.' He would also have us believe that the descendants of the officers were allowed to succeed them after their passing away on the basis of their hereditary rights such under the Khaljis and the first two Tughluq Sultans. There is no shred of evidence to substantiate it before the reign of Firuz Shah. Cf. S.B.P. Nigam, *Nobility Under the Sultans of Delhi*, Delhi, 1968, pp. 16, 17.
21. In the first version of the *Tarikh*, Barani refers to this unit as Sewistan instead of *arsa-i-Sind*. The unit of Sewistan was carved out by Sultan Alauddin out of the principality of the Muslim Sumra chief of Sind. The Sultan being annoyed by the powerful land chiefs in north India for their defiance of the Central authority, reduced them in power and resources by depriving them of half or more than a half of the ancestral territory. Rampur MS. pp. 268–9.

22. Probably Malik Gurshasp held the charge of the *diwan-i-ariz* for a short time because in the details of the reforms introduced by Tughluq Shah, Barani mentions Khwaja Haji of the time of Alauddin Khalji as the head of the *diwan-i-ariz* as will be discussed subsequently. Barani, p. 428.
23. The territorial unit, mentioned as *iqta-i-Zafarabad* was carved out by Sultan Alauddin out of the vast and unwieldy province of Awadh. The town seems to have been named after Zafar Khan, the renowned general.
24. Cf. Ishtiyaq Husain Quraishi, *The Administration of the Sultanate of Delhi*, Lahore, 1944, pp. 59–60 for the position and function of the *wakil-i-dar*.
25. Barani, pp. 426–7.
26. He is generally mentioned as Qutlugh Khan even in the account of the reign of Tughluq Shah, although he got this title from Sultan Muhammad bin Tughluq.
27. Barani, p. 428.
28. Earlier Barani mentioned Gurshasp as *amir-i-ariz* who was soon later sent to Samana as its governor and there faced with success the Mongol invaders. It seems that either Gurshasp remained *amir-i-ariz* in an honourary capacity or was replaced by Khwaja Haji.
29. Barani, p. 438.
30. Irfan Habib says: 'No harshness was to be shown to the Muqtis who took anything from one-tenth to one-fifth of the *kharaj* in exces of their sanctioned income.' Cf. *The Cambridge Economic History of India*, vol. I, ed. Tapan Ray Chaudhuri and Irfan Habib, Indian reprint, 1984, p. 72.
31. Rampur MS., p. 269.
32. Barani, pp. 430–1.
33. Ibn Battuta uses the term *Khazin*, which Gibb translates as the tax collector who was also paid handsome salary, i.e. one-twentieth of the revenue of the *iqta*. He also had quite large number of his subordinates under him. Some time, a quarrel could take place between the *wali* and the finance officer. Cf. *The Travels of Ibn Battuta*, vol. III, p. 763; *Rehla*, Arabic Text of Ibn Battuta's *Travelogue* (Beirut, 1964), p. 526.
34. He was the son of Nizam-ul-Mulk Junaidi, his original name has not been mentioned.
35. Barani, pp. 426–7.
36. Professor K.A. Nizami confuses him with Ain-ul-Mulk Mahru whom even Barani calls a non-warrior officer. Cf. K.A. Nizami, *On the History and Historians of Medieval India*, New Delhi, 1983, pp. 212–14; also Cf. Appendix A.
37. According to the contemporary writers, the *ulama* and Sufi saints of Delhi were also sent money by Khusrau Khan. They belonged to

Barani's first group of people who returned money to the state exchequer easily. Barani, pp. 432–3.

38. Barani, p. 438; *Futuh us-Salatin*, p. 390. Isami says that the armymen were paid by the order of Khusrau Khan two years' allowances in advance.
39. Barani, p. 438.
40. *Futuh-us-Salatin*, pp. 389, 390–1.
41. Barani, pp. 438–9.
42. Ibid., pp. 434–5.
43. The specimen documents composed by Amir Khusrau and incorporated in the *Ijaz-i-Khusravi* for the perusal of the elite not only aimed at displaying the author's competence to write in an ornate and rhetorical style but are also suggestive. Being a social and political thinker, Khusrau suggests to the Sultan and the members of the ruling elite what policy should be adopted with regard to the defence of the north-western frontier against the Mongols and that the regions of Maabar (Karnataḳa) and Dwarsamudra (Tamil Nadu) in the south should be annexed and brought under the direct control of the centre. Cf. Iqtidar Husain Siddiqui, 'Records of the Sultanate of Delhi', in Richard Britnell (ed.), *Pragmatic Literacy: East and West (1200–1330)*, The Boydell and Brewer Ltd., U.K., 1997, pp. 209–12.
44. In the first unrevised version, Barani says that the son of Malik Tigin and some of his followers were killed along with other culprits. In the second revised version, the reference to the rebels does not mention Malik Tigin's son. Rampur MS 276.
45. Malik Makh Afghan served in the Deccan where he again revolted during the reign of Sultan Muhammad bin Tughluq, as will be discussed later.
46. Barani, p. 458.
47. It is interesting to point out that the man who inscribed the text was Mohammad, the grandson of Minhaj Juzjani. Cf. *Epigraphica Indo-Moslemica*, 1939–40, p. 34, Plate 14A; Z.A. Desai, Katba Shanasi, *Dr. Yusuf Husain Commemoration Volume*, Urdu, Ghalib Institute, New Delhi, 2004, pp. 92–5; for the correct reading of the inscription.
48. Barani, p. 451; Ishwari Prasad, Allahabad, 1974, pp. 34–7; Agha Mahdi Husain, *Tughluq Dynasty*, pp. 74–6.
49. Cf. Perso-Arabic Sources of Information, p. 95, for Ikhtisan's account.
50. *Futuh-us-Salatin*, pp. 416–18.
51. Sultan Jalaluddin Khalji made Shahr-i-nau (Kailokhari) his capital because the residents of old capital (Delhi) were loyal to the house of Sultan Balban and regarded him an usurper. Sultan Alauddin also had a new capital founded at Siri for the same reason. Sultan Ghiyasuddin Tughluq Shah being a close-fisted ruler displeased people. Barani laments that the residents of Delhi disliked the virtuous Sultan without justification. In fact, the Sultan's policy towards the land-grantees and

taking back money, distributed by Khusrau Khan to people made the Sultan unpopular. They wished his fall. Barani, pp. 440–1.

52. *Futuh-us-Salatin*, p. 412.
53. Barani, p. 442.
54. Ibid., p. 450.
55. *The Travels of Ibn Battuta*, Eng. tr. Sir Hamilton Gibb, Cambridge, 1971, vol. III, p. 656.
56. Cf. Mehrdad Shokwhy and Natalie H. Shokwhy, 'Tughluqabad: The Earliest Surviving Town of the Delhi Sultanate', *Bulletin of the School of Oriental and African Studies* (BSOAS), vol. LVII, London, 1994, p. 423.
57. Ibid., p. 427.
58. Acording to Isami, Sultan Muhammad bin Tughluq ascended the throne after his father's death in 1324, but Barani says that Ulugh Khan did not occupy the throne until the *chehlum* (forty days' mourning period) rite was completed. After it, the preparations were made for the coronation on a grand scale. The coronation took place in the Daulat Khana (the old *darbar* hall), considered auspicious. *Futuh-us-Salatin*, p. 421; Barani, p. 456.
59. Barani, pp. 456–7.
60. *Futuh-us-Salatin*, p. 422.
61. *The Travels of Ibn Battuta*, vol. III, p. 736.
62. Isami writes that the Sultan had delivered the speech on the occasion of his coronation that every person would be done justice impartially. That he would treat the aged people like his father, the youth like his brothers and children like his own offspring because he felt bound to all the Indians by ties of blood and relation. And he would establish peace and bring prosperity to all and would like to be called *Shah-i-Jahan Parwar* (the King who cherishes the people of the world). *Futuh-us-Salatin*, p. 422.
63. Barani, p. 458.
64. The governor, called *muqta* or *vali*, had to keep his son or brother in the capital as surety for his good conduct in the province. Barani, pp. 411, 464–5, 483.
65. Isami is particular in applying the term *malikzada* to the sons of the nobles. *Futuh-us-Salatin*, pp. 386, 420.
66. Isami being hostile to the Sultan would have us believe that Malikzada Ahmad Bin Ayaz was involved in the conspiracy hatched by the heir apparent against his father. The pavilion for the reception of the Sultan on his return in triumph from Bengal and Tirhut was designed by the Malikzada in such a way that it would collapse and kill the Sultan. Accordingly, it collapsed on the Sultan and the latter was killed. In reward the Malikzada was made the *wazir.* However, he praises the *wazir* for his wisdom and sagacity. 'Though he was a

young man, he possessed the wisdom of old years.' *Futuh-us-Salatin*, p. 420.

67. Barani, p. 454; *The Travels of Ibn Battuta*, vol. III, p. 730.
68. Cf. Iqtidar Husain Siddiqui, 'Khan-i-Jahan Maqbool', *Encyclopaedia of Islam* (new edition), vol. IV, Leiden, 1978, pp. 1019 a-b.
69. Barani, pp. 454–5.
70. Isami uses the term *khadev* instead of *vali* or *wazir*, in order to imply that he had higher status than other governors on account of special powers granted to him. *Futuh-us-Salatin*, p. 422.
71. Barani, pp. 454–5; *The Travels of Ibn Batuta*, vol. III, p. 617.
72. Barani, p. 502.
73. Ibn Battuta says: 'People of India held the foreigners in hatred because of the Sultan's favouritism towards them.' *The Travels of Ibn Battuta*, vol. III, p. 726.
74. *The Travels of Ibn Battuta*, vol. III, p. 686.
75. Barani calls him Shaikhzada Bayazidi for he happened to be the descendant of Shaikh Bayazid Bistami. Ibn Battuta also mentions him as Azam Malik al-Bayazidi and the governor of Manikpur. The Indo-Persian historians calls this province either the *vilayat-i-Kara-o-Manikpur* or *Khitta-i-Kara-o-Manikpur* or even the *iqta-i-Kara-o-Manikpur.* Barani, p. 488; *The Travels of Ibn Battuta*, vol. III, p. 686.
76. *The Travels of Ibn Battuta*, vol. III, p. 693.
77. Ibid., vol. III, pp. 672–3.
78. Cf. Z.U.A. Desai, *Quest for Truth: A Collection of Research Articles of Dr. Z.U.A. Desai,* Ahmedabad, 2004, pp. 220–7, for inscriptions on their graves; also Nazir Ahmad, *Maqalat-i-Nazir*, New Delhi, 2002, pp. 20–4, 30, for the same inscription.
79. *The Travels of Ibn Battuta*, vol. III, p. 602.
80. In describing certain events, Ibn Battuta incidentally mentions the names of immigrants from countries as far as Spain. For instance, in his travelogue we find the names of Faqih Jalaluddin Maghrabi Gharnati (i.e. from Granada) and Shaikh Ibrahim Maldibi (i.e. from the Maldive Islands). Cf. *Ajaib ul-Asfar* (Urdu tr.), vol. 2, pp. 131, 272.
81. *Sirat-i-Firuz Shahi*, pp. 277–8.
82. *The Travels of Ibn Battuta*, vol. III, p. 599.
83. A careful study of the sources indicates that the governors were transferred frequently from one province to another. For instance, on his arrival in Multan, Ibn Battuta found Imad-ul-Mulk Sartez as the governor of Multan and Sind provinces, although he held the charge of *Diwan-i-arz* in the capital. After the destruction of Kishlu Khan the rebel, Imad-ul-Mulk was posted in this place for some time. Later on, Malik Maqbul Telangani, the naib *wazir*, replaced Imad-ul Mulk. Similarly, Aziz Khumar served in Amroha as its finance officer. In

1344, he was appointed as the governor of Malwa and a *shiqq* of the Deccan adjacent to Malwa, as will be discussed subsequently.

84. Since Khwaja Jahan remained the *wazir* until the end of the reign, Pira Mali must have been appointed either *mustaufi* (auditor general) or *mushrif* in the *diwan-i-wizarat.*
85. Barani, pp. 505–6.
86. *Futuh-us-Salatin*, p. 515.
87. Ibn Battuta paid a visit to Maqbal in Cambay and enjoyed his hospitality. Since Sir Hamilton Gibb's translation of the third volume comes to a close with the account of the traveller's departure from Delhi for the Deccan and its fourth volume is not available, I have utilized the Urdu translation for the events of the last years of the Sultan's reign. Cf. *The Travels of Ibn Battuta*, vol. III, p. 730; *Ajaib ul-Asfar* (Urdu translation), Maulvi Muhammad Husain, rpt., Islamabad, 1983, vol. II, pp. 280–1.
88. Cf. *Futuh-us-Salatin*, pp. 495–8, for the portrait drawn by Isami of Malik Ikhtiyaruddin Yal Afgan, a leading army general since the reign of Alauddin.
89. Barani uses the name of 'Afghanistan' in its literal sense. The compiler of *Tarikh-i-Muhammadi* says that Shahu Afghan went to the Sulaiman mountains where the Afghans of his tribe resided. Now this region forms part of the North-Western Frontier Province of present-day Pakistan. Barani, pp. 482–3; Muhammad Bihamad Khani, *Tarikh-i-Muhammadi*, MS. British Library, London, Or. 137, f. 401b; also Agha Mahdi Husain, *The Rise and Fall of Muhammad bin Tughluq*, p. 180.
90. Ibn Battuta, *Ajaib ul-Asfar* (Urdu trans.), vol. 2, pp. 259–60.
91. Cf. Iqtidar Husain Siddiqui, 'The Afghans and their Emergence in India as the Ruling Elite During the Delhi Sultanate Period', *Central Asiatic Journal,* Wiesbaden, 1982, vol. 26, nos. 3–4, pp. 241–61, 253–7.
92. *Ajaib ul-Asfar*, vol. 2, p. 260.
93. *The Travels of Ibn Battuta*, vol. III, p. 717.
94. He joined Hulajin in rebellion and was killed by Khwaja Jahan along with his ally. Barani, pp. 484–6. *Futuh-us-Salatin*, p. 471.
95. Barani, pp. 488–9; In certain stabilized provinces, the charge of government was held by civil officers like Aziz Khumar in Malwa. Bhairon is supposed to have been the commander of the army and the governor of the province as well. *Futuh-us-Salatin*, pp. 485–8.
96. *Futuh-us-Salatin*, pp. 522–9, 550.
97. Ibn Battuta says that Khwaja Jahan supervised the construction of the royal buildings since the reign of Sultan Ghiyasuddin Tughluq Shah, *The Travels of Ibn Battuta,* vol. III, pp. 654–5.
98. Cf. P.L. Madan, Adilabad—A Dream of Muhammad bin Tughluq,

Islamic culture, Quarterly, Hyderabad, vol. XXXVII, no. 1 January 1963, pp. 49–50.

99. *The Travels of Ibn Battuta*, vol. III, pp. 658–60.
100. *Qasid-i-Badr-i-Chach*, Kanpur, 1873, p. 20.
101. *Perso-Arabic Sources of Information*, pp. 113–14.
102. Cf. Hajib Khairat Dehlavi, *Dastur-ul-Afazil*, ed. Nazir Ahmad, Tehran, 1973, p. 40; also the editor's introduction, for Ustadabad. The compiler was in the service of the provincial *sadr* in Ustadabad. The inscription, discovered and reported in *Epigraphia Indo-Moslemica*, 1931–2, suggests, according to Z.U.A. Desai that the fort constructed near Gogi and the newly carved-out *shiqq* was called Khitta-i-Ustadahad. Cf. Z.U.A. Desai's note as cited by Nazir Ahmad in his introduction to *Dastur-al-Afazil*, p. 12.
103. *The Travels of Ibn Battuta*, vol. III, p. 644.
104. *Tarikh-i-Mubarak Shahi*, Calcutta, 1931, pp. 89–90.
105. Barani, p. 499.
106. *The Travels of Ibn Battuta*, vol. III, p. 657.
107. *Cf. Perso-Arabic Sources of Information*, p. 124.
108. *The Travels of Ibn Battuta*, vol. III, p. 736.
109. *Ajaib ul-Asfar*, vol. 2, p. 273.
110. Cf. Paul Jackson, S.J., *The Way of a Sufi: Shaikh Sharaf Uddin Maneri*, Delhi, 1987, p. 75, for details.
111. Ali bin Asad, *Jamiul-ulum* (Malfuzat of the Shaikh) Qazi Sajjad Husain (ed.), *Indian Council of Historical Research*, New Delhi, 1987, p. 257.
112. *Perso-Arabic Sources of Information*, pp. 96, 120.
113. Ibid., p. 96.
114. *The Travels of Ibn Battuta*, vol. III, p. 668.
115. *Perso-Arabic Sources of Information*, p. 122.
116. *Qasaid-i-Badr-i-Chach*, op. cit., p. 17.
117. *Perso-Arabic Sources of Information*, p. 122.
118. *The Travels of Ibn Battuta*, vol. III, pp. 752–3.
119. *The Travels of Ibn Battuta*, vol. III, p. 666.
120. *Perso-Arabic Sources of Information*, pp. 120–1.
121. *The Travels of Ibn Batuta*, vol. 1, pp. 71–2.
122. The pious saint referred to seems to have been Shaikh Nizamuddin Auliya, who died in the first regnal year of the Sultan's reign.
123. *Perso-Arabic Sources of Information . . .*, p. 123.
124. Ibid., pp. 125, 126–7.
125. Barani, pp. 462, 464–5.
126. Al-Umari calls the Indian dialect Hindi but the Indo-Persian writers refer to it as Hindwi. It is, however, important that the Sultan patronized Hindi poets and his successors maintained his traditions. Cf. *Perso-Arabic Sources of Information . . .*, p. 120.

127. Ibid., p. 93, *Tarikh-i-Muhammadi*, MS. British Library, London, Or 137, ff. 905 b-406a.
128. *The Travels of Ibn Battuta*, vol. III, pp. 676–7.
129. *Qasaid-i-Badr-i-Chach*, p. 12.
130. *Perso-Arabic Sources of Information* . . . , p. 123.
131. *Ajaib-ul-Asfar*, vol. 2, p. 453.
132. Cf. Iqtidar Husain Siddiqui, 'Fresh Light on Ziya Uddin Barani: The Doyen of the Indo-Persian Historians of Medieval India', *Islamic Culture*, Hyderabad (India), vol. LXIII, nos. 1–2, Jan.–April 1989, pp. 69–84, for Muhammad bin Tughluq's account as well as Barani's different approaches in the two versions of the *Tarikh-i-Firuz Shahi*.
133. Rampur MS, pp. 282–3.
134. Barani, pp. 465–6.
135. Rampur MS. pp. 283–4.
136. Barani, pp. 506.
137. Cf. *Perso-Arabic Sources of Information* . . . , p. 96; also Iqtidar Husain Siddiqui, 'Muslim Intellectual Life in India', *Medieval India: Essays in Intellectual Thought and Culture*, vol. 1, New Delhi, 2003, pp. 89–90.
138. *The Travels of Ibn Batuta*, vol. III, p. 676. It is noteworthy that the Maulana came to India to get money and not to propagate his teacher's religious philosophy. Professor Riaz ul Islam rightly remarks that if Ardwili had preached it, the stir caused by the Imam's radical views would not have escaped Barani's notice. Cf. *Sufism in South Asia: Impact on Fourteenth-Century Muslim Society*, Karachi, 2002, p. 294.
139. The *Hidaya* is a standard work on Hanafi law, compiled after Bazdawi and Qanduri, cf. *Perso-Arabic Sources of Information*, p. 123.
140. *Basatinul-Urs*, in *Perso-Arabic Sources of Information*, p. 96.
141. The remarks made by the Shaikh are found in a collection of his *Maktubat* (epistles) addressed to Qazi Shamsuddin. They were published by the Shaikh under the title *Maktubat-i-Sadi*. Cf. *Letters from Maneri: Sufi Saint of Medieval India,* Eng. tr. Paul Jackson, New Delhi, 1980. Letter no. 63, p. 254.
142. Ibid., letter no. 41, p. 156.
143. Barani, p. 466.
144. *Futuh-us-Salatin*, pp. 472, 510, 515.
145. Saiyid Muhammad Akbar Husaini, *Javami'ul-Kilem* (collection of the utterances of Shaikh Gesudaraz), Kanpur, AH 1356, pp. 175–6.
146. Paul Jackson, *The Way of Sufi: Sharaf Uddin Maneri*, Delhi, 1987, pp. 113–14, for details.
147. In 1930, Professor Mohammed Habib introduced a fragment of a document composed by Sultan Mahammad bin Tughluq and found appended to a manuscript copy of the *Tabaqat-i-Nasiri* in the British Library, London, calling it a part of the Sultan's autobiography.

Agha Mahdi Husain utilized it in the preparation of his work, *Rise and Fall of Muhammad bin Tughluq*. Later, K.A. Nizami questioned its genuineness on the basis of the condemnation by its author of the Sultans of Delhi who preceded Sultan Ghiyasuddin Tughluq Shah. But the discovery of Sultan Muhammad bin Tughluq's letter, sent to Sultan Abu Sa'id of Iran, in the same style and containing criticism of the past Sultans, with the exception of his father, leaves no doubt about its genuineness. It seems to be the fragment of a document, addressed to the elite after the diploma of authority was received by the Sultan from the Abbasid Caliph. The Sultan wanted to create the myth of the sanctity of the Abbasid Caliph. Its rotograph copy is available in the Library of the Department of History, The Aligarh Muslim University, Aligarh. Cf. *Collected Works of Mohammad Habib,* vol. 2, ed. K.A. Nizami, New Delhi, 1981, p. 271; K.A. Nizami, *Studies in Medieval Indian History and Culture,* Allahabad, 1966, pp. 65–72; also Chapter 5 of the present work for the letter of the Sultan addressed to the ruler of Iran.

148. Like Barani and other writers, Badr Chach also testifies about his royal patron's interest in Abu Sina's philosophy and the rationalism in his couplet.
149. *Al-Hisba fil-Islam,* as cited by Hamilton A.R., Gibb, *Studies on the Civilization of Islam*, Stanford J. Shaw and William R. Polk (eds.), London, 1962, p. 169.
150. Since the spirit in which Barani seems to have composed this treatise is not tormented, it can be assumed that it was brought to completion during the early years of Sultan Muhammad bin Tughluq. Barani's *Tarikh* was written when he suffered from torments caused by imprisonment and dismissal from the state service after the death of his royal patron, Cf. 'Fresh Light on Ziya Uddin Barani: The Doyen of the Indo-Persian Historians', *Islamic Culture,* vol. LXIII, nos. 1–2, op. cit., pp. 69–94.
151. Cf. Fatawa-i-Jahandari, ed. Mrs. A. Salim Khan, Lahore, 1972, pp. 139–40.
152. Rampur MS, p. 280.
153. Isami says: The emperor is friendly towards mean and hostile to Islam. He has gone astray and the *sharia* and the doctors of law have declared his destruction by people lawful. *Futuh-us-Salatin*, p. 515.
154. *The Travels of Ibn Battuta,* vol. III, pp. 696, 699–700, 701, 702, 704, etc.
155. Ibid., vol. III, pp. 692–3.
156. Ibid., vol. III, pp. 699–700, 703, 704, 705, etc.
157. *Futuh-us-Salatin*, p. 515.
158. Sagar is in Maharashtra where Gurshasp was posted in 1325 and revolted against the Sultan in 1316. Cf. Agha Mahdi Husain, *Tughluq Dynasty*, p. 213.

159. Cf. *Epigraphic Indica*, vol. XXXII (1956–57), p. 168.
160. Cf. Hiralal, *Descriptive List of Inscriptions in the Central Provinces of Berar*, Nagpur, 1916, p. 50; also *Tughluq Dynasty*, pp. 334–5.
161. Z.U.A. Desai correctly identifies Zafar Khan with the noble who was killed by the rebels in Gujarat. Barani mentions him in his *Tarikh-i-Firuz Shahi* on p. 516. Cf. Z.U.A. Desai, unpublished, 'Persian Inscriptions from the Baroda Museum and Picture Gallery', in *A Quest for Truth: A Collection of Research Articles of Z.U.A. Desai*, Ahmedabad, 2004, p. 557.
162. *Tughluq Dynasty*, Chapter XI, pp. 311–39, for the appointment of Jains on important posts, including that of the governor.
163. *Cf. Perso-Arabic Sources of Information . . .*, p. 96.
164. *The Travels of Ibn Battuta*, vol. 1, Cambridge, 1958, pp. 263–4.
165. Isami is the first Indian writer to use the term *pargana* as an administrative unit. For instance, he says that Delhi was a *pargana* headquarters of no importance before Sultan Iltutmish's reign. It emerged as a beautiful city and centre of learning and culture under Iltutmish. The later writers also use this term. Shaikh Rizq Ullah Mushtaqi says that a *pargana* contains villages from fifty to hundred. Cf. *Futuh-us-Salatin*, pp. 108, 398, 450; Afif, *Tarikh-i-Firuz Shahi*, p. 99; Iqtidar Husain Siddiqui, *Some Aspects of Afghan Despotism in India*, Aligarh, 1969, pp. 138–9, for Musḥtaqi and other later writers.
166. *The Travels of Ibn Battuta*, vol. III, p. 741.
167. Barani says that Ain-ul-Mulk Mahru and his brothers had no experience of warfare. Yet they revolted and also came out to give battle. They thought that the Sultan was unpopular, and that therefore the army would support them, but in vain. They were routed in the first charge. Barani, pp. 489–90.
168. The provinces of Malwa and Gujarat were annexed by Sultan Alauddin in 1305–6. The Maratha territory of Deogiri was finally brought under the direct rule of the Sultan during the reign of Sultan Qutbuddin Mubarak Shah, but effective control does not seem to have been established beyond the military headquarters; the countryside remained under the powerful land chiefs. It was really under Sultan Muhammad bin Tughluq that serious attention was paid to the consolidation of the centre's power. A number of centres, including Daulatabad, were founded with the planting of Muslim colonies. Barani is full of praise for Qutlugh Khan for consolidating the Sultan's power through his excellent conduct. Barani, p. 501.
169. Some of the veteran warriors such as Ali Shah Khalji and Makh Afghan served under Qutlugh Khan as *amiran-i-sada*. Ali Shah Khalji killed Bhairon, the *mutassarif* of Gulbarga, and Ibrahim, the governor of Bidar, seized the treasures and then declared his independence.

He was forced by Qutlugh Khan to surrender. The *amiran-i-sada* also started misbehaving in Malwa and Gujarat. Barani, pp. 488–9.
170. Ibid., p. 501.
171. Ibid., pp. 501–2.
172. Ibid., pp. 503–4, 507.
173. Ibid., pp. 507–8.
174. Ibid., p. 509; *Futuh-us-Salatin*, pp. 505–6.
175. *Futuh-us-Salatin*, pp. 506–8.
176. Ibid., pp. 512–14, Barani, p. 512.
177. Shaikh Ali Haidari resided in the port city of Cambay. Ibn Batuta says: 'He was held in high respect, well spoken of and of wide reputation. The sea-traders used to vow to give large sums to him, and on arriving in Cambay they would go first of all to salute him. He would show them that he knows what was in their minds; often one of them would make a vow and then repent of it, but when he came to salute the Shaikh, the latter would tell him first how much he had vowed and order him to fulfil it faithfully.' After the flight of the rebels to Daulatabad, the Sultan was informed of all those who had wished well of the rebels including Shaikh Ali Haidari. Cf. *The Travels of Ibn Battuta*, vol. III, pp. 705–6, 732.
178. *Futuh-us-Salatin*, pp. 515, 522.
179. Ibid., pp. 519–20; Barani, p. 514.
180. *Futuh-us-Salatin*, pp. 538–9.
181. Barani, p. 512.
182. Ibid., p. 483.
183. Ibid., p. 498.
184. Since the projects of the Sultan have been discussed in detail by different modern scholars, I have not discussed them here.
185. Cf. Chapter 5.
186. Though the Bahmani Sultan followed the Sultan of Delhi in conferring titles on the ministers and organizing his court, he pleased the nobles by decentralizing the power of the centre. He assigned *iqtas* to the nobles with the permission to maintain their own army contingents. Cf. *Futuh us-Salatin* pp. 556–7, 558.
187. Barani says that Malik Kabir and Khwaja Jahan whom the Sultan had left in Delhi to look after the affairs of the state during his absence jointly sent Barani to Daulatabad with greetings, petitions, and *khidmati* (offerings) for the Sultan. Barani met the Sultan on his way to Gujarat. The Sultan was pleased to meet him and showered favours upon him. He accompanied the Sultan and was consulted by him from time to time in the course of the journey from one place to another. He does not say that he was allowed to return to Delhi. Later, he appears to have been sent to Bhatner as a prisoner by Firuz Shah after the death of Sultan Mohammad bin Tughluq. See appendix related to the sources.

188. Barani, pp. 521–2.
189. Ibid., pp. 531–2.
190. In those days any person whose loyalty to the Sultan was doubtful and was condemned in some way, faced ostracism; even his relatives avoided him.
191. *The Travels of Ibn Battuta*, vol. III, p. 661.
192. Ibid., vol. III, p. 665.
193. Barani, pp. 493–4.
194. *Javami'ul Kilem*, op. cit., pp. 181–2, also Mir Khurd (Saiyid Muhammad Mubarak Kirmani), *Siyar-ul-Auliya*, Delhi, 1302 H, p. 246.
195. *Muntakhabut-Tawarikh*, vol. 1, p. 242.
196. *The Travels of Ibn Battuta*, vol. III, pp. 697–700.
197. Cf. Muhammad Bihamad Khani, *Tarikh-i-Muhammadi*, MS. British Library, London, No. Or. 137, ff. 159, lt-161a; also Iqtidar Husain Siddiqui, 'Muhammad Bihamad Khani's Approach to History', *Commemoration Volume of Professor S. Nurul Hasan*, Rampur Raza Library, Rampur, 2003, pp. 360–1.
198. Shams Siraj Afif, *Tarikh-i-Firuz Shahi*, Calcutta, 1891, pp. 29, 47, hereafter cited as Afif.
199. *The Travels of Ibn Battuta*, vol. III, p. 665.
200. Afif, pp. 51–2, also *The Travels of Ibn Battuta*, vol. III, pp. 660, 666.
201. Malik Khattab Afghan was one of the leading generals of the reign of Sultan Muhammad bin Tughluq. He held the charge of the *iqta* of Rapri, where he defeated the recalcitrant chiefs and succeeded in maintaining peace and order. Barani does not refer to his role in the struggle for the throne, but Afif, Muhammad Bihmad Khani, and Yahya Sirhindi fill this gap in our information. Ibn Battuta is full of praise for his bravery. Barani also says in the first version of his *Tarikh* that Malik Khattab was unrivalled in chivalry. Cf. Rampur MS., p. 322; *Ajaib ul-Asfar*, vol. 2, pp. 259–60, Afif, p. 50; Muhammad Bihamad Khani, *Tarikh-i-Muhammad*, op. cit., f. 406b; Yahya Sirhindi, *Tarikh-i-Mubarak Shahi*, Calcutta, 1931, p. 135.
202. Afif, pp. 43–6.
203. Saiyid Muhammad Mubarak Kirmani known as Mir Khurd, *Siyar-ul-Auliya*, Delhi, 1302 H., pp. 272–3, also *Tarikh-i-Muhammadi* (of Bihamad Khani), op. cit., f. 405b.
204. The credit for introducing the importance of Barani's work, *Na'at-i-Muhammadi*, as a source goes to the late Nurul Hasan. But the copyist whom he seems to have engaged for copying the relevant passages read Bhetner as Palilez. When I checked the manuscript copy in the Rampur Raza Library, I found the place name clearly written as Bhatner. Cf. S. Nurul Hasan, 'Sahifa-i-Na't-i-Muhammadi of Zia Uddin Barani', *Medieval India Quarterly*, Aligarh, vol. 1,

nos. 3–4, 1950, p. 100, fn. 4; *Na't-i-Muhammadi*, MS. Rampur Raza Library, Rampur, no. *Tarikh*, 127, ff. 4a-b.

205. Barani, pp. 547–8; Rampur MS, pp. 323–4.
206. *Tarikh-i-Mubarak Shahi*, pp. 122–3.
207. Afif, pp. 51–4.
208. Ibid., p. 46.
209. Barani, pp. 538, 539, 543.
210. Ibid., p. 538.
211. Cf. Peter Hardy, *Historians of Medieval India*, 1982; rpt., Westport, pp. 40–2, for details.
212. Afif, pp. 95–6; also *Sirat-i-Firuz Shahi*, pp. 161–2.
213. *Sirat-i-Firuz Shahi*, pp. 162–3; Iqtidar Husain Siddiqui, 'Khan Jahan Maqbul', *Encyclopedia of Islam*, vol. IV (new edition), Leiden, 1978, pp. 101a–b.
214. Afif, p. 505.
215. Ibid., p. 499.
216. Barani, pp. 556–7.
217. Afif, pp. 584–5.
218. *Sirat-i-Firuz Shahi*, pp. 164–5.
219. Barani, pp. 575, 585–6.
220. Since Barani could not write anything disparaging about Firuz Shah, he intimates his readers about the domination of low-born people in the account of Sultan Alauddin's reign. It is to Barani's credit that he informs us about the presence of low-born persons in Firuz Shah's nobility in this way. Barani, p. 366.
221. Ibid., p. 554.
222. *Tarikh-i-Mubarak Shahi*, pp. 136–43.
223. Rampur MS., p. 328.
224. Barani, pp. 587–8.
225. Ain-ul-Mulk Mahru, *Insha-i-Mahru*, ed. Shaikh Abdur Rashid, Lahore, 1965, document no. 6, p. 17.
226. Ibid., document No. 11, p. 23.
227. *Futuh-us-Salatin*, p. 602, Barani, p. 574.
228. *The Delhi Sultanate: A Political and Military History*, Cambridge, 1990, p. 287.
229. Cf. Chapter 8.
230. *Maktubat-i-Muzaffar Balki* (the spiritual successor of Shaikh Sharafuddin Yahya Maneri), MS. Acc. No. 185a, Khuda Bakhsh Oriental Public Library, Patna, pp. 503, 509.
231. *Futuh-us-Salatin*, pp. 556–7.
232. Cf. Iqtidar Husain Siddiqui, *Some Aspects of Afghan Despotism in India*, Aligarh, 1969, pp. 40–8.

CHAPTER 5

Foreign Relations

There appears to have been no exchange of any diplomatic missions or letters between the Khalji Sultans of Delhi and the neighbouring countries; at least the authentic information is wanting in this regard. As regards the so-called letters of Rashiduddin Fazl Ullah of Iran bearing on the exchange of emissaries between the Ilkhan of Iran and the Sultan of Delhi, they are to be rejected as forged.[1] There is no shred of evidence in the standard historical works compiled by Rashiduddin Fazl Ullah and his contemporaries in Iran to corroborate what we find in the fictitious statements contained in the letters.[2] The letters are full of factual errors. For example, in one of the letters Rashiduddin Fazl Ullah is said to have been sent by the Ilkhan, Arghun Khan (reigned: 1284-91), as envoy to the court of Sultan Alauddin in Delhi, although the latter seized the throne in 1296. Likewise, the statement contained in another letter about the large land grant made by Sultan Alauddin Khalji to Rashiduddin Fazl Ullah with the proviso that its annual income would be transmitted to him in Iran regularly is absurd. Had this been a fact, Amir Khusrau, Isami, and Barani would not have failed to mention it. Similarly, Rashiduddin Fazl Ullah and Wassaf also do not refer to the establishment of any friendly relations between Sultan Ghazan Khan and his Indian counterpart, Sultan Alauddin Khalji, in their respective histories.

The relevant passage in the *Tarikh-i-Wassaf* about the dispatch of an embassy to the Sultan of Delhi, Alauddin Khalji, is worth noting.

Khaluelchi and Mahmud Shah were appointed by Sultan Uljaitu (reigned: AD 1304–16) along with a royal letter with the purport that the kings of the country of India, both during the times of the victorious emperors Chinggis Khan and his successor, the generous Ogedei Khan, had shown friendship and obedience. [Yet] it looks rather strange that since my auspicious succession to the throne of royalty and the shining of the sun of the Kingdom of Islam on the horizons of the world, Sultan Alauddin has not traversed the path of established sincerity by stating his conditions and explaining the state of affairs, and has not expressed his feeling of pleasure (on my succession). Now he should strengthen the foundation of sincerity and faithfulness. He should give one of his daughters in marriage to the Sultan (of Iran).[3]

The letter was obviously offending. The Sultan of Delhi was addressed as if he were the vassal of Iran, although he considered himself greater in power and splendour and had already defeated the strong invading armies deputed by the Ilkhan's cousins, the Mongol rulers, Dua and Qaidu of Transoxiana and Khurasan. Second, it was also wrong to write that in the past the Sultans of Delhi had been obedient to Chinggis and Ogedei.[4] Offended by this letter, Sultan Alauddin Khalji had the Irani envoys and their companions, eighteen in number, trampled to death under the feet of elephants.[5]

It may, however, be pointed out that scholars and merchants were free to travel from one country to the other. There was no restriction on them to visit any country. Like their counterparts in other Muslim countries, Indo-Muslim scholars also had an internationalist attitude and visited foreign countries in search of knowledge and experience. Ibn Battuta met students and scholars from India in different countries.[6] Similarly, the merchants of Iran, India, and China carried on their overseas and overland trade without facing any hindrance. They were welcome in each others' country because their trade constituted an important source of income to the state. The relevant evidence furnished by Rashiduddin Fazl Ullah in his history reveals that Ghazan Khan was interested in promoting trade between his empire and foreign countries. He provided protection to foreign merchants against oppressive officers. Iran imported from India elephants and medicinal herbs, besides other commodities.[7]

Some words are in order here about the Mongol rulers of Transoxiana and eastern Khurasan (present-day Afghanistan) during the Khalji and Tughluq periods. Since Peter Jackson has discussed in detail the dissolution of the Mongol Empire, the internecine war between the descendants of Chinggis Khan and the invasions of India by the Chaghataid princes,[8] I need not repeat all this. It may, however, be pointed out that the Chaghataid and Ogedei princes who had turned against the central Mongol power after the selection of Monge Khan as the emperor in 1351 tried to expand their rule south of the *vilayet* of Ghazna. They occupied Indian territories up to the river Ravi (in the Panjab). Even Sultan Ghiyasuddin Balban had been unable to liberate these territories beyond the Ravi. It was in 1306 that Sultan Alauddin Khalji appointed veteran generals with strong provincial armies in the north-western frontier territories after his generals had defeated the last Mongol invaders of his reign. Ghazi Malik was entrusted with the government of the newly carved-out province of Depalpur and Lahore, as discussed earlier. Ghazi Malik is credited with having destroyed the Mongol military bases and established his firm control over the Hindu land chiefs in the Kuh-i-Jud region. Barani's statement that every year Ghazi Malik led expeditions to Kabul, Ghazna, Qandahar, and Girmsir, plundered and ravaged those regions, levied tribute on the inhabitants, and that the Mongols did not have the courage to defend themselves,[9] would have us believe that the frontier of the Sultanate was pushed ahead of the Indus. But we have to make allowance for Barani's exaggeration because his senior contemporary Amir Khusrau says in the official history *Tughluqnama* that Ghazi Malik seized Kuh-i-Jud from the Mongols, established his control over it, and then he would cross the Indus every year and carryout plundering raids against the Mongols.[10] Thus he makes it crystal clear that the region beyond the river Indus, called Binban, was still controlled by the Mongols. Since Amir Khusrau was concerned about the defence of the Sultanate against the invaders, he appears to have felt the need for the liberation of the region north of the Indus from the control of the Mongols. In a document patterned on the model of an *arzdasht* (petition or report), which is not in fact what it seems but had been designed as good counsel for the successor of Sultan Alauddin Khalji with regard to the defence of the north-western frontier,[11] said to have been written by Badr Hajib (certainly a fictitious person), Khusrau appears rightly to have considered the Sultan's control of the Hindu Kush to be essential for the defence of the Indian Sultanate against the Mongol invaders from the north; the Hindu Kush forms a natural boundary between Central Asia and the Indian subcontinent. Khusrau's counsel seems to have influenced Sultan Muhammad bin Tughluq's north-western frontier policy, as well be discussed later.

II

Of all the Sultans of Delhi, Sultan Muhammad bin Tughluq adopted a foreign policy that had the most far-reaching consequences. The relevant evidence available in miscellaneous sources tends to show that as a result of his policy India's foreign relations expanded and its prestige greatly increased in the outside world. The cornerstone of his foreign policy was to acquire effective control over the region in the north-west of the river Indus for ensuring the security of the people in the border area against the Mongol invaders from Central Asia, to create friends among the rulers outside India, and to promote overland and maritime trade between his Sultanate and foreign countries. Our analysis shows that the Sultan was successful, at least in the field of foreign affairs. The important outcome of his foreign policy was that the rulers of Central Asia either became his vassals or allies, while the rulers of other countries sought to establish close and friendly relations with him after they had been impressed by his resources and munificence.

We may first analyse the factors that led Sultan Muhammad bin Tughluq to adopt a definite policy towards the Mongol rulers of the neighbouring countries, identify the regions of strategic importance that had become the bone of contention between the Sultan of Delhi and the Chaghataid rulers of Central Asia, discuss the shift taking place in the policy of the Sultan towards the Chaghataid rulers from time to time, and then explain how friendly relations between the Sultanate of Delhi and the Central Asian rulers led to socio-economic growth in the Punjab. In addition, attention has also been drawn to the exchange of diplomatic courtesies and trade relations between India and the neighbouring countries ruled over by the descendants of Chinggis Khan.

The primary factor that influenced Sultan Muhammad bin Tughluq's foreign policy was his concern for border security against the Mongol invasions. Second, the Sultan also appears to have been interested in creating conditions favourable for the progress of overland trade between his Sultanate and the neighbouring countries. For a proper understanding of his achievements in this sphere, it is necessary to analyse briefly the state of affairs in the north-western region prior to his accession. This will help us re-evaluate the significance of the Sultan's historic role.

As discussed earlier, the little evidence available in the miscellaneous sources reveals that even after the liberation of the Kuh-i-Jud region by Ghazi Malik during his governorship, the Mongols retained their military bases beyond the Indus and in the vast areas around it, now included in the present-day districts of Gujarat, Mianwali, and Jhang in Pakistan and Sargodha in India. From these bases they sneaked in bands, plundered, and then returned, taking children and women as captives.[12]

After his accession to the throne, Sultan Muhammad bin Tughluq appears to have regarded the Mongol problem as one of prime importance. We do find clues to the Sultan's frontier and foreign policy in foreign as well as Indo-Persian sources. Sultan Muhammad bin Tughluq appears to have been determined to secure the natural frontiers for his empire. For this purpose, he planned to conquer and control the entire region up to the Hindu Kush mountains. According to Isami, the Sultan led a military campaign against the Mongol bases in the north-western region in the very first year of his accession. He stayed in Lahore, whence he deputed his generals with numerous troops, who first cleared the region of Kalanaur of the Mongols, pursued their fugitives across the Indus, occupied the town of Farshaur (present-day Peshawar), and took Mongol women and children as captives. The *khutbah* was read in every town there in the name of the Sultan. When the triumphant Delhi army marched towards Ghazna, the soldiers found neither fodder for their horses nor food grains for themselves, because the retreating Mongols used to follow a 'scorched earth' policy. Consequently, the Delhi army was forced to turn back. On the return of his generals, the Sultan punished the local chiefs who were in alliance with the Mongols in the Kalanaur region and then returned to Delhi after an absence of two months.[13] In Delhi, he planned to conquer, besides the trans-Indus area, the Himalayan kingdoms of Qarajil and Kashmir, and establish his domination there.[14]

Tarmashirin, the Mongol (Chaghataid) ruler of Central Asia, whose generals were driven away from the Indian territories, was not in a position to retaliate immediately, because he had to face the invasion of his territories by the army of Abu Said, the Ilkhanid ruler of Iran, soon (AD 1326).[15]

Upon the withdrawal of the Iranian general, Hasan bin Choban, from Ghazna in 1326, Tarmashirin was in a position to retaliate, either against Iran or India. The conditions in India seemed favourable for invasion. In 1327, the transfer of population from Delhi to Daulatabad (the former Deogiri) by the order of the Sultan was thought to have weakened the defences of the capital, for a large number of troops had also moved, escorting the people to the south. Tarmashirin, however, mobilized his forces in the border territories on such a large scale that even the Ilkhanid court in Iran was alarmed.[16] Having collected a huge army, Tarmashirin entered India, fully armed, on his way to Delhi. Isami, our contemporary authority, states that when the invader crossed the river Ravi, the Sultan was informed in Delhi about him. He at once came out from Delhi and encamped outside Siri where large forces gathered in no time. Ten thousand *sawars* were detached and dispatched to Meerut under the command of (Yusuf) Ibn Bughra. Ibn Bughra took the invader by surprise near Meerut and inflicted heavy losses on him. Tarmashirin suffered such a setback in the first encounter with the Delhi army that he gave up the idea of staying in India any longer, and started to retreat. The Indian army pursued him beyond the river Indus, finishing off the stragglers.[17]

Isami's testimony about Tarmashirin's invasion of India is not acceptable to Agha Mehdi Husain. He expresses the view that Tarmashirin never invaded India because Ibn Battuta found him a friend of the Delhi Sultan in 1333, and Barani, who served the Sultan for seventeen years as his *nadim* (counsellor), would not have failed to refer to it had it ever taken place.[18] No doubt, Isami being an enemy of Sultan Muhammad bin Tughluq portrays him differently, yet he is more generous in giving details of the events of his reign than other contemporary or near-contemporary writers. It is also worth noting that the printed text of Barani's *Tarikh-i-Firuz Shahi* is a revised version, and in it the contemporary historian fails to refer to Tarmashirin's invasion, although he had mentioned it in some detail in the first recension (or unrevised version) released two years earlier. The first recension of the *Tarikh-i-Firuz Shahi*, as mentioned, comes to a close with the account of the fourth regnal year of Sultan Firuz Shah's reign. In this recension Barani writes:

Upon the transfer of the citizens (from Delhi) to Daulatabad, the Sultan stayed in Delhi for two years. During this time Tarmashirin marched into India at the head of a huge army. He arrived (without meeting any resistance) in the Mian-i-doab (Meerut). Thereupon, the Sultan collected his forces. In the meantime, the officers and notables from Lakhnauti (Bengal) sought to go back to their region and foment trouble there. The Sultan fought a fierce battle against Tarmashirin. The latter, having given a good account of his fighting prowess, retreated to Tirmiz.[19]

It is not difficult to explain the reason for this omission by Barani in the second revised recension of his *Tarikh*. The internal evidence[20] in this (revised) recension tends to suggest that his praise of Tarmashirin's generalship—that he had given a good account of his fighting ability—as well as his portraying Sultan Muhammad bin Tughluq as the dominant mind of his age in the first recension had further embittered the reigning Sultan and his courtiers against him, for a reaction had already begun against the policies of the preceding regime, as already discussed.

Another contemporary of Barani, the anonymous author of the *Sirat-i-Firuz Shahi*, also refers, incidentally, to Tarmashirin's invasion, stating that the latter had arrived near Meerut.[21]

Yahya Sirhindi's statement about the same event seems to have been based on Barani's unrevised first recension as well as some additional information. He writes:

In the year 1328, Tarmashirin, the King of Khurasan and the brother of Qutlugh Khwajah, marched into the *vilayet* of Delhi at the head of a formidable army. He captured a number of forts on the way. People in Lahore, Samana, Indri (and the region) up to the border of Badaon (territory) were made captives. Having reached the bank of the Jamuna, he (Tarmashirin) had to withdraw. The Sultan (of Delhi), who had encamped between the city of (Old) Delhi and the Hawz-i-Khass, gathered numerous troops. When Tarmashirin crossed back the Indus vanquished, the Sultan reached Kalanaur in his pursuit. The fort of Kalanaur that was found in a dilapidated condition was entrusted by the Sultan to the charge of Malik Mujiruddin Abu Rija. The latter was ordered to have the fort repaired. (Moreover) the Sultan had also deputed a number of veteran generals to chase Tarmashirin (across the Indus). (From Kalanaur) the Sultan returned to Dar al-Mulk (Delhi).[22]

Likewise, Muhammad Bihamad Khani, who completed his *Tarikh* in 1438, also adds to the information about Tarmashirin's invasion contained in the earlier sources. He adds:

> During the reign of Sultan Muhammad bin Tughluq Shah, Tarmashirin entered India with a large army. But he had to retreat to Tirmiz, his capital, disappointed and defeated. He died there. Afterwards, when Amir Warghan ascended the throne, friendly relations were established between him and Sultan Muhammad Tughluq Shah. They remained friends and had mutual regard.[23]

In short, the Indian sources clearly show that the Delhi army was able to drive away the invader beyond the north-western frontier of the Sultanate. The Central Asian chronicler's statement that the Delhi Sultan having been frightened bought peace by making over costly gifts to Tarmashirin cannot be taken as authentic evidence.[24] In India, as well as in Central Asia, the official historians tend to suppress or distort facts disparaging their country's heroes.

Upon the withdrawal of Tarmashirin, Sultan Muhammad bin Tughluq took effective measures for strengthening the defence of the frontier territories and creating conditions favourable for their economic development.[25] Barani's *Tarikh-i Firuz Shahi*, if examined in conjunction with other sources, in particular, *Masalik al-Absar* and *Tarikh-i Mubarak Shahi*, tends to suggest that the vast liberated areas between the rivers Jhelum and Beas were separated from the unwieldy Kuh-i-Jud tract and then two new administrative-cum-fiscal units were formed with well-defined boundaries. These units were named the *vilayet* of Gujarat[26] and the *vilayet* of Kalanaur.[27] As regards the Binban tract extending to the north of the Indus and predominated by the Afghan tribes, it was made a dependency of the Kuh-i-Jud unit, which was already reduced in size.[28] Of the officers-in-charge of these territorial units, we find trace of only one in the historical record. He was Mujiruddin Abu Rija, the officer-in-charge of Kalanaur, mentioned by Yahya Sirhindi. At this time, the Sultan also decided to implement his plan for conquering Khurasan and make it the first line of defence of his Sultanate. The contemporary sources report that the Sultan wanted to destroy completely the non-Muslim Mongols in Khurasan. According to Mir Khurd, the Sultan had formulated his Khurasan policy in the first two years of his reign, but the implementation of the Deccan project was given priority.[29] The Sultan's letter written to Abu Said in 1328, the contents of which will be analysed subsequently, also refers to Khurasan as part of his plan for conquest. All this makes it necessary to discuss the geographical location of the region and what the Indo-Persian writers meant by the term 'Khurasan'.

Modern scholars have failed to escape certain pitfalls in identifying Khurasan, which Muhammad bin Tughluq had planned to conquer. They invariably identify it with the northern province of Ilkhanid Iran and thus fall into a historiographical error. The discovery of fresh evidence in the sources hitherto unknown calls for a reappraisal of the problem. The Khurasan mentioned by medieval Indo-Persian writers was certainly not included in Ilkhanid Iran. Rather, it formed a part of the Chaghataid empire of Central Asia.

In 1928, Sir Wolsely Haig identified Khurasan, mentioned by Barani and other medieval writers in their accounts of Muhammad bin Tughluq's scheme of conquest of foreign lands, with Persia.[30] Since then every scholar has followed him uncritically in this respect.[31] In 1964, K.A. Nizami pointed out in his contribution on Muhammad bin Tughluq's reign to the *Comprehensive History of India*, vol. 5, that 'the word Khurasan is often very loosely used and it is very difficult, therefore, to determine exactly the geographical area which Muhammad bin Tughluq had in mind'. Then he suggests that the Sultan intended to conquer both Iran and Central Asia and that the chaotic conditions in those countries might have encouraged him in this venture.[32] Probably inspired by Nizami, Peter Jackson propounded the hypothesis that the region of Khurasan that Muhammad bin Tughluq wanted to conquer embraced the land north-west of the Indus, i.e. the possessions of the Chaghataid ruler of Central Asia. In support of his hypothesis, he refers to the works of Ibn Battuta and Babur. Ibn Battuta says that in India 'all foreigners are called Khurasanis', while Babur writes, 'Just as Arabs call every place outside Arab (Arabia) Ajam, so Hindustanis call every place outside Hindustan Khurasan.'[33] Jackson's hypothesis is borne out by evidence available in miscellaneous sources.

Arab geographers invariably include Khurasan in the areas north-west of India and the vast region extending from the present-day province of Mashhad in Iran up to the Hindu Kush mountains.[34] The Ghaznavid Persian poets and Minhaj al-Siraj Juzjani also include the whole region west and north-west of India as part of Khurasan.[35] But the late thirteenth- and fourteenth-century Persian writers in India meant by Khurasan only the region north-west of the river Indus, including Balkh in present-day Afghanistan. For instance, in his account of Sultan Alauddin Khalji's military campaigns against the Mongol invaders from Central Asia, Amir Khusrau refers to Khurasan as being the area north-west of the Indus. He writes that after their defeat, the Mongols fled to the meadows of Khurasan.[36] Interestingly, Barani also helps us in this regard when he refers to the Khurasan project in his first version of the *Tarikh*. Explaining the circumstances that led to an increase in the state revenue demand in the Doab, he tells us that the Sultan needed a great deal of money for the conquest of Khurasan, for he wanted to win over people through generosity on his way to Ghazna.[37] Yahya Sirhindi calls Tarmashirin the ruler of Khurasan for the same reason as cited earlier. Another fifteenth-century work substantiates the fact that the region lying to the north-west of Binban was called Khurasan by the Indians. Describing the origin of the fifteenth-century Binbani scholars of Gujarat and the geographical location of Binban, the compiler of the *Jumaat-i Shahiyah* states: 'Binban is the *vilayet* lying between Multan and Khurasan. The group of people who are known as Binbani in the country of Gujarat have come from the *vilayet* (Binban). They are the descendants of Hazrat Abdullah bin Abbas.'[38] Shaykh Jamali Dihlavi's (d. 1537) use of Khurasan for Kabul and the area adjoining under Babur's rule conclusively establishes the fact that before Akbar's reign (1556–1605), the Indo-Persian writers called the present-day region of Afghanistan by the name of Khurasan. In his *qasidas* composed after Babur's victory over Ibrahim Lodi, Jamali says:

> From the region of Khurasan, the flag of the munificent King descended upon India like the cloud of God's blessing.[39]

> As you arrived in India from Khurasan, luck and success were on your right while victory and conquest were on your left.[40]

We may now analyse the contents of the letters exchanged between Sultan Muhammad bin Tughluq and Sultan Abu Said of Iran, for they cast fresh light on their policies towards the non-Muslim Chaghataid ruler of Khurasan and other parts of Central Asia. This correspondence between Delhi and Iran started just after Tarmashirin's invasion. In 1328, the Sultan of Delhi dispatched his emissaries along with a letter and costly presents to the court of Abu Said. In this letter, the Sultan first reminds Abu Said of the existence of friendship between India and Iran during the times of their predecessors, and then he refers to the duty of Muslim rulers to serve the cause of Islam. He writes that the infidels had taken possession of Khurasan and penetrated into the *vilayet* of Sind, which formed part of the country of Hindustan. According to him, all this happened because the preceding Sultans were incompetent rulers and none of them tried to drive away the infidels. 'Even today,' says he, 'the residents of the *vilayet* (of Sind) are not safe from their tyranny. They still suffer physical, material, and spiritual losses at their hands.' Further, the Sultan continues, he had made up his mind to save his people from their oppression. He also appeals to Abu Said in the name of Islam to join hands with him for destroying the Chaghataid power in Khurasan and also assures him of the success of their armies. He suggests that the enemies of Islam should be driven away across the river Oxus, so that the Muslims might enjoy peace and the laws of Islam be enforced. The letter also contains references to the difficulties, faced by merchant *caravans* and pilgrims to Mecca owing to the infidels' control over the land route (through Khurasan). Lastly, the Sultan states that he has dispatched the letter through his emissary in all sincerity for the purpose of fostering friendship with him (Abu Said). His emissaries were also directed to communicate other important information not contained in the letter. The date inscribed on the letter is 1328.[41]

The above letter evoked a favourable response from the ruler of Iran. Abu Said wrote a reply in 1330, and assured the Sultan of his friendship. First, he describes the conquests made by his ancestors in Iran and Iraq since the time of Hulegu (in Persian, Hulaku); that his illustrious ancestor (Hulegu), having crossed the river Oxus, led military campaigns into the regions of Iran, the wilderness of Rum (Anatolia), and the *vilayet* of Ghazna; that all the *vilayets* were conquered along with their strong and lofty forts. Of the rulers of his dynasty, he calls Ghazan Khan[42] (his uncle) and Uljaitu[43] (his father) pious rulers who had made the entire region the abode of Islam. They demolished the temples of infidels and restored the supremacy of the laws of Islam in their own dominions; that they were devoted to the cause of their faith and had exerted themselves to the utmost in suppressing heresies and other social evils. In the end, he appreciates the friendly gesture of the Delhi Sultan and also reciprocates the feeling of goodwill and friendship by calling him *Sultan-i Azam* (the great lord) and *Shahryar-i Mujahid* (the warrior of the faith). He closes his letter with the words that his emissaries would impart the necessary information verbally. His suggestion that emissaries and letters be exchanged frequently between the two courts shows how desirous he was to strengthen his ties with the Delhi court.[44]

Evidence contained in the contemporary Arabic and Persian sources, available in India as well as in foreign countries, further adds to our information about the exchange of diplomatic courtesies between the Ilkhanid and the Delhi courts from time to time. Extolling the excellent qualities possessed by Sultan Muhammad bin Tughluq, Shihab al-Din al-Umari tells us about the generous treatment meted out by the Sultan to the first Iranian envoy to his court. He writes:

> There was a person named 'Azd, son of Qazi Yezd, in the army of Sultan Abu Said, who had an ambition to become the vizir but did not possess the requisite ability. For the fulfilment of his ambition, he created dissensions among the vizirs and discontent in the army. The men in power found out a way to get rid of him by having him away from the centre. He was sent to Delhi as an envoy with the royal letter containing greetings, love and enquiries about the welfare of the Sultan (Muhammad bin Tughluq). In Delhi, 'Azd presented himself with the letter of Abu Said. The Sultan showered royal favours upon him. He was given money and proper arrangements were made for his comfortable stay.[45]

He was given a treasure and other costly gifts besides the gifts given to him by the Sultan separately for Abu Said. 'The gifts and treasure given to him amounted to eight hundred *tumans*, one *tuman* being equal to ten thousand *dinars* and one *dinar* to six *dirhams*. Thus all this was worth eight million *dinars* or forty-eight million *dirhams*.'[46]

The relevant evidence contained in the standard Irani source *Mujmal-i-Fasihi* is also worth quoting. Here also we find a bit of additional information about Saiyid Azd's visit to the Delhi court. Referring to the Indian envoy's visit to Abu Said's court bearing costly gifts, including the choicest products of India, Fasih Ahmad tells us that Abu Said also sent by way of courtesy his envoy, Saiyid Azduddin, with gifts and a letter. In India, when the envoy was conducted to the royal presence with the gifts, the Sultan was pleased. He showered high favours on the envoy. He ordered him to be taken inside the treasury and given whatever he would select for himself. He was taken there and told what the Sultan had ordered. To everybody's surprise, he did not care for anything but picked up a copy of the Koran. This had the desired effect on the Sultan. Impressed by his action, the Sultan showed him greater consideration. He was given a huge amount of money and numerous other gifts.[47] It is interesting to note that Qazi Saiyid Azd finds mention in Barani's *Tarikh* as well. Criticizing the generosity of Sultan Muhammad bin Tughluq to foreign dignitaries, Barani states that Sayyid Azd ud-dawlah was given 400,000 *tankas*.[48]

In short, Tarmashirin's invasion of India spurred Muhammad bin Tughluq to raise a large army, make friends with Abu Said, and fight for securing the natural frontiers of the Delhi Sultanate. His plan of conquest included the Himalayan kingdoms mentioned by medieval writers as Qarajil and Kashmir and the region north-west of Binban. In the north of India, the Hindu Kush mountains seem to have been considered by the Sultan as a natural barrier against the invaders of India. But the large army recruited for the conquest of Khurasan was disbanded after a year. In his account of this reign, Barani, who is more concerned with describing the consequences of the Sultan's ill-fated projects, fails to state why the Sultan changed his policy towards Tarmashirin.[49] It seems that Sultan Muhammad bin Tughluq's preparations on a large scale and his friendship with Abu Said frightened Tarmashirin. Moreover, the latter's conversion to Islam after his withdrawal might have induced him to improve his relations with the Sultan of Delhi, who also might have responded favourably.

No doubt, Tarmashirin's conversion to Islam seems to have

caused a change in his policy towards India; the exact time of its occurrence cannot be determined easily. He was a non-Muslim in 1328, as mentioned by Muhammad bin Tughluq in his letter to Abu Said (referred to above). In 1332–3, he was a zealous Muslim, as mentioned by Ibn Battuta.[50] Sharafuddin Yazdi calls him the first Muslim ruler of the Chaghataid dynasty and also credits him with having established the Islamic *sharia* in the empire.[51] However, Barani's description of the recruitment of the large army and its disbandment in the second year[52] supports the hypothetical date, 1329, as the year of Tarmashirin's conversion to Islam.

Another problem connected with the Sultan's frontier policy is the ill-fated Qarajil expedition. In analysing this problem, modern scholars again commit errors regarding the identification of the region, its approximate date, as well as the royal motives behind it. Ishwari Prasad is partly in agreement with Wolsely Haig that the expedition was a part of the Nagarkot conquest (1337–8). But he does not accept the view that western Tibet was to be conquered by the Sultan after Qarajil.[53] Rather, he holds the view that after the fort of Nagarkot had been reduced, 'the Sultan wished to complete the line of his northern frontier by conquering the hill states which were independent or wavered in alliance, and were not altogether unwilling to own the suzerainty of China'. Agha Mehdi Husain neither accepts the year 1338 as the date of the expedition nor does he consider it a part of the Nagarkot conquest. He sees no reason to not accept Barani's statement that it was a part of the Sultan's Khurasan expedition. Then he would have us believe 'that part of the same army which had been collected for the Khurasan expedition was utilized for the Qarachil expedition'.[54] Peter Jackson, in an attempt to add something new, identifies Qarajil with Kashmir. He states that Kashmir was known as Qarajil during the fourteenth century as no contemporary work refers to this region as Kashmir.[55] Let us re-examine the relevant evidence contained in the different sources.

No doubt, Barani links it with the Sultan's Khurasan expedition. In the first recension of the *Tarikh*, he calls the disastrous campaign of the Delhi army a calamity that befell the Sultanate. He also mentions the figures of the armymen as 30,000 to 40,000 troops detached from the main central army for subduing the mountainous region. This army met no difficulty in the beginning. But after it had penetrated deep, the Hindus emerged from their hideouts, closed the passage, and then the lines of communication and supplies were cut-off. Consequently, the army met with disaster, and only a few horsemen survived. In the second revised recension, Barani furnishes a more detailed account, but omits the figures of the horsemen. He states that after the preparations for conquering Khurasan and Mavaraulnahr (Transoxiana) had been completed, the Sultan decided 'that the Qarajil mountain through which runs the short route linking India with China, and since it exists as a wall between the two countries, should be brought under control, so that the road for the supply of horses and the movement of the army be rendered safe'. For this purpose, a large part of the experienced army was dispatched under veteran generals. The army entered the mountains, established *thanas* (military posts) at strategic points along the route according to the royal *farman*, and then penetrated deep; the important towns were easily occupied. Thereupon, the local chief, who had fled, returned and gained control of the passes. This happened when an epidemic broke out, and horses and *sawars* died in large numbers. Of this army, which had acquired fame for its invincibility, only a few persons could make good their escape.[56]

A comparative study of Barani's two recensions and other contemporary works helps us make the following points: First, Barani understates the figures of the *sawars* as 30,000 to 40,000[57] (deputed against Qarajil), while Isami exaggerates the figure as 100,000 and implies that the Sultan wanted them to be killed on account of his enmity towards Muslims.[58] Second, it is clear that the soldiers destroyed by the hill men were the war-experienced men who had nothing to do with the army newly recruited in 1328, for in the details of the disbanded army Barani mentions only Khurasan. There is no reference therein to Transoxiana. He categorically states that 380,000 inexperienced people were enrolled, supplied horses, and paid salary and allowances for one year. The following year, the entire army was disbanded because it could not be employed anywhere, although its maintenance had already caused a heavy drain on the exchequer.[59] But in his account of the Qarajil expedition, Barani links it with the Sultan's plan of conquering both Khurasan and Transoxiana. It needs to be pointed out here that Barani not only fails to describe the events in a chronological order but also often becomes rambling in his account. But it is implicit in the description that this expedition was organized under new circumstances around 1334–5 after the disbanding of the new Khurasan army had already become an event of the past. His reference to Transoxiana along with Khurasan in his account of the Qarajil expedition refers to a different situation created by the fall of Tarmashirin and the flight of his relations and supporters to India. Isami and Ibn Battuta help us explain this new situation in its correct historical perspective.

The sequence of events described by Isami suggests that the expedition was sent some time in 1334–5 after the murder of Tarmashirin when the latter's son, son-in-law, and other noblemen had arrived in India and the Kurt ruler of Herat and the officers of Ghazna had paid allegiance to the Delhi Sultan, as will be discussed subsequently. Ibn Battuta confirms this impression because the event took place after his arrival in India in 1333. According to him, the Qarajil ruler acknowledged the Sultan's suzerainty and paid annual tribute even after he had destroyed the invading army, for he could not retain the possession of the arable land in the foothills of the Himalayas without coming to terms with the Delhi court.[60]

Of the medieval Indo-Persian historians of the pre-Mughal period, only Yahya Sirhindi tells us that the Qarajil expedition was launched in 1338.[61] According to Badr Chach, the court poet of Sultan Muhammad bin Tughluq, this was the year when the fort of Nagarkot was reduced by the Sultan in person.[62] Certainly, Yahya confuses this date with that of the ill-fated expedition because the Sultan is not reported by any source to have moved out of his capital during this time. Therefore, the date 1338 may be pushed a few years earlier. The political development in the Chaghataid empire that took place after Tarmashirin's murder was quite encouraging for the Delhi Sultan, because the non-Muslim regicide Buzun had failed to consolidate his authority in the Chaghataid Empire. His usurpation was followed by anarchy; the Muslim officers in the western provinces, including Khurasan, combined together against him.[63] As the regicide stationed in the eastern part of the empire, the Sultan wanted to secure control over the Himalayan route running through Qarajil and Kashmir and enter Transoxiana directly without having any fear from the rulers of Herat and Ghazna, who had become his vassals. But the failure of the Qarajil expedition and the improvement in the situation in Central Asia after the fall of Buzun seem to have led the Sultan to abandon his scheme of conquering Transoxiana. Upon the restoration of Muslim rule in Transoxiana, friendly relations between its ruler and Sultan Muhammad bin Tughluq were re-established, as will be discussed subsequently.

In passing, we may refer to the migration of notables from Central Asia to India because they also seem to have helped the establishment of close ties between the two empires. Barani and Ibn Battuta mention a few of them while describing the Sultan's generosity towards the foreigners. Both men mention Bahram, the ex-governor of Ghazna, whom the Sultan received as a royal guest and lodged in a palace in Siri.[64] Likewise, Muhammad al-Charkhi, one of the prominent nobles of Tarmashirin, was also shown royal favour.[65] Malik Sanjar Badakhshani was paid 80,00,000 *tankas*, while the *qazi* of Ghazna was given so much in money and jewels that he could never have imagined in his life.[66] Many others seem to have arrived at the same time, but their names are not mentioned. Ibn Battuta also refers to the patronage extended by the Sultan to scholars from Central Asia and other countries.[67]

The numbers of foreigners, largely from Khurasan (present-day Afghanistan) and Transoxiana, increased so much that they constituted a force in themselves.[68] Foreigners were not only appointed to important posts in the administration of the empire but also given huge treasures. Many of them took the wealth to their own respective countries. The special recipients mentioned by Barani belonged to Khurasan, Iraq (Ilkhanid Iran), Trans-oxiana, Sistan and Harev (the kingdom of Herat), Egypt, Syria, and Mughlistan (Chinese Turkistan or Xinxiang). They came to India along with merchants, in ships and *caravans* both. They visited the Sultan with gifts, and in return received vases of gold studded with pearls and jewels, gold plates full of gold and silver coins, robes made of costly silk stuff such as *zarbaft* (silk woven with gold thread), imported horses, and expensive belts.[69]

As for the relations between Herat and Delhi, little relevant evidence contained in the contemporary sources about the acknowledgement of Sultan Muhammad bin Tughluq's suzerainty by the Kurt ruler of Herat after the death of Sultan Abu Said in 1334 is worth mentioning. In an account of the murder of a fugitive prince from Herat in India, Ibn Battuta informs us that King Husayn Kurt of Herat paid allegiance to Sultan Muhammad bin Tughluq, and had the *khutbah* read in the latter's name in his *vilayet.* 'The king of India,' writes Ibn Battuta, 'exchanged gifts with him and gave him the city of Bakr (Bhakkar) in Sind, whose tax yield is 50,000 silver *dinars* a year.'[70] The contemporary official documents not only corroborate but also supplement Ibn Battuta's statement. We come across two letters contained in the *Faraid-i-Ghiyathi,* a fifteenth-century collection of epistles.[71] One of the letters was written by Muinuddin Jami to Sultan Muhammad bin Tughluq on behalf of the successor of Sultan Husayn Kurt. In this, the Delhi Sultan has been informed about the chaotic conditions in Iran and the accession of Muizuddin (bin) Abu al-Husayn Kurt in Herat in 1349. The Sultan is also requested to send a *farman* along with his seal confirming the new ruler of Herat.[72] The second letter, drafted by another scholar, Malik Jamal al-Din Ikhtisan, was also addressed to the Delhi Sultan on behalf of the ruler of Herat in the same year. Again, the Sultan of Delhi is informed that the new ruler of Herat was placed on the throne by the *ulama*, saints, Sayyids, and leading citizens of Herat. It is further stated that order was restored everywhere in Khurasan. In the end, the Sultan is requested to confirm the new ruler as his vassal through the grant of the *farman.* It may be added that Sultan Muizuddin bin Husayn Kurt was soon able to establish his control over the territory of Ghazna also. Therefore, the Sultan of Delhi could consider the region of Herat within his own Sultanate and could exile non-desirable persons there.[73]

As regards Sultan Muhammad bin Tughluq's relations with the Muslim Mongol ruler of Khwarazm (the Golden Horde), Barani incidentally refers to the exchange of diplomatic courtesies and gifts between them. Unlike him, Ibn Battuta who had served the Khwarazm ruler, Amir Qutbul-Dumur, tells us that the Amir and his wife regularly sent gifts along with emissaries to Delhi and got in return what is said to have been many times the value of their own presents. He writes: 'The Khatun Turabak, wife of the Amir Qutbul-Dumur, the ruler of Khwarazm, had sent this (Abdullah) as the bearer of gifts to the king of India. . . . (The latter) accepted the gift and gave in return one many times its value, which he sent to her. But the envoy of hers chose to remain at his court, and the King enrolled him among his familiars.'[74]

Barani is critical of Sultan Muhammad bin Tughluq's foreign policy because it had caused a heavy drain on the royal exchequer. He writes that every year the Mongol commanders of *tuman* (ten thousand), *amiran-i-hazarah* (commanders of one thousand horsemen), the *khatuns* (royal ladies), and other notables arrived (in India) and crores and hundreds of thousands of *tankas*, in addition to robes, well-equipped horses, jewels and pearls were given to them. Moreover, every year banquets were hosted in their honour. Elaborate arrangements were made for their comfort and entertainment. The Sultan had no other work but to shower favours upon them for two or three months in the winter.[75] It may also be pointed out that Sultan Muhammad bin Tughluq is reported to have enforced prohibition in his empire, but the Mongol immigrants could imbibe wine in their houses, even though they had become Muslims.[76]

It is also worth recalling that the exchange of diplomatic courtesies between Iran and India was disrupted after the death of Abu Said in 1335. Our sources do not mention any such exchange of diplomatic correspondence. Only Ibn Battuta mentions one of the cousins of Abu Said, Haji Kawun, who arrived in Delhi as the representative of his brother, Musa. The latter was accepted as the Sultan of Iran by a section of the country's nobility. In Delhi, the Haji was extended royal hospitality and also loaded with costly gifts. He returned to Iran after his brother was killed in 1337.[77] On the fall of the Ilkhanid dynasty, Iran suffered from anarchy, and diplomatic relations with neighbouring countries could not be maintained. After some time, Abu Ishaq, who had consolidated his rule in Shiraz and the area around, seems to have sought friendship with the Delhi court. During the last years of his reign, Sultan Muhammad bin Tughluq is reported to have sent his sophisticated chief *dabir*, Ikhtisan, to Iran on a diplomatic mission. On his return to India in 1351, he joined his patron Sultan. He was either killed or died as a prisoner. He was one of those who was accused of misleading the late Sultan.[78]

Likewise, the disruption of the exchange of diplomatic courtesies between the Sultan of Delhi and the Chaghataid ruler of Central Asia was brief. After the fall of Buzun, the kingmaker Qazaghan maintained friendly relations with Sultan Muhammad bin Tughluq. Like the Kurt ruler of Herat, he also seems to have become an active ally of the Sultan of India and got financial support from him. He sent a strong military contingent under the command of Altun Bahadur to India for serving under the Sultan. Barani does not tell us when and in what capacity he had sent this contingent, but his reference to its presence in the royal army camp in Thatta suggests that it must have been dispatched some time after the year 1346 when Amir Qazaghan had emerged all powerful in Transoxiana.[79]

A word may be added here about the progress of overland as well as maritime trade between India, Iran, and the countries of Central Asia. It is worth recalling that the leading merchants commanded great respect in the countries they visited and would act as emissaries between different rulers. The Sultan of Delhi utilized the services of foreign merchants both for the progress of trade and to enhance his prestige abroad.

The contemporary Arabic sources furnish detailed information about the expansion of India's trade with the outside world during the period under review. The merchants, Indian as well as foreign, mentioned therein appear to have been leading wealthy men of their age. According to Shihabuddin al-Umari, they sailed in ships or moved in *caravans* to different countries. Silk fabric from China, Iraq and Alexandria (in Egypt), horses from Bahrain, Persia and Central Asian lands, and fruits, fresh as well as dry, from Khurasan and Bukhara were supplied to India in plenty.[80] Ibn Battuta supplements *Masalik al-Absar* in this regard. Sultan Muhammad bin Tughluq is reported by him to have showered royal favours upon these merchants. Of the foreign goods in demand in India, Ibn Battuta also mentions the delicious fruits from Khurasan, Bukhara, and Khwarazm, weapons such as swords and bows and arrows, costly fabrics, and war animals. His description of Multan and the port cities of Cambay in Gujarat and Lahri Bandar in Sind shows how crowded they were by foreign merchants and how they yielded huge revenues in the form of custom duties.[81]

To conclude: Sultan Muhammad bin Tughluq was far ahead of his age in adopting an enlightened foreign policy. He gave up the offensive policy against the Chaghataid ruler of Khurasan (present-day Afghanistan) and Mavraulnahr (Transoxiana) after he had become convinced that friendship would not only ensure security and peace to his people in the frontier region but also go a long way in promoting overland trade between the Sultanate and the Central Asian countries. It was an outcome of his statesmanship that the kingdom of Herat and the Chaghataid Empire became the satellites of his Sultanate, while the rulers of Iran and Khwarazm remained his good friends.

It may also be emphasized that the exchange of gifts between different rulers, which comprised the choicest products of their countries as well as gifted slaves, both male and female, led to diversity in culture and the improvement of arts and crafts. Sultan Muhammad bin Tughluq's enlightened attitude and generosity not only brought civilized countries closer to India but also attracted men of talent and learning from abroad. All this enriched the Delhi Sultanate's cultural heritage.

III

Besides Iran and the Central Asian countries, the Delhi Sultan also appears to have had diplomatic and trade relations with the Middle Eastern and Far Eastern countries, as far as Egypt in the west and China in the east, at least since the time of Sultan Muhammad bin Tughluq. After Sultan Iltutmish, Muhammad bin Tughluq was the second ruler to receive the investiture with the mandate of authority from the Abbasid Caliph in Egypt. The latter's ancestor, who had survived the sack of Baghdad in 1258, had been given protection by the Mamluk Sultan of Egypt. The latter declared him the caliph, but used him as a figurehead. The caliph could not grant audience to any foreign emissary without the permission of the Sultan of Egypt. The latter's permission was sought by foreigners along with the presentation of costly gifts. Thus, the maintenance of the caliph was a source of prestige and income to the Sultan. Barani tells us that during his stay in Surgdwari (1338–42), the Sultan had enquired from the travellers about the presence of the Abbasid Caliph in Cairo. He decided to send his emissaries to him and obtain the investiture from him. On his return to Delhi, the Sultan sent his emissaries under the leadership of Haji Rajab Barqai to Egypt. They carried money and other costly gifts both for the caliph and the Sultan of Egypt. In his own Sultanate, Muhammad bin Tughluq started issuing coins in the name of the caliph and suspended the Friday congregational prayer until the investiture was received two years later, in 1344.[82]

The relevant evidence contained in the Arabic sources reveals that the envoys from India visited the caliph and Sultan Al-Nasir for the first time in 1331.[83] Haji Rajab Barqai returned with the envoys of the Caliph, Al-Mustakfi Billah Abu Rabi Suleiman. The envoys were Haji Sarsari, Saiyid Ziad, Mubashir Khilafati, and Muhammad Sufi. They brought for the Sultan the sword, the robe, and the mandate in 745 AH, corresponding to AD 1345. The Sultan is said to have proceeded from the capital on foot along with his leading nobles to receive the mandate in a ceremonious way. The envoys returned with treasure, including rare diamonds, pearls, etc.[84]

Now the question that arises is whether Sultan Muhammad bin Tughluq seriously attached any importance to the grant of investiture by the caliph to him. No doubt, the caliph being the descendant of the uncle of the Prophet commanded immense respect among Muslims the world over, yet the fact that the adventurous military men in Muslim lands could defy the Abbasid Caliph even before the sack of Baghdad in 1258 should not be lost sight of. Even in India, Sultan Iltutmish had received the investiture from the caliph in 1229, but soon after Balka Khalji had revolted against him in Bengal (as already discussed). However, a close examination of the sources suggests that Muhammad bin Tughluq was in predicament on account of the *ulama's* opposition to his state policy. The *ulama* being religious leaders influenced public opinion. The rebellions by the governors forced him to seek the investiture from the nominal caliph, even though he was a non-entity and lived at the mercy of the Sultan of Egypt.

As regards diplomatic relations between India and other Arab countries, the relevant evidence shows that the Sultan had friendly relations, including trade, with the rulers of Bahrain, Aden, and Yemen. Ibn Battuta calls Aden the seaport of Indians. According to him, the ships that sailed from Cambay, Hannur, Thana, and Goa (Sindapur) anchored here. Besides Indian merchants, Egyptian merchants also resided here. The merchants were wealthy people who engaged in overseas trade. Aden's *bazaars* exported rice and cotton textiles imported from India.[85] Ibn Battuta also informs us about the establishment of diplomatic relations between the king of Aden and Sultan Muhammad bin Tughluq Shah. They exchanged gifts.[86] Shihabuddin al-Umari adds: 'Ali bin Mansur of Bahrain told me: Our envoys visit India frequently and we are well informed about the affairs of this country. . . . The Sultan is a very generous man and shows his munificence to the foreigners.' The merchants of Bahrain also supplied Arab horses to the Sultan.[87] Similarly, trade relations between China and India had existed for a long time.[88] The emperor of China is reported to have sent his emissaries to the court of Sultan Muhammad bin Tughluq with customary gifts, such as one hundred bales of *kamkhuab* (Chinese silk), one hundred slaves (male and female both), five robes studded with jewels, and weapons. The Sultan was also requested to grant permission for the reconstruction of temples at Buddhist pilgrim centres in the Himalayan region. In return, the Sultan sent gifts several times costlier along with his emissaries under the leadership of Ibn Battuta.[89]

We are also informed by Ibn Battuta about the visit made by the envoy of the Sultan of Sumatra to the court of Sultan Muhammad bin Tughluq. On Ibn Battuta's visit to Sumatra on his way to China, its Sultan treated him as his guest because the Delhi Sultan was held in high esteem by him.[90] In short, India's fame had reached far and wide, and its trade and cultural relations had expanded all over the world. Indeed, the reign of Muhammad bin Tughluq forms a watershed in the history of India's foreign relations during the Delhi Sultanate period.

Sultan Firuz Shah also attached importance to the mandate of authority received from the caliph. He received the caliph's envoys from time to time, and they returned with money and costly gifts. The investiture and the mandate were first received in 1353. It is not known whether the caliph sent them after the Sultan of Delhi had made a request for them. In 1364, the caliph's envoys came for the third time with the mandate, in which the Sultan was called Saiyid us-Salatin (the chief of the Sultans) and was also assured that the mandate of authority was not issued to any Indian monarch except the occupant of the throne of Delhi. In response, Sultan Firuz Shah deputed his trusted man, Mahmud Shams Kurd to accompany the caliph's envoys on their return journey with precious gifts and the *waqfnama* for getting sanction from the caliph. The *waqfnama* was a statement of the endowments 'made from the *imlak* consisting of the dead lands brought to life in the empire of India, of the dams built and canals dug, of mosques, inns, *madrasas*, *khanqahs*, passes (across hills), forts and palaces built by him, and of the proceeds of *imlak* being apportioned in fixed shares amongst these public works, for their expenditure'.[91] In 1369, Mahmud Shams Kurd returned with the caliph's envoys, Qazi Najmuddin Qureshi and Khwaja Kafur Khalifati, to deliver the caliph's approval of the Sultan's *waqfnama*. Emphasizing its importance, the official historian states: 'No Sultan had received from the caliphate such authoritative and definite proof of the rightfulness of the empire and the *waqf*. This is the unique fortune of His Majesty Firuz Shah.'[92] As for Sultan Firuz Shah's relations with the rulers of other countries, the sources of information do not help us, although trade relations with different countries seem to have continued as merchants were shown due consideration everywhere.

NOTES

1. In 1946, Reuben Levy examined the *Maktubat-i-Rashidi* and found it wrongly ascribed to the famous Ilkhani historian, Rashiduddin Fazl Ullah. He observes: 'Not only do they lack the characteristic marks of Rashid al-Din's style and language, amply displayed in the *Jami-ul Tawarikh*, but they are filled with anachronisms and improbabilities and phrased in the vaguest and most palpably exaggerated fashion.' He also opines that 'the letters seem to be of no earlier date than the fifteenth century and, at a guess, of Indian provenance'. Some Indian scholars, like K.A. Nizami have utilized them uncritically. Cf. Reuben

Levy, 'Letters of Rashid al-Din Fadl-Allah', *Journal of the Royal Asiatic Society of Great Britain and Ireland*, 1946, p. 74; K.A. Nizami, 'India's Contact with the Outer World during the Sultanate Period', in *Studies in Medieval Indian History and Culture*, Allahabad, 1966, pp. 1–12.

2. *Maktubat-i-Rashidi*, ed. Muhammad Shafi, Lahore, 1947, pp. 163–4.
3. *Tarikh-i-Wassaf*, Bombay, AH 1269, p. 528.
4. There is no authentic evidence contained in any standard source to suggest that there were established friendly relations between Chinggis Khan or Ogedei and the Sultan of Delhi. Rashiduddin Fazl Ullah may be quoted in support of this claim. He writes that once a merchant from India presented tusks of elephant to Ogedei. The latter was pleased and rewarded the merchant with treasure. Ogedei's courtiers objected to his generosity because the merchant was from an enemy country. He snubbed them and is reported to have remarked that he did not regard anyone in his own land as his enemy. Cf. Rashiduddin Fazl Ullah, *Jamiul Tawarikh*, MS. British Library, London, Add. 7628, f. 553a.
5. *Tarikh-i-Wassaf*, pp. 528–9.
6. Cf. *Ajaibul-Asfar* (Urdu tr.), vol. 1, pp. 265, 269, 304, 351.
7. Rashidudin Fazl Ullah, *Tarikh-i-Mubarak Ghazani*, ed. Karl Jahn, London, 1940, pp. 150, 206–7.
8. Cf. Peter Jackson, *The Delhi Sultanate: A Political and Military History*, Chapters 6 and 11, pp. 103–22, 217–31.
9. Barani, pp. 322–3.
10. *Tughluqnama*, verses, 2660–71, p. 138.
11. According to this *arzdasht*, the city of Ghazna was captured by the army of Sultan Alauddin Khalji, and the *khutba* (Friday sermon) was read in the name of the Indian ruler. This is a figment of Amir Khusrau's imagination and was intended to induce the Sultan to conquer the region of present-day Afghanistan for the defence of his Sultanate. I do not agree with Peter Jackson when he describes it as an intelligence report and calls it a memorial casting light on the disintegration of the principality built up by Qutlugh Qocha south of the Oxus during the years 1306–8. As a matter of fact, Amir Khusrau's prose work *Ijaz-i-Khusravi* contains examples of the *farman*, *fathnama* (victory letter), and *arzdasht* (petition or report on some given condition) as well as private letters. The study of these records, in conjunction with the contemporary historical literature, suggests that all these texts, with the exception of the personal letters written by Khusrau from Awadh to his friends in Delhi in the years 1285–6, were fiction because the events mentioned in them occurred much later. Khusrau uses them to suggest what the Sultan should do with respect to certain regions, how the governors should perform their functions, etc. It may be emphasized that had Ghazi Malik penetrated the region beyond Binban up to Ghazna, Amir Khusrau would not have failed to mention it in the *Tughluqnama*. Cf. Iqtidar Husain Siddiqui, 'Records of the Sultanate

of Delhi, 1206–1330', in *Pragmatic Literacy, 1200–1330*, ed. Richard Britnell, The Boydell Press, Woodbridge, 1997, pp. 206–15, 209–12; *The Delhi Sultanate: A Political and Military History*, p. 230.

12. Ibn Battuta, *The Travels of Ibn Battuta*, vol. 3, Eng. tr. Sir Hamilton Gibb, Cambridge, 1971, p. 578; also *Futuh-us-Salatin*, pp. 423–4.
13. *Futuh-us-Salatin*, pp. 423–4; also Iqtidar Husain Siddiqui, 'The Qarlugh Kingdom in north-western India during the Thirteenth Century', *Islamic Culture*, Hyderabad, April 1980, p. 80.
14. Mir Khurd provides us with insight into Sultan Muhammad bin Tughluq's north-western frontier policy. The Sultan persuaded the leading scholars of Delhi to move to Kashmir and convert the people to Islam to help him consolidate his rule there because he had decided to conquer Kashmir. Cf. Mir Khurd, *Siyar al-Awliya*, Delhi, AH 1302, p. 288.
15. Cf. Peter Jackson, 'The Mongols and the Delhi Sultanate in the Reign of Muhammad Tughluq (1325–51)', *Central Asiatic Journal*, vol. XIX, nos. 1–2, 1975, p. 126.
16. Loc. cit.
17. *Futuh-us-Salatin*, pp. 462–5.
18. Cf. Agha Mehdi Husain, *Rise and Fall of Muhammad bin Tughluq*, London, 1938, pp. 100–8; also idem, *Tughluq Dynasty*, Calcutta, 1963, pp. 119–43.
19. It may be pointed out that the Bodleian Library Manuscript, no. 173 (Elliot Collection 353) utilized by Peter Jackson is defective at places. Peter Jackson has translated the passage wherein Tarmashirin's invasion has been mentioned in these words: 'After the citizens (of Delhi) had been dispatched to Daulatabad, he (Sultan Muhammad) remained in the city for two years. During this time Tarmashirin invaded Hindustan with numerous troops and advanced into the Doab. Sultan Muhammad too gathered many forces. In this emergency, the amirs and nobles of Lakhnauti sought to depart and return to their own territory and stir rebellion. . . . And he (Tarmashirin) withdrew with his army to Timidh.' Cf. *Central Asiatic Journal*, 1975, nos. 1–2, op. cit., p. 123.

    The passage in the Raza Library, Rampur, copy is fair and complete. Cf. *Tarikh-i Firuz Shahi*, MS, Raza Library, Rampur, no. 1846, pp. 287–8; folios are not marked. Hereafter cited as the Rampur MS.
20. Barani states in the revised recension: 'If the *Tarikh-i-Firuz Shahi* had been compiled during the reign of Sultan Mahmud (of Ghazna) or Sultan Sanjar (Saljuq), his fame would have surely spread throughout the world.' Here Barani indirectly refers to the first recension of his *Tarikh* (Barani, p. 124). (References to Barani in this work mean the printed text of the *Tarikh-i Firuz Shahi*.)
21. Anonymous, *Sirat-i Firuz Shahi*, facsimile, Khuda Bakhsh Library, Patna, pp. 180–1.
22. Yahya Sirhindi, *Tarikh-i Mubarak Shahi*, Calcutta, 1931, p. 101.

    Yahya's testimony was accepted by Ishwari Prasad, who says: 'Barani may have preferred to keep silent over the discreditable occurrence, but it must be remembered that Barani is not a detailed chronicler who attempts to supply information about everything relating to Muhammad's reign. The nearest successor of Barani who mentions this invasion is the author of the *Tarikh-i-Mubarak Shahi*.' Cf. *A History of the Qaraunah Turks*, Allahabad, 1974, rpt., pp. 95–6.

23. *Tarikh-i Muhammadi*, MS, British Library, London, Or, 137, f. 328b.
24. Sharaf Ud-din Yazdi, *Muqaddimah*, MS, British Library, London, Add. 6538, f. 99b.
25. The Mongols used to convert everywhere large tracts of arable land into pastures for their war animals, horses and camels. They also did not keep the old forts under repair because they loved to reside in tents. In India as elsewhere they had turned agricultural land into vast pastures. Having driven away the Mongols, the Delhi officers encouraged people to bring the land under the plough again. Cf. Iqtidar Husain Siddiqui, 'Politics and Conditions in the Territories under the Occupation of Central Asian Rulers in North-western India, 13th and 14th Centuries', *Central Asiatic Journal*, vol. 27, nos. 3–4, 1983, pp. 294–8.
26. Barani, p. 601.
27. Shihab al-Din al-Umari, *A Fourteenth-Century Arab Account of India under Sultan Muhammad bin Tughluq* (being the English translation of the chapters from *Masalik-ul Abasarfi Ma-malik-ul Amsar* by Iqtidar Husain Siddiqui, Aligarh, 1971), p. 30.
28. See Iqtidar Husain Siddiqui, 'The Qarlugh Kingdom in North-western India during the Thirteenth Century', *Islamic Culture*, Hyderabad, April 1980, pp. 76–7, for the identification of the Kuh-i-Jud and Binban units.
29. Mir Khurd states that in those days when the Sultan decided to shift the population of Delhi to Deogiri, he met the leading citizens of Delhi in a spacious tent pitched outside the palace. In his speech delivered on the occasion, the Sultan emphasized the need to destroy the non-Muslim Mongols outside the border. On the same day, he said to Shaykh Fakhr al-din Zaradi, one of the spiritual successors of Shaykh Nizam al-Din Awliya: 'We wish to destroy the descendants of Chinggis Khan. Would you cooperate with me in performing this task?' Cf. *Siyar al-Awliya*, pp. 271–2.
30. Cf. Sir Wolsely Haig, *Cambridge History of India*, vol. 3, London, 1928, p. 151.
31. Ishwari Prasad and Agha Mehdi Husain in their respective works have no doubt extended our understanding about different aspects of Sultan Muhammad bin Tughluq's reign, yet they also identify Khurasan with Persia. Cf. Ishwari Prasad, *A History of the Qaraunah Turks*, pp. 118–24; Agha Mehdi Husain, *Tughluq Dynasty*, pp. 138–43.
32. *A Comprehensive History of India*, ed. Mohammad Habib and K.A. Nizami, vol. 5, New Delhi, 1982, rpt., p. 521.

33. Peter Jackson, 'The Mongols and the Delhi Sultanate', *Central Asiatic Journal*, 1975, op. cit., pp. 128–33.
34. Cf. Anonymous, *Hudud al-Alam*, Eng. tr. V. Minorsky, London, 1937, pp. 102, 109–10, 112.
35. In a *qasidah* composed by Unsuri in praise of Sultan Mahmud of Ghazna on the latter's victory over Jaypal of India in AD 1001 the victor is mentioned as the King of Khurasan: *The Lord of Khurasan* (Mahmud) on the plain of Peshawar scattered his enemies in one attack. Cf. *Diwan-i Ustad 'Unsuri Balkhi*, ed. Muhammad Dabir Sayaqi, Tehran, 1342 AH, p. 117.

    Describing the battle of Peshawar between Jaypal and Sultan Mahmud in AD 1001, Minhaj states: 'Jaypala, who was the greatest of the rais of Hind, he (the Sultan) made prisoner and kept him at Manyazid in Khurasan, and commanded that he might be ransomed for the sum of 80 *dirhams*.' (*Tabaqat-i Nasiri*, Eng. tr. Major Raverty, vol. I, p. 82.)

    The Manyazid of Minhaj al-Siraj Juzjani is identified with Miran Shah, a small town between Ghazna and Bannu (in present-day Pakistan). Here the Sultan seems to have received the ransom and released the Indian ruler. Abdur Rahman is correct observing, 'Unsuri is borne out by Firishta, who says that Jaypal and the other prisoners were released when Mahmud was on his way back to Ghazna. Obviously, the prisoners were not sent to distant Khurasan.' Cf. *The Last Two Dynasties of the Hindu Sahis*, Islamabad (n.d.), p. 146.
36. Amir Khusrau, *Khazain al-Futuh*, ed. Wahid Mirza, Calcutta, 1953, p. 42.
37. *Tarikh-i Firuz Shahi*, Bodleian MS, ff. 201b–202a.
38. *Jumaat Shahiyah* (collection of utterances of the fifteenth-century Sufi saint Shah Alam), as quoted by Sayyid Baqar Ali Timidhi in his Urdu article, 'Mawlana Abd al-Malik Binbani Muhaddith', *Ma'arif* (Urdu quarterly), Azamgarh, October 1950, pp. 281–2.
39. Shaikh Jamali Dihlavi, *Diwan*, MS. Hbib Ganj Collection, Aligarh, f. 41b.
40. Ibid., f. 43b. In another *qasida* composed in praise of Humayun he says: 'India again has gained lustre from your dazzling face. You have returned from Khurasan like the shining sun. Cf. *Diwan*, f. 48a; Humayun had returned from Kabul in 1530 before Babur expired.
41. Muhammad bin Tughluq's letter found in the *Bayad-i Tajuddin Ahmad Wazir*, ed. Iraj Afshar and Murtada Timur, *Danishgah-i Isfahan*, no. 137, 1351 Shamsi, pp. 404–8.
42. Ghazan Khan was the first Mongol ruler of Iran who embraced Islam. His reign lasted from 1295 to 1304.
43. Uljaitu was the younger brother of Ghazan Khan. On his accession to the throne in 1304, he adopted the Shi'i faith and made Shi'ism the state religion. He died in 1316. His son Abu Said was a Sunni Muslim. Agha Mehdi Husain wrongly calls him a Shi'i.

44. *Bayad-i Taj al-Din Ahmad Wazir*, p. 409.
45. Shihab al-Din al-Umari, *Masalik al-Absar fi Mamalik al-amsar*, Eng. tr. Iqtidar Husain Siddiqui, *A Fourteenth-Century Arab Account of India under Sultan Muhammad bin Tughluq*, Aligarh, 1971, pp. 47–8.
46. Loc. cit.
47. Fasih Ahmad bin Jalal al-Din Muhammad Khawafi, *Mujmal-i Fashihi*, ed. Muhammad Farrukh, Iran, n.d., pp. 39–40.
48. Barani, p. 461.
49. Ibid., pp. 476–7.
50. *The Travels of Ibn Battuta*, vol. 3, p. 555.
51. Sharaf al-Din Ali Yezdi, *Muqaddimah*, MS British Library, London, Add., 6538, f. 90a.
52. Barani, pp. 476–7.
53. *A History of the Qaraunah Turks*, p. 136.
54. *The Tughluq Dynasty*, pp. 178–80.
55. In fact, the learned scholar has not bothered to explore evidence about Kashmir in different fourteenth-century works produced in Delhi. Even Ibn Battuta's reference to the geographical location of Qarajil has escaped Jackson's notice. Describing his visit to Amroha (Moradabad district in present-day Uttar Pradesh), Ibn Battuta says that the river Sarju (Ramganga) comes down from the Qarajil mountain. It is clear that by Qarajil or Qarachil the medieval writers mean the Garhwal-Kumaon mountainous region. As regards the references to Kashmir in the contemporary fourteenth-century Indo-Persian works, Mir Khurd refers to Kashmir as cited above. Ikhtisan, the *dabir-i khas* of Sultan Muhammad bin Tughluq, describes the romance between the princess of Kashmir and the prince of Ujjain in *Basatin al-Uns*, dedicated to the Sultan. Cf. Peter Jackson, The Mongols and the Delhi Sultanate in the Reign of Muhammad bin Tughluq, *Central Asiatic Journal*, vol. XIX, pp. 141–3; *The Travels of Ibn Battuta*, vol. 3, p. 763; Ikhtisan, *Basatin al-Uns*, MS. British Library, London, Add. 7717; Bodleian MS. of Barani's first recension, ff. 193a–b.
56. Barani, pp. 477–8.
57. In the first recension, Barani writes as a defender of his patron, Sultan Muhammad bin Tughluq. He is not at all critical of his state policies. In the second recension, his approach becomes quite different.
58. *Futuh-us-Salatin*, pp. 466–8.
59. Barani, pp. 476–7.
60. *The Travels of Ibn Battuta*, vol. 3, p. 763.
61. *Tarikh-i Mubarak Shahi*, pp. 103–4.
62. Badr Chach, as cited by Agha Mehdi Husain, *The Tughluq Dynasty*, New Delhi, 1976, p. 179.
63. *The Travels of Ibn Battuta*, vol. 3, pp. 565–7.
64. Ibid., p. 682. Barani says that he was paid one lakh *tankas* annually. Barani, pp. 461–2.

65. *The Travels of Ibn Battuta*, vol. 3, p. 589.
66. Barani, p. 462
67. *The Travels of Ibn Battuta*, vol. 3, pp. 571, 580–1.
68. Ibid., p. 722.
69. Barani, pp. 461-2.
70. *The Travels of Ibn Battuta*, vol. 3 pp. 579–80.
71. This is an important collection of Persian epistles. It contains more than 800 letters and royal documents written by 200 important persons from the eighth century to the reign of Shah Rukh. The compiler, Jalal al-Din Yusuf Ahal Jami, dedicated the volume to Shah Rukh's *wazir*, Ghiyath al-din Pir Ahmad, in AD 1433. Hence, its title *Fara id-i-Ghiyathi*. The first two volumes have been printed in Iran. The third volume still remains unpublished. The last volume contains letters dispatched by Shah Rukh to the Indian Sultans of north India, such as the Sultans of Delhi, Malwa, Gujarat, Jaunpur, and Bengal.
72. Jalal al-Din Yusuf Ahal Jami, *Fara id-i Ghiyathi*, ed. Hashmat Moyyad, vol. 1, Tehran, 1977, letter no. 32, pp. 147–8.
73. Ibid., letter no. 41, pp. 183–4, Cf. Ibn Battuta, *Ajaib ul-Asfar*, Urdu tr. Ataur Rahman, Delhi, 1348 AH, vol. 1, p. 325, for the Kurt ruler; Barani, pp. 488–9, for the banishment of the rebels.
74. *The Travels of Ibn Battuta*, vol. 2, Cambridge, 1962, p. 311.
75. Barani, p. 499.
76. Akbar Husayni, *Javami al-Kelim*, Kanpur, 1356 AH, p. 250.
77. In Iran, Haji Kawun rebelled against the rival of his brother Sulayman but he was killed. Cf. *The Travels of Ibn Battuta*, vol. 3, pp. 677–9.
78. *Tarikh-i Muhammadi*, f. 405b; also *Perso-Arabic Sources of Information . . .*, pp. 91–3.
79. Barani, pp. 536–7; also Peter Jackson, The Mongols and the Delhi Sultanate in the Reign of Muhammad bin Tughluq, *Central Asiatic Journal*, vol. XIX, nos. 1–2, 1975, pp. 154–5.
80. *A Fourteenth-Century Arab Account of India under Sultan Muhammad bin Tughluq*, pp. 39, 40, 46.
81. *The Travels of Ibn Battuta*, vol. 3, pp. 672–3, 730, 733–4.
82. Barani, p. 491. The coins issued in the name of the caliph bear the dates 742, 743, and 744 AH. See also *The Tughluq Dynasty* for more details. Barani is corroborated by the anonymous compiler of the *Sirat-i-Firuz Shahi*: 'Due to the honesty of his purpose and his wide study of books, he (Sultan Muhammad bin Tughluq) found out the truth and arrived at the firm opinion that the sanction of the rightful caliph must be obtained so that he may rule over the people rightfully and the darkness of illegal dominion may be transformed with the light of legal authority. For this reason, the use of the title of Sultan, the delivery of sermons, the receiving and granting (of money), and the enforcement of laws were all suspended.' *Sirat-i-Firuz Shahi*, the passage relating to the

grant of investiture, and translated into English by Shaikh Abdur Rashid, *Medieval India Quarterly*, Aligarh, vol. 1, no. 1, July 1950, pp. 66–71.

83. Cf. Maqrizi, *al-Suluk*, vol. II, part 2, Cairo, 1942, p. 333, as cited by Jackson, *The Mongols and the Delhi Sultanate in the Reign of Muhammad bin Tughluq*, op. cit., p. 131, f.n.7.
84. Barani, p. 492–3 *Sirat-i-Firuz Shahi*, pp. 271–5.
85. *Ajaib ul-Asfar*, vol. 1, pp. 359–60.
86. Barani, p. 517.
87. Cf. *Perso-Arabic Sources of Information*, op. cit., p. 136.
88. Ibid., p. 119.
89. Loc. cit.
90. Cf. Tatsuro Yamamoto, 'International Relations Between China and the Countries Along the Ganga in the Early Ming Period', *Indian Historical Review* (*IHR*), July 1977, vol. IV, no. 1, pp. 13–14.
91. *Ajaib ul-Asfar*, vol. 2, pp. 243–4, 392–3.
92. *Sirat-i-Firuz Shahi*, the long passage relating to Firuz Shah's relations with the caliph, translated into English by Shaikh Abdur Rashid in Firuz Shah's Investiture by the caliph, *Medieval India Quarterly*, vol. 1, no. 1, July 1950, pp. 66–71.

CHAPTER 6

Intelligence Apparatus

The state apparatus developed by Sultan Mahmud of Ghazna provided a reference point to the Ghurids and the Sultans of India in organizing an elaborate network of intelligence service as well. It is noteworthy that by the time the Sultanate in India was founded, the politico-social system inherited by the early Sultans of India had become a complex phenomenon. In the absence of a rapid means of transport and communication, the law and order situation and the activities of the governors in the far-off provinces could be known and checked by the centre on the basis of the intelligence reports sent by the intelligence officers of the provinces. The intelligence agents acted for the good of the people and in the interests of the people. The maintenance of an elaborate network of spies was considered necessary for the maintenance of peace and order.

No doubt, in the Indian environment the old institutions appear to have gained a new meaning. New elements were added to the Central Asian heritage, yet there was a long continuity of administrative practice. It is also true that the recruitment by the rulers of spies was as old a practice as the state system that had existed since ancient times.[1] In the Islamic world also, the Abbasid caliphs had a well-organized espionage system. But the evidence available in the contemporary sources of information for the Ghaznavid period tends to reveal that Sultan Mahmud of Ghazna organized a central intelligence bureau under a *sahib-i-barid* (officer-in-charge of intelligence), who enjoyed the status of a minister at the centre. As the Sultan had a stake in the security and well-being of the people, not only would the ruler arrest criminals and oppressive officers in the country but he would also ensure impartial justice to all. The *barids* (intelligence officers) were posted in the provinces along with a number of spies, their subordinates. They were posted to keep watch on the officers holding important positions in the capital as well as in places visited by people, such as hospices and shrines of Sufi saints because the nobles and other disgruntled elements could meet there and plot the overthrow of the government. The spies communicated information to the *barid* about everything that was thought worth reporting, and the latter immediately passed it on to his chief at the centre. The Sultan was informed by the chief, called the *sahib-i-barid*. In short, the Sultan could centralize political power with the support of a central standing army and a well-organized bureaucracy. According to Fakhr-i-Mudabbir the Ghaznavid historian, the officers who belonged to the intelligence bureau formed a part of the bureaucracy. As the relevant evidence casts light on the importance that the Sultan attached to this office, we may summarize it:

> One of the important functions of the state is the establishment of the department of *barid* (intelligence network), which concerns the collection of news about different occurrences, incidents, and developments (in the empire). The employees attached to this department are to inform the king about them, no matter whether it is day or night. Every event is to be reported in detail faithfully.
>
> The spies should not put down any matter in the diary unless they verify its truth. Neither should they act against anyone out of malice, nor should they allow people to go scot free by taking bribes. Criminals and anti-social elements are to be suppressed. Therefore, righteous and honest persons must be entrusted with the office of the *barid*, so that the ruler be supplied correct information and innocent people saved from tyranny. The chief *barid* at the centre should select honest men known for their integrity of character to work as his subordinates in the capital as well as the provinces. They should be free from greed and remain satisfied whatever salary they receive.

Further, Fakhr-i-Mudabbir informs us about the elevation of the central *barids* to the highest position in the official hierarchy on account of their competence. He calls the office of the *barid* one of the pillars of the state and notes that the *barids* who had become distinguished for their services were promoted to the post of *wazir* under the Ghaznavids. Some of them are said to have written books on different subjects, including history.[2]

Barani, the political thinker of the Delhi Sultanate, also discusses the importance of the role of the *barids* in the maintenance of law and order in the country. He devotes a separate chapter to this subject in his treatise, *Fatawa-i-Jahandari*. First, he mentions the requisite qualifications to be possessed by the *barid*. He states that besides his noble birth, his honesty and integrity of character should be vouched for to ensure that he would act in a non-partisan way and that whatever was put down in his report was nothing but the truth. Because the *barid* was required to keep watch on all and sundry in the *qasbas*, cities, *arsas* (provinces or *vilayets*) and inform the centre about every development, at times steps were taken on the basis of his report to prevent a situation from taking a serious turn and causing widespread disturbances. Therefore, in Barani's view the Sultans of strong personality, like Sultan Mahmud of Ghazna, considered it their foremost duty to keep themselves well informed about every serious matter in the Sultanate through an elaborate network of *barids*. In concluding his advice, Barani suggests that competent *barids* should be employed because their existence was necessary for the maintenance of the *dabdaba-i-badshahi* (royal splendour and fear). The Sultan was also to be feared and not just respected.[3]

Like the Ghaznavids, the Sultans in India also appear to have had a well-organized intelligence service department, headed by the *sahib-i-barid*. Amongst the early thirteenth-century writers of the Delhi Sultanate, Sadiduddin Muhammad Awfi informs us that the first independent Sultan of India, Qutbuddin Aibek, selected a favourite Hindu *rana* (land chief) from the territorial unit of Benaras for the post of *sahib-i-barid* (chief *barid*) after his accession to the throne (AD 1206). Upon his elevation to this important position, one of the courtiers of the Sultan, Majd-ul-Mulk Bahauddin Aljamji, expressed his resentment by reciting a quatrain that he had composed off-hand, but in vain.[4] The references contained in *Tabaqat-i-Nasiri* reveal that the intelligence service remained effective under the successor of Sultan Qutbuddin Aibek.[5] Sultan Shamsuddin Iltutmish (ruled: AD 1211–36) seems to have posted spies in the guise of officials in every ministerial department at the centre and in the provinces as well. Even a trivial matter was reported to the Sultan. For instance, once a Turk slave who had been elevated to the position of *sar-i-jandar* (chief of the royal bodygua1rds) looked unhappy at the time of the payment of his salary for the first time, although it was an occasion of great joy for others. This being reported, the Turk was asked by the Sultan to explain the reason for his having detested the payment.[6] The Sultan also got information from the provinces about the wealth hoarded by the state officers. The law of escheat was applied in such instances where officers were found guilty of misappropriating the state share.[7]

The dangerous precedents set by the Turk slave generals and the Tajik officers after the death of Sultan Iltutmish against his sons aroused in the minds of the later Sultans a pathological anxiety for their own safety. The nobles had become kingmakers. Five Sultans came to the throne in ten years after the death of Sultan Iltutmish. Therefore, Sultan Ghiyasuddin Balban (ruled: AD 1266–87) reorganized a network of spies and *barids* who worked in the capital, *vilayets* and *shiqqs* (territorial units), and even inside the houses of the nobles. The king was informed about the activities of people, both loyal and seditious. In an attempt to reduce the high-ranking military generals, *muqtas* and *walis* (governors) to complete subservience to the throne, the Sultan took drastic measures against ambitious nobles. He got assassinated all the powerful nobles of doubtful loyalty and appointed trusted men to all important posts in the Sultanate. To be certain of their good conduct, he appointed men of intelligence and integrity for spying even on his loyal subjects. Barani says:

> During his reign, he appointed trustworthy spies in all the *vilayets*, *iqtas* and throughout all the territories; he also appointed them to important cities and large and distant towns. He never entrusted anybody with *baridi* (spying) unless he himself judged him as an honest and upright man. . . . For the fear of the spies, the *muqtas*, officers, and *amils* (revenue collectors), or their sons, dependants and slaves dared not distress any innocent person throughout his empire.[8]

The Sultan was so strict in this matter that he sent *barids* to watch over the conduct of his second son, Bughra Khan, whom he had entrusted with the government of the vilayet-i-Samana. Bughra Khan was an ease-loving prince addicted to wine drinking, therefore the Sultan spared no effort in setting him right. At the time of his appointment as the *muqta* of vilayet-i-Samana, the Sultan threatened him with dismissal and non-appointment to any post if he did not mend his ways. At last, the prince had to give way.[9]

Similarly, the *barids* were severely punished if they failed in informing the Sultan about any matter. For instance, the spy stationed in Badaon to watch its *muqta*, Malik Baqbaq, was hanged over the gate of the city for he did not report to the Sultan the killing by the *muqta* of his servant in a state of drunkenness.[10] In the list of the leading nobles of Balban's reign, Barani mentions Malik Jamaluddin Aitigin as the chief *barid* at the centre.[11]

Sultan Jalaluddin Khalji, though very liberal and kind to his nobles, was very serious about keeping himself well informed about the malicious activities of influential people in his capital. He is reported to have pardoned his nobles when they spoke ill of him. But he did not spare the lives of Sidi Maula and other malcontents, for they had seriously conspired against his life as already discussed.[12] The *sahib-i-barid* during his reign was Malik Ulghu, a Mongol convert to Islam and the Sultan's son-in-law, whose report was taken seriously because it was based on a thorough investigation. Sidi Maula's *khanqah* was visited by a large number of people, including nobles and foreign merchants.[13]

By the time of Sultan Alauddin Khalji, the number of spies appears to have increased considerably. He organized a network of spies that made it possible for him to implement his administrative and economic plans and reforms. The Sultan seems to have organized systematically the intelligence department, which continued during the succeeding period also.

Shihabuddin al-Umari collected information from travellers, foreign merchants, and Indian pilgrims to Arabia and, after having verified it, he included it in his work about different aspects of the culture and polity in India under the Sultan of Delhi. He states:

> Allama Sirajuddin Abul Safa al-Shibli related to me that the Sultan makes special arrangements to keep himself well informed about the affairs of his empire, army, and people. He has a department of intelligence (service), and the officials belonging to it are called *munhiyan* (spies). They have several grades. Some of them are posted in the army, while others keep watch on the public. When the spy comes to know of something which has to be reported to the Sultan, he conveys the information about it to his immediate superior. The latter passes it on to

the officer above him. In this way, the information reaches the Sultan through the highest officer.[14]

All this finds corroboration in the eyewitness account furnished by Ibn Battuta. It also bears testimony to the fact that the intelligence machinery was organized under a supreme officer called *malik al-mukhbiran* (Arabic equivalent of the Persian *sahib-i-barid*), that he was a man of high dignity and enjoyed the status of a *malik* as his title shows. He was entrusted with the charge of all the royal slaves stationed with the nobles in the capital, the *vilayets*, and the *iqtas* for spying in addition to other secret reporters appointed in his department. Ibn Battuta throws important light on the matter when he says:

> It is the custom of the King of India to set along side every amir, be he great or small, a mamluk of his to spy upon him and keep him informed of everything to do with him. He also places slave girls in their houses, who act as spies for him upon his amirs, as well as women whom they call sweepers, who come into the houses without asking permission. The slave girls pass on their information to those women and the sweepers in turn pass that on to the King of intelligence (i.e. *malik al-mukhbiran*), who then informs the Sultan of it.[15]

Besides the above-mentioned reporters, Sultan Alauddin Khalji is reported to have deputed underage boys serving in the royal pigeon houses in the *bazaars* of Delhi to get information about the malpractices of shopkeepers and merchants. As the shopkeepers could not charge more than the rates fixed, they started cheating people in weight. The boy spies used to buy miscellaneous things in the *bazaars* and then attended on the Sultan. It was ascertained whether the shopkeepers were honest in their dealings with the innocent people. If any one of them was found guilty of selling commodities underweight, he was severely punished.[16]

As a result, all the shopkeepers and traders became honest and refrained from giving people short weight. As Barani says:[17] 'For the dread of the spies, people and the traders, big as well as small, turned to honesty and thoroughly became submissive and obedient.'

Likewise, Haji Abd-al-Hamid, who completed his work *Dastur al-Albab fi Ilm al-Hisab* in AD 1358, also supplements our information about the intelligence service during the medieval period. His work shows that there were men of different categories employed for the work of espionage. There were the spies of the rank of officers about whom he says that they should be of noble birth. They should have a smiling face and a cheerful countenance without which people would not like their company. Being noble-born persons they could easily be familiar with the nobles and exalted personages. He says: 'If men of integrity and intelligence are appointed to this job, they would easily judge by their ability the conduct of the nobles from their words and acts. None but they could bring the secrets of the *maliks*, and *amirs,* the *sardars* and the *wazirs* from their hearts.'[18] As a matter of fact, the appointment of the noble-born and cultured people to high posts in the intelligence service was necessary. It was really difficult for low-born people to behave properly in the presence of high-ranking nobles or sophisticated foreigners whom they met on their arrival in the country.[19]

Below them were the spies who attended regularly to their work in the markets, thoroughfares, and other public places and performed their duties without any greed. To contact the spy slave girls working inside the houses of the nobles, trusted women were employed, who went to the houses of the nobles in the guise of maidservants or perfume dealers. These women reported to their superiors, who in turn sent their reports to the chief.[20]

The working of the system at its best seems to have begun from the time of Sultan Alauddin Khalji. He successfully controlled every aspect of human life in the name of the emergency caused by the Mongol menace. In an attempt to eradicate social evils and to keep state officers under restraint, he organized such a good network of spies that no action of men, whether good or bad, was concealed from him. No one could stir without his knowledge. Consequently, the nobles, high and low, did not have the courage to speak to their fellow nobles in the Hazar Satun palace. If they had to say anything, they communicated it by signs. 'The dread of the spies,' says Barani, 'made them (nobles) tremble day and night even inside their own houses. They refrained from doing anything which might result in their destruction or disgrace.'[21]

But those who dealt in the trade of wine proved to be very

difficult to put right. The enforcement of prohibition of wine failed in creating a sense of respect for the law in the minds of the people. Those who had any sense of self-respect at once gave up drinking but the reckless and 'vile characters' used to distil wine from sugar inside their houses for personal consumption and to sell it at a high price. They also used to supply wine to Delhi from neighbouring areas.

Despite the posting of *naqibs* and their assistant spies[22] at all the gates of Delhi, the wine dealers brought in the wine by deceiving them. They used to fill wine either in the *mashk* (a leather container used for carrying water) or concealed it in the loads of hay, fuel, and such other things and then carried it on asses. But the spies succeeded in arresting them. The offenders were severely punished and the people gave up drinking.[23]

In short, the system was so perfect and elaborate that credulous people attributed the Sultan with supernatural power. They thought that nothing could be concealed from him. Our contemporary historian says:[24] 'They imbued him with miraculous power. Whatever information he gave about the expeditions led (against the independent territories), victories and conquests, they attributed (its source) to his miracle and revelation.'

The study of the reigns of the later Sultans also shows that they successfully maintained the good traditions of Sultan Alauddin Khalji for keeping themselves well informed about the affairs of their nobles and the people as well. Sultan Muhammad bin Tughluq is said to have studied the reports of his intelligence officers very carefully. His intelligence officers took the utmost care in sending him detailed reports. If some foreigner entered the empire, they wrote to him that a certain man of such an appearance and dress had arrived, and also noted the number of his companions, slaves, servants, and others, his behaviour both in action and at rest, and all his doings. The foreigner was asked to stay in Multan until the royal order was received regarding his entry and the degree of hospitality to be extended to him. Foreigners were accorded honour according to their external appearances, actions and conduct, because no one knew anything of their family, lineage, or actual status in their own countries.[25]

The other relevant references contained in the contemporary literature from the reigns of Sultan Muhammad bin Tughluq and

Sultan Sikandar Lodi are interesting as they indicate that even the matters discussed between the nobles and their women, while in bed at night, were reported to the Sultan. 'Once an *amir* was in bed with his woman with whom he liked to be intimate. She begged him not to be so, conjuring him by the head of the Sultan. But he did not hear her. In the morning, the Sultan sent for him and told him about it. This became the cause of his destruction.'[26] The circumstantial evidence contained in the same source may also be cited. The Sultan's slave, Malik Shah, was posted to keep watch on Ainul Mulk. He reported to the Sultan as soon as Ainul Mulk went across the Ganges at night and revolted. The Sultan was perturbed because 'horses, elephants, grain, all of them, were with Ainul Mulk, and his own troops were widely scattered'.[27]

Similarly, Sultan Sikandar Lodi tried to get information through his spies about the activities of his nobles, for he also feared that any of them might conspire against him. Rizq Allah Mushtaqi's statement reveals that he also benefited from the services rendered both by male and female slaves. He says:[28]

> Moreover, the intelligence system was so perfect that if someone conversed in one's own house, it was reported to the Sultan. It is said that once Bhikkan Khan Lodi was sleeping on the roof of his house. When it started raining, he carried the cot into the room with the help of his wife as there was no slave girl or maidservant. Next morning when he came to the royal audience, he found (the Sultan) telling the others, such high nobles have no servants with them and carry the cot themselves into the room.

In short, the Sultan, like the early powerful Sultans, kept a vigilant eye on all that happened in his empire. His spies remained with the nobles whether they were stationed at the centre, the *sarkars*, or the *vilayets*, or were deputed on military expeditions, and provided him with intelligence about all the happenings as soon as possible. Once Masnad-i-Ali Azam Humayun Sarwani marched against the raja of Batha and proceeded so far in search of the fugitive raja that no information could be sent either to his relations in Agra or to the Sultan for seventeen days. His son Fath Khan was deeply worried about him, but the Sultan sent a man to tell him that his father was safe and would return to his *vilayet* victorious after a few days.[29] As a result, people thought that the Sultan possessed supernatural powers or had access to some kind of magic lamp, which on being lighted produced two geniis to inform him about every matter.[30]

As regards Sher Shah, he was very particular about having very able spies in his service even before his rise to power. In 1532, his spies informed him that Bahadur Shah of Gujarat had conquered the kingdom of Malwa and would soon declare war against the Mughals to seize Delhi. After his rise to power, he became even more particular about getting secret intelligence about all the matters whether concerning the nobles, the people, or the functioning of the state machinery throughout his empire. Everyone of the nobles, no matter howsoever great or loyal he might be, was strictly watched by the royal spies. Once Masnad-i-Ali Shujat Khan, the *muqta* of Malwa, was surprised to know that the king got information about his quarrel with the royal *khasa Khail* soldiers[31] (the central army men, posted in the province) over land grants, although he had persuaded them not to send their complaint to the king by redressing their grievances.[32]

A word may also be added here about the postal service as it was also linked with the intelligence service. The *barids* had their agents posted at the postal stations, called *dak chauki*. Shihabuddin al-Umari informs us that the *dak chaukis* were established along the highways linking the provinces with the centre.

> The distance between two *chaukis* is four bow-shots or even less. There are posted ten runners at every *dak chauki*. One of them whose turn comes takes the dispatch and runs with utmost speed to the next station, where the other runner receives it and passes it on to the next man in the same manner. After the dispatch is handed over to the other courier, the runner returns to his post with ease. Thus the dispatches reach from one remote place to the other remote place within a short time and earlier than the *dak* horses and camels.[33]

Ibn Battuta corroborates al-Umari, for he also mentions couriers and *dak* horses both. He adds that the mounted couriers travelled on the royal horses, with relays every 4 miles, while the couriers on foot had to run with all speed, holding rods one and a half yards long with brass bells at the top in one hand and holding the letter in the other. Hearing the sound of the bells, the men in waiting at the next *chauki* would rush to receive it.[34]

The espionage system continued unchanged under Islam Shah also because he required the services of the spies in dealing with his conflict with the nobles of his father.[35] But on his death it must have suffered a setback when the entire administrative machinery was paralysed due to widespread anarchy.

To conclude, the department of intelligence service performed an important role during the Sultanate period. In fact, the medieval polity could not function successfully without the help of this department because the ambitious and dissatisfied nobles were wont to aspire for the throne. They could also gang up and foment rebellion against the Sultan. The intelligence officers informed the Sultan about the activities of the nobles, the general public, maltreatment or good treatment by the officers of the people, the nature of their relations with their fellow officers, and the arrival of foreigners in their territories. The system continued during the subsequent period under the Mughals as well.

NOTES

1. Cf. Nagendra Nath Ghosh, *Early History of India*, Allahabad, 1981, rpt., pp. 186–7.
2. Muhammad bin Mansur, known as Fakhr-i-Mudabbir, *Adab al-Muluk wal Kifayat al-Mumluk*, pp. 25–8.
3. *Fatawa-i-Jahandari*, pp. 118–30.
4. *Lubab al-Albab*, ed. E.G. Browne and Muhammad Qazwini, London, 1906, part II, pp. 113–15; also Iqtidar Husain Siddiqui, *Perso-Arabic Sources on the Life and Conditions in the Sultanate of Delhi*, New Delhi, 1992, p. 7, for the translation of Awfi's work.
5. Minhaj Juzjani, *Tabaqat-i-Nasiri*, ed. Abdul Hai Habibi, Kabul, 1963, vol. I, p. 492.
6. Malik Saifuddin Aibek was unhappy because he was assigned the duty to kill undesirable nobles and deprive their sons and dependants of their assets. The Malik being a God-fearing man detested the job. *Tabaqat-i-Nasiri*, Kabul, 1964, vol. II, p. 8.
7. Sadiduddin Muhammad Awfi, *Jawami'ul Hikayat wal Lavami'ul Rivayat*, Eng. tr. I.H. Siddique, *Perso-Arabic Sources on the Life and Conditions in the Sultanate of Delhi*, op. cit., p. 32.

8. Barani's references to the *barid* and the *munhiyan* show that the former was an intelligence officer while the latter was a spy who passed on information about everything to the *barid*. The *barid* sent his report to the *sahib-i-barid* at the centre whose responsibility was to pass it on to the Sultan immediately if necessary. Ishtiyaq Husain Qureshi, identifying the *barids* with modern newspaper reporters, states: 'the newswriters can be broadly divided into two categories: the *barid* resembled modern newspaper reporters and sent their letters, and the extraordinary agents and spies sent on special mission', I.H. Qureshi, *The Administration of the Sultanate of Delhi*, 1944, p. 212.

   The difficulty in accepting this view is that the entire purpose of appointing *barids* would be defeated if a rebel *muqta* could either win them over to his side or, failing to do this, arrest them. As a matter of fact, the *barids* worked secretly in disguise. Both Ibn Battuta and medieval Indian writers support our view, as will be later discussed.
   Tarikh-i-Firuz Shahi, Calcutta, 1862, p. 45.
9. Barani, p. 81.
10. Ibid., p. 40.
11. Ibid., p. 24.
12. Iqtidar Husain Siddiqui, 'The Nobility under the Khalji Sultans', *Islamic Culture*, vol. 37, no. 1, Jan. 1963, p. 57.
13. Yahya Sirhindi, *Tarikh-i-Mubarak Shahi*, ed. Muhammad Hidayat Husaini, Calcutta, 1931, pp. 65–7.
14. Cf. *Perso-Arabic Sources of Information on the Life and Conditions in the Sultanate of Delhi*, p. 131.
15. Ibn Battuta, *The Travels of Ibn Battuta*, vol. 3, p. 721.
16. Barani, p. 308. Here Barani refers to the *barid* of *munhiyan*, i.e. the officer of the spies.
17. Ibid., p. 315.
18. *Dastur al-Albab fi-Ilm al-Hisab*, rotograph of the Raza Library MS., ff. 54a–b.
19. *The Travels of Ibn Battuta*, vol. 3, p. 595. The chief of the intelligence service in Multan called on Ibn Battuta and also took him to the governor after his arrival there.
20. *Dastur al-Albab fi-Ilm al-Hisab*, f. 56a.
21. Barani, p. 284.
22. Ibid., p. 285.
23. Ibid.
24. Ibid., p. 324.
25. *The Travels of Ibn Battuta*, vol. 3, pp. 595–6.
26. Ibid., p. 721.
27. Ibid.
28. Shaikh Rizq Ullah Mashtaqi, *Waqiat-i-Mushtaqi*, Eng. tr. Iqtidar Husain Siddiqui, New Delhi, 1993, p. 36. See also *Tarikh-Daud*, Abd Allah, Aligarh, text, p. 64.

29. *Waqiat-i-Mushtaqi*, Eng. tr., pp. 47–8.
30. Shaikh Muhammad Kabir Batni, *Afsana Shahan*, rotograph of the MS, British Library, London, f.34b; Ahmad Yadgar, *Tarikh Shahi*, Calcutta, 1939, p. 44.
31. The *Khasa Khail* soldiers belonged to the royal army under the immediate command of the king. Cf. *The Administration of the Sultanate of Delhi*, p. 139.
32. *Tarikh Sher Shahi*, ed. S.M. Imam al-Din, Dacca, 1964, pp. 229–30.
33. *Perso-Arabic Sources on the Life and Conditions in the Sultanate of Delhi*, pp. 131–2.
34. *The Travels of Ibn Battuta*, vol. 3, pp. 594–5.
35. Ahmad Yadgar, *Tarikh-i-Shahi*, ed. M. Hidayat Husain, Calcutta, 1939, p. 250.

CHAPTER 7

Provincial Organization

The history of the evolution of the territorial units, extensive as well as small, deserves a closer study than has so far been made. The well-defined administrative units called *khitta, vilayet, arsa, shiqq*, and *iqta* came into existence after the consolidation of Muslim power as a result of an evolutionary process. The land potentates who held large tracts under their control seem to have acquiesced to the authority of their conquerors for the time being; they sided with the overthrown rulers against the Sultan whenever an opportunity arose. It may, however, be pointed out that the garrisons posted in the important cities and forts and located at strategic places played a vital role in the gradual shaping of the state system.

The process of the evolution of the larger or provincial units started from the north-western region of the Panjab.[1] It was here that Muslim power was consolidated for the first time. Consequently, the units of Binban,[2] Kuh-i-Jud,[3] Sialkot, Lahore, and Multan became the pattern to be followed in the other regions of the Sultanate with regard to provincial organization. The extensive territorial units of Binban, Kuh-i-Jud (later the *shiqq* of Bhera), Sialkot, and Lahore were formed during the Ghaznavid period, while Multan had existed as a well-demarcated unit since the time of its Ismaili Qaramita rulers. The unit of Sialkot seems to have extended up to hills of Jammu, the raja of which was hostile to Khusrau Malik, the last Ghaznavid ruler, and had allied with Sultan Muizuddin Muhammad bin Sam. The *khitta* of Lahore lay along the river Ravi up to the boundary of the Multan unit. The territories of Hansi and Tabarhinda that once formed a part of the Ghaznavid dominions in India were seized by the Rajput ruler of Ajmer.[4] It may also be pointed out that the trans-Sutlej territorial units had well-defined boundaries, which were determined by the rivers. Of them the unit of Jalandhar lay between the Sultej and Beas rivers and was thus an ideal one. It was governed by a senior noble.[5]

With the conquests made by Sultan Muizuddin Muhammad bin Sam and his lieutenants after the second battle of Tarain in AD 1192, the whole of northern India came under the control of the Sultan, and the forts and strategic places were garrisoned under the command of competent generals. But no attempt seems to have been made to demarcate the boundaries of the territories seized from the Rajput rulers, for the land potentates who happened to be the allies of the overthrown *rais* had to be reconciled to the alien rule. The demarcation of the boundaries of the units in the cis-Sutlej region and the Doab began under Sultan Iltutmish. The unit of metropolitan Delhi[6] was bound on the east by the river Jamuna, on the north 'by the Siwalik hills, or rather by the line of forest at their feet, and on the south it marched with Mewat, a fluctuating boundary, because at times the turbulent Mewatis threatened Delhi itself'.[7] On the west, the *khitta* of Delhi shared its boundary with that of Kuhram and Sunam (later called Samana-o-Sunam).[8] It included almost the whole of present-day Haryana and the *sarkar* of Sirhind of the Mughal period. Like them, the territorial units of Mian-i-Doab, with Meerut as its headquarters, and Badaon, which encompassed the region of Katehar (or Rohilkhand of the British period), were divided into two separate units by the river Ganga. The Khitta-i-Mian-i-Doab included the present-day districts of Meerut, Muzaffarnagar, and Roorki.[9] Apart from them, the other territorial units, particularly of the eastern region, were not touched in this regard.

The position of the *sipahsalar* (or *wali*), the officer-in-charge of the army contingents placed in the towns, the headquarters of the territories, remained precarious in the beginning. As already mentioned, the only established territorial units during the time of Sultan Muizuddin Muhammad bin Sam were those of Binban, Kuh-i-Jud, Sialkot, Lahore, Multan, Uchh, Khitta-i-Tabarhinda, Khitta-i-Kuhram and Sunam, and Khitta-i-Delhi. Unlike these territories, the territories of Meerut, Baran, Koel, Awadh, Benaras, Kalinjar, Bayana, Gwalior, Ajmer, and Nagore (mentioned by the chroniclers as *khitta* or *vilayet*)[10] took time to be pacified during the latter half of the thirteenth century. It is, however, to the credit of the Khalji nobles that they were able to reconcile the local land chiefs of Bihar and Bengal, and as a result a friendly policy was followed by them towards the local people; they had secured their cooperation and then established their firm politico-military control over them.[11]

The Consolidation of Muslim Rule and the Evolution of Territorial Units

It appears from the military campaigns led by Aibek's successor, Sultan Shamsuddin Iltutmish (reigned: 1210–36), that the territories around Delhi up to the border of Bihar had to be wrested from Muslim rivals and land chiefs.[12] Having destroyed his Muslim rivals, Tajuddin Yildoz and Sultan Nasiruddin Qubacha in the north-western territories and Sind, and the Khaljis in Bihar and Bengal, Sultan Iltutmish established his rule over the whole of northern India, conquered and ruled over by Sultan Qutbuddin Aibek.[13] The *sipahsalars* appointed by him in the territories played an important role in consolidating the Sultan's rule. They maintained their hold over their territorial units, established peace, won over the confidence of the local people, and thus laid down the foundations of the administrative units, which developed into *shiqq*, *arsa*, and later *sarkar* (under the Lodis and Sher Shah Sur).

The large territories re-annexed by Sultan Iltutmish to the Delhi Sultanate remained under the effective control of the *sipahsalars* during the reign of his successors also. Though the Rajput chiefs rose in arms time and again in the Doab and Rajputana (present-day Rajasthan), they failed in finally expelling the Muslim garrisons. Their gains in some territories were short lived. For instance, Timur Khan, the *sipahsalar* of Awadh, led successful expeditions against the hostile chiefs of Bhatgorah (Bundelkhand), Malik Tajuddin Sanjar Qutlugh subjugated the recalcitrant elements in the Katehar region, while Bahauddin Balban is reported to have crushed the *ranas* and *rais* in the territories around Delhi.[14]

It is also noteworthy that the death of Sultan Iltutmish in 1236 provided an opportunity to the nobles to decentralize power and assume the role of kingmakers. The nobles posted as *sipahsalars* in the *khittas* became almost autonomous, and each one regarded the unit held by him as his *iqta*, with the right to keep its revenue as his share in the Sultanate. But they continued to maintain nominally their link with the centre as it was in their interests to do so. An open rebellion by a noble against the Sultan could provide his rivals at court an opportunity to join hands against him. In this way, his hold over the *khitta* remained firm. With the weakening of the centre, the whole of the Sultanate became a sum of *iqtas* and the former *sipahsalars* became *muqtas*. The most prominent of the *muqtas*, each holding sway over a resource-rich and extensive territory, were Malik Izzuddin Kabir Khan, the *muqta* of Multan; Malik Saifuddin Kuchi, the *muqta* of the combined *khittas* of Hansi, Kuhram and Sunam; Malik Alauddin Jani, the *muqta* of Lahore; who maintained peace and order in their respective *iqtas*.[15] Similarly, the powerful *muqtas* of the Doab region, Malik Izzuddin Muhammad Salari in Badaon,[16] Malik Nusratuddin Taisi in Awadh,[17] Malik Izzuddin Balban-i-Kishlu Khan in Nagore, Mandore, and Ajmer successfully governed the turbulent territorial units under them. In addition, there were also posted some princes of the blood in the important outlying territories along with competent nobles to help them in the administration. Their guides and followers exerted themselves not only in guarding them but also in creating conditions favourable for progress.[18] In short, there were sporadic efforts made by the dispossessed *rais* and *ranas* to recover their lost power and territories, but their attempts could not crystallize into a mass movement against the Muslim rule imposed on them. By this time the administrative institutions of the Sultanate appear to have taken a definite shape, though the territorial units were still under evolution, without fixed boundaries.

The following *khittas* (also called *iqta* and *vilayet*) appear to have existed during the first half of the thirteenth century. Some of the *khittas* included more than one extensive territorial unit, which were later separated and organized into *shiqqs* with demarcated boundaries.

1. *Khitta-i-Binban*[19]
2. *Khitta-i-Kuh-i-Jud*[20]

3. *Khitta-i-Lahore*, which included the region up to the boundary of Multan along the river Ravi
4. *Khitta-i-Multan*[21]
5. *Khitta-i-Uchh*[22]
6. *Khitta-i-Tabarhinda*
7. *Khitta-i-Kuhram* and *Sunam*
8. *Khitta-i-Hansi*[23]
9. *Khitta-i-Delhi* (later Haveli-i-Hazrat Delhi)
10. *Khitta-i-Meerut* (later Shiqq-i-Mian-i-Doab)[24] *Khitta-i-Baran*[25]
11. *Khitta-i-Kol* (also mentioned as *vilayet*)[26]
12. *Khitta-i-Sambhal* (later merged into the unit of Amroha).[27]
13. *Khitta-i-Badaon*, which included within its boundaries the entire tract from Hardwar, and the whole of Katehar along the foothills of the Himalayas (now divided into the divisions of Bareilly and Moradabad). The leading nobles were entrusted with its governance. Moreover, a large colony of foreign immigrants was also planted there. The references contained in the *Fawaid ul-Fawad* reveal that Badaon became the hometown of the scholars, Maulana Raziuddin Sighani, the compiler of the celebrated *Mashariq ul-Anwar* (a collection of *hadith*), Maulana Alauddin Asuli, the teacher of Shaikh Nizamuddin (Auliya), and Maulana Sirajuddin Tirmizi. Besides these scholars of eminence, the leading Sufi saints, poets, merchants, and craftsmen also took up residence in the town, with the result that it also assumed the role of an integrative nucleus in Katehar, known as western Uttar Pradesh.[28] Surrounded by dense forests but linked with Delhi and other parts of the Sultanate through a highway, it was a peaceful place and therefore held a fascination for scholars and poets. Shihab Mihmara, the leading early thirteenth-century poet, requests his royal patron, Sultan Ruknuddin Firuz Shah (killed in 1336) in a panegyric to grant him a maintenance land grant near Badaon:[29]

    O the elephant-bestower, I desire a place in the wilderness of Badaon,
    Even though this region is the abode of the wolf, the rhinoceros, and the lion.

May your enemies be left without life like the lions, elephants, wolves, and rhinoceros at the end of the story line in the bath.

14. *Khitta-i-Qanauj*,[30] which comprised the area of the present-day district of Farrukhabad and parts of Ettah and Mainpuri districts of Uttar Pradesh. The town of Qanauj was a large urban centre with big mansions. Ibn Battuta calls Qanauj an important and large city containing an impregnable fort and lofty city walls. It was famous for its sugar, which was produced in huge quantities and transported to Delhi. It is also mentioned as a city known for its elite, the members of which served in important positions in the Sultanate.[31]
15. *Khitta-i-kara-o-Manikpur*.[32]
16. *Khitta-i-Bahraich*, which extended over the region from the Ghagra River and was bound in the north by the dense forest of Gorakhpur.[33]
17. *Khitta-i-Bihar*, which included the districts of south Bihar.[34]
18. *Iqlim-i-Lakhnauti* (also mentioned as the *vilayet* of Lakhnauti or Bengal).[35]
19. The *khittas*, lying to the south of Delhi were those of Bayana, *Mehar-o-Mahavan*,[36] Gwalior, Nagore, Ajmer, and Ranthambore. The latter seems to have been evacuated during the reign of Sultan Raziya.[37]

Of the aforesaid territorial units, now included in present-day Rajasthan, Bayana, Gwalior, Ajmer, and Nagore could be retained by the nobles of the Sultan, although their writ does not seem to have run in the dependencies held by the Rajput chiefs in the interior.

Reorganization of the Territorial Units into *Shiqqs*

The organization of extensive territorial units called *shiqqs*, with fixed boundaries, may be traced to the reign of Sultan Balban. It was some time in AD 1279 when Sultan Balban led military expeditions against the rebel governor Tughril, and took Bughra Khan with him, that he parcelled out the outlying *vilayet* of Samana and Sunam into two *shiqqs*, those of Samana and Hansi, so that the governor other than a prince of the blood might not turn rebel for having been put in charge of a large and resource-rich territory. Barani says: 'He (the Sultan) divided the *vilayet* of Samana and Sunam into *shiqqs* and assigned them to the nobles and army (into maintenance *iqtas*).'[38] The Sultan is also reported to have appointed Malik Sonj as Sar-i-Jandar, that is, as the commander of the army posted in Samana.[39]

As regards the territorial units of Baran and Kol (present-day Aligarh), they seem to have been smaller in area and were generally assigned in *iqtas* to the high-ranking nobles who held ministerial posts at the centre. Unlike them, the territorial unit of Badaon was unwieldy and problematic, and the Katehariya chiefs still remained unsubdued. The Sultan is reported to have led a punitive expedition against the chiefs, ravaged their villages, and carved out a separate unit named iqta-i-Amroha, and placed it under the control of the centre as *khalsa* territory. He appointed a number of officers with specified duties.[40] From that point on Amroha began to develop into a flourishing city. Ibn Battuta found it a small but beautiful city, with a number of officers, including the Shaikh ul-Islam, who looked after the management of the *khanqah* (the charity house). There were 1,500 villages, grouped into *parganas* (or *sadis*); their revenue amounted to 60,00,000 *tankas* per annum.[41] Like Ketehar, the *khitta* of Qanauj also received royal attention for it abounded in highwaymen and recalcitrant land chiefs. It encompassed a vast region, including the present-day districts of Ettah, Etawah, Farrukhabad, and Hardoi. As pointed out earlier, the *thanas* established by the Sultan around Qanauj helped in the consolidation of the centre's rule and rendered the road safe for the movement of merchant *caravans* between Delhi and Bengal. Some of the *thanas* founded by Balban developed into important townships and served as the *pargana* headquarters during the Khalji period. Ibn Battuta found Kanpil with a fort that was known for its strength.[42] He describes Jalali a city with fortifications.[43] Ibn Battuta's description of the city of Qanauj is also interesting because it reveals that the old demographic pattern was not disturbed anywhere but that a new element was added to it. A separate colony of Muslim immigrants comprising soldiers, scholars, and merchants was planted. According to Ibn Battuta, Qanauj was a large city with an impregnable fort and enclosed with lofty walls. In it sugar was produced in abundance, sold at low prices, and transported to

Delhi. Shaikh Muin Bakharzi resided there and acted as the Shaikh ul-Islam. A feast was arranged by him to entertain Ibn Battuta. The governor of the unit was Firuz Chobin, a descendant of Kisra. The sons and grandsons of Sharaf ul-Mulk resided in Qanauj. They were respected for their learning and noble qualities. Sharaf ul-Mulk served in Daulatabad as chief *qazi* during the reign of Sultan Alauddin Khalji. He was held in esteem for his humanism and integrity of character.[44]

As for the eastern region, the extensive territorial units of Awadh, Kara, Bihar, and Bengal, they appear to have been left by Balban untouched in their boundaries, although each one of them was unwieldy. The land chiefs in these territories were powerful enough to defy the central authority.

With the advent of the Khaljis to power in the Delhi Sultanate, the Sultanate polity underwent important changes. The re-organization of the extensive territorial units took place during the reign of Sultan Alauddin. As the Sultan was annoyed with the powerful land chiefs in northern India for their defiance of the centre, he seems to have reduced their power and resources by depriving them of parts of their estates. For example, the *shiqq* of Sewistan was created in the arsa-i-Sind out of the principality of the Muslim Sumera chief.[45] In Awadh also, a new unit called by Barani the *iqta-i-Zafarabad* was constituted out of the area of its chief.[46] It is also noteworthy that all the outlying and unwieldy territorial units appear to have been divided into controllable units, each named as *shiqq*, the boundaries of which were determined in the light of geographical conditions. It was difficult for *walis* (governors) to control their overly extensive units, extending in some cases even beyond the large and unfordable rivers, particularly during the rainy season. But the information available is so meagre that much cannot be said with certainty about the demarcation of the boundaries of the different *shiqqs*. It is also to be pointed out that Barani's only reference to *shiqq* under Sultan Alauddin Khalji is found in his account of the strict state control exercised over the revenue officials posted in the *shiqqs*. He states: 'Very often the *mutassarifs* and *amils* of the *shiqqs* were thrown into prison and were kicked and flogged.'[47] The other important reference to the *shiqq-i-Awadh* as a territorial unit in the same work occurs in the account of Sultan Muhammad bin Tughluq.[48] But very often Barani avoids this term for the well-defined provincial units and frequently uses the terms *vilayet* and *iqta* instead as their use had become popular. However, the fourteenth- and fifteenth-century inscriptions found at different places in Gujarat leave no doubt about the fact that *shiqq* was the official term used for the provincial unit.[49] As for the *arsa*,[50] it occurs as the name of a larger unit, containing a number of *shiqqs*.

Also worth mentioning is the restoration of the north-western territories as separate units and the selection of Depalpur as the headquarters of the *shiqq* in place of Lahore, which had lost its importance after its sack by the Mongol invaders in 1241. Besides the *shiqq* of Sewistan, the unit of Uchh was separated from the unit of Multan, which was reduced to its previous size during the reign of Sultan Iltutmish. In each unit, a veteran general was entrusted with its administration and the command of the provincial army. Similarly, the newly conquered region of Malwa was divided into the two *shiqqs* of Dhar and Chanderi. The list of the provincial units given by Barani, though incomplete, casts light on the reorganization of the Sultanate into centralized polity.[51]

The *iqlim*[52] (or *arsa*) of Gujarat was entrusted to Alap Khan, Multan and Sewistan to Taj ul-Mulk Kafuri, Depalpur to Ghazi Malik (later Tughluq Shah), Samana and Sunam to Malik Akhurbeg Naik, Dhar and Ujjain to Ain ul-Mulk Multani, Jhain (eastern Rajasthan, near Jaipur) to Izz ul-Mulk Maisarati, Chittor to Malik Abu Muhammad, Chanderi and Iraj to Malik Timar, Badaon, Koila (Gola) and Karak[53] to Malik Dinar, the Shahna-i-Peel, Awadh to Malik Baktan, Kara to Malik Nasiruddin Sotlia, while (the territorial units of) Kol, Baran, Meerut, Amroha, Afghanpur and Kabero,[54] i.e. the entire tract of the Doab, was brought under a uniform administrative system and thus made a part of the *khalsa*.[55]

It is also noteworthy that the territories of Gujarat, Dhar and Ujjain (Malwa), Chanderi, Chittor and Jhain were annexed to the Sultanate by Sultan Alauddin Khalji during the years 1301 and 1306. The new state system and culture did not take a long time to spread; its roots began to develop quickly; the cities and towns were studded with mosques, *madrasas*, *bazaars*, and other institutions, which had a civilizing effect. All the territories, with the exception of Chittor, which was left to the Rajput rulers afterwards, flourished in peace and prosperity as the provinces of the Sultanate. Ibn Battuta's eyewitness account of the development of Chanderi into a beautiful provincial headquarters is worth quoting:

> It is a large city. The bazaars there are found thronged with people. The officer-in-charge of the entire region is Amir ul-Umara Izzuddin Multani, who is entitled as Azam Malik. He resides in Chanderi. Being a generous man of learning, he likes the company of the learned. Among his associates are included Faqih Izzuddin Zubairi and Wajihuddin of Bayana and Qazi Shamsuddin. The officer-in-charge of finance (of the province) is Qamaruddin, while the provincial army is commanded by Saadat Tilangi, who is famous for his chivalry. He looks after the affairs of the army. As for Azam Malik, he comes out only on Friday.[56]

A word may be added here about the *shiqqs* left out by Barani in his list because they had continued to remain under the governors of the Sultanate since the thirteenth century. Mention should be made of the *shiqqs* of Qanauj (in the Doab), Bayana, Ranthambore, Gwalior (in present-day Madhya Pradesh) Ajmer, Nagore, and Jalore in present-day Rajasthan, all omitted by Barani. All these provincial units were stabilized ones. The Khalji and Tughluq inscriptions from these places refer to the rule of Sultan Muhammad bin Sam, Alauddin Khalji, Sultan Qutbuddin Mubarak Shah Khalji, Ghiyasuddin Tughluq Shah, Sultan Muhammad bin Tughluq, and Sultan Firuz Shah. The epigraphical evidence is interesting in that we find insights into the welfare measures taken by the officers on behalf of the Sultan in having step-wells, artificial lakes, and other buildings of public utility constructed.[57]

As regards the Tughluq period, both Sultan Ghiyasuddin Tughluq Shah and Sultan Muhammad bin Tughluq appointed separate *walis* in the *shiqqs* of Bihar and Bengal and also parcelled out the regions of south India that had been conquered and annexed to the Delhi Sultanate during their reigns. On the conquest of Bengal, Nasiruddin, the Bengal prince, was assigned the territory of Lakhnauti as a vassal, while the territories of Satgaon and Sunargaon were separated and each was entrusted to a separate noble.[58] Isami fills the gap left in Barani's *Tarikh* about the conquest of Tirhut (north Bihar) and its annexation to the Sultanate for the first time. According to Isami, the Sultan having seized the region of Tirhut, deputed army generals to subdue the land chiefs not willing to acquiesce. When the entire region was pacified, Ahmad bin Talbagha was entrusted with the government of Bihar.[59] Ikhtisam adds to Isami's account regarding the policy of the Sultan towards the land chiefs. According to him, all those *muqaddams* (*zamindars*) who agreed to acknowledge his suzerainty were not only left untouched but also favoured with additional land for maintaining an increased number of soliders for the service of the Sultan.[60] Likewise, on the conquest of Telangana by the heir apparent, the region was parcelled out into a number of *shiqqs* and in each one separate officers mentioned by Barani as *muqtas*, *mutasarifan* (plural of *mutassarif*) and the latter's subordinate *umal* (revenue collectors) were posted.[61] Sultan Muhammad bin Tughluq is also reported to have parcelled out the Maratha region into four *shiqqs* and selected Malik Sarduatdar, Malik Mukhlis ul-Mulk, Yusuf Bughra, and Aziz Khumar to take over the charge of the units assigned to them respectively.[62] In Maabar also, a number of *shiqqs* were carved out as the references to them contained in the sources suggest. For example, Barani incidentally refers to the territorial units of Gulbarga and Bidar in the account of the rebellion by Ali Shah Khalji.[63] In short, all the *arsat*[64] (plural of *arsa*) seem to have been divided into controllable extensive units for the sake of administrative convenience during the reigns of the first two Tughluq Sultans. They remained unaltered during the reign of Firuz Shah. We find mention of the following *shiqqs* in the *arsa* of Gujarat: (1) the *shiqq* of Cambay (also called *iqta*); (2) the *shiqq* of Bharoach; (3) the *shiqq* of Baroda; (4) the *shiqq* of Sorath (Saurashtra) with Mongrol as its headquarters.[65]

Also worth mentioning is the reorganization into provincial units of the region cleared by Sultan Muhammad bin Tughluq of the Mongol military bases around the Kuh-i-Jud up to the hills of Jammu in the beginning of his reign. He drove away the Mongols beyond the river Indus and then two new *shiqqs* were constituted. They were called the *shiqqs* of Gujarat[66] (now in Pakistani Panjab) and Kalanaur[67] respectively. As regards the officers posted in the new *shiqqs*, we find the trace of only one of them in the historical sources. Malik Mujir Abu Rija was entrusted with the governance of Kalanaur in 1327. He was ordered to have the fort repaired and to rehabilitate the towns and village, destroyed by the Mongols.[68] That is why Shihabuddin al-Umari could include the Kalanaur unit in his account of India on the basis of the information supplied to him in Damascus by an Indian traveller[69] a few years later. The following twenty-three units of the Delhi Sultanate under Muhammad bin Tughluq are mentioned in the incomplete list given by Shihabuddin al-Umari: (1) Delhi; (2) Deogiri (Daulatabad); (3) Multan; (4) Kuhram;[70] (5) Samana; (6) Sewistan (arsa-i-Sind); (7) Uchh; (8) Hansi; (9) Sarsuti (present-day Sirsa in Haryana); (10) Kalanaur; (11) Lahore;[71] (12) Badaon; (13) Awadh; (14) Qanauj; (15) Kara; (16) Bihar; (17) Lakhnauti; (18) Malwa (Dhar); (19) Gujarat; (20) Jajnagar (Orissa);[72] (21) Telangana; (22) Maabar (Karnataka); and (23) Duarsamaudra (Tamil Nadu).

The above list is incomplete. The important *shiqqs* in present-day Rajasthan and a few in present-day Uttar Pradesh and Madhya Pradesh do not find any mention. The *shiqq* of Ajmer,[73] the *shiqq* of Nagaur, the *shiqq* of Jalore, the *shiqq* of Bayana in Rajasthan, the *shiqq* of Kol, the *shiqq* of Amroha, the *shiqq* of Baran, the *shiqq* of Mian-i-Doab (Meerut), the *shiqq* of Rapri,[74] the *shiqq* of Zafarabad, the *shiqq* of Bahraich in Uttar Pradesh,[75] and the *shiqq* of Gwalior and the *shiqq* of Chanderi and Errach in Madhya Pradesh also need to be included to make the list complete.

Though the successor of Sultan Muhammad bin Tughluq, Sultan Firuz Shah was not interested in recovering the lost provinces of Bengal and south India where the rebels had established independent kingdoms, he tried to keep a stronghold over all those territories that could be governed easily through the *muqtas* from Darul Mulk Delhi. His *wazir*, Khan Jahan Maqbul (defect ruler) seems to have taken a keen interest in the administrative set-up of the Sultanate. During Firuz Shah's reign the whole of the Sultanate was parcelled out into well-defined *shiqqs*. The Sultan also got new capital cities constructed for certain *shiqqs*. The *vilayets*, *shiqqs*, and *iqtas* under Firuz Shah were: (1) Multan and Uchh; (2) *Shiqq-i-Samana* (also called *Khitta-i-Samana*);[76] (3) *Shiqq-i-Hisar Firuza*, which was formerly called *Shiqq-i-Hansi* in the state papers. But the Sultan founded the city of Hisar

Firuza after his return from Bengal, constructed two canals, one from the Jumuna and the other from the Sutlej for irrigating this region, and also shifted the provincial capital from Hansi to this new city.[77] (4) *Shiqq-i-Sirhind*, which was constituted in AD 1360 out of the vast *shiqq* of Kuhram by Sultan Firuz Shah, who also constructed a strong fort in Sirhind. Shortly afterwards, the city of Sirhind developed into a populous centre.[78] (5) *Shiqq-i-Salura* and Khizrabad, which comprised some portions of Ambala and Saharanpur districts;[79] (6) *Shiqq-i-Sambhal*;[80] (7) Mian-i-Doab;[81] (8) *Shiqq-i-Kol*;[82] (9) *Shiqq-i-Badaon*;[83] (10) *Khitta-i-Etawah* (also called *vilayet*);[84] (11) *Iqta-i-Reprint*;[85] (12) *Shiqq-i-Firuzpur*;[86] (13) *Iqta-i-Chanderi*;[87] (14) *Shiqq-i-Bayana*[88] (15) *Shiqq-i-Gwalior*; (16) *Shiqq-i-Mewat*; (17) *Iqta-i-Dhar* (mentioned as *shiqq* and *khitta* also);[89] and (18) *Vilayet-i-Gujarat*.[90] The *shiqqs* and *iqtas* in eastern Uttar Pradesh were the *Iqta-i-Sandila* (Hardoi and Lucknow districts);[91] *Shiqq-i-Dalmau*,[92] *Iqta-i-Qanauj*,[93] *Iqta-i-Awadh (shiqq)*,[94] *Khitta-i-Kara*,[95] *Iqta-i-Jaunpur-o-Zafarabad*,[96] *Iqta-i-Bihar*,[97] and *Iqta-i-Tirhut*.[98] But the important *shiqqs* of Depalpur and Bahraich have been almost left unmentioned in Firuz Shah's account, while he is said to have paid visits to both the cities, that is, Depalpur and Bahraich.[99]

Now the following facts can be deduced with regard to the evolution of the *vilayet* or *arsa*, *shiqq*, *khitta*, and *iqta* under the Sultans of Delhi.

The chroniclers have used the aforementioned terms for the extensive administrative units more or less in the same sense, but the references to them in the state papers leave us with the impression that *vilayet* or *arsa* was officially the largest unit (province) and that the *shiqqs* were constituted out of the *vilayets* or *arsas* under the strict control of the centre, while the *iqta* appears to have been a smaller unit than the *shiqq*, lying either inside a *vilayet* or a *shiqq* or as a separate unit consisting of a few *parganas*.[100] For instance, the *iqta* of Rapri remained a separate unit ever since its inception, but Firuz Shah made its *muqta* subordinate to the *muqta* of the *shiqq* of Firuzpur. On the death of Firuz Shah, it again became a separate unit because the *shiqq* of Firuzpur was seized by the rebel chiefs of Etawah and Bhogaon. Therefore, Sultan Muhammad Shah, son of Firuz Shah, had to constitute the *shiqqs* of Kalpi and Mahoba, which he assigned to

Mahmud Khan, son of Malikzada Firuz Turk, with orders to crush the rebel *rais*.[101] As regards the *khitta*, it was a common term which appears to have been used by the chroniclers for any extensive territorial unit.

As for the smaller unit, a number of which were grouped to form a *shiqq*, this is generally mentioned by the Indo-Persian writers as a *pargana*.[102] Unlike them, Ibn Battuta states that under Sultan Muhammad bin Tughluq the fiscal unit composed of one hundred villages was called *sadi*, as already discussed. It seems that probably the use of the term *sadi* for the fiscal-cum-administrative unit probably remained confined to the revenue ministry, and did not gain popularity among the public. Therefore, Isami avoids its use and continues to prefer the general term of *pargana* in his narrative throughout.[103] Similarly, Afif and other later writers also use the term *pargana*, in which a number of villages were included.[104] For the Lodi period, Shaikh Rizqullah Mushtaqi says that each *pargana* comprises fifty to one hundred villages.[105] The officer-in-charge was a Muslim officer as described by Ibn Battuta (already quoted), but seems to have been designated *shiqqdar*. The important reference in the *Tarikh-i-Firuz Shahi* to the *shiqqdar* along with the *faujdar*, in connection with the rebellion of the land chiefs caused by the increase in land revenue during Muhammad bin Tughluq's reign, provides us with a clue to an understanding of the position of the *shiqqdar*. The Sultan was annoyed by the disobedience of the *zamindars*, and he ordered the *shiqqdars* and the *faujdars* of the Doab regions to chastize them. Barani says: 'In those two years when the Sultan remained at Delhi (1327–8), the *vilayet* of the Doab was brought to ruin by the heavy taxation and numerous other cesses. The Hindus (*zamindars*) set fire to the stocks of corn and turned out their cattle. The Sultan ordered the *shiqqdars* and the *faujdars* to destroy them. Some of the *muqaddams* and *khuts* were killed and others were blinded.'[106] The relevant evidence contained in the *Tarikh-i-Mubarak Shahi* tends to show that the *faujdar* was superior to the *shiqqdar* in status and position, as he held the *shiqq* or *vilayet* in his charge and combined in himself the office of an army commander as well as an executive officer. Yahya Sirhindi mentions the appointment of Daulat Khan as the *faujdar* of the *shiqq* of Mian-i-Doab in 1404.[107] The position of the *shiqqdar* and also of the *faujdar* remained unchanged during the later period.[108]

Now some words are in order about the provincial government under the Sultans of Delhi. Apparently the re-introduction of the payment of salary and allowances to the state officers and armymen in lieu of land assignment or *iqtas* led to important changes both at the centre and at the provincial level. By the time of the reign of Sultan Ghiyasuddin Tughluq Shah, the Delhi Sultanate had become quite a centralized entity, and the complete bureaucratization of the administrative machinery was possible. Ibn Battuta's account of India and the *Malfuzat* of Shaikh Sharafuddin Yahya Maneri contain supplementary as well as corroborative evidence that helps us reconstruct a fairly accurate portrait of the provincial government of the Sultanate of Delhi.

Previously, the appointment of a *wali* or *muqta* carried with it a number of obligations along with privileges. No doubt the province that the noble was appointed to rule was treated as his *iqta* (revenue assignment), but he was, in fact, also charged with the duty of maintaining peace and order in addition to its defence, both against external invaders and internal rebels. He also had to maintain his own military contingent. With the bureaucratization under the Khaljis and the first two Tughluqs, the *iqta* system was given up; a number of officers were appointed in each province with specified powers and functions independent of each other but each accountable to the centre. In every province, finance and the judiciary were separated from the executive (or governor's sphere). The revenue officer-in-charge of the province was designated as *mutasarrif*, the supreme judicial officer as *hakim*, and the governor as *faujdar*, *naib* or *wali*.[109] Ibn Battuta informs us that the governor and the controller of revenue were each paid one-twentieth of the income from the province.[110] His description of the administrative set-up in a provincial unit also shows that the *faujdar* and the *mutasarrif* were independent of each other, and that a quarrel could also take place between them.[111]

Finally, we may take up for analysis the document entitled *Ahadnama*, regarding the agreement of loyalty to the Sultan signed by the governor. Everyone is said to have made a pledge in writing to serve the state and obey the royal *farman* (order) with unwavering loyalty at the time of his appointment as a minister at the centre or as a governor in a province. The *Ahadnama* document available belongs to the reign of Firuz Shah, but it shows that this was an age-old practice in the Sultanate. The phrases and terms that are contained in the document are of religious nature and attach religious significance to it, so that it could be binding on the state officer concerned.[112] But in certain circumstances, the governor felt constrained to ignore his oath and rise in revolt against the Sultan. In 1376, Shamsuddin Damghani promised Sultan Firuz Shah that he would increase the revenue from Gujarat to 40,00,000 *tankas* for the royal treasury if he would be entrusted with its government. His offer was accepted by the Sultan. But he revolted in Gujarat after he found it impossible to fulfil his undertaking.[113] It is noteworthy that the Sultanate polity was decentralized by Firuz Shah, yet he retained the old pattern of the provincial government. The *naibs* (or *walis*) and other officers as well as the *hakims*, *mutasarrifs*, and *kotwals* of cities and towns continued to function; they were assigned *iqtas* in place of cash salary.[114] The assignment of *iqtas* even to the troops of the provincial army was made on a hereditary basis, at least in practice if not in theory. This practice not only weakened the Sultan's power but also affected discipline and the fighting capacity of the soldier. Allowed full powers, the governors built up their strength and base in their provinces and defied the central authority towards the close of Firuz Shah's reign when Prince Muhammad acted as regent.

NOTES

1. The name 'Panjab' given to the entire region of the rivers Sutlej, Beas, Ravi, Chenab, and Jhelum is a later adoption. During the Delhi Sultanate period, the extensive units of this region were called after the names of their respective provincial headquarters, such as Lahore, Multan, etc. Ibn Battuta calls the site 'Panjab' where the waters of the five rivers met the Indus River. *The Travels of Ibn Battuta*, vol. 3, p. 592.
2. In 1980, I was able to correct the historiographical error regarding the name of the vast territorial unit lying in the north-west of the Indus. This was called Binban and not Banian, as deciphered by Elliot in his work *History of India as Told by Its Own Historians*, vol. 3. Peter

Jackson and André Wink are in agreement with me in their respective works, *The Delhi Sultanate* and *Al-Hind*, vol. 2. Cf. Iqtidar Husain Siddiqui, 'The Qarlugh Kingdom in North-western India during the Thirteenth Century', *Islamic Culture Quarterly*, Hyderabad, vol. LIV, no. 2, April 1980, pp. 76–7.

3. Bhera is situated on the western bank of the Jhelum in the Salt Range was the provincial headquarters during the Delhi Sultanate period.
4. Cf. *The Foundation of Muslim Rule in India*, pp. 35–6.
5. *Tabaqat-i-Nasiri*, vol. 2, p. 25.
6. *Tarikh-i-Fakhr-i-Mudabbir*, p. 29.
7. *The Agrarian System of Muslim India*, p. 23.
8. This vast territory was entrusted to the charge of Malik Qutbuddin Aibek in 1192, as already discussed. Aibek was designated as *sipahsalar* (i.e. military governor). *Tarikh-i-Fakhr-i-Mudabbir*, pp. 21–2; *Tajul-Masir*, Eng. tr. Bhagwat Saroop, Delhi, 1998, p. 72; *Tabaqat-i-Nasiri*, vol. I, p. 40; see also Chapters 2 and 3 for details.
9. In 1255, Malik Kishli Khan (Saifuddin Aibek) was assigned the charge of the Khitta-i-Mian-i-Doab. He led an expedition from Meerut against the rebel chiefs, chastized them, and forced them into submission. The entire region from Badaon up to Roorki and the tract was pacified. *Tabaqat-i-Nasiri*, vol. II, pp. 46–7.
10. The early thirteenth-century writers generally use the term *khitta* for an extensive territorial unit. Later on, Minhaj Juzjani, mentions the large territorial unit as *vilayet* and also *iqta*. These terms are invariably used by the Indo-Persian writers as synonyms. It is also to be pointed out that in Iran and Central Asia the *khitta* was an extensive unit with fixed boundaries, as mentioned in the *Tajul Masir* and the fourteenth-century lexicon, *Farhang-i-Lisan ul-Shuara*. Cf. *Tajul-Masir*, MS, British Library, London, Add. 7623, f.10a; Ashiq, *Farhang-i-Lisan ul Shu'ara*, ed. Nazir Ahmad, New Delhi, 1995, pp. 91, 159.
11. *Tajul Masir*, f. 10a, *Tabaqat-i-Nasiri*, vol. I, pp. 422, 438.
12. The combined territory of Kalinjar and Mahoba was the first to be captured by the Chandela chief. After it, Gwalior fell to the Parihara chief, while Harish Chandra re-established himself in the Doab, and ultimately seized even Badaon, sometime after AD 1210. Cf. *The Foundation of Muslim Rule in India*, pp. 102–3.
13. *Tabaqat-i-Nasiri*, vol. I, pp. 445–7.
14. Ibid., vol. II, pp. 18, 26, 54, 60, etc., pp. 445–7.
15. Ibid., vol. II, pp. 6–7, 9; vol. I, pp. 455, 456, 459.
16. Ibid., vol. II; vol. I, pp. 456, 459.
17. Ibid., vol. I, p. 458; vol. II, pp. 11–13.
18. Ibid., vol. I, p. 470.
19. Ibid.
20. A fifteenth-century scholar of Gujarat states about Binban while

discussing the origin of the Binbani scholars (in Gujarat): 'Binban is the vilayet lying between Multan and Khurasan.' Cf. *Juma'at-i-Shahija*, cited by Nazir Ahmad, *Islamic Culture Quarterly*, Hyderabad, vol. XXX, no. 4, October 1956, p. 345. The author of the *Tarikh-i-Sadr-i-Jahan* also belonged to this Binbani family of Gujarat. Cf. Faizullah Binbani, *Tarikh-i-Sadr-i-Jahan*, ed. Iqtidar Husain Siddiqui, Aligarh, 1988, pp. 3–6 (Introduction).

20. The Kuh-i-Jud tract is identified with the Jhelum district in the Salt Range in Pakistan. Its south-eastern boundaries were demarcated by the river Ravi. Its headquarters was Nandanah, situated in the Pin Dadu Khan subdivision, S. 32° 43′ N. 73° 17′ E, in the Salt Range. Bhera became its headquarters during the fourteenth century. Cf. Ata Malik Juvaini, *Tarikh-i-Jahan Qusha*, ed. Mirza Muhammad Qazvini, Leiden, 1911, vol. II, p. 147; Shihabuddin Nasawi, *Sirat-i-Jalaluddin Mangbarni*, a fourteenth-century anonymous Persian translation, ed. Minovi, Tehran, 1456 Shamsi, pp. 121, 122, 237.
21. Minhaj-i-Siraj Juzjani calls the unit Khitta-i-Multan. Since the units of Uchh and Sind (or Sewistan) were included in it by Ghiyasuddin Tughluq Shah, Barani mentions it as Arsa-i-Sind-o-Multan.
22. The first *sipahsalar* of Uchh appointed by Sultan Muizuddin Muhammad bin Sam was Nasiruddin Artan. On his fall in the battle of Andkhud in 1204, the Sultan sent Nasiruddin Qubacha to Uchh as its new governor (*sipahsalar*). *Tabaqat-i-Nasiri*, vol. I, p. 19.
23. It formed part of the *khitta* of Kuhram and Sunam during the period of Sultan Miuzuddin Muhammad bin Sam. Later, it seems to have become a separate unit, with the town of Hansi as its headquarters. Cf. *Tabaqat-i-Nasiri*, vol. I, pp. 401, 486–7; in the eighth regnal year of Sultan Nasiruddin Mahmud, the *khitta* of Hansi was held by Ulugh Khan Balban (later Sultan).
24. The description by Hasan Nizami of the fort and town of Meerut tends to suggest that it was a large urban centre. It had a strong fort, some parts of which were firm and 'solid like a lofty mountain, and surrounded by a wide moat boundless like an ocean'. A *kotwal* was appointed to maintain peace and order in the town. *Tajul Masir*, Eng. tr., pp. 101–2.
25. Baran was a separate unit and Iltutmish was entrusted by Aibek with its charge before he was promoted to the governorship of Badaon. Cf. *Tabaqat-i-Nasiri*, vol. I, p. 443; vol. II, pp. 6, 11, 24, 26.
26. On its conquest, Aibek appointed his lieutinent, Hussamuddin Oghalbak as its *sipahsalar*. *Tabaqat-i-Nasiri*, Eng. tr., p. 177.
27. Sambhal was a small unit surrounded by the rebel Rajputs of Katehar. It was held by the *sipahsalar* of Badaon as an additional charge until Balban included it in the newly carved-out unit of Amroha. *Tabaqat-i-Nasiri*, vol. I, p. 482; Barani, pp. 36–7.
28. Hasan Sijzi, *Fawaid ul-Fuad* (Malik Sirajuddin, Lahore, 1966), pp. 79,

83, 158, 179, 181, 227, 228, 245, 257, 261, 266, 278, 280, 288, 290, 291–2, 332, 349, 351, 361, 367, 381, 401.

29. Iqtidar Husain Siddiqui, *Medieval India: Essays in Intellectual Thought and Culture*, vol. 1, p. 46.
30. It was conquered by Sultan Muizuddin Muhammad bin Sam in AD 1194–5. In 1243–4, Prince Jalaluddin was released from prison and assigned the governorship of the *khitta* of Qanauj. *Tabaqat-i-Nasiri*, vol. I, pp. 401/ 470; vol. II, pp. 17, 31, for the appointment of different governors under the successors of Iltutmish.
31. *Ajaib ul-Asfar*, vol. 2, pp. 256–7.
32. *Tabaqat-i-Nasiri*, vol. I, pp. 481–2, 451.
33. Minhaj Juzjani also calls it *iqta* in the sense of *khitta* or territorial unit. *Tabaqat-i-Nasiri*, vol. II, p. 690.
34. Cf. *The Foundation of Muslim Rule in India*, p. 140.
35. As mentioned above, Bihar and Bengal were conquered by Muhammad Bakhtiyar Khalji and then annexed to the Sultanate of Delhi. On Iltutmish's death, the governor of Bengal became independent for all practical purposes. It was Sultan Balban who re-imposed central control over the combined provinces of Bihar and Bengal.
36. It comprised the region of Mathura district. Iltutmish is reported to have assigned its charge to Malik Nusratuddin Taisi, who already held the governorship of the Bayana unit. *Tabaqat-i-Nasiri*, vol. II, pp. 10–11.
37. Ibid., vol. I, p. 460.
38. Barani, p. 85.
    Barani's statement that Malik Sonj, *Sar-i-Jandar*, was appointed as the commander of the provincial army suggests that the *shiqq* of Samana was governed by the centre and that the armymen were not paid in cash. Like the soldiers of *hashm-i-ala* (central army), they were assigned the revenue of the villages around a *qasba* (town) that is mentioned as a *pargana* since the times of the Khaljis, as will be discussed subsequently.
39. Kishli Khan, the *amir-i-hajib*, held the *iqta* of Kol for his maintenance while the *iqta* of Baran was assigned to Malik Tuzaki, the *amir-i-arz*. Sultan Kaiqubad also assigned the *iqta* of Baran to Jalaluddin Khalji at the time of his elevation to the post of *amir-i-arz*. Cf. Barani, pp. 113–14, 170.
40. Barani, pp. 68–9.
41. *The Travels of Ibn Battuta*, vol. III, p. 722.
42. *Ajaib ul-Asfar*, vol. 2, p. 248. *The Travels of Ibn Battuta*, vol. 3, p. 723.
43. *Ajaib ul-Asfar*, vol. 2, pp. 247–8.
44. Ibid., pp. 256–7.
45. The *shiqq* of Sewistan is found mentioned in our sources since the Khalji period. Malik Muhammad Shah held Sewistan during the reigns of Alauddin Khalji and Qutbuddin Mubarak Shah. Cf. *Tughluqnama*, p. 57.

46. Barani mentions the iqta-i-Zafarbad in his account of Sultan Ghiyasuddin Tughluq Shah for the first time. His reference to it suggests that it had existed as an extensive territorial unit during the preceding period because its charge had been given to Tatar Malik just after the Sultan's accession to the throne. Barani, p. 428.
47. Barani, p. 289.
48. Ibid., p. 587.
49. Cf. Inscriptions edited by Z.A. Desai, in *A Quest for Truth: A Collection of Research Articles* by Z.A. Desai, Ahmedabad, 2004, pp. 164, 404, 456.
50. An inscription in Gujarat uses the term *arsa* for the whole region of Gujarat. Gujarat was divided into several *shiqqs*. Ibid., p. 405.
51. The *shiqqs* of Uchh, Ajmer, Nagore, and Jalore are not mentioned by Barani in the list. The inscriptions found and published by Z.A. Desai and his colleagues leave no doubt about the fact that the territorial units of Ajmer, Nagore, and Jalore were firmly controlled by the governors of the Khalji and the Tughluq Sultans. Cf. *Epigraphia Indica: Arabic and Persian Supplement*, 1967, pp. 1–24.
52. Barani uses either *iqtim* or *Arsa* as synonyms for a region parcelled out into a number of *shiqqs*.
53. Koila and Karak were small towns called *parganas*. They were included in the *shiqq* of Badaon. They are now included in the Khiri Lakhimpur and Shah Jashanpur districts of Uttar Pradesh respectively.
54. Afghanpur is present-day Aghwanpur in the district of Moradabad. Ibn Battuta mentions it in the account of his visit to Amroha. It seems to have been founded by Sultan Balban as a *thana* when he carved out the *iqta* of Amroha for keeping the Katehriya rebels under check.
55. Barani, pp. 323–4.
56. *Ajaib ul-Asfar*, vol. 2, p. 272.
57. Cf. *Annual Report on Indian Epigraphy (ARIE)*, for 1955–56, nos. D.119, 138, 155; ibid., 1962–63, nos. D. 198, 204; ibid., 1965–66, nos. D. 338, 341, 343, 349; Z.A. Desai, 'Khalji and Tughluq Inscriptions from Rajasthan', *Epigraphia Indica: Arabic and Persian Supplement*, 1967, pp. 1–24.
58. Barani, p. 451.
59. *Futuh us-Salatin*, pp. 416–18.
60. *Perso-Arabic Sources...*, pp. 94–5, for Ikhtisan's *Basatin ul-uns*.
61. Barani, p. 450.
62. Ibid., p. 501.
63. Incidentally, Barani mentions the territorial unit of Bidar in the account of the rebellion by Shihab Sultani entitled Nusrat Khan, and that he got the territory on farming (*muqata*) and pledged to pay 1,00,00,000 *tankas* per annum to the state treasury. As he failed to pay the due amount, he revolted. Again, he refers to the territories of Bidar and Gulbarga while describing the revolt of Alishah Khalji, and that he first

killed Bhairon, the *mutassarrif* of Gulbarga, occupied it, and thence proceeded to Bidar. In Bidar, he killed the *naib* (i.e. governor) and seized it also. Barani, pp. 481, 488–9; *Futuh us-Salatin*, pp. 476–80, 485.

64. Barani uses the term *arsat* for the vast regions such as Gujarat, Bengal, Deccan, etc. Barani, p. 469.
65. Barani, pp. 502, 516; Inscriptions edited by Z.A. Desai in *A Quest for Trust*, op. cit, pp. 163–4, 166, 263, 264, 370, 388–9, 404, 405, 406, 407, 457–8.
66. It should be pointed out that Barani mentions the unit of Gujarat in the account of the Mongol raids during Firuz Shah's reign. The Timurid historian, Sharafuddin Yazdi, also refers to it in his account of Tarmashirin's invasion. Barani, p. 601. *Zafarnama, Muqaddima*, MS, British Library, London, Add., 6538, f. 99b.
67. *Perso-Arabic Sources of Information . . .*, p. 113.
68. *Futuh us-Salatin*, pp. 423–4; *Tarikh-i-Mubarak Shahi*, p. 101.
69. The name of the Indian traveller has been mentioned as Ṣirajuddin al-Awadhi. *Perso-Arabic Sources of Information . . .*, p. 12.
70. Shihabuddin mentions Kuhram as a separate province, although it had been included in the *shiqq* of Samana and Sunam during the reign of Balban. It now seems to have been separated along with a number of *parganas* of eastern Punjab and made the headquarters of a separate *shiqq*.
71. Lahore formed part of the *shiqq* of Dipalpur, as already mentioned.
72. The Raja of Orissa is said to have acknowledged the suzerainty of the Sultan. Barani, p. 450.
73. The inscription of the period refers to Ajmer as Mamura-i-Ajmer also. Cf. *Epigraphia Indica: Arabic and Persian Supplement*, 1967, ed. Z.A. Desai, p. 12.
74. The territorial unit of Rapri was of strategic importance and was held by the veteran general, Malik Khattab Afghan, who was highly praised by Ibn Battuta for his courage and first-rate generalship. Cf. Iqtidar Husain Siddiqui, 'The Afghans and their Emergence in India as the Ruling Elite during the Delhi Sultanate Period', *Central Asiatic Journal*, Wiesbaden, vol. 26, nos. 3–4, 1982, p. 254.
75. Afif, p. 272. *Tarikh-i-Mubarak Shahi*, p. 161.
76. Afif, pp. 292–5.
77. Ibid., pp. 117–18.
78. *Tarikh-i-Mubarak Shahi*, pp. 130, 176, 189 and 190.
79. Afif, pp. 305, 308, 330, 430.
80. *Tarikh-i-Mubarak Shahi*, p. 136.
81. Afif mentions it as iqta-i-Mian-i-Doab, while Yahya Sirhindi calls it khitta-i-Meerut or shiqq-i-Mian-i-Doab, Afif, pp. 237–8; *Tarikh-i-Mubarak Shahi*, pp. 160, 167, 168.
82. *Tarikh-i-Mubarak Shahi*, pp. 133 and 175. The author mentions the unit of Kol as *khitta* and *shiqq* both.

83. Afif, p. 340.
84. Yahya Sirhindi uses the terms *iqta* and *vilayet* both for Akhal and Etawah, while the author of *Tarikh-i-Muhammadi* calls it khitta-i-Etawah. The author of *Tarikh-i-Muhammadi* says that the powerful *rai* of Etawah turned rebel during the reign of Sultan Firuz, who forced him to submit. On his submission, the Sultan got several mosques constructed in the khitta-i-Etawah. He also founded a town, Tughluqabad, and posted Malik Shah Afghan in-charge of the garrison and the *vilayet* of Etawah to keep watch over the turbulent *rais* there. Shortly afterwards, Malik Shah Afghan died and his son, Yal Khan, was allowed to succeed him to his *iqta* and office. *Tarikh-i-Muhammadi*, Muhammad Bihamid Khani, rotograph of the MS. B.M. London, f. 412a. According to Yahya Sirhindi, the powerful *rais* in the Etawah region were Rai Sabir, Adhran, Jeet Singh Rathore, Birbhan, the *muqaddam* of Bhogaon, and Abhi Chand, the *muqaddam* of Chandwar. They had built their power, joined hands with one another and shook off the suzerainty of the Sultan during the reign of Muhammad Shah, son of Firuz Shah, *Tarikh-i-Mubarak Shahi*, pp. 153–4.
85. The vast *iqta* of Rapri was held by Imad-ul-Mulk (Bashir), who had the rank of 5,000 *sawars* under Firuz Shah. He assigned *parganas* and villages to his officers there. Afif, pp. 483, 441.
86. The *shiqq* of Firuzpur was constituted by Firuz Shah in the *khittas* of Iraj and Kalpi, where he also constructed a fort on the bank of the river Jumuna, and Hasan Makhan was posted there. But the government of the new *shiqq* was entrusted to the charge of Malikzada Firuz, son of Tajuddin Turk. Malikzada Firuz established peace and order in the whole *shiqq* up to Bhogaon, Chandwar, and Phapoond as well as in Iraj, Ratha, and Shahpur. He appointed his eldest son, Mahmud Khan, as the paymaster general of the army of the shiqq-i-Firuzpur. *Tarikh-i-Muhammadi*, ff. 412 a–b.
87. Afif, pp. 237–8.
88. The *shiqqs* of Bayana, Gwalior, and Mewat have been omitted by chroniclers in their accounts of Firuz Shah, but they are mentioned in the accounts of his successors.
89. Afif, pp. 237–8. *Tarikh-i-Mubarak Shahi*, pp. 169, 170.
90. Afif, pp. 237–8. *Tarikh-i-Mubarak Shahi*, p. 168. Yahya Sirhindi calls the *vilayet* of Gujarat *vilayet* as well as arsa-i-Gujarat in the same sense.
91. Afif, p. 237. *Tarikh-i-Mubarak Shahi*, p. 133. It seems that the *iqta* of Lucknow was also included in the Sandila unit because it is no longer heard of as a separate unit after Muhammad bin Tughluq.
92. *Tarikh-i-Mubarak Shahi*, p. 133.
93. Afif, p. 237, Khitta-i-Qanauj in *Tarikh-i-Mubarak Shahi*, pp. 146–7, 170.
94. Afif, p. 237. The unit of Awadh seems to have remained intact in its boundaries from the days of Muhammad bin Tughluq, for no new unit

was constituted out of it during the reign of Firuz Shah. But Barani calls it *shiqq-i-Awadh*, as already mentioned.

95. *Tarikh-i-Mubarak Shahi*, p. 143 *Tarikh-i-Muhammadi*, f. 402 a; the unit of Kara also included Mahoba, but it seems to have been separated from it by Firuz Shah later on.
96. Afif, p. 237. *Tarikh-i-Mubarak Shahi*, p. 133. On the foundation of the city of Jaunpur, the capital of the unit was shifted from Zafarabad to it during Firuz Shah's reign.
97. Afif, pp. 237–8. The author of the *Tarikh-i-Mubarak Shahi* calls it khitta-i-Bihar, p. 140.
98. Afif, pp. 237–8.
99. Ibid., pp. 256, 372.
100. Ibid., p. 483.
101. *Tarikh-i-Muhammadi*, ff. 412a, 430a.
102. Isami says about Delhi before Iltutmish made it his capital: 'I have heard that Delhi was in those days one of the *parganas* of the region.' *Futuh-us-Salatin*, p. 108.
103. Ibid., pp. 450, 597, etc.
104. Afif, p. 99.
105. *Waqiat-i-Mushtaqi*, Eng. tr. Iqtidar Husain Siddiqui, New Delhi, 1993, p. 80.
106. In his account of Balban's reign, Barani refers to the creation of the post of *mutassarrif* along with a military governor in the *iqta* of Amroha, reserved for *khalsa*, i.e. the unit to be governed by the centre through officers appointed directly by the Sultan. As the armymen posted in such units were assigned the revenue of villages in lieu of cash salary, the military governor-in-charge of law and order might have been designated the *shiqqdar*: Later on, when the nobles and troops were paid in cash and not through the assignment of *iqta* under the Khaljis and the Tughluqs, the post of the *faujdar* seems to have been created. The *faujdar* held the charge of the extensive territorial unit (*shiqq*) and the *shiqqdar* became his subordinate in the *pargana* as the evidence contained in the later works suggests. Cf. Barani, pp. 36, 85, 479.
107. *Tarikh-i-Mubarak Shahi*, p. 175.
108. Cf. Iqtidar Husain Siddiqui, 'Position of the *Shiqqdar* under the Sultans of Delhi', *Islamic Culture Quarterly*, Hyderabad, vol. XLI, no. 4, October 1967, pp. 235–9.
109. Ibn Battuta, in the account of his visit to Amroha, mentions Aziz Khumar as the *wali al-kharaj* (officer-in-charge of revenue) and Shamsuddin Badakhshi as the *amir* (governor) of the territorial unit. Again, he refers to Aziz Khumar as *khazin* (treasurer). In fact, he seems to have translated the terms in vogue (in India) into Arabic. The *malfuzat* of the contemporary Firdausi Sufi saint, Shaikh

Sharafuddin Yahya Maneri, mentions the supreme officers of Bihar with their official designations. For instance, Malik Zaynuddin, entitled Majd ul-Mulk, was the *wali* of Bihar, while Khwaja Mahmud 'Iwaz held the office of *mutassarrif* in the *shiqq* of Bihar (south Bihar). Qazi Muinuddin is mentioned in the *Malfuzat* as a *hakim*, meaning chief justice. Barani also supports the *Malfuzat* of the saint with regard to the designations of different officers at the provincial level. Ibn Battuta, *Rehla* (Arabic text), Beirut, 1964, p. 526; Shaikh Zayn Badr Arabi, *Maadan al-Maani*, Bihar Sharif, 1884, vol. 1, p. 90, vol. 2, pp. 298, 352; Barani, pp. 505, 523.

110. *The Travels of Ibn Battuta*, vol. 3, pp. 602, 763.
111. Loc. cit.
112. Ainul-Mulk Mahru, *Insha-i-Mahru*, document no. 12, pp. 24–5.
113. Afif, pp. 499–501, *Tarikh-i-Mubarak Shahi*, p. 132.
114. Cf. Z.A. Desai, *A Quest for Truth*, op. cit., pp. 250, 251, 252, 384, 385, 387.

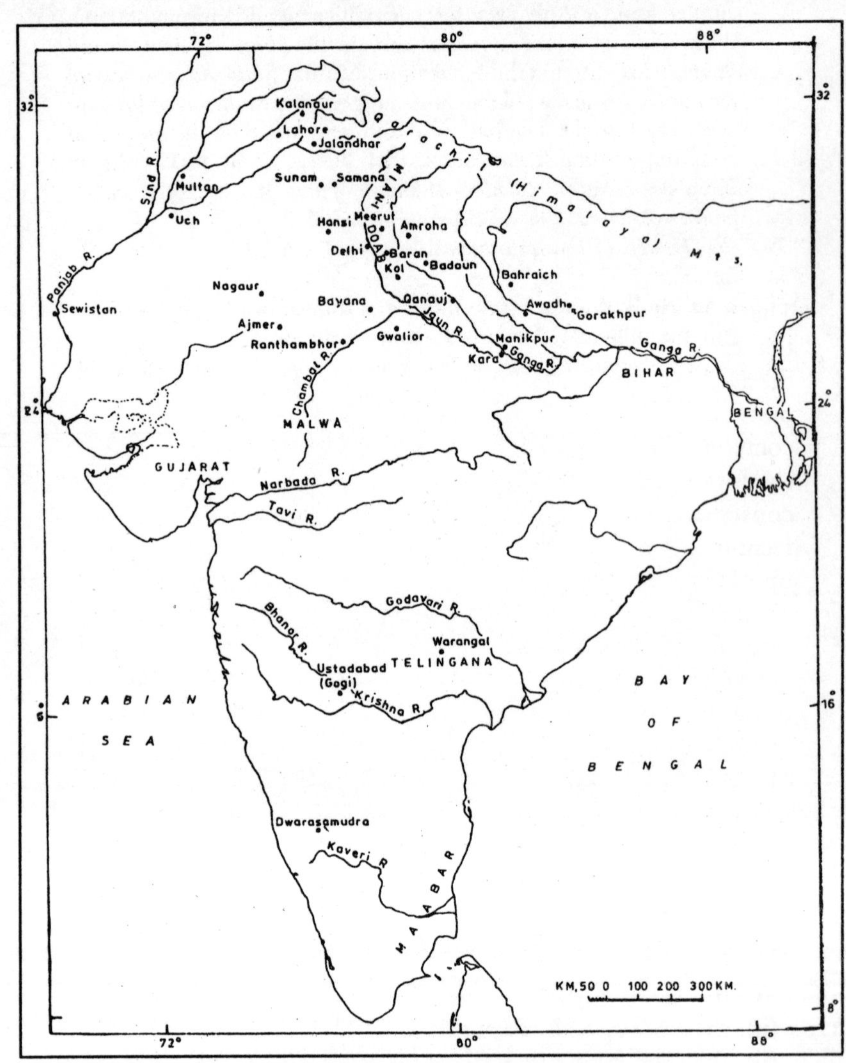

DELHI SULTANATE UNDER TUGHLUQ

CHAPTER 8

Waterworks and the Irrigation System

The construction of waterworks and the technological changes that took place in the traditional irrigation system in India during the Delhi Sultanate, hitherto neglected, need to be studied in a more scientific manner. The relevant evidence available in the contemporary Arabic and Persian works, though brief and sketchy, sheds interesting light on the engineering skill that went into the construction of waterworks and the changes that irrigation technology underwent from time to time. In particular, the setting up of the Persian wheel on wells and the construction of large artificial canals provide clues to the introduction of certain mechanical devices in the irrigation system employed during the period under review. They also offer insights into the regional disparities in the lives and conditions of peasants in different territorial units under the rule of the Sultans. In fact, the diffusion of advanced irrigation technology in the region brought about prosperity and also helped the growth of material culture. This chapter examines the evidence contained in miscellaneous sources about the construction of waterworks, the different modes of irrigation, and their possible relationship with the life of the people. This chapter is divided into three parts:

(i) the first is concerned with lakes, cisterns, and tanks;
(ii) the second with wells; and
(ii) the third with artificial canals.

I

The Khalji conquerors of Bengal were the first dividers of water from the land in this region of overwhelming rivers and boundless swamps. They are reported to have built dykes, roads, and tanks, which made the reclamation of vast tracts of land possible in the deltaic region of Bengal. According to Minhaj Juzjani, the dykes made the movement of people and cattle possible during the rainy season. Moreover, the water flowing through the channels could be diverted to paddy fields should the failure of the monsoon cause scarcity.[1]

The arid soil of Haryana and the torrid climate of Rajasthan (Rajputana) also attracted the attention of the rulers, who constructed tanks and lakes for irrigation purposes and also to provide relief to the *caravans* of travellers and passers-by. A contemporary Persian epigraph refers to the construction of a *haud* (lake) at Palwal. It was constructed by Badruddin Sunqar, the officer-in-charge of the town, in AD 1211 both for the benefit of people and cattle.[2] Evidence contained in a later source about an old *kolab* (water reservoir) built in Sialkot during the early period of the Delhi Sultanate suggests that reservoirs were meant for a variety of purposes. In Sialkot, the *kolab* served as the major source of water for domestic purposes. The local people preferred its water to that of the river Chenab, which flowed nearby.[3]

The first lake constructed in Delhi by Sultan Shamsuddin Iltutmish near the Idgah (usually unroofed enclosure where Muslims offer congregational prayer on the occasions of Id-ul-Fitr and Id-al-adha) and outside the Ghazni Gate deserves to be discussed in detail because the additions made to it from time to time to enhance its utility and beauty point to the development of architecture in the Delhi Sultanate during the thirteenth and fourteenth centuries. This was 2 miles in length by half that breadth.[4] It was meant for a variety of purposes. The medieval Indo-Persian writers mention it as a reservoir constructed for supplying drinking water to the city of Delhi, but Ibn Battuta's reference to the cultivation of seasonal fruits such as melons and vegetables along its sides during the summer shows that its water was used for irrigation also. Both Amir Khusrau and Ibn Battuta[5] say that its contents were collected from rainwater, but in addition to it a number of channels seem to have been led off from the Jamuna River and other springs, so that the supply of water to the population in the city could be maintained even during the summer. For example, Isami alludes to the Chashma-i-Aftab[6] (Sun Spring), i.e. the famous Suraj Kund near Delhi, as its source of water. The details furnished by Sultan Firuz Shah (1351–88) and the compiler of the *Sirat-i-Firuz Shahi* about the repair of the lake allude to the original channels through which the water from the Jamuna River flowed to the lake.[7]

It may also be noted that the Haud-i Sultani built by Sultan Iltutmish in Delhi became a beautiful recreation centre during the subsequent period. The buildings erected by the order of Sultan Alauddin Khalji in 1311 and later by his successors bear testimony to the progress made in the field of architecture. Referring to the repair of the old buildings by the order of Sultan Alauddin Khalji, Amir Khusrau incidentally refers to the construction of a lofty and beautiful dome over a platform raised in the centre of Haud-i-Sultani. Amir Khusrau praises the dome in his poetic style: 'The dome in the centre of the tank is like a bubble on the surface of the sea. If you see the dome and the tank rightly, you will say that the former is like an ostrich egg, half in water and half out of it.'[8] The graphic description given by Ibn Battuta reveals that certain buildings were added to the complex inside the lake during the reigns of the successors of Alauddin Khalji. We may quote Ibn Battuta at some length:

> Its western side in the direction of the *musalla* (Idgah) is constructed with stones, and disposed like a series of terraces one above the other, and beneath each terrace are steps leading down to the water. Beside each terrace there is a stone pavilion containing seats for those who have come out to visit the place and to enjoy its attractions. In the centre of the tank there is a great pavilion built of dressed stones, two stories high. When the reservoir is filled with water it can be reached only in boats. . . . Inside it is a mosque.[9]

Like Sultan Iltutmish, his nobles also evinced an interest in having lakes constructed in the areas where people suffered from the scarcity of water. A few inscriptions that have survived the ravages of time substantiate this fact. For instance, an inscription found at Bari Khatu (district Nagaur in Rajasthan state) mentions the construction of a lake by the officer Masud, son of Ahmad Khalji, in 1232. This must have provided relief both to cultivators and travellers in the torrid climate of the desert.[10] About the same time, a lake seems to have been constructed in the town of Badaon.[11]

The little information available about the excavation of lakes and tanks by the Sultans and their officers shows that the traditions set by Iltutmish were maintained during the subsequent period. Sultan Alauddin Khalji is credited with having taken an interest in developing the means of irrigation in his empire for the progress of agriculture. Barani states that a number of tanks were constructed along with other buildings.[12] The most important of the lakes was the Haud-i Khass, also called the Haud-i Ala'i (Ala'i lake).[13] This was built outside the new metropolitan city of Siri (near Delhi). It seems that Sultan Alauddin wanted it to be larger and more attractive than the old Haud-i Sultani, as Ibn Battuta's description reveals. 'Along its sides,' says Ibn Battuta, 'there are forty pavilions and around about it live the musicians. Their place is called *Tarababad* (city of music) and they have there a most extensive bazaar, a cathedral mosque, and many other mosques beside'.[14] Barani's reference to the bala-band-i-Siri (lofty dam at Siri) contained in his account of a number of beautiful buildings constructed there by Sultan Firuz Shah suggests that it was erected by Sultan Alauddin Khalji with strong and lofty embankments for the storage of rainwater in the area nearby.[15] Odd bits of information available in the later sources suggest that the Haud-i Sultani and the Haud-i Khass began to occupy an important position in the socio-cultural life of Delhi. They were maintained in good condition by the later Sultans.

In 1398, Amir Timur and his companions, the invaders from Central Asia, were fascinated by the beauty of these lakes.[16] Two interesting anecdotes related by Shaikh Rizqullah Mushtaqi in the *Waqiat-i Mushtaqi* show that both the lakes attracted people from different parts of the city by their scenic beauty.[17]

As regards the Tughluq period, it was marked by a great deal of improvement in the irrigation system obtaining in the Delhi Sultanate. Many lakes, tanks, and cisterns seem to have been excavated in Delhi as well as in the provinces. The details furnished by later writers about the lakes and cisterns of this period are indicative of the fact that the Tughluq Sultans paid greater attention than their predecessors to the architectural beauty of the lakes that they constructed. This reflects on the progress made in civil engineering during the fourteenth century. For instance, Ghiyasuddin Tughluq Shah (1320–4) had aqueducts built over the lake surrounding the royal tomb constructed in his lifetime for his burial after his death. The bridge that connects the tomb with the palace-fortress of Tughluqabad is still intact.[18] This indicates the kind of masonry that went into its construction. The traces of these works were noticed by later writers. They have mentioned that the waterworks included both *baolis* (step-wells) and cisterns.[19] The son and successor of Sultan Ghiyasuddin, Sultan Muhammad bin Tughluq, was very charitable. He took an active interest in works of charity and public utility as expected of a ruler. He had beautiful lakes and cisterns put up both in Adilabad (near Delhi) and Daulatabad (near old Deogiri in Maharashtra), the metropolitan cities founded by him. A huge lake was excavated below the hillock on which was erected the palace-fortress of Adilabad. It had an extremely beautiful location. Sir Syed Ahmad Khan having surveyed the ruins observes: 'As such it seems likely that it (Adilabad) was founded by the Sultan for merrymaking. A bridge connected it with the city of Tughluqabad.'[20]

About the same time when the Tughluq Sultans constructed lakes and tanks in Delhi and Daulatabad, certain *walis* or *muqtas* (governors) seem to have been equally active in constructing works of public utility in the territories under their administrative charge. Contemporary Persian epigraphs that have fortunately survived bear testimony to the construction of lakes and tanks at several places, for instance, in Bihar town[21] (present-day Bihar Sharif in Bihar), Garhmukteshwar[22] (district Ghaziabad in Uttar Pradesh), Manglore[23] (district Saharanpur, Uttar Pradesh), and Bari Khatu (district Nagaur, Rajasthan). The inscription found at Bari Khatu informs us that the *muqta* (governor) Malik Firuz bin Muhammad had a fairly large lake erected there and named it Firuz Sagar (Hindi *sagar*, meaning sea).[24]

As regards the long reign of Sultan Firuz Shah (1351–88), it was marked by great construction activity. Contemporary writers have noted with pride and joy that beautiful edifices were put up, including bridges, aqueducts, lakes, cisterns, and irrigation channels. In them we find references to some of the waterworks, the construction of which actually helped people in more than one way. The *Sirat-i-Firuz Shahi* and contemporary hagiographic sources refer to the important lakes such as the Haud-i-Tughluq

Shah, Haud-i Qutlugh Khan[25] (Sultan Muhammad bin Tughluq's teacher whom the latter had raised to the rank of a high noble), Haud-i Shahzada Mubarak Khan (son of Firoz Shah), and Haud-i Shahzada Fath Khan (eldest son of Firuz Shah). Of these the Haud-i Shahzada Mubarak Khan seems to have been the most magnificent lake built so far in Delhi. Beautiful villas were erected along its embankment. Moreover, Sultan Firuz Shah is reported to have had a big dam built for the storage of rainwater. Its walls were built with chiselled stone.[26]

The big cistern constructed by Sultan Firuz Shah in the fort of Hisar Firuza is also worth mentioning for its beauty and grandeur. According to Afif, it was so large, deep, and marvellous nowhere any lake could strike comparison with it. It was originally constructed to discharge water into the ditch excavated around the fortification.[27] Later, the ditch received the water from the canals Ulugh Khani and Rajwah.

It is worth recalling that the construction of cisterns was not a new development during the Delhi Sultanate period as they had existed since ancient times. Ibn Battuta visited a number of cisterns in the fort of Gwalior. He writes: 'Inside it there are cisterns of water and about twenty wells, attached to the castle by protecting walls. . . .'[28] Likewise, there were old lakes, artificial as well as natural, in different territories. Babur's description of the Kalda Kahar lake in the Kuh-i-Jud is graphic. We are informed that the prosperity of the area depended upon the water flowing from the lake. It was about 6 miles round, the ingathering of rainwater from all sides. Fields of densely growing corn were watered by it. It was rich in scenic beauty also. 'On the other side of this lake,' says Babur, 'lies an excellent meadow; on the hill skirt to the west of it there is a spring having the source in the highest overlooking the lake.'[29]

Sultan Firuz Shah was undoubtedly the first ruler who seriously thought of storing rainwater through the construction of dams in territories that suffered from scarcity of water. Firishta tells us that the Sultan constructed thirty huge reservoirs to promote irrigation in areas where canal water was not available. The contemporary historian Afif mentions the following dams in the territorial unit of Delhi: (i) the band-i Fath Khan (*band* means dam); (ii) band-i Maljah; (iii) band-i Mahipalpur; (iv) band-i

Wazirabad.[30] Near one of these dams was raised the hunting lodge of Firuz Shah, known as Kushik-i-Jahan Numa or Kushik-i-Shikar. The traces of the palace and the channels of water flowing from the dam could be found until the nineteenth century. Sir Syed writes on the basis of these ruins:

> Firuz Shah built a palace at a distance of 3 *kos* (6 miles = 9.66 km.) from Firuzabad. He named it Jahan Numa palace. He also built a strong dam to collect rainwater from the hills near the palace, traces of which are still available. In fact, it was a hunting lodge and was connected to the *Kushik-i-Firoz Shah* (situated in the Kotla) by an underground tunnel of 2 *kos* (4 miles = 6.44 km.) length. . . . The nobles also raised their mansions in its neighbourhood and thus a miniature city grew around it.[31]

It was intact during the Lodi period. Mian Zafaruddin, who had been posted in Delhi by Sultan Sikandar Lodi, used to visit it along with his harem and stayed there from time to time at short intervals.[32]

The break-up of the Delhi Sultanate into a number of regional kingdoms and principalities towards the close of the fourteenth century was paradoxically paralleled by the extension of Delhi imperial culture. In fact, their founders were the inheritors of the cultural traditions and aristocratic norms evolved at the Delhi court. In their newly founded capitals they not only raised beautiful edifices in the old traditions but also welcomed skilled workers from foreign countries for the introduction of new arts and crafts, with the result that new ideas came in and new features were added to the architecture and design of gardens and waterworks. For instance, the Kankariya lake constructed near Ahmedabad (capital of the Gujarat Sultanate) during the reign of Sultan Qutbuddin is said to have been unique in the subcontinent. A mini town sprang up around it because a number of villas were erected and pleasure gardens planted.[33] Likewise, the Sultans and governors of Malwa took an interest in this type of work. Babur praises the lakes and tanks built by them in Chanderi.[34]

The *Mathnavi*, *Arvat-ul-Wuthqa*, written by Shihab Hakim, a resident of Jaunpur during the reign of Sultan Ibrahim Sharqi (1401–40), reflects on the passion with which the rulers of these new kingdoms were seized to raise beautiful structures in their capitals. Shihab Hakim,[35] who was a remarkable man on several counts, furnishes useful information about the construction of what came to be called a Pani Mahal (water palace) under his own supervision and direction in one of the royal gardens. Besides a number of fountains and water channels, there were put up two beautiful cisterns with doors opening inside the gardens. Their water was diverted through channels to the groves of mango trees. All these constructions were marvellous. On his first visit to the Pani Mahal and the garden, the Sultan was so greatly pleased that he showered royal favours on Shihab. The latter was honoured with a royal robe, cap, belt, bales of *diba-i-rumi* (silken fabric imported from the Ottoman Empire), *zarbaft-i-chin* (Chinese silk woven with gold threads), eighty-one horses, and ten villages in perpetuity.[36]

Evidence available in the *Mulfuzat* of Shah Mina of Lucknow reveals that in certain towns the lakes constructed during the early phase of the regional dynasty became polluted with the rapid expansion of towns and cities in the Sharqi kingdom of Jaunpur. For instance, Nuruddin, a nobleman, constructed a pukka *haud* (tank) on the outskirts of Lucknow. Soon afterwards, the town grew into a city and the tank was enclosed by new quarters built by people belonging to different professions. Pigs owned by some local residents started bathing in it. This led others to give up using its water.[37]

In Nagaur, the administrative headquarters of a principality, several new lakes were excavated. Both the local rulers and the Sufi saints are reported to have constructed huge lakes to help people irrigate their fields and gardens.[38] Shaikh Husain Chishti Nagauri is reported to have constructed a lake and named it after the Prophet of Islam as Mustafa Sagar.[39]

Similarly, the Lodi and Sur kings and their nobles also built lakes at different places in their dominions. Mushtaqi incidentally refers to them in his account of the nobles. An inscription of Sher Shah Sur's reign refers to a *haud* constructed by Yusuf bin Jhakan, the *munsif* in the town of Chaund (Bihar). It was a beautifully patterned tank in a garden.[40] The famous tomb of Sher Shah in Sahasram was also constructed inside an artificial lake. The tomb and the lake are still intact.

We may now pass to considering the beginning of the construction of beautiful fountains in north India. This was a new development of great importance as it considerably added to the beauty and charm of royal gardens. It was started by foreign immigrants. The close cultural and commercial ties between India and foreign countries enabled Indo-Muslim rulers to utilize the services of men of skill from abroad whom they had always patronized. The arrival of these foreigners often led to the modification of traditional crafts and the adoption of new ones. This also encouraged new ideas and forms in architecture. A chronicler of Gujarat admits that the idea of constructing pleasure gardens with fountains and channels of running water in Gujarat came from Iran during the reign of Sultan Mahmud Begara.[41] In Malwa also, water palaces and gardens contained artificial waterfalls, channels, and fountains.[42] According to Mushtaqi, Araish Khan Shirazi (Iranian) supervised the construction of these royal edifices in Mandu and Ujjain.[43] In Jaunpur, Khan Azam Lad Khan Lodi Sarang Khani had cisterns and fountains constructed all around the Sabha Mandal (pavilion) inside the palace. Being a womanizer, the Khan Azam maintained a large seraglio full of beautiful ladies. At times he sat on the roof of the Sabha Mandal and looked at the ladies. When he cast his glance on them, he found houris and fairies moving all around in the midst of flowerbeds, fountains, and channels through which water flowed.[44] It may not be an exaggeration to say that the construction of fountains and other types of waterworks was undertaken by members of the ruling elite everywhere in a competitive spirit.

II

As to the construction of wells, they are mentioned in our sources either as *chah* or *bain* or *baoli*. The *chah* was a simple well, while the latter were step wells put up for the use of man and animals. Evidence available about the *chah* is interesting in so far as it reflects on the use of a gear device employed by Indians for lifting water from deep wells through Persian wheels in Delhi and the area around it during the early Sultanate period. It also provides a clue to the origin of the use of the Persian wheel in India.

In 1969, Irfan Habib suggested in his presidential address to the annual session of the Indian History Congress that the Persian wheel was introduced into India some time in the fifteenth century because there is no reference available to it in any work produced in India earlier than the *Baburnama*. 'There is in fact no explicit reference to gearing,' says he, 'until Babur described the mechanism with its gearing early in the 16th century. By then it was fully established in the Panjab up to Sirhind.'[45] Some modern scholars of ancient Indian history have accepted Irfan Habib's thesis, while others not only contradicted him but also tried to establish that the Persian wheel was indigenous to India.[46] It needs to be noted here that Irfan Habib's statement about the time of the diffusion of the gearing device that was employed for water lifting from wells is not correct; in fact, he has failed to explore evidence in the earlier sources. We do find useful evidence about the presence of the Persian wheel in Delhi and the area around it in the Arabic and Persian works compiled during the fourteenth century. They reveal the extent to which certain territorial units had become prosperous, because the possession of the Persian wheel was an expensive affair and its widespread use in a certain area points to general prosperity and affluence. Only rich farmers could afford the installation of this water-lifting device.

The fourteenth-century Arabic and Persian works contain references to the *saqiya* and *charkh* set up on the wells that were owned both by the state as well as private cultivators. For instance, the author of the *Masalik-ul-Absar* who collected information from Indian travellers in the beginning of Sultan Muhammad bin Tughluq's reign about the life and culture of India writes that people in and around Delhi set up Persian wheels on the wells to water their fields and gardens. He refers to the Persian wheel as *al-savaq*,[47] the plural of *saqiya*[48] (the Arabic equivalent of the English phrase Persian wheel). Contemporary Indo-Persian writers mention the Persian wheel as *charkh*, the short form of the *charkh-i-abkashi* and the Persian equivalent of the Arabic *saqiya*.

An interesting anecdote related in the *Javamial-Kilm* (the collection of table talks of Shaikh Muhammad Gesudaraz) about Shaikh Nizamuddin Auliya suggests that the Persian wheel had gained general acceptance in Delhi some time in the thirteenth century. It tells us that once Shaikh Nizamuddin Auliya came across a Persian wheel set up on a well. The cultivator who was driving the bullocks for lifting the water exhorted the animals, saying '*age barh, age barh*' (speed up, speed up) in a melodious tone. The sound produced by the revolving of the wheel and the voice of the cultivator had such an emotive effect on the Shaikh that he was immediately transported into a state of ecstasy. The allusion made in the anecdote to the pair of bullocks, the *charkh*, and the sound produced by its revolving leave no doubt about the presence of the perfect Persian wheel in the territorial unit of Delhi during the lifetime of Nizamuddin Auliya (d. 1325).[49]

Another fourteenth-century Persian work, the *Sirat-i Firuz Shahi*, furnishes relevant evidence in its account about the waterworks established by Sultan Firuz Shah (1351–88). It informs us that the *charkhs* (Persian wheels) were set up on the wells around the newly constructed Haudi-Shahzada-i-Mubarak Khan outside the capital city of Firuzabad. This lake was filled with water from wells when rainwater was exhausted. The author further informs us that the *haud* was just one of hundreds of charity trusts established by Sultan Firuz Shah because the income accruing from the sale of its water went to the poor. The account also contains references to buckets (*dalvs*) made of metal instead of *kuza* (pitchers or pottery vessels) hanging down the well fixed on a chain of ropes).[50] In addition, the Persian term *dulab* also occurs in the same passage, signifying the presence of the *noria* or surface wheels installed on the sides of the lake.[51]

By the turn of the fourteenth century, the device of lifting water through the Persian wheel seems to have diffused into different territories in north India. The evidence about the putting up of fountains in the gardens and palaces in Jaunpur during the early Sharqi and the Lodi periods suggests that they may have been made to work by the water in the cisterns flowing through the channels. These cisterns may also have been filled with water lifted from the wells through Persian wheels as no channel is ever reported to have been led off from the river Gomti on the bank of which Jaunpur was founded by Firuz Shah. Kabir who flourished during the fifteenth century makes mention of the Persian wheel in a metaphorical way in his verses. Emphasizing the importance of sincerity in love, he makes fun of the rosary used by the traditionalists. He likens it to the *rahat* (the Hindi word for the

Persian wheel) in these words: 'If by putting on a rosary one is to meet God, then you should see around the neck of the *rahat* (which has a chain of buckets, around the wheel). People do not develop the sentiment of devotion (which is the real thing); they should observe that the *rahat* also has a rosary around its neck (but does not get emancipation).'[52]

Like the Indo-Persian writers, Shaikh Zainuddin, the *sadr* (minister for religious affairs) under Babur, makes mention of the Persian wheel being used in India as *charkh*.[53] Babur refers to the Persian wheel twice in his memoirs. First, he refers to it in his account of the occupation of Bhera town in AD 1519. In Bhera and Khoshab, he found it a common mode of irrigation; the cultivation of profitable crops of sugar cane and rice depended on irrigation through the Persian wheel.[54] The second time that Babur refers to the Persian wheel in his description of the methods of irrigation in different parts of north India. His description of the Persian wheel reveals that when he found the device in India, he took it as a novelty and was amazed. Therefore, he furnishes full details about the structure and the working of the gear machine. He writes:

> They make two circles of ropes long enough to suit the depth of the well, first fix strips of wood between them and on these fasten pitchers. The ropes with the wood and attached pitchers are put over the well-wheel. At one end of the wheel-axle a second wheel is fixed, and close to it another on an upright axle. This last wheel the bullock turns; its teeth catch in the teeth of the second, thus the wheel with the pitchers is turned. A trough is set where the water empties from the pitchers and from this the water is conveyed everywhere.[55]

The impression created by Babur is that the use of the Persian wheel was confined to the territorial unit of Sirhind and that it did not spread eastward. But the evidence analysed above dispels this impression. Shaikh Zain's *Waqi'at-i Baburi* also serves as a corrective to *Baburnama*. Unlike his master Babur, Shaikh Zain writes that in India cultivators irrigate their fields with water from the well lifted through a Persian wheel in addition to other methods. According to him, water lifting through *charas* (leather buckets) was also a common mode of irrigation.[56]

The terms *bain* and *baoli* are of Indian origin and refer to what is called 'step well'. The sultans and the governors evinced an interest in the construction of these wells in cities and towns and along the highways. Ibn Battuta refers to a number of step wells that he found in different parts of north India. He also informs us that the *maliks* and *amirs* posted in the provinces tried to outdo one another in building *bains* on the roads for the benefit of travellers. He gives a detailed description of step wells in the territorial unit of Kol (present-day Aligarh district).[57] The epigraphical sources also yield interesting information in this regard. For instance, an inscription found in Balibagarh in the Damoh district of Madhya Pradesh, dated AD 1328, sheds interesting light on the religious policy of Sultan Muhammad bin Tughluq and his officers towards the Hindus. It records the construction of a cow temple along with a step well inside a garden by the order of the Sultan.[58] The fifteenth-century inscriptions noticed in the step wells show the continuation of old traditions by the regional Sultans and their officers in Gujarat, Malwa, Jaunpur, etc. Moreover, they were made parts of endowments made for the benefit of the people. An inscription found near the village of Mandavi, about 3 km. to the north-west of Champaner (Gujarat), records that Malik Sandal Sultani endowed two ploughs of land (200 *bighas*) for the upkeep of a step well, a mosque, and a mausoleum erected by him during the reign of Sultan Mahmud Begara.[59]

The survey of the traces of the fifteenth-century step wells in Malwa shows that they were multi-storied. Of the numerous *baolis* found in and around Chanderi, the Battisi Baoli deserves to be described in detail. This is a large square step well, 60 ft. each way, and sinks by four storeys.

Besides the principal stairway which is in the south side, there are two flights of steps in each of the four sides of each of the four storeys, thus making the number of stairs thirty-two—a figùre from which apparently the well takes its name. It is built of chisel-dressed stone and is said to have originally stood in the midst of a beautiful park, which perhaps justified the inscription on the well, exclaiming "If anyone visits this place, he will say 'It is Heaven'." This inscription records that the well was built in 890 AH (AD 1485) in the reign of Ghiyath Shah Khalji of Mandu.[60]

Likewise, a new phase started in the architecture of step wells built in Delhi and other cities and towns under the rule of the

Delhi Sultans during the Lodi period. The Sultans and their nobles built beautiful *baolis* consisting of more than one storey. We can refer to a few *baolis* of the period for the sake of brevity. The step well built by a *khwaja sera* (eunuch) of Sultan Sikandar Lodi named Mian Basti in Delhi contains arcades in several stories.[61] Another *baoli*, called Rajon ki Bain is situated in Delhi near the shrine of Shaikh Qutbuddin Bakhtiyar Kaki. It was constructed by the order of Daulat Khan Lodi in 1506. It also contains rooms built all around with chisel-dressed stones and lime mortar.[62] The same noble also constructed a beautiful *baoli* in Lahore.[63] Sher Shah Sur and his successor Islam Shah Sur (1545–53) also had step wells constructed; some of them are still extant in Delhi.[64]

III

The most important development that took place in the irrigation system was the harnessing of big rivers. Canals, big as well as small, were led off from rivers for the irrigation of the north-western territories that suffered from scarcity of water. The evidence available in the contemporary literature shows that the construction of large artificial canals began in the reign of Sultan Alauddin Khalji towards the close of the thirteenth century. Amir Khusrau incidentally refers to a deep and quite wide canal built by Ghazi Malik in the account of the mutiny of the Multan army against the governor, Mughlati. Attacked by his followers, Mughlati tried to run away, but he was drowned in the canal while crossing it. One gains the impression that the canal was cut from the river Ravi and that it watered the area between it and the river Jhelum.[65]

In addition, Ghazi Malik seems to have constructed a few more canals in the territories of Multan and Dipalpur where he served in different capacities during the Khalji period.[66] Barani states that in each territory assigned to his charge, he constructed canals for the progress of agriculture.[67] But he neither mentions the number of these canals nor provides any hints about the areas that were irrigated by them. Ain ul-Mulk Mahru, however, provides clues to the existence of three of these canals. In a *nishan* (official document issued by a governor), Mahru directs one of his subordinate officers, Kamal bin Taj, to carry out the repair work on the old canals. They are mentioned with their names, such as Ju-i-Nasirwah, Ju-i-Qutbwah, and Ju-i-Khidrwah. The *nishan* also instructs the officer Ali Quli to collect money from the cultivators to meet the expenditure in desilting the canals so that the money of *bait-ul mal* (state treasury) should not have to bear the burden. He justifies this action by citing the practices of the early Muslim rulers of the classical lands of Islam. According to him, the cultivators had to contribute to the expenses incurred on the repair of canals as their prosperity depended on them, and that any neglect shown by the state in keeping them intact would ruin the cultivation and the peasantry at large.[68]

Ibn Battuta also provides us with relevant evidence about a gentleman farmer who cut a small canal from the Jamuna for watering his farm near Delhi. The details furnished by Ibn Battuta give us insights into the life of the foreign immigrants who took an interest in agriculture. He states that Shaikh Shihabuddin al-Khurasani[69] occupied a fairly large tract of land at a distance of 6 miles from Delhi and brought it under the plough. In this tract, he excavated a cave and had bedrooms, storerooms, an oven, and a bath constructed, all underground. He also brought water from the river Jamuna through a channel, and the fields were irrigated by it. He earned a huge income from cultivation, particularly during the days of scarcity.[70]

It was in the reign of Sultan Firuz Shah that an ambitious project of constructing big canals in the region between the Sutlej and Delhi and the Doab was undertaken. Barani clearly implies that the canals built by Sultan Firuz Shah went a long way towards bringing about prosperity and paved the way for socio-economic growth in the areas through which they flowed, and that they also provided travel and transport facilities. He writes:

> During the auspicious Firuz Shah's reign, the canals, one hundred and one hundred twenty miles long, were led off from the rivers, the Jamuna and the Ganga. The water flowing through them irrigated the desert and desolate tracts where no well or lake existed (before). The depth and width (of certain canals) has made the use of boats possible; people travel in boats, covering the distance from the one to the other place.[71]

Barani's reference to the Ganga built by Sultan Firuz Shah is intriguing and has escaped the notice of modern scholars. Even the medieval writers Shams Siraj Afif and Yahya Sirhindi do not mention it among the projects undertaken by the Sultan. However, a clue provided by the contemporary work the *Sirat-i-Firuz Shahi* not only corroborates Barani's statement but also supplements it. The *Sirat-i-Firuz Shahi* incidentally alludes to the *Nahr-i-Gang* (Ganga canal) in the account about the damage caused by lightning to the Qutb Minar in Delhi in 1368. The Sultan got this sad news when he was out on a hunt at the place of origin of the Ganga canal.[72] It may also be pointed out that Firuz Shah had built *shikargahs* (hunting stations) around Delhi as far as Baran and Kol. The *Gang Nahr* (Ganga canal) had probably earlier irrigated this region, but it later ceased to flow either owing to silting or to the change of course by the river itself.

It is worth recalling that the contemporary sources indicate that the region that attracted Firuz Shah's attention for the first time were the territorial units of the *shiqqs*[73] of Samana and Hansi, now incorporated in the states of Haryana and the Panjabi Suba. These territories suffered from a scarcity of water and here only one crop in a year (i.e. the *kharif* or rainy season's crop) could be harvested. In 1354, the Sultan is reported to have laid down the foundation of the city of Hisar Firuza (present-day Hisar) and then constructed a double system of canals the headwaters of which were drawn both from the Jamuna and the Sutlej. The Sutlej canal named Ulugh Khani flowing through Rupar and Sirhind (towns) met the Jamuna canal called Rajiwah; the latter also passed via Karnal. At Hisar Firuza, they discharged their water through a single channel into the ditch around the city walls. Having filled the ditch, the water flowed through another channel and irrigated the area up to the town of Jhajhar (district Rohtak).[74] Another canal was excavated from the Ghaggar River that flowed past the fort of Sirsuti and irrigated the area up to Harnikhera.[75] The most important canal was the Jamuna canal, named Ju-i-Firozabad. It flowed up to the capital city of Firozabad. According to the compiler of the *Sirat-i-Firuz Shahi*, its headwaters were drawn from the Jamuna just below the foothills.[76] In addition, the canal dug out in the Siwalik hills received water from the Sirsuti and Salima streams and flowed past Shahabad town. It is now identified with the Khanpur ka Nala.[77]

All these canals were big and important and their construction can be considered an important feat of medieval engineering. Moreland is not correct in his assessment of the importance of these canals. He observes: 'During the rains, officers were specially deputed to report how far the floods caused by each canal had extended, and that the king was exceedingly pleased when he heard of the widespread inundation. The canals were thus of a somewhat elementary type, and should not be thought of in terms of those which now exist in the Panjab. . . .'[78] Afif's statement about the widespread inundation caused by the overflow of water from the canals during the monsoon[79] needs to be carefully examined. It implies that there was no provision to stop the flow of water in the canals through the use of shutters during the rainy season as it is today. Perhaps the use of shutters was not known to the people in Central Asia where generally lay the source of diffusion of new techniques and changes during the thirteenth and fourteenth centuries. It is also indicative of the fact that inundation did not cause any damage to human life and property; rather it was useful for cultivation.

As regards the levy of the irrigation tax (*haqq-i-sharb*), it was nominal and had to be collected to replenish the state treasury as a huge amount had already been spent on construction. It was one-tenth of the income accruing from the irrigated land and the yearly collection amounted to 2,00,000 *tankas*.[80]

Like Firuz Shah, some of his nobles also seem to have improved the water resources in their *iqtas*. The biographical details contained in the *Surat-i-Firuz Shahi* about the *wazir*, Khan Jahan Maqbul, indicate that he took measures to create conditions favourable for socio-economic growth in his *iqta*. A number of canals, *sarais*, and *bazaars* were constructed and gardens planted.[81]

We may now discuss the transformation of the landscape in the arid land of modern Haryana and Panjabi Suba (i.e. Indian Panjab). Barani, who does not appear to have survived beyond the sixth regnal year of Firuz Shah's reign,[82] states that peasants had started cultivating wheat, gram, and different varieties of sugar cane there. He emphatically points out that where the peasants could not even think of sowing the crops of wheat or sugar cane but could raise only one crop of *moth* (a kind of bean) and *til* (oilseeds) in a year, they would now harvest both the *kharif* (summer) and *rabi* (winter) crops.[83] Further, he states that sugar, wheat, and gram were supplied to this region from Delhi or other towns near Delhi.[84]

Afif's account of the affluence brought about by the progress of agriculture in the newly constituted shiqq-i-Hisar Firuza shows how the canals served as instruments of change and brought about affluence in the region. According to Afif, the travellers from Iraq (Iran) and Khurasan (Central Asia) used to buy water four *jitals*[85] per *seer* in the region included in the newly constituted *shiqq* (unit) of Hisar Firuza during the summer, for water was scarce.[86] But the availability of water from the new canals solved this problem. One could now see lush fields and gardens all around. There was an abundance of different types of fruits and flowers. Various types of sugar cane were grown such as *ponda* and black sugar cane. The sugar cane grown here was soft and juicy; one could easily remove its skin with one's teeth and suck its juice. 'Previously people,' says he 'harvested only the *kharif* crop; the *rabi* crop was not possible because the wheat (crop) needs enough water.'[87] This was not all. The presence of the canals made the construction of wells in the region easy. The water level was so raised that pukka wells would normally be only 4 yards deep.[88] The anonymous author of the *Sirat-i-Firuz Shahi* also gives a list of the fruits and flowers grown here.[89]

All the canals, with the exception of the Nahr-i-Gang, seem to have been kept under repair by the later Sultans of Delhi.[90] Babur's description of the irrigation system in India would have us believe that the canals in the north-western territorial units in the Delhi Sultanate had ceased to flow,[91] but this is not acceptable in view of the evidence contained in another contemporary work, the *Waqi'at-i-Baburi*. The latter serves as a corrective to the *Baburnama* and also indicates that new canals were built in certain regions during the fifteenth century. Shaikh Zain refers to one of the Firuz Shahi canals, watering the area around the town of Jhajjar.[92] In the same work we find graphic details of a number of villages and lush fields of corn in the hilly *pargana* of Jaiswal, held by Dilawar Khan Lodi's maternal uncle. This canal seems to have been built during the Lodi period. Babur also contradicts himself when he refers to the artificial channels of running water in the territorial unit of Chanderi.[94] It may be noted that the Sultans of Malwa constructed canals in their territories for a variety of purposes. They irrigated fields and pleasure gardens and also supplied water to the lakes surrounding the water palaces built in the cities of Mandu and Ujjain.[95] In fact, the rulers harnessed the rivers for irrigation purposes wherever it was possible. We find authentic evidence about the construction of dams over rivers even in pre-Mughal Orissa. Sulaiman Karrani came across canals in Orissa in the course of his military operations there in 1567.[96]

In the final analysis, it may be noted that the relevant evidence analysed earlier illustrates that India was quite an advanced country in irrigation technology. Indeed, people had made great progress in material culture. The construction of fountains, waterfalls, and water pavilions not only richly contributed to the traditions of material culture but also led to refinement in artistic taste. All these achievements reflect on the high civilization that formed the social milieu of Indian aristocracy in medieval India. The affluence enjoyed by the cultivators in Delhi, Haryana, and the Panjab regions during the Lodi period can be attributed to the advanced methods of irrigation. Likewise, the use of lime mortar begun by the Muslim immigrants from Central Asia in the thirteenth century made possible the construction of waterproof walls and floors for the pavilions and mausoleums erected inside the lakes. This was by all standards a great feat of engineering.

NOTES

1. Minhaj Juzjani, *Tabaqat-i Nasiri*, ed. Abdul Hai Habibi, Kabul, 1342 Shamsi, vol. 1, pp. 436–7.
2. Cf. *Epigraphia Indo-Moslemica*, 1911–12, ed. J. Horovitz, pp. 1–3.
3. Shaikh Zainuddin, *Waqi'at-i Baburi*, MS, British Library, Or. 1999, ff. 21b–22a.
4. Ibn Battuta, *The Travels of Ibn Battuta*, Eng. tr. Sir Hamilton Gibb, Cambridge, 1971, vol. 3, p. 624.
5. Amir Khusrau, *Khazain al-Futuh*, Eng. tr. Mohammad Habib, Madras, 1933, p. 19; *The Travels of Ibn Battuta*, vol. 3, p. 624.

6. Isami, *Futuh us-Salatin*, ed. A.S. Usha, Madras, 1948, pp. 114–15, hereafter cited as Isami.
7. Firuz Shah, *Futuhat-i-Firuz Shahi*, ed. Sh. Abdur Rashid, Aligarh, 1954, p. 12; Anonymous, *Sirat-i-Firuz Shahi*, MS, Khuda Bakhsh Library, Patna, ff. 79a–b.
8. *Khazain al-Futuh*, op. cit., pp. 19–20.
9. Ibn Battuta, *The Travels of Ibn Battuta*, vol. III, p. 624.
10. Cf. Z.A. Desai, 'Inscriptions of the Mamluk Sultans of Delhi', *Epigraphia Indica: Arabic and Persian Supplement*, 1966, pp. 5–7.
11. Mir Hasan Sijzi, the compiler of the *Fawaid al-Fuad*, relates that the residents of Badaon compared it in beauty and size with the Haud-i-Sultani of Delhi. When this was reported to Shaikh Nizamuddin Auliya, he did not agree that it was larger than the Haud-i-Sultani. However, it does imply that the lake of Badaon was also a large reservoir.
12. Ziauddin Barani, *Tarikh-i-Firuz Shahi*, ed. Sir Syed Ahmad, Calcutta, 1862, p. 341, hereafter cited as *Barani.*
13. Barani mentions the lake as Haud-i-Ala'i. Barani, p. 148.
14. *The Travels of Ibn battuta*, vol. III, p. 625.
15. *Barani*, p. 565.
16. Sharafuddin Yazdi, *Zafarnama*, Calcutta, 1888, vol. I, p. 109.
17. *Waqi'at-i-Mushtaqi* (Rampur, 2002), ed. Iqtidar Husain Siddiqui, p. 250.
18. Sir Syed Ahmad, *Athar u'l-Sanadid*, Eng. tr. R. Nath, *Monuments of Delhi*, New Delhi, 1979, p. 35, hereafter cited as *Monuments of Delhi.*
19. Sangin Beg, *Siyar-ul-Manazil*, Urdu tr. Naim Ahmad, Aligarh, 1980, p. 126.
20. *Monuments of Delhi*, p. 5.
21. Cf. Qayamuddin Ahmad, *Corpus of Arabic and Persian Inscriptions of Bihar*, Patna, 1973, p. 31.
22. Edward Thomas, *The Chronicles of the Pathan Kings of Delhi*, 1st edn. 1871, Delhi, 1971, p. 136.
23. *Epigraphia Indica: Arabic and Persian Supplement*, 1964, p. 136.
24. Ibid., 1967, p. 9.
25. This lake seems to have been constructed by Qutlugh Khan during the reign of Sultan Muhammad bin Tughluq as he does not seem to have survived his master. Shaikh Gesudaraz alludes to it as one of the important lakes of Delhi. Cf. Muhammad Husaini, *Juvami al-Kilem* (collection of the table talks of Shaikh Gesudaraz), Kanpur, 1356 AH, p. 241.
26. *Sirat-i-Firuz Shahi*, ff. 78b–79a, 91b, 106b, 107a; the facsimile's passage is too dim to be deciphered.
27. Shams Siraj Afif, *Tarikh-i-Firuz Shahi*, Calcutta, 1891, p. 126, hereafter cited as *Afif.*
28. *The Travels of Ibn Battuta*, vol. III, p. 645.
29. *Baburnama*, Eng., tr. Mrs. Beveridge, vol. I, p. 381.

30. *Afif*, p. 330; also Tatsuro Yamamoto, Mastsu Ara and Tokifusa Tsu Kinowa, *Delhi: Architectural Remains of the Delhi Sultanate Period, Water Works*, vol. 3, Tokyo, 1970, p. 120. Though we are not in a position to judge the merit of the Japanese work on account of unfamiliarity with the language, the beautiful plates contained therein show how ambitious and beautiful were the projects undertaken by the medieval rulers.
31. Cf. *Monuments of Delhi*, p. 7.
32. *Waqi'at-i-Mushtaqi*, p. 76.
33. Mahmud Bukhari, *Tarikh-i-Salatin-i-Gujarat*, ed. A.A. Tirmizi, *Medieval India Quarterly*, Aligarh, vol. 5, 1963, p. 59.
34. *Baburnama*, vol. 2, pp. 592, 596, 597.
35. His name was Ali bin Mahmud al-Kirmani, but he was famous as Shihab Hakim. He was Iranian by origin and had settled in Jaunpur during the reign of Sultan Ibrahim Sharqi. After the latter's death, he moved to Malwa where he compiled his history of Malwa, *Mathir-i-Mahmud Shahi*. Cf. *Mathir-i-Mahmud Shahi*, ed. Nurul Hasan Ansari, Delhi, 1968, pp. 3, 6–7.
36. Shihab Hakim, *Arvat-u'l-Wuthqa*, ed. Hafiz Mahmud Shirani, *Maqalat-i-Shirani*, Lahore, 1972, vol. 6, pp. 403–4.
37. *Malfuzat-i-Shah Mina*, compiled by Muhi al-Din al-Husaini, MS, Habib Ganj Collection, Aligarh, F.21/244, f.77a.
38. Shaikh Abdul Haque Dehlevi, *Akbar al-Akhyar*, Matba-i-Ahmadi, Delhi, n.d., p. 209, 210.
39. *Waqi'at-i-Mushtaqi*, p. 202.
40. *Corpus of Arabic and Persian Inscriptions of Bihar*, op. cit., p. 138.
41. Sikandar bin Manjhu, *Mirat-i-Sikandari*, ed., S.C. Misra, Baroda, 1961, pp. 139–40.
42. Cf. G. Yazdani, *Mandu: The City of Joy*, Oxford, 1929; also *Waqi'at-i-Mushtaqi*, f.79a.
43. *Waqi'at-i-Mushtaqi*, pp. 205, 208–9.
44. Ibid., p. 92.
45. Presidential Address, Medieval India Section, *Proceedings of the Indian History Congress*, XXXI Session, Varanasi, 1969, pp. 152–3.
46. Cf. Lallanji Gopal, *Aspects of History of Agriculture in Ancient India*, Varanasi, 1980, pp. 116–20, for the controversy over the presence of the Persian wheel in ancient India. It may, however, be pointed out that Lallanji Gopal's thesis is based on references to the garland of pots hanging down the wheel in the well that also occur in ancient works in a metaphorical sense. He himself admits: 'There is no clear reference to the gear system in the water-lifting device.' It is still reasonable to agree with A.L. Basham who says: 'The Persian wheel turned by an ox is nowhere clearly mentioned in the early sources, though it may have been used.' Cf. A.L. Basham, *The Wonder that was India*, 3rd edn., London, 1967, p. 194.

47. Shihabuddin al-Umari, *Masalik al-Absar-fi-Mamalik-al-Amsar* (Chapters on India), ed. under the title, *Du Jadid 'Ali Tarikh al-Hind*, by Khursheed Ahmad Tariq, Delhi, 1961, p. 23.
48. Thorkid Schioler has established that the *saqiya* was equipped with a pawl-mechanism for breaking the movement in reverse, and that by the year, AD 1100, it had reached Baghdad. Cf. Thorkid Schioler, *Roman and Islamic Water-Lifting Wheels*, Odense (Denmark), 1973, pp. 168–73.
49. *Juvami'al-Kilem*, op. cit., p. 150.
50. Anonymous, *Sirat-i-Firuz Shahi*, ff. 78b–79a.
51. The Arabic term for the surface wheel is *naura*, which has been anglicized as *noria*. In Persian it is called *dulab*. The *noria* or *dulab* operates on open water surfaces such as rivers, tanks, or lakes. It has pitchers or pottery vessels fixed on the rim of the wheel. It was turned by the hand of man and revolved horizontally. The Persian wheel, on the other hand, operates in deep wells. It comprises three wheels and a beam horizontally attached to a toothed wheel outside the well. To the outer end of the beam a pair of bulls or buffaloes is yoked. The animals move in a circular path, pulling the beam and thus making the wheels revolve. As the machine is turned, the buckets hanging in a chain dip, one by one, into the water. Again, they reach the top and then empty into a trough. The water flows through a drain to the fields, orchards, etc.
52. Quoting the Hindi verses with their English translation, Lallanji Gopal remarks: 'The analogy requires us to assume that buckets were tied, at regular intervals, to a long rope hanging around the wheel. This description suits a Persian wheel and not a *noria*.' Cf. *Aspects of the History of Agriculture in Ancient India*, op. cit., pp. 131–2.
53. *Waqi'at-i Baburi*, op. cit., ff. 52a–b.
54. *Baburnama*, vol. I, p. 388.
55. Ibid., vol. II, pp. 486–7. The passage translated by Mrs Beveridge does not contain the names of the Sirhind territory along with those of Lahore and Dipalpur where Babur found the Persian wheel as a common mode of irrigation. But Abdur Rahim Khan Khanan's translation of *Baburnama* (Persian) mentions Sirhind also. Cf. *Baburnama*, Persian tr. Abdur Rahim Khan Khanan, ed. Muhammad Shirazi, *Malikal-Kutab*, Bombay, 1308 AH, p. 191.
56. *Waqi'at-i Baburi*, ff. 52a–b.
57. Ibn Battuta, as quoted by Jamal Muhammad Siddiqui, *Aligarh Survey*, (from ancient times to 1803), Delhi, 1981, p. 59.
58. Cf. W.H. Siddiqui, 'Religious Tolerance as Gleaned from Medieval Inscriptions', *Proceedings of the Seminar on Medieval Inscriptions*, Aligarh, 1970, p. 50.
59. 'Mandevi Step-well Inscription at Champaner', ed. and tr. V.H. Sonawne, *Journal of the Oriental Institute*, vol. XXI, no. 3, Baroda, 1972, pp. 224–7.

60. *Annual Report of the Archaeological Department, Gwalior State* for the year 1924–5, 1981 VS, p. 5.
61. Sir Syed Ahmad, *Athar U'l-Sanadid*, Eng. tr. R. Nath, *Monuments of Delhi*, New Delhi, 1979, p. 44.
62. Ibid., p. 45.
63. Cf. M. Abdullah Chaghtai, 'The Oldest Extant Muslim Architectural Relics at Lahore', *Journal of the Pakistan Historical Society*, vol. XII, 1964, p. 70.
64. Cf. Mirza Sangin Beg, *Sair ul-Manzil*, Urdu tr. Naim Ahmad, Aligarh, 1980, p. 50; also *Monuments of Delhi*, op. cit., p. 48.
65. Amir Khusrau, *Tughluqnama*, Hyderabad, Deccan, 1933, verses 1201–2, p. 63.
66. Amir Khusrau informs us that Ghazi Malik entered the service of Ulugh Khan after the murder of Sultan Jalaluddin Khalji (1296). Soon after, Ulugh Khan was deputed to seize Multan from the sons of Jalaluddin Khalji. Having occupied Multan and posted his men there, Ulugh Khan came back to Delhi. He might have left Ghazi Malik in Multan as his deputy. Ibn Battuta also mentions a mosque constructed by Ghazi Malik during the same period. In 1306, Ghazi Malik was appointed as the officer-in-charge of the border tract. *Tughluqnama*, op. cit., pp. 136–7; also *The Travels of Ibn Battuta*, vol. III, p. 649.
67. *Barani*, p. 442.
68. Ain-ul Mulk Mahru, *Insha-i-Mahru*, ed. Sh. Abdur Rashid, Lahore, 1965, letter no. 114, pp. 204–5.
69. The immigrants from Afghanistan and Transoxiana were known as Khurasanis in India during the pre-Mughal period. The Persian writers of pre-Mughal India invariably apply the term 'Khurasan' to the region now included in present-day Afghanistan. Cf. Iqtidar Husain Siddiqui, 'The Qarlugh Kingdom in North-western India—13th Century', *Islamic Culture*, Hyderabad, vol. LIV, no. 2, 1980, pp. 76, 88, fn. 3.
70. Ibn Battuta, p. 698.
71. *Barani*, 567.
72. *Sirat-i-Firuz Shahi*, ff. 790–b.
73. The *shiqq* was an extensive territorial unit with well-defined boundaries. This official term was replaced by a new term *sarkar* during the Lodi period. Cf. Iqtidar Husain Siddiqui, 'Evolution of the *Vilayet*, the *Shiqq*, and the *Sarkar* in Northern India, AD 1210–1555', *Medieval India Quarterly*, Aligarh, vol. V, 1963, pp. 14, 18–19, 26–7.
74. Afif, *Tarikh-i-Firuz Shahi*, Calcutta, 1891, pp. 124, 126–7; Yahya Sirhindi, *Tarikh-i-Mubarak Shahi*, Calcutta, 1931, pp. 125–6.
75. *Tarikh-i-Mubarak Shahi*, op. cit., p. 126.
76. *Sirat-i-Firuz Shahi*, ff. 106b–107a.
77. R.C. Jauhri, *Firuz Shah Tughluq*, Agra, 1968, p. 105.
78. W.H. Moreland, *The Agrarian System of Moslem India*, rpt., Delhi, 1968, pp. 59–60.

79. *Afif*, p. 130.
80. Ibid., pp. 129–30.
81. *Sirat-i-Firuz Shahi*, f. 76a.
82. Cf. Peter Hardy, *Historians of Medieval India*, rpt., 1982, pp. 20–2.
83. Barani, pp. 567–8.
84. Ibid., pp. 568–9.
85. *Afif*, p. 125.
86. *Jital* was a copper coin and one-sixteenth part of the silver coin called *tanka*. Cf. *A Fourteenth-Century Arab Account of India Under Sultan Muhammad bin Tughluq*, op. cit., p. 59.
87. *Afif*, pp. 127–8.
88. Ibid., p. 128.
89. *Sirat-i-Firuz Shahi*, ff. 80a–82a.
90. We find references to some of these canals in the official histories compiled during the reigns of Akbar and Shah Jahan. When they were reopened, the English officers also found them flowing during the nineteenth century. 'The old line of the Jumna branch was carefully traced by Col. Colvin in 1833, and may be followed on the modern maps from Badshah Mahal at the debouchement of the river from the outer range of the Himalayas by Chichroli and Buriah to Karnal through the cutting below Uncha Samana, into the eastern branch of the Chitrang river, near Sufidun, and thence through the old bed of the Chitrang to Hansi and Hisar.' Cf. Edward Thomas, *The Chronicles of the Pathan Kings of Delhi* (1st pub. in 1871), Delhi, 1971, pp. 294–5.
91. *Baburnama*, vol. II, p. 487.
92. *Waqiat-i-Babri*, ff. 45b–46a.
93. Ibid., ff. 42a–b.
94. *Baburnama*, vol. II, pp. 596–7.
95. *Waqi'at-i-Mushtaqi*, pp. 205–6.
96. Iqtidar Husain Siddiqui, *Mughal Relations with the Indian Ruling Elite—16th Century*, New Delhi, 1983, pp. 155–6.

APPENDIX A

Ain ul-Mulk Multani and Ain ul-Mulk Mahru

Generally, Ain ul-Mulk Multani and Ain ul-Mulk Mahru have been regarded as one individual, a noble who supposedly rose to prominence under Sultan Alauddin Khalji and continued to serve in high positions until his death during the reign of Firuz Shah.[1] In 1977, I was requested to contribute a short note on Ain ul-Mulk Multani to the supplement of the *Encyclopaedia of Islam.* I examined the sources and found that Ain ul-Mulk Multani and Ain ul-Mulk Mahru were different persons and belonged to different generations. The publication of this note prompted Peter Jackson to study the problem afresh, and he added an appendix on the subject in his excellent work *The Delhi Sultanate: A Political and Military History.* Jackson is in agreement with me.[2] Now I find that the relevant evidence contained in the sources provides us with new insights into the changes that the system of governance underwent after the reign of Alauddin Khalji. It is desirable to include this information in an Appendix here.

Ain ul-Mulk Multani appears to have begun his career as a civil servant. He was first employed by Ulugh Khan, the brother of Sultan Alauddin Khalji, to serve as his *dabir* (secretary in-charge of correspondence).[3] In his capacity as *dabir*, he had to accompany his employer on military expeditions in order to write reports on matters connected with the army and the situation in alien territories. In Ranthambore he appears to have played an important role as a statesman and warrior. Since his meteoric rise in the nobility is traced from the conquest of Ranthambore in 1300–1, Amir Khusrau says in his praise, 'Although he was a man of the pen, in the battlefield also he stood very tall.'[4]

Mention is made by Barani of Ain ul-Mulk Multani for the

first time in the account of the consultation held by the Sultan about the measures to be taken for the prevention of disturbances after Haji Maula's revolt in Delhi. Ain ul-Mulk participated in the discussion along with other nobles. On their advice, the Sultan imposed restrictions on the nobles. They were forbidden to enter into matrimonial alliances among themselves, forbidden to arrange the marriage of sons or daughters without royal permission, and forbidden to host banquets or hold convivial gatherings to entertain fellow nobles. Spies were posted to keep watch on them.[5] Amir Khusrau corroborates Barani about the time when Ain ul-Mulk Multani impressed the Sultan and shot into prominence. Khusrau's statement contained in the *Khazain ul-Futuh* suggests that having been impressed by his qualities of military leadership, the Sultan selected him to command the army in Malwa and sent him there with the title of Ain ul-Mulk.[6] The ruler of Malwa, Rai Malik, was a powerful chief but he did not succeed in driving away the invader. Having lost the battle in the open, he shut himself up in his impregnable fort of Mandu. Ain ul-Mulk Multani's diplomacy and pragmatism soon enabled him to capture the fort with local support. This was not all. He not only established the political control of the Sultan over Malwa (called the *vilayet* or *arsa* of Dhar), but also persuaded the chiefs of the neighbouring territories to acknowledge the suzerainty of the Delhi Sultan. The success achieved by him was so great that the Sultan went out of his way to do him special favours. The Sultan raised him above other nobles by giving him the town of Ujjain as his personal reward, in addition to the charge of the government of Malwa.[7] It was really an extraordinary favour because no noble, excepting Malik Naib (Kafur), is reported to have been given any land, town, or *iqta* in *inam* (reward). It is also noteworthy that Amir Khusrau tells us that Ain ul-Mulk Multani got the charge of the province with the designation of *mutassarif*, and not of *wali* or *faujdar*.[8] This implies that the *mutassarif* could hold the combined charge of the governor and the finance officer, in case he was considered capable of providing leadership to the army.

In Malwa, Ain ul-Mulk Multani served until 1313, when he was transferred to Deogiri (in Maharashtra) from where Malik Naib was called to Delhi to look after the ailing Sultan. Ain ul-

Mulk successfully controlled the Maratha region. On Sultan Alauddin's death in 1316, he was ordered to proceed to Gujarat against the followers of Alap Khan whom Malik Naib had treacherously murdered. Alap Khan's supporters revolted in Gujarat. He complied with Malik Naib's order, but was still on his way when the news was received about the assassination of Malik Naib in Delhi. He halted in Chittor for more than a month, waiting for the situation to settle down at the centre.[9] After some time, Prince Mubarak Khan ascended the throne under the title of Sultan Qutbuddin Mubarak Shah. He sent robes of honour to Ain ul-Mulk Multani and other generals in his company and also directed them through his *farman* to go to Gujarat and deal with the followers of Alap Khan.[10]

In Gujarat, Ain ul-Mulk Multani tried to resolve the problem diplomatically. He wrote to the leaders of the rebellion that the murder of Alap Khan had already been avenged by the assassination of Malik Naib and that they should not persist in their rebellion. He also warned them of dire consequences in case they did not submit to the new Sultan. His persuasion had the desired effect on many rebels. Many joined his camp. Only Haidar and Zirak fought against the royal army, and they were easily routed. Having settled the affairs of Gujarat, he then returned to the capital. In Delhi, he was showered with royal favours. The other nobles who had accompanied him were also presented with robes. Malik Shahin got the charge of Gujarat province along with the title of Zafar Khan.[11]

In 1318, Ain ul-Mulk was sent to Deogiri as the *wazir* of the entire region after the rebellion of Malik Yaklakhi had been suppressed there. Besides him, Malik Tajuddin, son of Khwaja Ata, was appointed the *mushrif* and Malik Mujruddin Aburija the *naib wazir* of the territorial unit of Deogiri.[12] But Ain ul-Multani's presence in Delhi on different occasions suggests that the work of the *wizarat* in Deogiri was looked after by the *naib wazir*, Mujr Aburija. In his condemnation of moral laxity on the part of Sultan Qutbuddin Mubarak Shah, Barani writes that the Sultan gave up observing court etiquette and that his slave girls turned up on the roof of the *Hazar Satun* palace (the thousand-pillared palace) and hurled abuses at the nobles; even senior and respectable nobles like Ain ul-Mulk Multani and Malik Qarabeg were not spared.[13] Also in 1320, he was present in Delhi when Sultan Qutbuddin Mubarak Shah was killed by the allies of Khusrau Khan. Though he was not in alliance with Khusrau Khan, the latter honoured him with the title of Alam Khan in order to win him over to his side.[14]

Of all the senior nobles, only Ghazi Malik, the *muqta* of Dipalpur, was determined to organize a movement against Khusrau Khan the regicide who had assumed the royal title of Sultan Nasiruddin, seeking revenge for the murder of Sultan Qutbuddin Mubarak Shah. Ghazi Malik persuaded all the important nobles, including Ain ul-Mulk Multani, to help him. Ain ul-Mulk, afraid of Khusrau Khan's agents, showed Ghazi Malik's letter to the regicide and thus assured him of his loyalty. Ghazi Malik, anxious to win him over, again wrote a letter to him. This time Ain ul-Mulk Multani expressed his sympathy with Ghazi Malik's undertaking and promised not to participate in the battle against any party because he was in Delhi, surrounded by the allies of Khusrau Khan and could not take up arms against him. Accordingly, on the day of battle outside Delhi, he fled away to Ujjain, causing dismay in the rank and file of the army of Delhi.[15] On achieving the throne, Ghazi Malik assumed the title of Sultan Ghiyasuddin Tughluq Shah. He appears to have retained all the nobles who did not join any side in the war against the regicide. Barani includes Ain ul-Mulk Multani among the leading nobles of Tughluq's reign,[16] but he is not mentioned in the account of any event of the region recorded by Barani in his *Tarikh*. According to Isami, Ain ul-Mulk joined Ulugh Khan (later Sultan Muhammad bin Tughluq) on the Warangal expedition in 1322; the siege of Warangal became prolonged, and Ulugh Khan insisted on capturing the citadel. Correspondence between the court of Delhi and the camp was disrupted for some time. Rumours were spread by mischief mongers of the death of the Sultan in Delhi. Some officers who became suspicious of Ulugh Khan mutinied, yet Ain ul-Mulk and many others remained loyal and joined Ulugh Khan in his retreat to Deogiri.[17] But Isami is not corroborated by any other source in this matter.

As regards his namesake Ain ul-Mulk Mahru, who is confused by modern scholars with Ain ul-Mulk Multani, he was another noble who started his career under Sultan Muhammad bin

Tughluq. Isami calls him Ainuddin Mahru while describing his revolt in the combined provinces of Awadh and Zafarabad. He also informs us that on the arrival of the *wazir*, Khwaja Jahan, and the veteran generals Mujir Aburija and Malik Khattab Afghan from the adjoining territories, the Sultan marched and gave the rebel, battle outside Qanauj. The brothers of Ain ul-Mulk, Shahrullah and Nasrullah, were killed and Mahru was arrested. He was forgiven and taken back into the royal service.[18] The description by Barani of Mahru's revolt is more important in that we find a further clue to the fact that in the stabilized provinces of north India the governors were appointed from amongst non-military men, and that the provincial army was made subordinate to them. Barani writes that Mahru held the charge of the combined provinces of Awadh and Zafarabad.[19] His two brothers assisted him in maintaining law and order in the entire region. He rendered service to the Sultan by maintaining a regular supply of food grains and money during his stay in Swargduari during the years of famine. The Sultan was pleased, reposed full confidence in him, and favoured him with the status of a courtier and companion. As there was a complaint of misappropriation by the subordinates of Qutlugh Khan of state revenues in the Deccan, the Sultan decided to appoint Mahru as the governor-general of the Deccan. Informed of the Sultan's decision, Mahru's brothers became apprehensive about their future. They thought that Qutlugh Khan being held in high esteem by the Sultan could not be removed from his place and that their brother was to be eliminated in the Deccan on account of some misunderstanding. On their instigation, Mahru fled away from the court at night and revolted. Further, Barani writes contemptuously that he and his brothers belonged to the class of scribes and had no experience of warfare, yet they thought that the army would support their cause because of the unpopularity of the Sultan, but in vain. They were routed in the first assault. Ain ul-Mulk Mahru was arrested while his brothers and other supporters were killed. Mahru was pardoned and again assigned important positions.[20] Ibn Battuta is also worth quoting in this regard. According to him, when the Sultan was informed by the intelligence officer of the flight of Ain ul-Mulk, he was perturbed because the troops were widely scattered. He consulted his nobles about the course to be taken.

'The Amirs of Khurasan and foreigners,' says he, 'were in the greatest fear of this rebel, because he was an Indian, and the people of India hold the foreigners in hatred because of the Sultan's favouritism of them.' The nobles suggested to the Sultan that he should attack the rebel without delay. He was defeated and his brothers were killed in pursuit. Later, he was pardoned and made the superintendent of the Sultan's gardens. He was honoured with robes and horses and also given a fixed daily allowance.[21]

The *qasidas* (panegyrics) composed by Muthar of Kara in praise of Mahru, his patron during his stay in Awadh, shows that he was in the prime of his career, and the poet visualized his further rise in the official hierarchy:[22]

He is a promising and fortunate young man,
He is the bestower of wealth and the adorner of the realm.

In the following couplet, Muthar refers to the interest evinced by his patron in extending patronage to men of learning and talent. Mahru seems to have gathered around him a fairly large number of scholars and artists:[23]

At times, subtleties of poetry and music are discussed.
At other times, theories related to the calendar and astrolabs are taken up for discussion.[24]

In another couplet, Muthar of Kara refers to Ghazipur, which formed part of the territorial unit of Zafarabad:[25]

The sorrow afflicts since long,
Because the Malik of the East is in Ghazipur.

Similarly, the near-contemporary historian Afif presents Mahru as the creation of Muhammad bin Tughluq. According to him, Mahru produced a number of treatises on different sciences during the reigns of Muhammad bin Tughluq and Firuz Shah. One of them is the celebrated work entitled *Tarsul-i-Ainul-Mulk* (perhaps the *Insha-i-Mahru*).[26] Sultan Firuz Shah appointed him *Ashraf-i-Mumalik*[27] in the *diwan-i-Wizarat* after his accession to the throne in Delhi. As differences arose between him and the *wazir*, Khan-i-Jahan (d. 1368), over the question of jurisdiction, he was first removed from the state service and then entrusted with the governorship of the combined provinces of Multan, Uchh, and Sewistan.[28]

Lastly, it may be stated that most of the letters and documents contained in the *Insha-i-Mahru* were drafted during the period of Firuz Shah's reign, and only a few belong to the time of Muhammad bin Tughluq; there is no letter written by Mahru during the reign of the latter's predecessors. In short, Ain ul-Mulk Multani and Ain ul-Mulk Mahru were two different persons belonging to different generations.

NOTES

1. Cf. Shaikh Abdur Rashid, Introduction to the edited text of *Insha-i-Mahru*, Lahore, 1965; S.B.P. Nigam, *Nobility Under the Sultans of Delhi*, pp. 10–11, 13, etc. K.A. Nizami, *On History and Historians of Medieval India*, pp. 211–16.
2. *Delhi Sultanate: A Political and Military History,* Appendix IV, p. 329.
3. Barani, p. 337.
4. *Dewal Rani Khizr Khan*, p. 68.
5. Barani, pp. 283–4.
6. His name was probably Ainuddin. Khusrau states that after the grant of the title he became Ain ul-Mulk. *Khaz Ain-ul-Futuh*, Eng. tr., p. 44.
7. Ghazi Malik is said to have written in his letter to Ain ul-Mulk Multani that Sultan Alauddin (Khalji) had raised him above other nobles by rewarding him with the grant of Ujjain as a reward, in addition to the charge of Dhar province, and that therefore he should cooperate with him against Khusrau Khan, who had killed his benefactor's sons. *Tughluqnama*, p. 66.
8. *Khazain ul-Futuh*, Eng. tr., pp. 44–6.
9. *Futuh-us-Salatin*, pp. 347–8; Barani, pp. 388–9.
10. *Futuh-us-Salatin*, pp. 355–7.
11. *Futuh-us-Salatin*, pp. 358–60; Barani, pp. 388–9.
12. Barani, pp. 397–8; *Futuh us-Salatin*, p. 369.
13. Barani, p. 396.
14. Ibid., pp. 410–11.
15. *Tughluqnama*, pp. 67–8; Barani, p. 419.
16. Barani, p. 424.
17. *Futuh-us-Salatin*, pp. 393–6.
18. Ibid., pp. 473–6.
19. It may be recalled that Tatar Malik was the governor of Zafaraba'd *iqta* during the reign of Sultan Ghiyasuddin Tughluq. Tatar Malik was trained as a military general, and led the advance guard of the Sultan's expedition against Bengal in 1323. He was replaced by Muhammad bin Tughluq some time after his accession to the throne.

20. Barani, pp. 489, 490–1.
21. *The Travels of Ibn Battuta*, vol. 3, pp. 720–1, 722–7.
22. Cf. *Diwan-i-Muthar*, ed. Abdur Razzaq, Patna, 1998, p. 15.
23. Ibid., p. 24.
24. Loc. cit.
25. *Diwan-i-Muthar*, p. 131.
26. The officer-in-charge of the department was called *mushrif*, and was charged with the duty of maintaining the records of the different types of taxes levied and their collection under various heads.
27. Afif, pp. 409–10.
28. Ibid., pp. 416–17; *Insha-i-Mahru*, document no. 3, pp. 11–12.

APPENDIX B

Nature of Source Material

I need not go into details about the historical works composed by Muhammad bin Mansur, known as Fakhr-i-Mudabbir,[1] Hasan Nizami[2] and Minhaj-i-Siraj Juzjani[3] because adequate attention has been paid by modern scholars to them. The only exception among the early writers whose works still await the attention of modern scholars, interested in the study of history and culture of the Delhi Sultanate period, is Sadiduddin Muhammad Awfi. His literary works contain interesting information, both of corroborative and supplementary nature about important events that occurred in the Sultanate until AD 1230. Therefore, I would like to start my discussion with Awfi's works.

Sadiduddin Muhammad Awfi was born in Bukhara. The Mongol conquest of his home land led him to turn to India for refuge.[4] On his arrival in India, sometime in the 1220s, he completed his Persian translation of Qazi Al-Tanukhi's Arabic classic, *Kitab ul-Faraj ba'd ul-Shidda* and presented it to Sultan Nasiruddin Qubacha. In its introduction, Awfi praises Nasiruddin Qubacha for his benevolence towards people in general and refugees from the lands, conquered by the Mongols in particular. Another work that he dedicated to 'Ain ul-Mulk Ashari' is the celebrated Persian Tazkira *Lubab ul-Albab*, an anthology of the early Persian poets. This work contains also notices of the Persian poets who flourished in India since the Ghaznavid period and played an important role in different fields. The interesting information contained in the notices of the emigrant Persian poets who joined Sultan Qutbuddin Aibek's and his successor's courts provide us with insights into the court culture. The third work, written by Awfi is his magnum opus *Javami ul-Hikayat wa-Lavami ul-Rivayat*. This is divided into four volumes, each containing a number of chapters, based on a careful study of the

Arabic classics, early Persian histories, author's own personal observations and the information collected from the traders and friends about the life and conditions in different countries, including India. Its encyclopaedic nature and range made it worthy of notice for every educated man even during the lifetime of its author.[5] It is really this work that led Ziauddin Barani, the doyen of medieval Indo-Persian historians to included Awfi among the early historians of the Sultanate of Delhi.[6]

Strangely enough, the modern scholars of medieval Indian history and culture have not paid any attention to the *Jawami ul-Hikayat wa-Lavami ul-Rivayat* (hereafter cited as *Javami ul Hikayat*). Unlike them the European scholars Barthold and Bosworth used it in the preparation of their works on the history of Central Asia and Ghaznavids respectively. Barthold writes:

> Muhammad Awfi's anthology, called *Collections of Anecdotes and Brilliant Tales* was written in India. The author travelled much in his youth, and had visited Bukhara and Khorezmia. Of the anecdotes quoted, those of the greatest importance for us are the fairly numerous tales about the Qarakhanids, especially Tamghoch Khan Ibrahim b. Nasr. In addition to anecdotes, the book contains a Chapter of history (part I, Ch. 5), and another of geography (part IV, Ch. 16); in the latter special interest attaches to his accounts of the Eastern Asiatic and Turkish Tribes; for instance, the author is the first Persian writer to mention the Uighurs.[7]

Equally important are the anecdotes related to the early Muslim rulers of India. Besides, the traditions, set by the early rulers in different Islamic Countries and incorporated by Awfi in the *Jawami ul-Hikayat* it served as a source of inspiration for the rulers and the ruling elite in India. These traditions help us trace the origin and development of certain institutions of cultural and political importance in the Sultanate of Delhi. For instance, we find references to the *karkhanas* (store-cum-workshops) maintained by men of means in Central Asia.[8] These *karkhanas* appear to have been established by the Muslim conquerors in India in the beginning of their rule.[9] The most important institution of public utility that the Sultan established in Delhi after it had been made the capital of the Sultanate was the hospital, called either *Dar-ul-Shafa* or *bimaristan.* Our author incidentally refers to the *bimaristan* in Ghazna where the patients suffering from mental trouble were treated[10] but the later Indo-Persian writers furnish a somewhat detailed description both of the private and government hospitals in Delhi during the fourteenth century.[11]

As for the additional information about events in India, available in the *Jawami ul-Hikayat*, it can be cited briefly. Only two events will be mentioned here, in order to show how this work adds to our knowledge. The first event to be selected by me for comment is the second battle of Tarain, fought between Prithviraj and Sultan Muizuddin Muhammad bin Sam. Awfi's description of the battle is more detailed than that furnished by Minha Juzjani of the new strategy and tactics adopted by the Sultan. Awfi writes.

> When the martyred Sultan appeared to fight second time, he knew that the enemies kept their elephants in battle array on the field before (his) horses that got frightened by their sight. It was the cause of his defeat (in the first battle). When the rival armies came face to face and the camp fires were visible on either side, the Sultan ordered his men to collected plenty of wood and set it on fire in front of the royal tent and the tents of the nobles and kept it ablaze throughout the night, so that the enemy could regard it the camping ground. Thereafter, the sultan marched off in a different direction with his main army. Seeing the fire burning, the infidels thought that (the Sultan's) army still encamped there. The Sultan marched all the night and got in the rear of the rival army. At day break, the Sultan suddenly fell on the rival army and put a large number of the people to death. Thrown in confusion, Kola (Prithviraj) decided to retreat, but neither he could maintain his forces in order nor his elephants could be brought under control. The ranks of his army were broken and he was taken prisoner. The Muslims gained complete victory and then the Sultan returned in triumph.[12]

The second event for comment is the rebellion of Balka Khalji against Sultan Shamsuddin Iltutmish in 1229–30, which was also described by Minhaj Juzjani. This is the last event, mentioned by Awfi in the *Jawami ul-Hikayat*. The details furnished by Minhaj are brief and laconic. Awfi helps us fill the gap in our understanding of the political developments in eastern India after the annexation of Bihar and Bengal to the Sultanate of Delhi in 1226. We are informed by Awfi that Balka Khalji who held no important position in Bengal prior to its conquest by Prince Nasiruddin Mahmud was favoured by Sultan Iltutmish and allowed to rule over a vast territory (in Bengal) as a vassal with the royal title of

Daulat Shah. The latter continued to acknowledge Iltutmish's suzerainty till 1229, the year when the Crown Prince and the viceroy of eastern territories, Nasiruddin Mahmud fell ill and passed away. On his death, Daulat Shah Khalji declared his independence from the Sultan of Delhi. He drove away the officers of Iltutmish from Bengal and punished those who had collaborated with the latter. Awfi states that he was a non-entity before Sultan Iltutmish did him favour and installed him as his vassal. 'The devil', says he, 'led him (Daulat Shah) astray. Upon the death of the peerless Prince, Malik-i-Malik ul-Sharq Nasir ul-Hawue wad-Din Mahmud, ingratitude and ambition led Daulat Shah to repudiate his allegiance to the Sultan. He seized the entire *vilayet* of Lakhnauti, considering sovereignty an easy choice. His rebellion and the reign of terror started by him spurred the Sultan to march against him. He ordered the army to proceed both by the land and the Sea (the Ganga). On the arrival of the Sultan, Daulat Shah also came out to fight. According to Awfi, he was killed by the Sultan's soldiers before the Sultan reached the battle-field.'[13]

Mention should be made here of Amir Khusrau also because he started his literary career during the later half of the thirteenth century. Apart from the controversy whether he was a historian by inclination or not,[14] his writings provide us insights into the life and culture of the Sultanate of Delhi. Undoubtedly, Khusrau was the most gifted and entertaining of medieval writers who wrote on contemporary history in prose and verse, in addition to Persian poetry in general. The epistles and specimen documents composed by him and incorporated in the five volumes of his *Ijaz-i-Khusravi* provide us with insights into different aspects of life and culture which are not found elsewhere. Deeply concerned with the fate of his own world of the Delhi Sultanate which he depicts in his poetry and prose, as being threatened with the frequent Mongol invasions on the one hand and strained by the conflict between the Centre and the Hindu chiefs on the other, Amir Khusrau gave serious thought to these problems and offered solution through specimen documents, written by him for the perusal of the ruling elite. The study of these specimen records, *arzdasht* (petition), *fathnama* (victory letter) and *farman* (royal order) in conjunction with the contemporary historical literature suggests that all of them, with the exception of personal letters, were designed as good counsel. Being a political and social thinker, Khusrau uses them to suggest what the Sultan should do with respect to certain territories whose rulers were independent, how the governors should perform their functions in the provinces, the treatment he should mete out to traders engaged in foreign trade, and the strategy that was to be adopted for the defence of the north-western frontier against the Mongol invaders from Central Asia.[15] No doubt, the documents are futuristic and suggestive, they were composed by Khusrau for the perusal of the ruling elite. The first-two Tughluq Sultans appear to have been inspired by Khusrau's views expressed therein. Sultan Ghiyasuddin Tughluq Shah and his son established their direct rule over the regions of south India. Sultan Muhammad bin Tughluq, like Amir Khusrau, thought that the defence of the north-western frontier was not possible without the establishment of his control over the Hindu Kush Mountain, the natural boundary between India and Central Asia, as discussed in the preceding chapter on foreign relations.

Also interesting is the information available in the *Ijaz-i-Khusravi* about the concept of political economy and public welfare, held by the elite of the Sultanate. In one of the epistles Khusrau praises Sultan Alauddin Khalji for enforcing the price control. He says that the Sultan stood unrivalled as regards his mastery over *ilm-i-maishat* (economic science), and that he had gained precedence over the kings of the past (by introducing far-reaching economic reforms).[16] The use by him of the term *ilm-i-maishat* tends to reveal that economics formed part of political philosophy of the elite and the standard of education and learning was high. Likewise, Khusrau's critique of Sultan Alauddin Khalji's state policy, contained in an epistle on *fiqh* (Islamic jurisprudence) is important in that we find evidence about Sultan Alauddin Khalji's political behaviour and the socio-political changes that resulted from it. Khusrau is critical of the Sultan's niggardliness in rewarding the scholars and men of talent with money lavishly and also appointing people of low-birth to important posts in the army and administration. To Khusrau education and merit were not enough to qualify people for important positions. But the Sultan met the need of the expanding sultanate by recruiting competent persons irrespective of birth as discussed earlier. In short, Khusrau's works, poetical and prose both, enable us to reconstruct the picture of life and culture of the Sultanate Delhi and they cannot be ignored.

The contemporary but much younger poet Isami wrote the history of Muslim rule in India in verse and entitled it *Futuh-us-Salatin*.[17] His narrative begins with the history of Sultan Mahmud of Ghazna (d. 1030), containing popular legends devoid of any factual basis. Influenced by Firdausi Tusi's *Shahnama*, he fails to make any distinction between fiction and history, even the part, related to the Sultans of Delhi is marred by the inclusion of unhistorical material, fables and stories. It is, however, in the richness of details of the military expeditions led and conquests made since the reign of Sultan Alauddin Khalji and the graphic description of the emergence of cities of Delhi and Daulatabad (former Deogiri) that one finds the *Futuh-us-Salatin* to be of absorbing interest. The alusions to the territorial units contained in the details of the rebels of Sultan Muhammad bin Tughluq provide us with hints about the re-organization of vast regions into manageable *shiqqs* and different officers posted in each one.

Another young contemporary of Amir Khusrau is Ziauddin Barani, the author of the celebrated history, *Tarikh-i-Firuz Shahi*. Besides his *Tarikh*, some other works written by him are also extant, such as the *Fatawa-i-Jahandari* and *Naat-i-Muhammadi* (the biography of the Prophet). As much has been written on Barani's *Tarikh-i-Firuz Shahi*, I need not describe his career and the merits and demerits of his work, and confine my discussion to the manuscript copies of the first version (or recession) of the *Tarikh-i-Firuz Shahi* and a bit of Barani's concept of time reflected in the *Fatawa-i-Jahandari*. The rare copies of the first version are available in the libraries of UK and India.

The first version of the *Tarikh-i-Firuz Shahi* was published by Barani some time in the fifth regnal year of Firuz Shah's reign,[18] i.e. two years earlier than the second revised version which is available in print.[19] The first version covers the period from the reign of Sultan Ghiyasuddin Balban (AD 1266-87) up to the fourth regnal year of Sultan Firuz Shah's reign. My study of the two versions enables me to discuss the abridgement as well as enlargement of historical materials in the two versions, marked, at least, from the reign of Sultan Alauddin Khalji (AD 1296-1316). Details of certain events contained in the first version and omitted in the second revised version, or vice versa, certainly extend our understanding of the important problems connected with the history of the Sultanate of Delhi. Our comparison of the two versions helps us analyse the interaction of the author's mind with the material he treats and study the internal dynamics of the work as well. Barani's account of Muhammad bin Tughluq's reign tends to suggest that he decided, in particular, to portray the Sultan, his benefactor in bright colours. He is all praise for his royal patron, Sultan Muhammad bin Tughluq and focuses on his greatness as a Sultan in the first version. Two years later he was constrained to reverse his approach in such a way that a case could be made for his own defence against his enemies who held sway in the court of Sultan Firuz Shah and accused him of misleading the deceased Sultan (Muhammad bin Tughluq) with regard to state policies. Barani served Muhammad bin Tughluq as his *nadim* (friend and companion) but after his death, he was arrested and imprisoned in Bhatner as discussed earlier. After his release, he was an outcast as it happened to all those discarded by the reigning Sultan as undesirable persons. In the revised second version he incidentally and very briefly mentions his own imprisonment in the fort of Bhatner after the death of Sultan Muhammad bin Tughluq.[20] But he mention his plight in some details in his work *Naat-i-Muhammadi* as discussed in the fifth chapter. In short, in the death of his patron Sultan the present replaced the past for him, with its usual effect of boredom and disenchantment. His second version shows that he wanted to please the reigning Sultan at every cost. Probably his first version was not liked by the Sultan and the purpose of winning the royal favour was not fulfilled. He revised his *Tarikh* and added the account of two more years of Firuz Shah's reign. In this revised version his approach to the reign of Muhammad bin Tughluq changes, the rationalist thinkers are blamed for misleading the Sultan from the right path. In the first version the religious policy and ideology of the Sultan is not criticized at all. Moreover, the second version contains cryptic statements about certain important events. All this divergence requires us to read Barani's two accounts and do some reading between the lines. The different terms and expressions in these versions also necessitate a hermeneutic approach and a closer scrutiny.

In the prologue to his Persian translation of the *Tarikh-i-Al-i-Baramikah* (Barmecides), Barani indirectly advises Sultan Firuz Shah that the old aristocratic families, known for their generosity and services rendered to the state and society for generations should not be ruined because any harm done to them affects the popularity of the Sultan as it did in the case of Caliph Harun Rashid.[21]

As for Barani's *Fatawa-i-Jahandari*, it does not seem to have been written by him when he suffered torment during the reign of Firuz Shah. His forceful expression in this work rather suggests that being an ambitious man, he was sure to impress the reigning Sultan, Muhammad bin Tughluq with this work and get an agreeable position at the royal court in reward through its presentation. Because Barani's advocacy of the need for the Sultan to formulate state rules and regulations regardless of the *sharia* but in accordance with the requirements of changed times could be appreciated by the Sultan.[22] Further, he calls time the creator of new conditions, implying that the change in time throws challenge to which the man of dynamic personality rises.[23] All this could have appeal to the philosopher king, Sultan Muhammad bin Tughluq. It also tends to suggest that Barani subscribed to the concept of linear time and was opposed to the view of cyclic time.

Barani influenced the historians who compiled histories during the subsequent period. Like Barani, the anonymous writer of *Sirat-i-Firuz Shahi* and Shams Siraj Afif describe in detail social cultural and economic developments of their age, besides political events. The rare manuscript cop1y of the *Sirat-i-Firuz Shahi*, available in the Khuda Bakhsh Oriental Public Library, Patna does not contain the name of its compiler but it reads as an official history of Firuz Shah's reign from his accession to the throne in 1351 up to the year 1370–1. It avoids to describe in any detail the succession crisis, caused by the death of Sultan Muhammad bin Tughluq in the course of military expedition in Sind. Such other events the narration of which could tarnish the image of Firuz Shah are left unmentioned. It is, however, an interesting source for the history of Firuz Shah's reign. Besides the details of military and hunting expeditions, led by Sultan Firuz Shah, it contains detailed information about religious sects, sufis, *ulama*, popular sciences, such as astronomy, medicines, pharmacology, and works of public utility. The construction of the *dar-ul-shafa* (hospital), *khanqahs* (rest houses for the comfort of wayfarers), canals and water reservoirs, the foundation of new cities and towns and repair of old monuments are described in details. An effort has been made to describe Firuz Shah as an ideal Sultan whom none of the preceding Sultans could match in taking measures for the welfare of the people.

As regards Shams Siraj Afif, he belonged to an old aristocratic family, the members of which served the Sultanate of Delhi for generations. He was born and brought up during the reign of Sultan Firuz Shah. He compiled four volumes on the history of the Sultans of Delhi from Sultan Ghiyasuddin Tughluq Shah to Sultan Muhammad bin Firuz Shah, each devoted exclusively to one particular reign.[24] Of these volumes only one, devoted to the reign of Firuz Shah is extant. It was brought to completion after the sack of Delhi and the devastation of vast region around it by Timur in 1398. Suffering from nostalgic regrets, caused by the foreign invasion, he portrays Firuz Shah as a saintly ruler whose presence on the throne saved Delhi from every calamity. Therefore, he wrote this volume in the form of *manaqib* (collection of virtues) like that of the spiritual biography of a sufi saint. The title of *Tarikh-i-Firuz Shahi* has been given to it by the editor of its text.[25] It is worth noting that the posterity preserved only this volume of Afif for the comprehensive information which it contains about socio-economic development that resulted from the state policies followed by the *wazir* of Firuz Shah. Because it covers the entire long reign and could serve as a source of inspiration and enlightenment to the posterity. It is a vital source of information for us also as its use by me in the preceding chapters shows.

On the dissolution of the Delhi Sultanate in the wake of Timur's invasion, a number of regional sultanates and principalities arose in its provinces. The capital of each regional sultanate took the place of Delhi as the Centre of learning and culture. The regional Sultan emulated the Sultans of Delhi in patronizing the men of learning and talent, in order to enhance the grandeur of his capital. Some of the scholars associated with the courts of the regional Sultans compiled histories of their patrons. The extant histories, produced by them generally begin with the early Muslim rulers of India. These compilers appear to have largely used the works of Hasan Nizami, Minhaj Juzjani and Ziauddin Barani in the preparation of the account of Delhi Sultans. The bits of information of supplementary nature in these regional histories point to the availability of some other sources to their compilers but lost afterwards. Of the fifteenth-century regional histories, mention may be made of Yahya Sirhindi's *Tarikh-i-Mubarak Shahi*,[26] Muhammad Bihamad Khani's *Tarikh-i-Muhammadi*[27] and Shihab Hakim's *Maasir-ı-Mahmud Shahi*,[28] for they yield bits of additional information.

In addition, the poetical works of the thirteenth- and fourteenth-century Indo-Persian poets, the Persian lexicons, *insha* (writings) and the *malfuzat* (collections of utterances of the Sufi saints) serve as useful sources for the students of medieval Indian history and culture. The *masnavis* and *qasidas* (panegyrics) composed by the poets on special occasions illuminate the feel of life and culture around the court of the Sultan and in the metropolis of Delhi. Amidst all this Amid Lowiki Sunami, a late thirteenth-century poet, incidentally provides us with insight into prison conditions, coins, rates of interest, charged by moneylenders, etc. The moneylenders charged 20 per cent interest per month. He was charged of having embezzled state money and thrown into prison. Pleading not guilty, he states: 'No one has seen half a dang (copper coin) weight of gold in my possession. And even if he has, I would not willingly undergo imprisonment for the sake of it. Gold has no value in my sight, how could I pledge it like a userer so as to get twelve for every ten.'[29] The lexicographers help us in understanding the significance of certain administrative and cultural terms, while the *insha* collections contain official as well as specimen documents, casting light on the state apparatus.

The *malfuzat* of Shaikh Nizamuddin (Auliya), Shaikh Nasiruddin Chiragh-i-Dilli, Shaikh Sherafuddin Yahya Maneri (Firdausi), Shaikh Jalaluddin Bukhari, known as Jahaniyan-i-Jahangasht and Shaikh Muhammad Gesudaraz reflect the socio-economic conditions which prevailed during the lifetimes of the sufi saints. Evidence contained therein not only provide us with insights into the currents and cross-currents of thought but also helps us correct the historiographic errors committed by modern scholars. For instance, the medium of exchange in the Sultanate of Delhi was the token copper coin called *jital*. According to Minhaj-i-Siraj, the nobles and state officers were paid their salaries and allowances in *jitals* and not in silver *tankas*. Minhaj himself was rewarded with thousands of *jitals* by Sultan Nasiruddin Mahmud and Ulugh Khan Azam (later Sultan Balban) for compiling the *Tabaqat-i-Nasiri*.[30] The evidence contained in Barani's *Tarikh-i-Firuz Shahi* suggests that *jital* remained the medium of exchange until the reign of Sultan Jalaluddin Khalji. By the time of Sultan Alauddin Khalji the conditions had improved and new fractions of silver *tankas*, were introduced. The wealth brought from the conquered territories in south India and the progress of trade and commerce increased the circulation of money on the one hand and gave rise to consumerism among the elite on the other. For the convenience of traders and people, different silver coins, called *gannis* were brought into circulation. But no chronicler mentions the value of *jital* in relation to the silver *tanka* or its different fractions. Generally, the view held by modern scholars on the basis of conjecture is that the *jital* changed at 1/48th of a silver *tanka*. But Shaikh Nizamuddin Auliya told his disciples that once Shams Dabir, the poet visited his preceptor, Shaikh Fariduddin Ganj-i-Shakr and presented about 50 *jitals* as *futuh* (offering). The Shaikh distributed them among his disciples. He further told them that one *jital* was equivalent to the present day one *ganni*.[31] According to Shibahuddin al-Umari 16 *gannis* made are *tanka*. Similarly, we find interesting information about movements of thought and feeling available in the comments made by the Sufis on them. All this literature has been used critically in the preparation of this work.

NOTES

1. Fakhr-i-Mudabbir's two works, '*Shajra-i-Ansab*' and '*Adab ul-Muluk wa-Kifayat ul Mamluk*' form an important part of the Indo-Persian historical literature produced during the Sultanate period. The *Shajra-i-Ansab* is a book of genealogies. This contains a detailed *Muqaddima* in

which the author has narrated the conquests made by Qutbuddin Aibek after his appointment as *sipahsalar* of the territorial unit of Kuhram. Aibek's accession to the throne in the city of Lahore in 1206, the reforms introduced by him and the state policy followed by him during his reign are also described in detail. This *muqaddima* reads like an official history because the work was presented to Aibek after his accession to the throne. In view of its importance as the first history written in India, E. Denison Rose separated the *Maqaddima* from the *Shijra-i-ansab* and published its edited text under the wrong title *Tarikh-i-Fakhruddin Mubarak Shah Marvarrudi*, confusing its author with his contemporary poet, Fakhruddin Mubarak Shah Marvar-rudi, the court poet of Sultan Ghiyasuddin Muhammad bin Sam of Ghur. The latter composed in verse the genealogy of the dynasty and called his work *Silsilah-i-Ansab* which is not extant. I have cited this *Muqadma* as *Tarikh-i-Fakhr-i-Mudabbir.* As for the *Adab ul-Muluk wa-Kifayat-ul-Mamluk*, it is a voluminous work, containing forty chapters of unequal length, dealing with kingship, different ministerial departments at the centre (under the Ghaznavids), mode of warfare, war-horses, etc. Each chapter is found designed on the pattern of episodic historiography, a tradition set by the Arab historians. Later on thirty-six chapters were separated from this work by some scribe, perhaps at the instance of some bookseller and introduced under the title *Adab ul-Harb wal-Shuja'a* in order to make it look a different work. I have utilised the printed copies of both the works.

2. Hasan Nizami's *Tajul Masir*, written in ornate Persian also begins with the second battle of Tarain in 1192. Hasan Nizami wrote it to gain royal reward after Aibek's accession to the throne. After the untimely death of Aibek in 1210, Hasan Nizami seems to have discontinued writing it because the *Tajul-Masir*, contains a gap of the period from 1197 to 1202, the events that occurred during this period are omitted. The description of the events that took place since 1202, seems to have been written after Iltutmish had consolidated his power in Delhi because Iltutmish is given therein credit for every conquest instead of Aibek. Moreover, more than half of the work has no relevance to the history of the period covered therein, as has been pointed out by so many scholars.
3. The *Tabaqat-i-Nasiri*, compiled by Minhaj-i-Siraj is an important work. Generally its *tabaqat* on India have been used as an important source by modern scholars. It needs to be pointed out that the *tabaqat* from the sixteenth *tabaq* onward contain interesting information about India in the details of refugees who fled to India after the fall of the Khwarazm Shah dynasty.
4. Cf. Iqtidar Husain Siddiqui, *Perso-Arabic Sources on the Life and Conditions in the Sultanate of Delhi*, New Delhi, 1992, pp. 1-4.
5. Ibid., pp. 5-9.

6. Barani, *Torikh-i-Firuz shahi*, p. 14.
7. W. Barthold, *Turkestan Down to the Mongol Invasion*, Eng. tr. T. Minorsky, ed. C.E. Bosworth, London (1968 edn.), p. 36.
8. *Jawami 'ul Hikayat*, vol. III, part II, pp. 467-68.
9. Barani, p. 50.
10. *Jawami'ul Hikayat*, vol. III, part I, p. 155.
11. *Cf. Shihab Uddin al-Umari, Masalik, ul-Absar fi-Mamalik al Absar*, Eng. tr. Iqtidar Husain Siddiqui in *Perso-Arabic Sources of Information on the Life and conditions in the Sultanate of Delhi*, New Delhi, 1992, p. 116
12. Cf. *Perso-Arabic Sources of Information on the Life and Conditions in the Sultanate of Delhi*, pp. 23-4; also *Tabaqat-i-Nasiri*, vol. 1, p. 400-1, for comparison.
13. *Jawami'ul-Hikayat*, vol. I, part 2, pp. 552-6.
14. Peter Hardy does not consider Khusrau a historian by inclination. He is of the opinion that Khusrau wrote on history of his times only to fulfil an aesthetic purpose. Among Hardy's critics, Syed Hasan Askari may also be mentioned. He agrees with Kunwar Muhammad Ashraf in calling Khusrau a historian of contemporary history and cites by way of example *Taghluqnama* as a complete history of the war of succession between Ghazi Malik and Khusrau Khan in 1320. Cf. Peter Hardy, *Historians of Medieval India* (rpt. 1982), p. 114; Syed Hasan Askari, *Amir Khusrau: As a Historian*, *Historians of Medieval India*, ed. Mohibbul Hasan, Meerut, 1968, pp. 22-36.
15. Cf. *Ijaz-i-Khusravi*, 5 vols., Lucknow, 1876, vol. 4, pp. 119-40, vol. 5, pp. 5-13.
16. Ibid., vol. 4, p. 236.
17. Peter Hardy and K.A. Nizami have discussed at length Isami's approach and the value of his *Futuh-us-Salatin* in their respective works. Peter Hardy, *Historians of Medieval India*, op. cit., pp. 94-110; K.A. Nizami, *On History and Historians of Medieval India*, New Delhi, 1983, pp. 107–23.
18. There are three manuscript copies of this version, known so far. One is available in the Bodleian Library, Oxford, Elliot Collection, No. 353, other in the Raza Library, Rampur (India) while the third one belongs to the personal collection of Simon Digby (MS. 57). I have utilized the Bodleian and Rampur copies.
19. *Tarikh-i-Firuz Shahi*, ed. Sir Syed Ahmad Khan, Calcutta, 1862.
20. *Tarikh-i-Firuz Shahi* (printed text), p. 534.
21. Ziauddin Barani, *Tarikh-i-al-i-Baramikah*, Bombay, 1889, pp. 4-5.
22. *Fatawa-i-Jahandari*, ed. Mrs. A. Salim Khan, Lahore, 1972, pp. 139-40, 218.
23. Ibid., p. 137.

24. Cf. Peter Hardy, op. cit., pp. 40-55, for details.
25. Cf. Shamsuddin bin Sirajuddin Afif, *Tarikh-i-Firuz Shahi*, ed. Maulvi Vilayat Husain, Calcutta, 1891.
26. Yahya Sirhindi *Tarikh-i-Mubarak Shahi*, ed. Muhammad Hidayat Husain, Calcutta, 1931.
27. Muhammad Bihamad Khani, *Tarikh-i-Muhammadi*, MS, British Library, London, Or. 137.
28. Ali bin Mahmud al-Kirmani known as Shihab Hakim compiled the history of the Sultans of Malwa and did not devote any space to the Sultans of Delhi, yet he incidentally refers to the latter. Moreover, he provides us with insight into the expansion of Delhi's imperial culture with the emergence of regional Sultanates in the fifteenth century. Cf. *Maasir-i-Mahmud Shahi*, ed. Nurul Hasan Ansari, Delhi, 1968.
29. Cf. Iqtidar Husain Siddiqui, 'The Intellectual and Historical Dimensions of the Indo-Persian Poetry of the Thirteenth Century Poetry', in idem, ed., *Medieval India, Essays in Intellectual Thought and Culture*, New Delhi, 2003, p. 49.
30. *Tabaqat-i-Nasiri*, vol. 2, pp. 8, 220.
31. *Fawaid ul-Fuad*, pp. 127-8.

Select Bibliography

Abbas Sarwani, *Tuhfa-i-Akbar Shahi*, known as *Tarikh-i-Sher Shahi*, ed. S.M. Imam Uddin, University of Dacca, Dacca, 1964.

Abdul Haque Muhadis, *Akhbar ul-Akhiyar*, Matba-i-Mujtabai, Delhi, 1914.

_____, *Tarikh-i-Haqqi*, MS, Maulana Azad Library, Aligarh.

Abdul Qadir Badaoni, *Muntakhab-ut-Tawarikh*, vol. 1, Bibliotheca Indica, Calcutta1864; Eng. tr., vol. 1, G.S.A. Ranking, Calcutta, 1895.

Abu Bakr bin Ali Usmani al-Kasani, *Farsi Tarjuma-i-Kitab ul-Saidna* of Al-Baruni, ed. M. Satudeh and Iraj Afshar, Bunyad-i-Farhang-i-Iran, Tehran, 1325 Shamsi.

Abul Fazl Muhammad al-Baihaqi, *Tarikh-i-Masudi*, known as *Tarikh-i-Al-i-Subuktigin*, Tehran, 1324 Shamsi.

Abu Nasr Muhammad al-Jabbar al-Utbi, *Tarikh al-Yamini*, Arabic text, Lahore, 1300 H., *Tarikh-i-Yamini*, thirteenth-century Persian translation by Abu-s-Sharaf al-Jurbazqani, ed. Jaffar Shiyar, Tehran, 1345 Shamsi.

Afif, Shams Siraj, *Tarikh-i-Firuz Shahi*, ed. Wilayat Husain, Bibliotheca Indica, Calcutta, 1891.

Ahmad bin Umar Ibn Ali an-Nizami al-Aruzi, *Chahar Maqala*, ed., Mirza Muhammad Qazvini, Tehran, reprint, 1348 Shamsi.

Ali bin Hamid al-Kufi, *Fathnama-i-Sind*, known as *Chachnama*, ed. Nabi Bakhsh Baloch, Islamic University, Islamabad, 1983.

Ali bin Mahmud al-Kirmani, known as Shihab Hakim, *Maasir-i-Mahmud Shahi*, ed. Nurul Hasan Ansari, Indo-Persian Society, Delhi, 1968.

Amid Loeki Sunami, *Diwan-i-Amid Loeki*, ed. Nazir Ahmad, Majlis-i-Taraqi-i-Adab, Lahore, 1984.

Anonymous, *Sirat-i-Firuz Shahi*, Facsimile, Khuda Bakhsh Oriental Public Library, Patna, 1999; also MS, Khuda Bakhsh Oriental Public Library, Patna.

_____, *Hudud al-Alam*, Eng. tr. V. Minorsky, entitled *The Regions of the World*; 2nd edn. GMS, no. XI (London, 1970).

_____, *Bayaz-i-Tajuddin Wazir*, ed. Iraj Afshar and Murtaza Timur, Danishgarh, Isfahan, No. 103, 1351 Shamsi.

Arabi, Zain Badr, *Khwan-i-Pur Ni'mat* (*Malfuzat* of Shaikh Sharafuddin Yahya Maneri), Patna 1321 H.

____, *Maadan al-Ma'ani* (*Malfuzat* of Shaikh Sharafuddin Yahya Maneri), 2 vols., Bihar Sharif, 1884.

Ata Malik Juvaini, *Tarikh-i-Jahan Gusha*, ed. Muhammad Qazvini, Leiden, 1911, Eng. tr. J.A. Bryle, entitled *The History of the World Conqueror,* 2 vols., Manchester, 1958.

Awfi, Sadiduddin Muhammad, *Javami'ul Hikayat wa-Lavani'ul Rivayat*, vol. 1, Parts I and II, ed. Muhammad Nizamuddin Ahmad, Hyderabad, A.P., 1965–6; vols. II and III, ed. Amir Bano Musaffa and Mutahir Musaffa, Bunyad-i-Farhang-i-Iran, Tehran, vol. IV, MS, Khuda Bakhsh Oriental Public Library, Patna.

____, *Tarjuma* (Persian), *Kitab ul-Faraj bad ul-Shidda*, MS, India Office Library, London, Ethe no. 1432.

____, *Lubab ul-Albab*, ed. E.C. Browne and Mirza Muhammad Qazvini, Leiden and London, 1903–6.

Badr Chach, *Qasaid-i-Badr-i-Chach*, Newal Kishore, Lucknow, 1279 AH.

Barani, Ziauddin, *Fatawa-i-Jahandari*, ed. Mrs A. Salim Khan, University of the Punjab, Lahore, 1972.

____, *Nat-i-Muhammadi*, MS, No. Tarikh 127, Raza Library, Rampur.

____, *Tarikh-i-Firuz Shahi*, ed. Saiyid Ahmad Khan, Bibliotheca Indica, Calcutta, 1862.

____, *Tarikh-i-Firuz Shahi*, unrevised first version, MS, Bodleian Library, Elliot Collection, No. 353, Oxford, and Ms. Raza Library, Rampur. Muhammad, Bihamad Khani, *Tarikh-i-Muhammadi*, MS Or. 137, British Library, London.

Dharma Swamin, *Biography of Dharma Swamin* (chaglo tsa-ba chos-rje-dpal), vol. II, Eng. tr. G. Roerich, K.P. Jayaswal Research Institute, Patna, 1959.

Fakhr-i-Mudabbir, Muhammad bin Mansur, *Adab ul-Harb, wal-shuja*, ed. Ahmad Suhaili Khwansari, Tehran, 1346 Shamsi.

____, *Adab ul-Muluk wa-Kifayat ul-Mamluk*, ed. Muhammad Sarwar Maulai, Bunyad-i-Farhang Iran, No. 212.

____, *Muqadima of Shajra-i-Ansab*, ed. Denison Ross, and published under the title *Tarikh-i-Fakhruddin Mubarakshah Marvar-rudi*, London, 1927. It has been cited by me as *Tarikh-i-Fakhr-i-Mudabbir.*

Fakhruddin Mubarak Shah, known as Qawwas Ghaznavi, *Farhang-i-Qawwas*, ed. Nazir Ahmad, Raza Library, Rampur, 1999.

Faiz Ullah Binbani, *Tarikh-i-Sadr-i-Jahan*, ed. Iqtidar Husain Siddiqui, Academic Books, Aligarh, 1988.

Fazl Ullah, Rashiduddin, part relating to India, ed. Karl Jahn under the title *Rashiduddin's History of India*, The Hague, 1965.

Firishta, Muhammad Qasim Hindu Shah, *Gulshan Ibrahimi,* known as *Tarikh-i-Firishta*, Newal Kishore Press, Lucknow, 1281 H.

Firuz Shah, *Futuhat-i-Firuz Shahi*, ed. S. Abdur Rashid, The Aligarh Muslim University, Aligarh, 1954.

Gardezi, Abu Said, *Zain al-Akhbar*, ed. Abdul Hai Habibi, Iran, 1347 Shamsi.

Hajib Khairat Dehlavi, *Dastur ul-Afazil*, ed. Nazir Ahmad, Bunyad-i-Farhang-i-Iran, Tehran, 1352 Shamsi.

Hamid Qalandar, *Khair ul-Majalis*, ed. K.A. Nizami, Aligarh, 1959.

Harvi, Saif Jam, *Majmua-i-Lataif-o-Safina-i-Zaraif*, MS Or 4110, British Library, London.

Hasan Nizami, *Taj ul-Maasir*, MS. Add. 7623, British Library, London, English tr. Bhagwat Saroop, published by Sand Ahmed Dehlavi, Delhi, 1998.

Hasan Sijzi, *Fawaid ul-Fuad*, Newal Kishore Press, Lucknow, 1302 H; also Malik Siraj Uddin & Sons, Lahore, 1966.

Ibn Battuta, *The Travels of Ibn Battuta*, vol. III, Eng. tr. Sir Hamilton Gibb, Cambridge University Press, Cambridge, 1971; Urdu tr., vol. I, *Ajaib ul-Asfar*, Maulana Ata-ur-Rahman, Rahmani Press, Delhi, 1348 H; *Ajaib ul-Asfar*, vol. 2, Maulvi Muhammad Husaini, rpt., Islamabad, 1984.

Ikhtisan, Muhammad Sadr Ala (bin) Ahmad Hasan Abdusi Dabir, *Basatinul-Uns*, Ms. No. Add. 7717, British Library, London, English tr. with comments, Iqtidar Husain Siddiqui, in *Perso-Arabic Sources on the Life and Conditions in the Sultanate of Delhi*, Munshiram Manoharlal, New Delhi, 1992.

Isami, *Futuh us-Salatin*, ed. A.S. Usha, Madras University Islamic Series No. 9, Madras, 1948.

Jajarmi, Majduddin Abul Maali Muaiyid bin Muhammad, Farsi Tarjuma Ihya-ul-Ulum-ud-Din of Imam Ghazzali, MS Or 8194, British Library, London.

Jalaluddin Ahal Jami, *Faraid-i-Ghiyasi*, ed. Hashmi Moyyid, Bunyad-i-Farhang-i-Iran, Tehran, 1974.

Jamali Kambo, *Qasaid-i-Jamali*, MS Maulana Azad Library, Aligarh.

Juzjani, Minhaj-i-Siraj, *Tabaqat-i-Nasiri*, 2 vols., ed. Abdul Hai Habibi, *Anjuman Tarikh-i-Afghanistan*, Kabul, 1963–4, Eng. tr. H.G. Raverty, 2 vols., Calcutta, 1897.

Khusrau, Amir, *Ijaz-i-Khusravi*, 5 vols., Newal Kishore Press, Lucknow, 1865-7.

_____, *Khazain ul-Futuh*, ed. Wahid Mirza, Calcutta, 1953; Eng. tr. Mohammad Habib under the title *The Campaigns of Alauddin Khalji*, D.B. Taraporewala Sons and Co., Bombay, 1931.

_____, *Masnavi Dewal Rani Wa-Khizr Khan*, ed. Rashid Ahmad Salim, Aligarh, 1917.

_____, *Masnavi Miftah ul-Futuh*, ed. Shaikh Abdus Rashid, Aligarh, 1954.

_____, *Masnavi Qiran al-Sadain*, ed. Muhammad Ismail, Aligarh, 1918.

_____, *Masnavi Nuhsiphr*, ed. Wahid Mirza, Oxford University Press, Calcutta, 1950.

_____, *Tughluqnama*, ed. S. Hashmi Faridabadi, Aurangabad, 1933.

Khwafi, Fasih Ahmad bin Jalaluddin Muhammad, *Majm'ul Fasihi*, vol. III, ed. Mahmud Farrukh, Tehran, 1339 Shamsi/1960, 3 vols.

Mir Khurd, Saiyid Muhammad Mubarak Kirmani, *Siyar ul-Auliya*, lith., Delhi, 1302 AH 1885.

Muhammad bin Ali al-Ravandi, *Khulsa-i-Rahat ul-Sudur-o-ayat ul-Surur*, ed. Nazir Ahmad, in *Qand-i-Parsi*, no. 9, Iran Cultural House, New Delhi.

Mushtaqi, Rizq Ullah, *Waqiat-i-Mushtaqi*, eds. Iqtidar Husain Siddiqui and Wiqarul Hasan Siddiqui, Raza Library, Rampur, 2003; Eng. tr. Iqtidar Husain Siddiqui, Indian Council of Historical Research, New Delhi, 1993.

Muthar Kara, *Diwan-i-Muthar*, ed. Abdur Razzaq, Khuda Bakhsh Oriental Public Library, Patna, 1998.

Nizamuddin Ahmad Bakhshi, *Tabaqat-i-Akbari*, Bibliotheca Indica, Calcutta, 1911.

Nizam ul-Mulk Tusi, *Siyasatnama*, ed. Jaffar Shiyar, Tehran, 1348 Shamsi.

Saiyid Muhammad Husaini, *Javami'ul-Kilem*, ed. Muhammad Hamid Siddiqui, lith., Kanpur, 1356 H.

Shaikh Sharafuddin Yahya Maneri, *Maktubat-i-Sadi*, Eng. tr. Paul Jackson under the title *Letters from Maneri*, Horizon India Books, New Delhi, 1992.

Sirhindi, Yahya bin Ahmad, *Tarikh-i-Mubarak Shahi*, ed. M. Hidayat Husain, Bibliotheca Indica, Calcutta, 1931.

Yazdi, Sharafuddin, *Muqadima-i-Zafarnama*, MS., Add. 6538, British Library, London.

_____, *Zafarnama*, Bibliotheca Indica, Calcutta, 1888.

Modern Works

Aziz Ahmad, *Studies in Islamic Culture in the Indian Environment*, Oxford, 1967.

Aziz Ahmad, Muhammad, *Political History and Institutions of the Early Turkish Empire*, Lahore, 1949.

Barthold, W., *Turkestan Down to the Mongol Invasions*, Eng. tr. V. Minorsky, ed. C.E. Bosworth, London, 1968.

_____, *Four Studies in the History of Central Asia*, Eng. tr. V. and T. Minorsky, Leiden, E.J. Brills, 1956.

Bosworth, C.E., *The Ghaznavids: The Empire in Afghanistan and Eastern Iran*, Edinburgh, 1963.

_____, *The Later Ghaznavids: Splendour and Decay*, rpt., Munshiram Manoharlal, New Delhi, 1992.

Chaudhuri, Tapan Ray and Irfan Habib (eds.), *Cambridge Economic History of India*, Orient Longman, rpt., Delhi, 1984.

Digby, Simon, *War Horse and Elephant in the Sultanate of Delhi*, Oxford University Press, Karachi, 1971.

Habib, Muhammad, *Politics and Society in Early Medieval India*, (Collected Works), 2 vols., ed. K.A. Nizami, New Delhi, 1974 and 1981.

_____, ed., *Comprehensive History of India: The Delhi Sultanate*, vol. V, Delhi, 1970.

Habibullah, A.B.M., *The Foundation of Muslim Rule in India*, rpt., New Delhi, 1972.

Hardy, Peter, *Historians of Medieval India*, Greenwood Press, Westport, Connecticut, 1982.

_____, 'Didactic Historical Writings in Indian Islam: Ziauddin Barani's Treatment of the Reign of Sultan Muhammad bin Tughluq', in *Islam in India*, ed. Y. Friedmann, Jerusalem, 1984.

_____, 'The Duty of the Sultan (in the Sultanate Period): To Further the Material Welfare of his Subjects', *The Concept of Duty in South Asia*, ed. Wendy Doniger O' Flaherty and J.D. Derrent (eds.), New Delhi, pp. 147–65.

Hodivala, S.H., *Studies in Indo-Muslim History*, Bombay, 1939.

Husain, Agha Mehdi, *Tughluq Dynasty*, Calcutta, 1963.

Jackson, Paul, S.J., *The Way of a Sufi: Sharaf Uddin Maneri*, Delhi, 1987.

Jackson, Peter, *The Delhi Sultanate: A Political and Military History*, Cambridge University Press, 1999.

_____, 'The Mongol and the Delhi Sultanate in the Reign of Muhammad bin Tughluq', *Central Asiatic Journal*, vol. XIX, nos. 1–2, Wiesbaden, 1975, pp. 118–56.

Lal, K.S., *History of the Khaljis*, rpt., New Delhi, 1980.

Majumdar, R.C. (ed.), *The History and Culture of the Indian People: The Struggle for Empire*, Bombay, 1975.

Mirza, M. Wahid, *Life and Works of Amir Khusrau*, Calcutta, 1935.

Moreland, W.H., *The Agrarian System of Moslem India*, Cambridge, 1929, rpt., New Delhi, 1968.

Nazim, Muhammad, *The Life and Times of Sultan Mahmud of Ghazna*, rpt., New Delhi, 1971.

Nigam, S.B.P., *Nobility under the Sultans of Delhi*, New Delhi, 1968.

Nizami, K.A., *Studies in Medieval Indian History and Culture*, Allahabad, 1966.

_____, *Some Aspects of Religion and Politics in India during the Thirteenth Century*, 3rd rpt., Delhi, 1978.

Prasad, Ishwari, *History of the Qaraunah Turks*, rpt., Allahabad, 1974.

Qureishi, I.H., *The Administration of the Sultanate of Delhi*, Lahore, 1944.

Shokoohys, Mehrdad and Natalie Shokqohy, 'Tughluqabad: The Earliest Surviving Town of the Delhi Sultanate', *Bulletin of the School of South Asian Studies* (*BSOAS*), London, pp. 516–50, vol. LVII, 1994; and part 3, 1999, pp. 421–61.

Siddiqui, Iqtidar Husain, *Perso-Arabic Sources on the Life and Conditions in the Sultanate of Delhi*, 1992.

_____, Eng. tr., *Waqiat-i-Mushtaqi* of Shaikh Rizq Ullah Mushtaqi, Indian Council of Historical Research, New Delhi, 1993.

_____, *Islam and Muslims in South Asia: Historical Perspectives*, Adam Publishers, Delhi, 1987.

_____(ed.), *Medieval India: Essays in Intellectual Thought and Culture*, vol. 1, Manohar, New Delhi, 2003.

Tripathi, R.P., *Some Aspects of Muslim Administration*, Allahabad, 1936.

Index